Social Justice and Community College Education

This book explores the central role community colleges play in American social justice. The United States has long-standing social and cultural structures that perpetuate inequality along race, ethnicity, and income lines. The primary role of American community colleges is to disrupt these structures on behalf of the students we serve. In this sense, community colleges are called to play a subversive role in contemporary society, but it is a good kind of subversion.

Social Justice and Community College Education makes four very important contributions to this conversation:

- First, the book helps us quantify and understand the size and dimension of the equity gaps in higher education by tracking ten specific student groups from historically underserved communities.
- Second, the book summarizes best practices research and literature with regard to pedagogy, services, programs, and leadership in community colleges, presenting practical strategies for implementation.
- Third, through a national survey of community college personnel, the book covers significant new territory in the discussion of work we need to do collaboratively as community colleges.
- Fourth, this book captures the unique and special mission of American community colleges. Our work is the work of social justice, and we carry this work out in society at a greater volume, with greater intentionality, and through greater expertise than any other sector of higher education. In this arena, community colleges should lead.

Bryan Reece is the Chancellor of Contra Costa Community College District (4CD). Located in the San Francisco Bay Area, 4CD is one of the largest districts in California, serving a regional population of over one million residents, with more than 52,000 students. 4CD's three colleges, Contra Costa College, Diablo Valley College, and Los Medanos College, have long and proud histories serving students from historically underserved communities.

Social Justice and Community College Education

Bryan Reece

Routledge
Taylor & Francis Group
NEW YORK AND LONDON

First published 2022
by Routledge
605 Third Avenue, New York, NY 10158

and by Routledge
2 Park Square, Milton Park, Abingdon, Oxon, OX14 4RN

Routledge is an imprint of the Taylor & Francis Group, an informa business

© 2022 Bryan Reece

The right of Bryan Reece to be identified as author of this work has been asserted by him in accordance with sections 77 and 78 of the Copyright, Designs and Patents Act 1988.

All rights reserved. No part of this book may be reprinted or reproduced or utilised in any form or by any electronic, mechanical, or other means, now known or hereafter invented, including photocopying and recording, or in any information storage or retrieval system, without permission in writing from the publishers.

Trademark notice: Product or corporate names may be trademarks or registered trademarks, and are used only for identification and explanation without intent to infringe.

Library of Congress Cataloging-in-Publication Data
Names: Reece, Bryan, author.
Title: Social justice and community college education / Bryan Reece.
Description: New York, NY : Routledge, 2021. | Includes bibliographical references and index.
Identifiers: LCCN 2020056758 (print) | LCCN 2020056759 (ebook) | ISBN 9780367675608 (hardback) | ISBN 9780367675585 (paperback) | ISBN 9781003131786 (ebook)
Subjects: LCSH: Social justice and education—United States. | Community colleges—Aims and objectives—United States. | Educational equality—United States.
Classification: LCC LC192.2 .R43 2021 (print) | LCC LC192.2 (ebook) | DDC 370.11/5—dc23
LC record available at https://lccn.loc.gov/2020056758
LC ebook record available at https://lccn.loc.gov/2020056759

ISBN: 978-0-367-67560-8 (hbk)
ISBN: 978-0-367-67558-5 (pbk)
ISBN: 978-1-003-13178-6 (ebk)

Typeset in Baskerville
by Apex CoVantage, LLC

I spent 30 years at three community colleges. Colleagues from Cerritos College, Crafton Hills College, and Norco College brought great joy to my professional life and helped shape many of the ideas poured into this book. As I step into the work of Chancellor for Contra Costa Community College District, I look forward to the professional relationships and friendships to come. In particular, I am grateful for the help that Mark Snowhite and Nick Owchar extended, providing meaningful insight regarding the shape of this book.

A group of volunteers helped me tremendously with the national polling that informed major elements of the book. These individuals included Alva Acosta, Laura Adams, Saeed Ahmad, Paulo Amarol, Riley Araujo, Carlos Arce, Stan Arterberry, Maria Barragan, Kevin Bash, Tracie Burruel, Peggy Campo, Al Cathouse, Gregory Coker, Francine DeFrance, Debbie DiThomas, Vicki Downey Novak, Eloy Garcia, Cyndi Gundersen, Jeffery Hahn, Jane Harmon, Ashlee Johnson, Andrew Jones, Diane Keenan, Sam Lee, Rachel Lee, Jackson Lennon, Richard Linfield, Sherrie Loewen, Richard Mahon, Jeff Marshall, Donna Miller, Farshid Mirzaei, Peter Moloney, Barbara Moore, Terrance Mullins, Sunday Obazuaye, Kay Osorio, Nick Owchar, Kevin Palkki, Jason Parks, Judy Perry, Elizabeth Reece, Barry Russel, Nadeya Sara, Susan Scott, Shanti Scribe, Mark Snowhite, Gio Sosa, Eric Stano, Yong Tan, Kaneesha Tarrant, Marisa Taylor, Sylvia Thomas, Esmeralda Vazquez, Char Weakley, and Keith Wurtz.

I am grateful to have had two wonderful parents who loved me unconditionally and filled me with the confidence to move forward with a sense of optimism, unafraid to tackle challenges like this book. My parents gave their professional lives to service through the church. I have followed in their footsteps in many ways, dedicating my professional life to service through the academy.

The entire Hafliger family played a role in my life that is hard to overstate. Mr. Hafliger (Henry), Mrs. Hafliger (Dorothy), Hank, John, Mike, Robin, Mark, and Lisa were all important people at a vulnerable time in my life. They truly helped change the trajectory of my life. I reflect often on their investment in my life. Much of this book was inspired by their generosity.

My wife, three daughters, and son-in-law were greatly supportive during the writing and research of this book. They were patient with the hours it took from our private lives. They were helpful with the exchange of ideas throughout the process. Much of this book talks about implementing change in higher education, and doing this kind of work can be very difficult at times. All five of these individuals in my life have been great examples of the strength and resolve we need in order to fight for change on behalf of students.

Bio

Bryan Reece is the 9th Chancellor of the Contra Costa Community College District (4CD). Located in the San Francisco Bay Area, 4CD is one of the largest districts in California, serving a regional population of over one million, with more than 52,000 students. 4CD's three colleges, Contra Costa College, Diablo Valley College, and Los Medanos College, have long and proud histories serving students from historically underserved communities.

Dr. Reece has been working in higher education for over 30 years, with 15 years of academic and private sector leadership experience. He taught political science as a tenured community college faculty member for 19 years. As a college leader, he has a documented record of moving community colleges in directions that improve academic success for students across all groups and has particular expertise with student populations from disfavored communities.

Dr. Reece holds bachelor of arts, master of arts, and doctorate degrees in political science from the University of Southern California.

Bryan Reece, Ph.D.

Contents

1 A Good Kind of Subversion   1
2 Community Colleges and Upward Mobility   6
3 How Big Are the Gaps?   22
4 Adding Academic Capital to Students' Lives   61
5 Funding Higher Education Equitably   76
6 Establishing Best Practices   93
7 Creating Intuitive and Supportive Transitions   109
8 Placing Historically Underserved Students in Selective Universities 135
9 Developing Leaders Who Can Effect Institutional Change   152
10 Implementing the Work of Social Justice in Our Colleges   168
11 Social Justice Reform in the Community College Ecosystem   182
12 Caution and Courage   204

   Works Cited   211
   Index   220

1   A Good Kind of Subversion

During my early years as a political science instructor, I spent a lot of time developing lectures, trying to design a classroom experience that was dynamic and engaging. I felt that a great classroom experience would inspire students academically. For a solid decade, I worked on this idea, developing lecture content, honing my speaking skills, curating video clips, designing PowerPoint slides, and building collaborative learning activities. Ten plus years into my teaching career at Cerritos College, I felt I still was not getting the results I wanted in terms of student performance, so one summer, I devoted a great deal of time going back through my lectures, tightening up the content and reworking the corresponding slides for my Introduction to American Government course. I entered the following fall semester confident about the new material and particularly eager to see the midterm results. I was fully expecting to see a jump in student performance, hoping for academic success that would cut across the entire class. I remember being eager to grade the mid-term exams, but as I moved through them, I felt my hope slip away with each score—D, F, D, C, C–, D, C+ . . . It was one of my more discouraging moments as a faculty member.

On the day I was to return their exams, I walked up the three flights of stairs to the classroom with the graded mid-terms tucked under my arm. I could feel my frustration rising as I thought about the time I had pulled from my wife and daughters to prepare the new materials and how this work didn't seem to make a difference. If anything, the scores were worse than they had been the semester before. By the time I made it to class and was handing out the exams, I was angry. I lost my temper with the students and said things to them I still regret. I dismissed class abruptly after passing out the exams. It took 48 hours for me to cool off.

During the next class session, I apologized to my students, and we agreed to a reboot for the semester. But that moment was a turning point for me. I felt like my aspirations for student success were eluding me, and I could feel myself starting down a path I had seen several colleagues take—a path of focusing on the few students who were ready to learn and providing less attention to the students who were not fully committed to learning.

A few months later, I found myself at a training session put on by the California State Academic Senate. It was running a three-day session for new faculty senate leaders or individuals considering a leadership position. I had agreed to attend the meeting, but I was not there with the best frame of mind. Several colleagues at Cerritos College had been encouraging me to run for academic senate president, and I had repeatedly indicated I was not interested. The position seemed very political to me, and as a long-serving senator, I had not personally experienced an academic senate president who had a strong academic focus or any kind of real impact on student learning. But my colleagues' persistence eventually wore me down, and I agreed to attend the training session.

I started the session expecting to confirm my attitudes about the senate as predominantly a political organization, but toward the end of our first day, a speaker laid out the powers of the senate and proceeded to discuss how those powers could be used to enhance the success of our students and elevate the overall teaching and learning environment at our institutions. The presentation had a tremendous impact on me, so much so that I needed to find a quiet place to sit and think about what she had suggested. I was truly shocked. I did not expect to discover the idea that teaching could be enhanced through a collaborative effort and that the college academic senate president could help organize this approach. I felt like this suggestion was a solution to many of the problems I had been struggling with in the classroom, so a few months later, I ran for academic senate president and won with a platform titled *Agenda for Student Success*. Sitting on that bench by myself at the State Academic Senate training session was the start of a long process. A straight line can be drawn from that moment to this book. It's a line that traces two decades through a range of programs, positions, and initiatives organized around the singular idea of doing collaborative work to strengthen the teaching and learning process and thereby effect greater student success.

Collaborative solutions in higher education are very effective. They can have positive impacts on student learning. Many colleagues have found this to be true with the implementation of learning communities, supplemental instruction, guided pathways, and similar programs. I have found most of these collaborative efforts fruitful in every position I have held since I was academic senate president. However, while I have seen programs and projects generate success for students through collaborative approaches, I have yet to experience a collegewide surge of success through this approach. Like many state legislators, governing board members, education researchers, and higher education leaders, I am frustrated with the state of community college completion rates. While we have seen pockets of remarkable success in assorted programs, success rates for community college students in general and success rates for community college students from disfavored communities in particular are disturbingly and unacceptably low. The National Center for Education Statistics finds that only 13 percent of community college students finish their "two-year degrees" within two years, 22 percent within three years, and 28 percent within four years (Chen G., 2020). When community college students are tracked all the way through completion of their "4-year degrees," we find that only 16.7 percent complete within six years—with Asian students completing at 26.4 percent, White students at 21.6 percent, Latinx students at 13.8 percent, and Black students at 9.9 percent (Community College Research Center, 2020a).

I have listened to the concern of education leaders about these disappointing rates for decades and have watched the results remain relatively flat the entire time, while the barriers that hinder success remain. I have gone from faculty member, to academic senate president, to dean, to vice president of instruction, and college president, watching these stubborn rates persist.

To make significant progress on college completion rates for students from historically underserved communities, we need to push past the approach of incremental reform that characterizes so much of higher education. Incremental change leads to incremental improvement, but our students need substantive leaps forward in success rates if we hope to address the enduring equity gaps that persist in American society. For example, we do not need to spend energy and time in efforts that move African American success rates from a 9.9 percent BA/BS completion rate to a 12 or 13 percent rate. The voices calling for social justice today are asking institutions across America to "reach equity," not "reach for equity." They (we) are rightfully impatient with incremental, dispassionate reform. Pointing to the modest changes that come from incremental reform is synonymous with asking people to wait for equity, or, as Dr. King said in "Letter from a Birmingham Jail," "Justice too long delayed is justice denied." To "reach equity" in higher education, we need community colleges in particular to move all disproportionately impacted groups to the 60 percent or higher completion rates that students from upper-income families enjoy, and to achieve improvements of this magnitude, we need big, disruptive solutions. We need an agenda for change with sufficient scope, we need to implement this work together, and we need team members from all constituent groups at our colleges to be engaged in this work.

To move in this direction, we need to recognize the critical role community colleges play in social justice. In the United States, we have long-standing social and cultural structures that perpetuate inequality along race, ethnicity, and income lines. The central role of American community colleges is to disrupt these structures on behalf of the students we serve and improve them. In this sense, community colleges are called to play a subversive role in contemporary society, but it is a good kind of subversion. It is the kind of subversion that the late Congressman and civil rights leader John Lewis called making "good trouble." Community colleges serve the majority of undergraduates from historically underserved communities. Our students are disproportionately students of color, students with recent immigrant histories, students from cycles of low income if not poverty, students from Indigenous communities, and students from first-generation families.

The intended impact of our work with these students is to empower the powerless, enrich the poor, vest the misappropriated, seat the disenfranchised, and center the marginalized. To be successful in this work, we need to break old discriminatory structures, and this kind of work has historically been characterized by the people who benefit from these structures as "causing trouble." So, I believe that if you work in the community college sector, it is important for you to recognize and embrace the idea that you are in the business of making *good trouble*.

Coming out of a community college presidency in 2019, I was just starting to realize this important role we play in society and the disruptive nature of our calling (implementing disruptive reform is probably the reason I was coming out of a presidency in the first place, but more on that later). I had a strong sense of the magnitude these challenges represent regarding student success. I knew the work we needed to do was sizeable, I knew we would only be able to implement the work through collective efforts, and I knew we needed to do work that would scale. But I did not have a comprehensive framework for the full scope of work that community colleges need to complete if we want to close the equity gap in our colleges and impact this achievement gap throughout society. So, in mid-2019, with a year of time in front of me, I decided I would start building the framework and see if I could at least outline the work community colleges need to pursue in our effort to move student success forward and close the equity gap.

I started with a TEDx Talk in the early fall of 2019 that worked out the idea of academic capital, or private resources in students' lives that can assist with their academic journeys, and how our institutions can add capital into the lives of students who lack these resources. I followed up with a few posts/essays on student success (see www.bryan reecephd.com). I eventually decided to combine some of the essays into the development of a white paper that I thought might become a discussion piece in the 2020 presidential campaign dialogue. As I wrote the white paper, it grew and grew, outstripping the typical parameters of such a paper, and it became increasingly clear that the mounting collection of ideas would need the breathing room of a book-length manuscript. Several months later, Routledge (a publisher with a strong education list) and I decided to partner in the publication of what became *Social Justice and Community College Education*.

As I think back on the year of writing and research, there are four things I really learned from the development of this book. First, there is a fairly thorough body of literature discussing internal best practices we need to implement as academic institutions. There is impressive research and discussion about pedagogy, services, programs, and leadership in community colleges that can help our students experience much greater academic success and create an environment where our institutions achieve equity. The book captures these ideas in one place and helps present a practical approach to implementing them in a manner that accelerates equitable student success without overwhelming an institution with too much change.

Second, the book covers significant new territory in the discussion of work we need to do collaboratively as community colleges. There is good work being done collaboratively in many states, the source of most community college funding. But the work we need to do collaboratively at the national level is not as fully defined. There are a few national organizations (e.g., ACCT, ACE, AACC) that do advocacy work in Washington and carry policy agendas; however, on the research front, there is much less work in this space. For instance, there are few substantive articles written around national policies for community college effectiveness in comparison to the articles many of us read regarding policy recommendations at the state level. This book reviews the literature on national policy and collaborative recommendations and pulls opinion data from a national survey of community college personnel. In so doing, we are able to construct a national policy agenda for community colleges that may be the most comprehensive to date. This is one of the more significant contributions of the book.

Third, writing this book helped answer the question, "What makes community colleges unique in higher education?" I have been frustrated with answers to this question for a very long time, and community colleges have suffered from narratives that explain our work in pejorative terms. For most of my career, I received definitions and narratives of community college work that felt externally constructed and derivative of university work. I was presented with (and accepted this for a long time) the notion that community colleges are primarily filled with students and personnel who could not make it to the university. I struggled with the narrative that our students, faculty, staff, mangers, and board members were not up to levels found in four-year universities. This is a common refrain held in popular culture and echoed across the university system where most of us are trained. I knew in my gut for many years that this was a definition given to us by external sources and knew it was inaccurate, but I could not find the central idea that captures the unique expression of community colleges.

Writing this book helped me capture the unique and special mission of American community colleges. We are not ineffectual renderings of the university; rather, community colleges are institutions of higher education whose central role is equity. The work of the community college is the work of social justice, and we carry out this mission in society at a greater volume, with greater intentionality, and through greater expertise than most of our four-year colleagues. The idea of promoting social mobility through education is unconditionally and uncompromisingly embraced by community colleges at levels that are not seen in most of our four-year institutions. In this sense, community colleges are central to a national strategy to end systemic inequality, discrimination, and racism.

The fourth thing I learned from this book adds nothing new to our literature, it adds nothing to our understanding of community colleges, but it added something meaningful to my personal development. Writing this book reinforced the timeless message that growth requires struggle. The initial ideas for this book started during a dark time in my life. The first month or so after I left Norco College was difficult. I was uncertain about my future. I doubted my professional expertise. I experienced the embarrassment of public failure. I felt like I let the people of Norco College and my immediate family down. It was a difficult time, but as I started to pull out of the uncertainty, I realized I had been given the gift of time and could use it to work on a set of problems I would never have had the time to address had I remained in the presidency. In this sense, I am grateful to the Chancellor and the Board who bought out my contract, the college/community members who opposed the decision, and the public clamor that transpired. While it was all personally difficult, the rough outlines of important and fundamental questions emerged alongside a boisterous demand for answers to these questions. What is the scope and scale of community college work? What is the highest purpose of a community college? These two questions hung in the air as I left Norco College and largely shaped the year that followed.

We all need people in our lives who push us in uncomfortable directions. These people encourage us (sometimes in difficult ways) to explore challenging terrain. The Chancellor and the Board of the Riverside Community College District played this role in my life. They set me on a course and prompted me to make the case that community colleges are central to American social justice, central to establishing equity throughout society, and in need of expansive development and support. They pushed me to define our scope of work, develop a national policy agenda, identify and articulate areas of collaboration, and place the work of community colleges into the larger context of America's ongoing struggle to grow access and establish equity. A journey I did not intend to start began from a difficult place, broke through to one of the most productive/fulfilling years of my professional life, and brought me to a deeper understanding of the institutions I love. I hope you learn as much from reading this book as I did from writing it.

2 Community Colleges and Upward Mobility

When I was in high school, I worked on the Hafliger Dairy farm in San Jacinto, California. My job was to bring cows in from their corrals to the milk barn, clean the cows' udders before they entered the barn, help the cow milker transition from one corral to the next, help feed the cows, and do other jobs around the dairy as needed. My shifts varied. Sometimes I worked about 20 hours per week after school or before school started. During the summers, I was able to work full time.

Toward the end of my senior year, I decided to approach the manager of the dairy and ask if I could continue working for him as a full-time cow milker. To me, cow milkers had a steady job, and the pay seemed enough to carve out a living. So, on an early morning winter day, at the end of my shift, with a bright new sun over the horizon and a crispness in the air, I stood on the concrete slab outside the manager's office waiting for him to arrive. As he approached, I mustered up the courage to ask him the question, "I am going to be graduating in a few months, and I was wondering if I could milk cows for you full time after graduation?"

Feeding Dairy Cows

The manager was Hank Hafliger, the oldest son in the Hafliger family. He was a no-nonsense kind of person, in his late 20s or early 30s, with a young family and a house on the dairy property. He stopped as I approached him, listened to my question, and replied without hesitation, "You can't work for me unless you go to college." I remember being shocked by his reply. I was not expecting that answer, and while I stood there blinking in the early morning sun, he followed up, "Do you want to go to college or not?"

I had wanted to go to college. This was something I had hoped for throughout high school. I took college prep courses. I was a pretty good student, receiving mostly As and Bs on report cards. On top of that, I was a very strong basketball player. During my junior and senior years of high school, I was contacted by college basketball coaches across the country inviting me to come play for them. Despite all of this opportunity, I somehow wound up deep into my senior year with no concrete plans on how to go to college. I hadn't followed up with any coaches. I hadn't applied to any colleges. I could not seem to connect all the dots. They seem so obvious to me now as a mature adult, but at the time, I was lost.

When he asked me if I wanted to go to college, I answered without hesitation, "Yes, I definitely want to go to college." Hank then turned around, walked into his office, and called the Dairy Science Department at California Polytechnic University in San Luis Obispo. He spoke with the chair of the department, found out that there were five more student openings in the department, and arranged for an application to be sent to me, telling the chair that he had an employee who would be applying and asked that they hold a slot. When I received the application in the mail, I filled it out, turned it in, and was accepted to Cal Poly San Luis Obispo.

In the months leading up to Cal Poly, Hank, his dad Henry, and his mom Dorothy helped me prepare. They took me on a visit of the campus, encouraged me to follow through, made sure I started my freshman year, and more. They continued to follow up with me throughout my initial years. They helped me out financially from time to time. They helped me with summer jobs and work over breaks. They were not relatives. They were not people I had known for multiple years. They were not boosters for Cal Poly. They were just kind people who decided to help a young man get his start.

I think about that morning with Hank often. I wonder what might have happened had he agreed to give me the job or, worse yet, told me there was no opening for a new full-time cow milker and left it at that. What he did for me, in such a brief encounter, was nothing short of changing the trajectory of my life and subsequently all the people connected to me thereafter.

Many of our students come to us in a situation very similar to this. They are standing on their own slab of concrete asking us to help with their futures. Like me, they may come from families that love them very deeply, but the students who come from families that do not have college-going traditions struggle to navigate the basics of a college education; they do not have people in their lives who know academic processes. This is particularly true for students from historically underserved communities and therefore very common in a community college setting. We need to stay ever conscious of the precious nature each student encounter may have. They are at very tenuous moments in their lives, and even the slightest acts of kindness, warmth, and direction can have profound impacts on their lives. We need to bring this consciousness into our teaching, services, management, and leadership; it needs to be integrated into the operations of our colleges. While our individual and group interactions with students may seem small, like placing a phone call to Cal Poly San Luis Obispo, they are often profound in the lives of our students.

I did not have immediate success in college. In fact, I ended my freshman year on academic probation and returned my sophomore year knowing I had to figure out how to be a more serious student. Success eventually came with hard work and a series of individuals who took an interest in my academic life, wrapping themselves around me and showing me how to be a good student. Faculty, staff, and other students were gracious, empathetic, and generous with their time. Because of them and because of individual hard work, I eventually found my footing academically, transferred to the University of Southern California (USC), changed my major to political science, entered an honors program, and made it onto the Dean's List for academic excellence.

In graduate school, as I was starting to think about my career, I did not have a specific career idea, but I knew that I somehow wanted to replicate what others had done for me as many times over as possible. This is what I was thinking about when I became a professor of political science. It is what I was thinking about when I became a dean. It is what I was thinking about when I became VP of academic affairs. It is what I was thinking about when I became a college president. It is what I have been thinking about during the writing of this book.

There are millions of Americans caught in a similar situation to the one I described. They have an awareness of what is possible in America but are not sure how to move toward these possibilities and need someone (actually a group of people) who can help set them on their path. Awareness of these opportunities is pretty common. Many people who experience extreme poverty live close to equally extreme wealth in many U.S. communities. For those who live in more isolated settings, they may not encounter wealth and privilege in their day-to-day lives, but it is inescapable if they have access to television, the internet, film, or radio. Every day, year after year, we see a common narrative play out in American entertainment, telling stories that have the idea of opportunity baked into them, if not a major theme in the story itself. American television is filled with stories that reinforce this idea. Our sitcoms, dramas, news vignettes, reality programming, and more constantly reinforce the idea that living an honest life and working hard lead to a comfortable existence that includes a nice home, a satisfying job, access to healthcare, and participation in democratic societies with opportunity for all who are willing to do the work.

The promise of America has captured imagination from its inception. Engineering a country around the goals of equality and opportunity for all remains appealing the world over, and our celebration of this idea through American entertainment—one of our greatest exports—has sold it to domestic and international audiences alarmingly well. In certain respects, I like the idea of promoting and celebrating these ideals through entertainment media. Communicating ideas through storytelling is as old as humanity. We are wired to follow and remember stories. Stories that reinforce our commitments to equality, opportunity, individualism, community, family, hard work, and democracy are good in the sense that they communicate complex ideas to a mass audience and have the potential to bring us together around shared values.

The dangerous part about communicating these ideas through entertainment lies in the distinction between normative ideals and empirical reality. Normative ideals are important to society. They help us understand where we are headed. They help us visualize and agree upon what *should be* in society. Empirical reality, on the other hand, is a description of what *is*. It describes how things actually are. As a faculty member, I always tried to start with this idea in my lectures on American government. It is critical to understand where we are headed (what America *should be*) and where we are (what America *is*). Having a clear sense of these contrasting views—our normative goals and our empirical reality relative to these goal—informs the individual of the scope and scale of reform that is needed in society.

For example, if you believe that our empirical reality in the United States is very close to our normative goals, you are probably a person who calls for incremental change. You see the need to do fine-tuning. If you are a person who believes our empirical reality is far from our normative goals, you are probably a person who calls for significant reform. The dangerous part of our entertainment being filled with these normative ideas is that people start to believe that the fictional programming they watch is a reflection of reality. The sitcom where racism is never a part of life suggests to some that racism is not part of America. The reality television program demonstrating that prosperity comes to those who are willing to work hard suggests to many that such success is a reality in American. The drama that shows seamless integration of recent immigrants suggests to many that such is the reality in America. The belief that these values are a reality in the United States can become so entrenched that individuals are not capable of receiving data that reveal the contrary.

The history of America can be understood as a collective march (sometimes fight) toward our ideals. We have made admirable progress in some areas, but the state of our society, the empirical reality of today, is of course far from achieving these ideas. Every social science discipline in American higher education is working in this space, documenting inequitable access to the promise of America. Individual, cultural, and institutional bias against people from marginalized communities is an overwhelmingly consistent finding across these disciplines. People of color, recent immigrants, low-income families, other-abled individuals, the LGBTQ+ community, Indigenous Americans, and more have long histories of suffering discrimination, and with little more than a click, we can watch current incidents of this suffering play out in our daily news feeds.

A majority of Americans (58 percent) believe race relations in the United States are bad, and most (56 percent) believe this problem is getting worse (Horowitz, Brown, & Cox, 2019). A clear majority of Americans indicate they do not want racism to be part of our society, and a recent survey found that 75 percent of Americans believe diversity strengthens our society and should be nurtured (Horowitz et al., 2019).

A major shared value in the United States is equality. It is celebrated throughout our society. At the same time, as demonstrated previously, we have the presence of inequality in society. Eliminating the inequality of opportunity we find in reality and moving toward our ideal of equality of opportunity without exception is the goal of our social justice work. Great civic and political reforms have been accomplished in the United States under the banner of social justice. The American Revolution, the Civil War, Emancipation, and women's suffrage can be seen as struggles to address social injustices.

However, major components of our American heritage are marked by the development of wealth and power through the deliberate engineering of inequality. A significant portion of our country's development has been built on the back of social injustices. Slavery, Jim Crow laws, Indian reservations, Japanese internment, repatriation, and red-lining have been government-authorized programs that take resources from one group to enrich another. Part of our struggle to move toward the ideal of equality requires direct confrontation of social structures that work in opposition to equality. Unfair discrimination is one of those structures. Race-based, income-based, and other group-based discrimination is part of the American fabric holding threads that are over 400 years old. With many of these threads still loaded in the loom today, we have considerable work to do to establish a more equitable society. Removing inequities from American society is essential to building a better union and is the central goal of social justice.

Unrest in the United States related to social justice issues is on the rise. Mass shootings in the United States hit an all-time high in 2019. Violent hate crimes are rising. Citizens of color continue to be killed in disproportionately high numbers (ACLED, 2020). There are a range of other indicators that point to this unrest. The causes for the rise range from anxiety related to the pandemic; the government's more militarized response to protests; a heightened use of us-them politics emphasizing race, ethnicity, immigration, and religion; stark partisanship; and stoking of culture wars. I believe these are accurate reasons, but they are secondary. The surface reason that fuels the underlying approaches that in turn create unrest is a half-century trend in growing inequality that has diminished the very idea of an American Dream.

The American Dream is an aspirational idea suggesting that the United States is a place where opportunity is not restrained by social conventions like birthright or class or any of the cultural restrictions humans put on each other to privilege some and limit others. The American Dream is an idea that has been associated with the geography of North America for hundreds of years, drawing an eclectic mix of individuals from stifled conditions to this place where freedom, equality, and individualism are core values. The American Dream promises that prosperity comes from individual effort and ingenuity, and over a long history, this land has lured people into her open spaces and urban centers with the idea that opportunity is available to each individual willing to work hard.

One way to think of American history is through the lens of the American Dream. The United States was established on this core idea, and our history can be seen as a struggle to live up to the idea, embedding it in our institutions, in our stories, and in our struggles to expand the number of people who are permitted to enjoy the American Dream.

In contrast, class, gender, race, ethnicity, nationality, and religion have all been instruments used to limit who has access to the American Dream. Our most significant struggles in U.S. history have been efforts aimed at confronting and breaking these limitations on access to opportunity. The American Revolution, Civil War, Labor Movement, Women's Suffrage, Civil Rights, MeToo, and others have been conflicts centered around a privileged group holding power and an underprivileged group insisting that power be redistributed in a more equitable manner. The moral underpinning of each of these conflicts has been the American Dream, the idea that we are all supposed to have access to the pursuit of happiness.

While access to opportunity in the United States has expanded in certain respects, it has been contracting over the last 50 years, and this backward trend has been swelling frustrations from one generation to the next, as the idea of prosperity in the United States grows more and more elusive for many segments of the population. There is no place where this frustration is more evident than in our recent civic dialogue. Many voters and their elected representatives across the political spectrum are expressing rhetoric on a routine basis that is alarming. We commonly hear language that has punched through the ceiling of our traditional civic dialogue. We have seen recent public protests leading to physical harm (even death). We have government officials openly accusing each other of the worst intentions—even criminal intentions. Many have gone well beyond a passionate disagreement over ideas and have dug in around partisan lines where actors from both sides publicly demonize their opposition. Some observers have called this behavior a "cold civil war." I believe much of this frustration stems from an economy that is changing fundamentally, leaving significant pockets of our population behind, and causing widening inequality across the entire country.

From the mid-60s forward, a gap has been growing between the wealthy and the middle class, between the wealthy and the poor. A wide range of academics, journalists, and government leaders (on both sides of the aisle) have pointed to this trend. In a recent report by the Urban Institute (Signe-Mary McKernan, 2017), researchers found that in 1962, wealthy Americans (in the 90th percentile of income) earned two times more than middle-income Americans (in the 50th percentile of income) and seven times more than poor Americans (in the 10th percentile of income). Tracking the differences between wealthy, middle class, and poor Americans over a 50-year period, the study found that gaps grew consistently throughout the half-century. By 2016, wealthy Americans earned 3 times more than middle-income Americans and 13 times more than poor Americans. Furthermore, with income in the United States breaking down along race and ethnicity lines, there is also a disturbing pattern associated with Americans of color. When filtered for Black and Latinx income, the study found that there is a similar widening trend between White earnings and earnings for people of color, so much so that by 2016, White Americans earned on average ten times more than Black Americans and eight times more than Latinx Americans. While the American economy has expanded dramatically since the 1960s, individuals in the

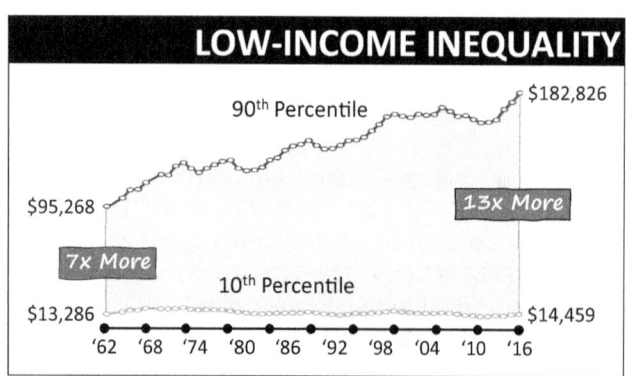

upper income brackets (predominately White) have taken a disproportionate share of this growth, while middle- and low-income Americans have realized very small gains over the same period.

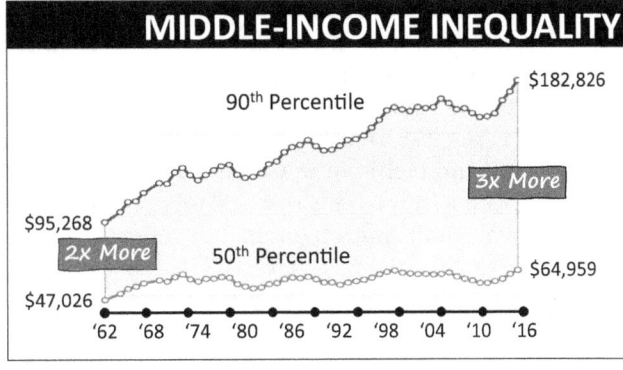

This economic inequality is not only *seen*, but it is *felt* by many Americans. Many Americans are watching the stock market and similar economic indicators hit record highs over extended periods of growth but have not seen this translate into their lives or their family's lives. Increasingly, working-class and low-income Americans are finding themselves stuck with relatively flat wages and rising costs of living. This makes it highly difficult and extremely stressful to sustain a livelihood and even agonizing as they watch many of their children follow family traditions only to find standards of living that slip below that of their parents.

Since the 1960s, leaders across the political spectrum have come and gone with rhetoric aimed at solving this problem. Nearly every president has called out this inequality to one degree or another. But for 50 years, this trend has consistently grown, and with it a general feeling of resentment and distrust among those who suffer from this widening inequality. Their frustration explains the energy and traction that left and right ideas have captured in contemporary America. It explains "Feel the Burn" and "Make America Great Again." It explains diesel truck owners' coal-rolling drivers in electric cars. It explains the passion behind "Black Lives Matter." It explains the misplaced suspicion of immigrants and Muslims. Many Americans are watching an economy that provided for their families over generations turn into something they do not recognize. It is leaving them behind. Desperation is settling in, and we are seeing the worst in us prevail as pockets of America displace blame and misplace frustrations on groups that don't look like them.

A study released at the 2019 World Economic Forum in Switzerland provides a basis for understanding these issues (Woetzel, 2019). The report looked at all jobs in the United States and Europe, assessing their demand between 2016 and 2030 (projected). With the findings from their analysis, we can categorize jobs into two categories: jobs that are on the rise and jobs that are in decline.

The grey box in Figure 2.4 summarizes the findings for jobs in decline. The study estimates that in 2016, there were the equivalent of 153 million full-time jobs. These jobs are trending down, so much so that by the time the United States and Europe reach 2030, this category will have lost the equivalent of 23 million full-time jobs, and individuals who remain in those jobs will likely experience wage stagnation. Jobs in the black box are expected to grow. The study estimates that in 2016, there were the equivalent of 160 million full-time jobs. These jobs are trending up, so much so that by the time the United States and Europe reach 2030, this category will have added the equivalent of 38 million full-time jobs, and most individuals employed in these jobs will experience healthy wages.

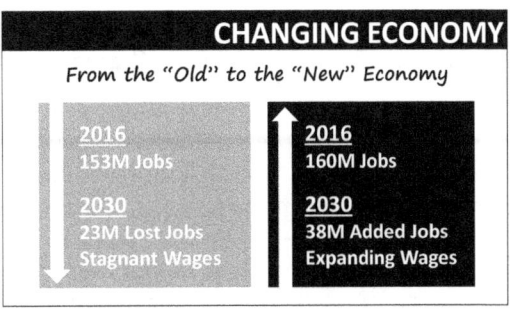

Jobs in decline include those that require manual labor, low cognition, low skills, and repetitive tasks. Jobs that are on the rise tend to require technology expertise, people and management skills, high levels of cognition, elevated skills, and creativity. These jobs are predicted to continue growing.

The study suggests that the primary reasons the economy is changing in this way are globalization and technology. Global markets are larger and more connected than they have ever been in human history, and technology is more widespread and capable than it has ever been. Globalization has had the effect of moving "grey box" jobs to markets with low labor costs and away from markets like the U.S. Technology has had the effect of replacing "grey box" jobs with automation. The growing jobs, "black box" jobs, are those that cannot be done by low labor and cannot be automated. Combined, these two forces are altering the nature of work, the work that is needed in society today, and the work that will be needed tomorrow. Furthermore, as globalization and digital technology continue to accelerate—and they are accelerating—"black box" jobs will continue to expand, while "grey box" jobs continue to shrink, especially in the United States.

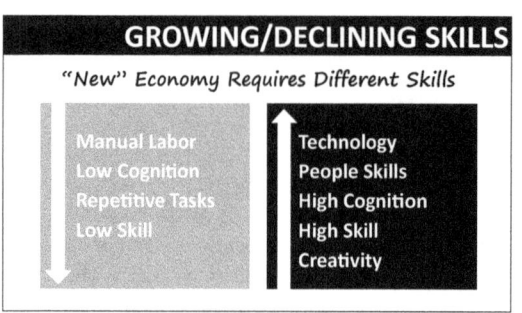

When I look at these trends from a personal perspective, I tend to have a sense of optimism. Most of my career has been in the growth areas. My wife's career is in the growth area. Our kids are preparing for careers in the growth area. Most of my friends and colleagues are in this growth area. But if your livelihood is in the box that is diminishing or if you were born into a family that has traditionally worked in these industries, you have a very different perspective on these trends. What these individuals often experience is job loss or the fear of job loss, community blight, and economic hardship. This is hitting pockets of rural and urban America especially hard, and this coincides with some of the angriest dialogue in the United States. These places are upset and desperate as they watch their livelihoods diminish, all the while seeing people in the "black box" prosper and flourish.

During difficult economic times, during times of major economic turmoil, too many Americans turn to an uglier side and start looking for scapegoats to blame all their troubles on. At the same time, politicians who speak to these fears and articulate policy positions that support scapegoating rise in popularity and amplify a toxic message that divides us and perpetrates further discrimination against racial and socio-economic minority groups. This dynamic has happened throughout our history and is playing out in contemporary America as the effects of growing inequality are being felt across major segments of the American public.

Social Injustice in the United States

When I look at racism, homophobia, xenophobia, sexism, and all the other forms of discrimination that oppress vulnerable groups in the United States, I see it stemming from four distinct sources. The first source is individuals or groups. Individuals and groups that overtly believe in supremacy (e.g., white supremacy) have always been part of American society. This is probably the easiest source of discrimination in the United States to identify, because they are upfront about their beliefs. They openly publish hate-based rhetoric in their social media feeds. They have mission statements that tell us what they stand for.

White nationalism in particular is experiencing a rise in the United States and other countries. According to the Anti-Defamation League (ADL), white nationalist propaganda has surged over the last four years. Tracking propaganda incidents across the country between January and July of the last four years, ADL found fewer than 250 incidents in 2017, over 500 in 2018, about 1,200 in 2019, and over 2,700 in 2020 (Johnson & Urquhart, 2020).

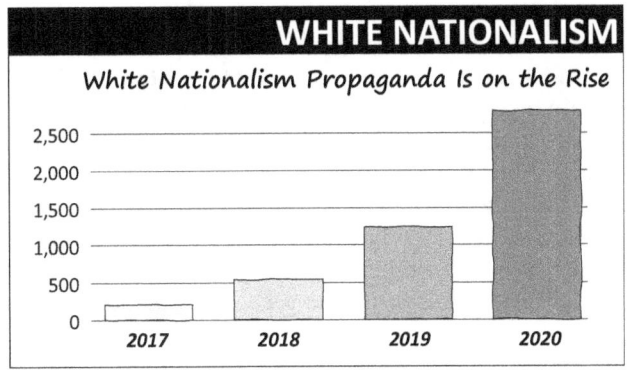

A second major source of discrimination in the Anti-Defamation League (ADL) comes from public policy. This country has a history filled with examples of official laws and long-standing precedents that have codified unfair discrimination. Laws that established and enforced segregation did not allow for mixed-race marriage, prohibited same-sex marriage, suppressed voter turnout, and much more. These public policies are a stain on the country, but our collective work in legislatures, courthouses, and ballot boxes to remove and overturn these policies is something we can also be proud of as a nation. The removals of many of these public policies occupy major markers in our historical development (e.g., *Brown v. Board of Education*). With that said, we still have discriminatory policies at the local, state, and federal levels that remain and need to be removed.

A third major source of discrimination comes from cultural norms. All of us live by a very complex and long list of rules. Many of the rules we live by are official. They are written down and held by official bodies. For example, a wide range of rules address how we are required to drive, what taxes we are required to pay, ways we are required to behave in the wilderness, lines we are not allowed to cross with regard to private property and much more. These are all official rules. But there is even a longer list of *un*official rules we all live by that are not written down by an official body. These are the rules imposed on us by our culture. These rules govern how we eat, how close we stand to each other, how long we are to hold eye contact with each other (if at all), how we interact in professional settings vs. romantic settings, and much more. We learn these rules through acculturation. As we grow, the influential adults and peers in our lives teach us thousands and thousands of subtle rules that heavily influence how we behave. These cultural rules are so embedded in us that we give little thought to them in our daily routines. For example, people from the same culture easily, almost automatically, establish the appropriate amount of space when they are talking to each other. And when two people with different cultural definitions of conversation space address each other, there is often an awkwardness that neither can explain. The awkwardness stems from a collision between deeply held cultural rules we subconsciously try to follow as we move through our daily lives.

Most of the cultural rules that we receive during our formative years are inconsequential. Some cultures encourage eating with an open mouth; others encourage eating with the mouth closed. Some cultures find brief eye contact between strangers to be a sign of respect and acknowledgment; other cultures discourage this kind of eye contact, seeing it as an invasion of privacy. Some cultures encourage quiet during the screening of a movie; others encourage verbal engagement. Is one right and the other wrong? Of course not. They are just different, and these differences are inconsequential. They are not very relevant to improving the human condition.

But when the given rules, norms, or beliefs that we impose on members of our culture support discrimination, support poor treatment of some groups and privileged treatment of others, the impact on society can be profound. If you are raised, for example, to believe certain groups are more violent, less honest, less capable of leadership, prone to distraction, lawless, and so on, you are likely going to treat members of these group worse than those in the groups you believe to hold more admirable traits. You may not even know you are behaving in this manner because these beliefs (in this case biases) are so deeply held they seem *natural*, or indisputable. This is how people who insist they do not discriminate against any group act in a discriminatory manner. This source of discrimination is insidious and very difficult to even recognize, let alone change.

When I was a college student, I was definitely homophobic. I held attitudes that were anti-gay. I did not develop these beliefs reasonably and thoughtfully. I had not spent a lot of time thinking about sexuality and come to a conclusion that supported this stance. If you had asked my in that period of my life why I held those beliefs, I probably would have given you a memorized cliché. A couple of times after high school, I had been asked out by gay men. From time to time, I would bring these incidents up in the company of friends and tell the stories from a very pejorative frame.

I remember sitting in a car with a friend at Venice Beach one day. We were both undergraduates, hanging out at the beach, enjoying the day. In the course of our conversation, I told her about one of these encounters. I told the story as I always had. I didn't tell the story with hate, but I did communicate it with surprise and a degree of disgust. I remember she listened to the story that I had intended to be humorous. She didn't laugh. Instead, she asked me why I found these encounters so offensive. She asked me why I didn't see another man asking me out on a date as a compliment. I remember her saying, "When a guy asks you out on a date, he is just indicating that he finds you attractive and would like to spend some time with you. Where is the insult? Why don't you see this as a compliment?"

In that moment, sitting in the passenger seat of her car, I was able to access a deeply held belief and look at it with a more critical eye and from a different perspective. I was able to see a bias, an irrational belief with much greater humanity. We all have these cultural biases. They are difficult to locate and more difficult unpack. I am grateful for that conversation in the car and lucky to have encountered a friend who could so skillfully help me introspect and address an unconscious belief that only added discord to society rather than community.

A fourth major source of discrimination in the United States is institutional racism/discrimination. In my opinion, this is the most difficult kind of discrimination to address in society. It is difficult for many to see, difficult for the individuals who work in these institutions to accept, and highly complicated to eradicate. Many institutions or sectors in society have long-established ways of carrying out their responsibilities. Similar to the discussion of culture previously, these institutions/sectors have official policies and practices, often put in place many years ago, and norms and attitudes baked into the culture of the organization that are often as old as the institution itself.

Police departments, corporations, churches, schools, universities, healthcare institutions, and government agencies have histories that have been passed down to contemporary employees. When these histories are long, it is not difficult to see how they reach back to eras when blatant discrimination was accepted, even encouraged. The individuals who ran these institutions during these periods were part of an America that was starkly different than the one we live in today. They wrote policies and established cultural norms that often remain and continue to generate biased outcomes which cut against disfavored communities. This is how we find ourselves in a society where an institution can be filled with individuals who do not want discrimination to prevail despite the institution they belong to generating outcomes that have a discriminatory effect on society.

Institutional discrimination is the kind of discrimination most frequently discussed in this book. We look at practices inside our institutions as practices that prevail in the higher education ecosystem that continue to stack the deck against students of color, students with recent immigrant histories, LGBTQ+ students, first-generation students, poor students, and others.

As a political scientist, I have been aware of these injustices for decades. The forces in society responsible for them were the main reason I was drawn to the discipline. Social justice was a major theme baked into the courses I taught as a faculty member. This theme has been paramount as I have moved into every leadership position I have held, believing in the central idea that higher education can be the Great Equalizer.

The Great Equalizer

Horace Mann (1796–1859), one of the earliest advocates for public education, thought of education as essential to our general civic development and advocated for it as an attorney and later as an elected legislator from Massachusetts. Mann referred to public education as the "Great Equalizer," a moniker we have held for education to this day. Higher education prides itself in this light, claiming that the surest onramp to the middle class, the surest way to achieve the American Dream, is to secure an education—in today's economy, that generally means a bachelor's degree.

Using data collected by Raj Chetty (Harvard) and his team, the *New York Times* recently ran an article (Gregor Aisch, 2017) showing the equalizing impact higher education has on society. The study looked at the income level of children's families and compared that to the income level these children achieve when they reach their mid-30s. The study starts with an analysis of all children in the United States, regardless of education levels achieved, and follows them into their mid-30s. This analysis shows that those from a low-income family are much more likely to end up in poverty themselves, whereas those from a high-income family are much more likely to end with a salary that is at an upper-income level. The study then looks at children grouped by levels of education. When the data are controlled for education, it is evident that a bachelor's degree has an equalizing impact on graduates. For example, students 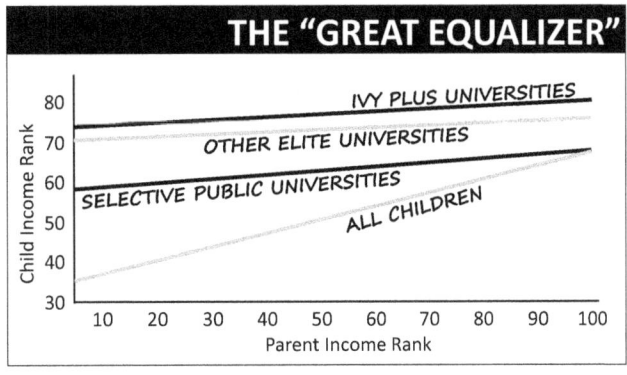 who graduate from Ivy League and similar institutions tend to end up with similar incomes by the time they reach their mid-30s. The same holds for graduates from other elite universities and selective public universities. Graduates from affluent families still tend to do a little better economically than their peers who come from low- and moderate-income families; however, there is a dramatic equalizing effect. This analysis is very encouraging news for those who see education as the Great Equalizer.

But, when we look at the number of students who move through these institutions to receive degrees, when we look at the volume of students from high-income backgrounds who complete bachelor's degrees and compare it to the volume of students from middle- and low-income backgrounds who complete bachelor's degrees, the differences are stunning. According to the National Center for Education Statistics and College for America, about 60 percent of freshman students from high-income families will complete their bachelor's degree, while approximately 29 percent of freshman students from middle-income families will finish with that degree, and roughly 14 percent of freshman students from low-income families will receive a bachelor's degree. Although the economic impact on students who complete their degrees has an equalizing effect, the success rate of students from different economic backgrounds continues to seriously inhibit social mobility in the United States. For a myriad of reasons (we will explore these later), higher education is helping affluent families maintain their privileged places in society and predominantly keeping lower-income families from accessing the American Dream.

I do *not* think this result is intended by my colleagues who work in the colleges and universities across the United States, but it is the clear impact higher education continues to have. The institutions we rely on to create an environment where social mobility is real, the colleges and universities we rely on to make the American Dream accessible to all, are actually part of the problem in contemporary American society. American institutions of higher education are systematically, albeit unintentionally, part of the inequality problem in the United States.

With this knowledge of higher education's impact on society, our national imperative, our national challenge, becomes very clear. We need to make changes across our college and university systems that cause more historically underserved students to go to college, succeed in college, complete college, and enter middle-income (or higher) jobs. We must define and embrace a reform agenda that changes the academic odds of success for students of color, for student from backgrounds of poverty or low income, for students with recent immigrant histories, for students from Indigenous communities, for students from foster care backgrounds, for students where no one in their family has gone to college. When we are able to effect change in higher education that moves these students from a 14 percent completion rate of bachelor's degrees to a 40, 50, or 60 percent rate, then we will be able to truly live up to Horace Mann's aspiration of American education as the Great Equalizer.

> **OUR PRIMARY CHALLENGE**
>
> How do we get more <u>historically underserved</u> students into college, through college, out of college, and into middle-class (or above) jobs?

Students from historically underserved communities who complete their bachelor's degree take a range of paths on their way to success, but the most common pathway starts at a public K–12 institution, moves into a community college, transfers to a university, and ends at the job market, although for some, additional education will lead to other jobs. There are a series of hurdles laid out across this journey, and some of these hurdles reduce the pipeline of students dramatically as they try to work their way through this journey. To begin with, onboarding at the community college is problematic. Many colleges see more than a 50 percent drop-off through the onboarding process, where over half the students who indicate an interest in attending the college by starting the applications process fail to complete the entire process. Once underserved students are registered in class, more than 75 percent of them at community colleges fail to complete their program. This means that more than 75 percent do not complete an associate degree or certificate or achieve enough units to become transfer ready. For the few that make it to transfer-readiness, many (in the range of 50 percent at some colleges) do not apply for transfer to a university. Finally, when students do transfer, very few apply for or are accepted by select universities. For example, the top ten universities this year according to *U.S. News and World Report* on average have 18.8 percent of their student body from middle, lower-middle and low-income backgrounds. This percentage is critical, because many of the large employers in the United States look to the most selective universities for employees, and with these universities biased so heavily toward students from upper-income families, social mobility for students from low-income families will continue to lag.

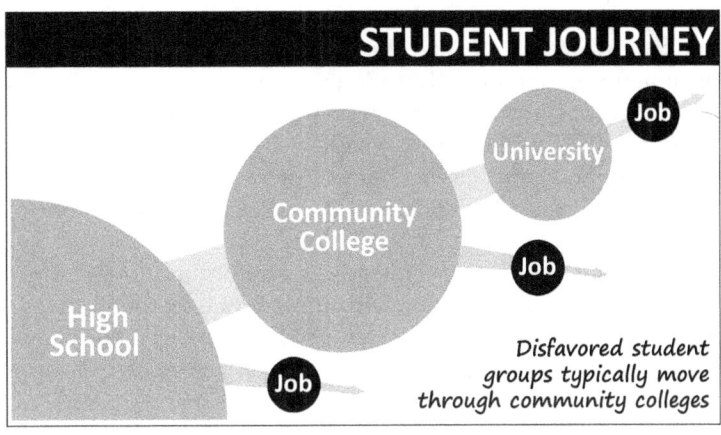

While these hurdles continue to cause significant problems for many students, it is important to note that there are many elements in the pathway from high school through higher education that are working. It is an impressive infrastructure and national asset that is the envy of the world in many respects. We annually invest over $700 billion on public elementary and secondary schools in the United States (National Center for Education Statistics, 2019a) and nearly $600 billion on degree-granting postsecondary institutions (National Center for Education Statistics, 2019b). We spend nearly $1.3 trillion on this pathway annually. On top of this impressive commitment to education, I can categorically say that in my 30-year career in higher education, almost every person I have worked with has been unequivocally committed to helping students succeed. But still, we have a few critical choke points in the process causing students from historically underserved communities to stall, if not drop out altogether.

Given that higher education is the most common route to positions of influence in society, and given that community colleges work with more students from historically underserved communities than any other sector of higher education, the special role community college plays in society becomes clear. We are at the center of social justice in the United States. In order for us to achieve social justice at a faster rate, we need to make sure community colleges are successful. But right now, many community colleges are struggling to deliver on this important mission.

I recently conducted a rather straightforward assessment to see how effectively we have been in addressing these issues throughout the state of California. For three full decades, I have been engaged with a large group of colleagues in California's community college system trying to build systems, processes, and practices that elicit greater student success. This has included a desire to see all students find greater success and in particular increase success rates in a manner that lowers the equity gaps between student populations that is prevalent across the United States. We have been in a serious dialogue about these issues for most of my career. As a system, we have been talking about student success and equity for a long time. We have identified proven best practices strategies we need to implement. We have baked these goals and aspirations into our strategic and planning documents across the California community college system. With this significant push, I wanted to see how much progress we have made.

I decided to apply a basic analysis I have used in college-level assessment, looking at course retention and success rates for students, and disaggregate the data by race/ethnicity. However, instead of collecting these data for a single college or district, I would apply this analysis to the entire state. Pulling course success and retention data for fall terms for all public community colleges in California between 1992 and 2019, I was able to access over 44 million student enrollments in over four million sections/courses (California Community College Chancellor's Office, 2020a). Focusing only on in-person courses (no distance education courses) and exclusively on degree-applicable courses, I was able to track the statewide course retention and success trends over 27 years. As might be expected, some of the trends are promising, while others are surprising, if not frustrating.

In the most general terms, the California Community College system appears to be headed in the right direction. When all students are assessed over the 27-year history, course retention and success trends are moving up. For all students in the fall of 1992, the course retention rate (students who finished with a grade of A, B, C, D, F, P, NP, I, IPP, INP, FW) was 78.4 percent. This number grew in a fairly linear fashion over 27 years, ending with a fall 2019 rate of 87.7 percent. With regard to course success (students who finished with a grade of A, B, C, P, IA, IB, IC, IPP), the rates went from 66.0 percent in fall of 1992 to 72.3 percent in fall of 2019. Over 27 years, both trendlines were moving in a positive direction, with retention and success rates growing by 9.3 percent and 6.3 percent, respectively.

When the data are disaggregated by race/ethnicity, a similar trend is found for Asian, Black, Indigenous, Latinx, Pacific Islander, and White students. Assessing data from the fall term of 1992 through the fall term of 2019, Asian students went from 79.7 percent to 90.0 percent for course retention rates and 68.4 percent to 79.3 percent for course success rates. Black students went from 72.1 percent to 84.0 percent for course retention rates and 55.2 percent to 63.4 percent for course success rates. Indigenous students went from 75.7 percent to 86.0 percent for course retention rates and 61.5 percent to 68.4 percent for course success rates. Latinx students went from 76.0 percent to 86.5 percent for course retention rates and 60.3 percent to 68.3 percent for course success rates. Pacific Islander students went from 76.2 percent to 85.9 percent for course retention rates and

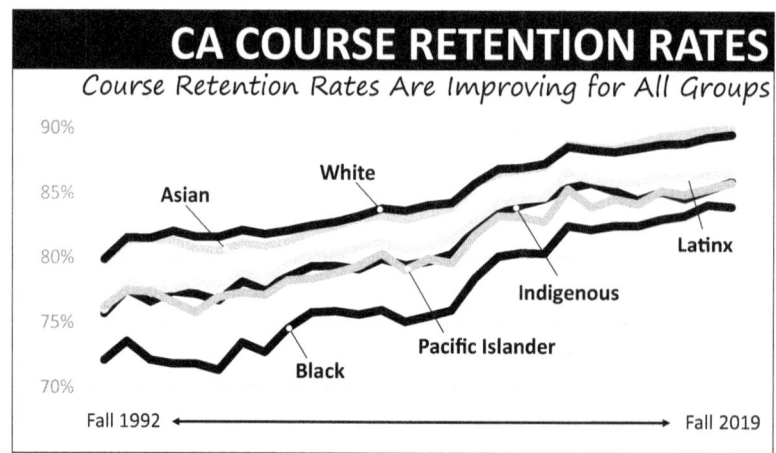

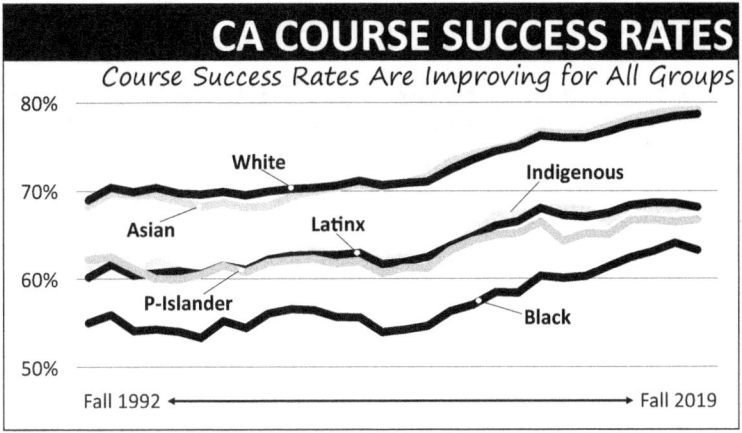

62.4 percent to 66.8 percent for course success rates. Finally, White students went from 79.9 percent to 89.6 percent for course retention rates and 69.1 percent to 78.8 percent for course success rates. All six groups have shown ongoing improvement with regard to course retention and course success over the last 27 years. As demonstrated in the corresponding graphics, all six historical lines for course retention and success are moving in positive directions.

Equity Gaps: Course Retention

To determine the course retention equity gaps (course retention means to finish a course), we need to assess the relative difference between the top-performing group each year from 1992–2019 and the lower performing groups. In every year, the highest-performing group was Asian or White. In the earlier years, the top performer tended to be White; in the later years, the top performer tended to be Asian. For each year, I measured the gap between the top performer and the lower-performing groups (Latinx, Black, Pacific Islander, and Indigenous students). In this assessment, the findings are hopeful. In the 27-year period of analysis, the trendline for African American students shows a steady narrowing of the gap, with a 1992 gap of 7.8 percentage points below the top-performing group and a 2019 gap of 6.0 points. Latinx students demonstrated a trend toward narrowing the gap with a 1992 gap of 3.9 percentage points below and a 2019 gap of 3.5 points below. Pacific Islander students trended in the positive direction (the trend was only slight, but positive nonetheless), even though they started at 3.7 percentage points below and ended at 4.2 points below. Indigenous students demonstrated a similar pattern, showing a slight positive trend toward narrowing the gap, despite starting at 4.2 percentage points below and ending at 4.1 points below. For all four groups, the data show trendlines that are moving in the right direction. The rate of change needs to be accelerated, but the gaps appear to be narrowing with regard to course retention.

Equity Gaps: Course Success

To measure course success equity gaps, I used the same strategy, identifying the top-performing group for each year from 1992–2019. Again, in every year, the highest-performing group was Asian or White, with the earlier years mostly showing the top-performing group as White students and the latter years predominately Asian students. Measuring the

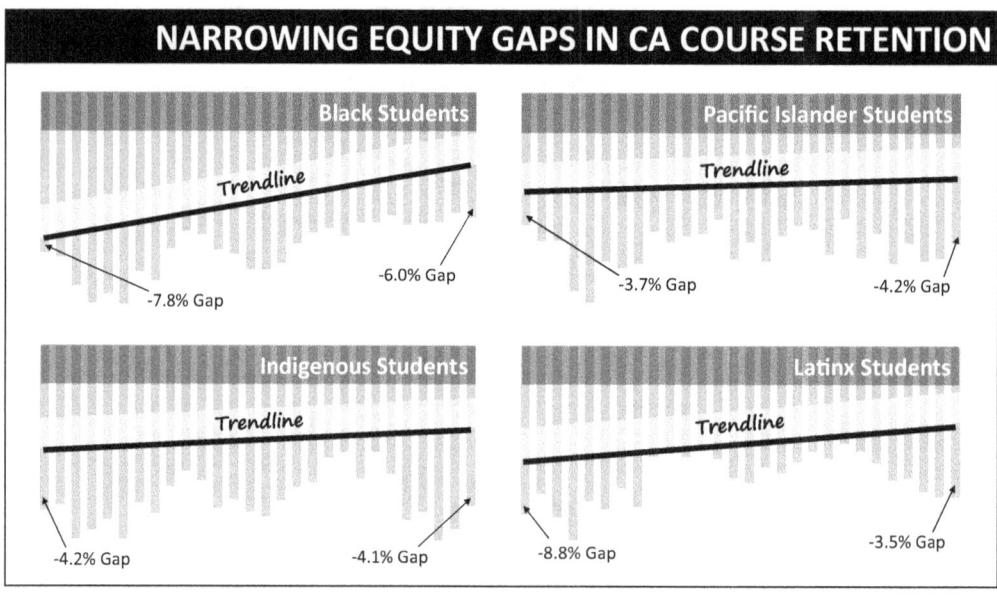

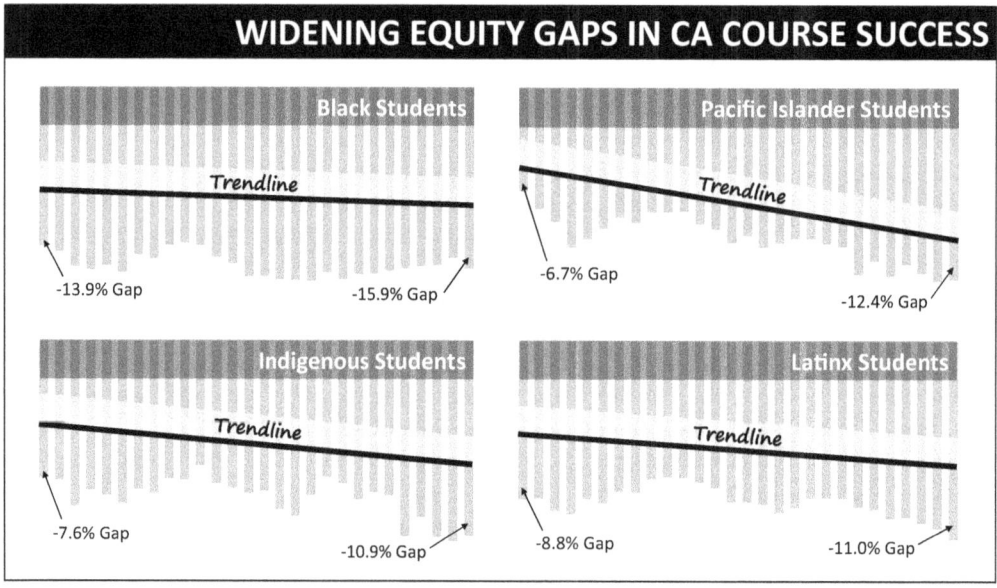

gap between the top-performing group and the lower-performing groups (Latinx, Black, Pacific Islander, and Indigenous students) over 27 years, it is evident that equity gaps have expanded for all four groups and are generally larger than the course retention gaps.

Over the 27-year history, Black students have experienced a negative trend, with the equity gap widening. In 1992, Black students were 13.9 percentage points below the top-performing group, and by 2019, the gap had grown to 15.9 points below. Latinx students have also trended in the wrong direction, starting at 8.8 percentage points below in 1992 and expanding to 11.0 points below by 2019. Pacific Islander students trended in a negative direction at the most rapid rate for all four groups, starting at 6.7 percentage points below and expanding to 12.4 points below. Indigenous students trended in the wrong direction over the 27 years, starting at 7.6 percentage points below and ending at 10.9 points below.

The data showing these trends for course success are surprising and frustrating. As a state system, we have declared equity one of our major goals. We have openly and collectively stated that we want to narrow and eventually close these persistent academic gaps. However, when the data are tracked over a 27-year period, we see that the trends for course success are moving in the wrong direction. This is worth repeating. Over the last 27 years, the success gaps for Black, Latinx, Pacific Islander, and Indigenous students have grown. These students have fallen further behind relative to their Asian and White colleagues.

We have talked and talked and talked about this issue at conferences, in strategic planning meetings, in board meetings, in senate meetings, in union meetings, in management meetings, and more. We have dedicated considerable time and resources to this effort, and while course retention and success have improved for all groups, and while the relative gap for course retention has declined, the gaps for course success have worsened.

Conclusion

As a country, we are still working out the implementation of equality. We have successfully bent the arc of our own history in the direction of equality, but we are also clearly nowhere near the end of this work, with social injustices persisting in the United States. A major role academia needs to play in this campaign is the role of moving students from historically underserved communities into positions of prominence, power, and influence in society. In rooms where decisions are made, we need proportionate numbers of individuals of color, people from low-income backgrounds, individuals with recent immigrant histories, and so on. We all bring our individual histories to work, to leadership. When we have board members, trustees, legislators, CEOs, executives, business owners, partners, supervisors, and commissioners who reflect the diversity of America, the diversity of America will in turn be more fully reflected in the operations of our institutions. To achieve this goal, higher education needs to ensure that the path to academic success is available to all groups, and the sector of higher education that works with students from historically underserved communities more than any other is the American community college.

The balance of this book looks at the structural problems that keep historically underserved students from succeeding, with an emphasis (not exclusively) on the role community colleges play in this campaign. We will address some of the underlying problems that give rise to the particular hurdles causing problems for these students. We will look at practical strategies to lower or eliminate these hurdles. As you read through these chapters, I encourage you to continually remain conscious of the challenge we are addressing. Discrimination based on race, ethnicity, income, religion, national origin, and other characteristics has a 400-year history in the United States, and while we have made significant strides in some social justice areas, economic inequality in the United States has been on the rise for the last six decades, adding new fuel to age-old ideas that stoke division. The challenges we face are stubborn and large; our response needs to be proportionate. The ultimate goal of this book is to expand upward mobility for students from disfavored communities with a forward-looking response from higher education—especially community colleges.

3   How Big Are the Gaps?

Crafton Hills College holds a reception every semester for students on the Deans' List. The reception is called Tea with Deans, and it celebrates students who are enrolled full time and performing at a very high academic level. As the vice president of instruction, I always attended the ceremony and made opening comments to the group. The event was primarily a social gathering, allowing academic managers and students to meet each other and get better acquainted. At one of these events, I met Adam Diaz, a remarkable student who came to influence my life significantly. He is literally the student I most often think about before I step on a stage or enter a meeting to discuss issues that I know will be difficult to navigate but are significant in students' lives. I often imagine him sitting in the back of the audience and listening to what I have to say. It helps me keep student concerns at the center of these conversations. He personifies the difficult circumstances so many of our students struggle with in their day-to-day encounters. He and all the other students with similar lives call us to develop innovative solutions that will eliminate or mitigate the hurdles that stand in the way of their academic success.

With Adam in my Office

Adam grew up in one of the poorest areas of Orange County, California. He was the oldest sibling in his family and was raised by two very religious parents. His father was the leader/minister of a small religious group that practiced a faith of extreme abstinence based in a distrust of modern society. He did not attend public schools, did not watch television, and did not listen to popular music. His early education was almost exclusively provided by his two parents, who both had limited educations themselves. In the absence of peers, the absence of teachers, and the absence of popular media, Adam grew up with a very high degree of ignorance in the truest sense of the word. Living in the middle of Southern California—one of the most affluent, well-educated, and populated places on earth—Adam had the knowledge base of a person cut off from the world. This isolation characterized his childhood until early adolescence, when Adam's parents divorced and his father abandoned their family, taking his already meager income with him, and leaving Adam, his siblings, and mom in jeopardy. With no margin for financial setback, the family quickly fell into a life of poverty.

Adam spent the next few years moving in and out of public education, and he was surprised to find himself far behind in basic learning. He struggled with many of the problems that arise in hardships of this nature. He lost all sense of faith and became angry with his father, God, and society at large. He lashed out with a self-destructive lifestyle and spiraled to a low point that he once described to me as sleeping in a park and desperate for a fix. The turnaround in his life was similar to many stories like his. At his bottom, someone recognized his pain and offered to help, and with no other options, Adam accepted. He ended up living in a spare room in Redlands, California, with encouragement from his host family to enroll in Crafton Hills College.

Many students in community colleges come to campus with deeply complicated personal lives like Adam's. Many of these complications are not as severe, and a few are worse, but most face difficulties. Our students typically need to hold part-time or even full-time jobs to put food on the table and cover rent and other necessities. Many students are in multigenerational homes, required to fulfill major commitments to their families by caring for relatives, preparing meals, running errands, and even serving as interpreters. Many are first-generation students who likely come from loving families but have low or no academic capital to rely on. We have single moms, recovering addicts, foster care kids, high school dropouts, and formerly incarcerated students sitting next to valedictorians, wealthy international students, professors' children—students with generations of academic capital piled up in their families. All of them file into our classrooms, labs, and lecture halls, looking like college students and making it difficult for us to see the challenges that they face in their daily lives.

"Tea with Deans"

Adam was a bright student with a deep curiosity and an eagerness to tell his story within the context of academia. His personal life was a rich and unique case study that he enjoyed running through the lens of humanities and social sciences disciplines. When I first met him, he seemed like a fairly typical bright student. But in our first conversation, it became clear that he was exceptional for many reasons. As I learned his story and the role education was playing in his life in real time, I was drawn to him, and so were many others. Faculty, staff, and students came to know him as a major personality at the college. Many of us felt like we adopted him as one of our own. We found on-campus work for him. We helped him move into academic honors programs. We encouraged him to apply to some of the country's most selective universities. We wrote letters and made calls on his behalf. It was evident to all of us involved in his life that we were watching and participating in a person's life as he made a dramatic and positive trajectory change.

The last time I saw Adam was on a Thursday afternoon in my office. He was a few months away from graduating and in the middle of applying to transfer. He had applied to a few Ivy League universities and some highly ranked private institutions. He was applying to several institutions in the University of California (UC) system and a few in the California State University (CSU) system. On that particular afternoon, he stopped by my office to tell me about a road trip he was going to take to the San Francisco Bay Area. He wanted to visit his number-one hope for transfer, UC Berkeley. I had been helping him with some of the college application fees, and during our conversation, I learned he was out of money but still had a few more applications to submit. Toward the end of our conversation, we walked over to the ATM machine across campus, and I pulled out some cash for him to cover the remaining application fees. I reminded him that I would have never made it through college without people helping me and that he needed to be more comfortable with telling me when he needed help. I told him that he would do the same thing for students like him when he finished school and landed in a career. We talked a little while longer near the cafeteria and said goodbye. He was excited to be on his way, and I was excited for him.

The next morning, about 10:00 AM, I was meeting with a colleague outside my office when the phone rang. I answered, and a soft voice asked, "Is this Bryan Reece?"

"Yes," I said. Her tone was a little abrupt, but I waited.

"Are you a friend of Adam Diaz?"

I again replied with "Yes," sensing something odd.

"I am sorry to tell you Adam died in a car accident last night," she said as she started to cry.

I couldn't process the information and didn't know who she was. She told me he was on his way to the Bay Area and hit an oncoming car in a head-on collision. She told me Adam had been living with her and her husband for the last two or three years. We talked awkwardly for a short time. She gave me her contact information. We ended the call.

News of Adam's death spread throughout the college community quickly. Much of the campus mourned his loss. We shared stories about Adam with each other for weeks. We held a remembrance on campus. We raised money to help pay for his funeral. We attended his simple ceremony. About a month after Adam's death, Crafton Hills College held a dinner and ceremony to celebrate outstanding students. The annual event was an evening to talk about our best students and celebrate their acceptance to a range of universities. It was always a joyous event as faculty bring students to the podium, speak to each student's accomplishments, and discuss their transfer plans. I was the evening's host and emcee. Many managers, faculty, and staff attended, along with a roomful of students and family members. At the end of the evening, we all remembered Adam with happiness and sorrow as the college's transfer coordinator announced he had been selected as one of our outstanding students and was accepted for transfer to UC Berkeley.

The Lives Our Students Live

At the end of my typical workday, I usually say good night to anyone left in the immediate vicinity of my office, walk to my car parked in a spot reserved for the president, drive home, park the car in the garage, and spend some time with my wife, Kathi. The close of my workday and the transition into my family life each evening is vastly different from the day-to-day environment that many of our students navigate. Being constantly immersed in the professional and private life I have built up around me, I find it alarmingly easy to lose awareness of our students' lives. My personal journey included many of the same hurdles that our students encounter, but those hurdles are now so far removed and my life is so completely different that I frequently lose the awareness of their struggles. As

I drive home each evening in the comfort of my car, some of our students are cold and homeless. Some are hungry or tired from a day of studying and a night of physical work. Many feel displaced, uncertain of their future, moving with insufficient direction and guidance. Most struggle with too many demands on their time. Our students, the students that often attend community colleges, face a complicated array of personal hurdles that they must navigate on top of the academic challenges already built into undergraduate studies.

I've been in front of countless academic audiences over the years, talking about our students. I know that many of our faculty, staff, and managers struggle with the same difficulty. Being mindful of our students' difficult lives is something we must fight for. We need to keep this awareness in our collective consciousness. Without this understanding, our aspirations for equity are lost, and we will lack the direction and kind of urgency that come when we are present and aware of the hurdles our students encounter. We simply cannot address equity issues in society and in higher education unless we have a personal, ongoing, and palpable sense of the challenges our students continually live with. We need to somehow be ever mindful about where our students are starting, the disparate nature of those starting points, and the wildly divergent journeys in front of them.

Many of our students, especially those from historically underserved communities, start their academic journey further back. They will need to run a longer and more complicated race. They will need to do it at a faster pace to keep up. And they will need to do all of this with less agency. If we—the people who work in community colleges—lose our sense of this, if we slip into a kind of indifference or complacency, we won't be able to measure the requisite scope and scale of our work, we won't bring a sense of urgency to the work, and we will collectively break apart when the work becomes too challenging and difficult. Social justice work is hard. The only way it can be achieved is if the people doing the work are palpably conscious of the social injustices they are trying to address.

In 2016–17, 8.7 million unique students enrolled in community colleges throughout the United States. Of all the 2016–17 undergraduates attending higher education institutions, 38 percent were community college students, with a little over two-thirds of them enrolled part-time and a little under one-third enrolled full-time. Community college enrollments skew toward students from historically underserved communities. While 38 percent of undergraduates are enrolled in community colleges, 55 percent of poor undergraduates (dependent students with family incomes below $30,000) attend community college; 49 percent of African American students and 51 percent of Hispanic students start at a two-year public college, while only 38 percent of Asian students and 36 percent of White students start at a community college (Community College Research Center, 2020b). In the most general sense, community colleges work with more students from disfavored communities than typical four-year institutions. Like Adam, many of these students come with complicated lives that make succeeding in college more difficult than it is for students who arrive without these issues. With that said, these students are the primary reason I have remained engaged with community college work for over three decades. Working with them is a source of joy and pride that I share with many of my colleagues.

Inside of this very large population are groups that bring unique challenges. Finding ways to help these groups succeed is difficult but rewarding, admirable, and squarely down the middle of social justice work in the United States. The list of special populations is long, but some of the more prominent include students of color, recent immigrants, working adults, foster care students, military veterans, Indigenous students, inmates, formerly incarcerated students, low-income students, LGBTQ+ students, and first-generation students. Students from these groups are more likely to have complications in their lives that make academic success difficult and therefore less likely. These groups are not exclusively whom we work with in community colleges, but they encompass the majority of our students.

African American Students

Being a person of color in the United States means you are tied to a deep and disturbing history. It is a history filled with slavery, discrimination, displacement, intolerance, abuse, injustice, and denial. It is a dark history, and while conditions for the Black community have improved with important gains like emancipation, suffrage, and civil rights, there are stubborn sociological constructs that remain, cultural attitudes and norms that persist, and hate-filled hearts that continue to shape the experience of African Americans, Asian Americans, Latinx Americans, Native Americans, and other Americans of color.

African American students enter higher education with a long and difficult history in the United States that extends over 400 years, with many scholars pointing to a journal entry by Virginia colonist John Rolfe as the first record of African slaves brought to one of the colonies. Some historians point to earlier origins of slavery in the United States. Regardless, the history of Africans in American is older than the country itself, and there is no dispute over the brutality slaves from Africa suffered. Emancipation in 1863 marked the official end of slavery in the United States, but African Americans continued to suffer deep, hate-filled discrimination, with examples of this treatment still available on our news feeds. With White Americans dominating positions of authority since our founding, many of these attitudes and norms have become embedded in our public and private society, baking racism, bias, and discrimination into many American institutions.

From slavery to the present day, African Americans have had to fight for access to college. Higher education admissions for Black students started in the early and middle 1800s with a handful of institutions. Shortly after the Civil War, historically Black colleges and universities (HBCUs) began to emerge. In 1954, *Brown v. Board of Education* forced more colleges and universities to admit Black students. By 1962, James Meredith became the first African American student to enter the University of Mississippi, creating backlash so intense that President Kennedy sent 5,000 federal troops to the campus to keep the peace. The push for access continued through the Civil Rights Movement of the 1960s, and while demonstrable gains have been made with regard to African American education, significant inequities remain today.

According to the U.S. Census Bureau, 13.4 percent of the American population in 2019 was African American (U.S. Census Bureau, 2020). In 2018, educationdata.org looked at all undergraduates in the United States and found that 13.8 percent were Black (educationdata.org, 2020a). This finding demonstrates significant progress with regard to access, with the Black undergraduate percentages basically equal to the overall Black population in the United States.

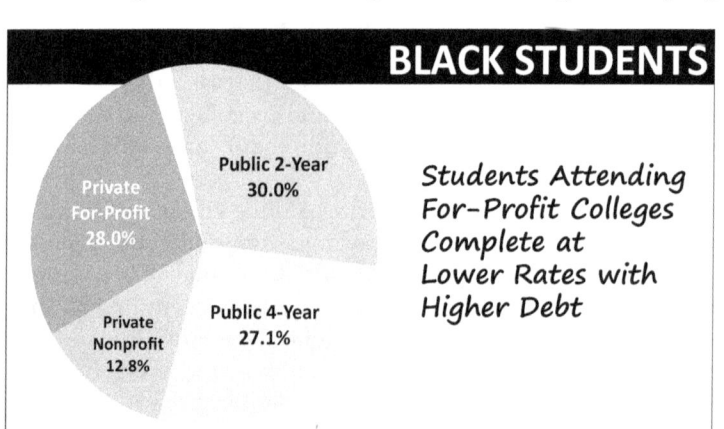

The work we need to focus on now with regard to African American education involves the types of educational institutions African Americans attend or have access to and their completion rates relative to other groups experiencing greater success. Black students are more likely to attend for-profit private institutions than all other race and ethnicity groups. Assessing students who completed degrees or certificates between 2013 and 2015, Black students were more likely to graduate from for-profit schools than other race or ethnicity groups, with 28 percent of Black students completing their degrees at for-profits (Libassi, 2018). This is highly significant because for-profit students complete at lower rates with higher debt (Espinosa & Baum, 2019). Regarding completion, African Americans have a six-year completion rate of 46 percent, while White students have a 72 percent completion rate. And when we look exclusively at Black students starting in community colleges, the six-year completion rate for a bachelor's degree is less than 10 percent (Community College Research Center, 2020b).

With community colleges serving such a significant portion of Black students, we need to make sure all institutional barriers and many social barriers are identified and removed to generate greater success for Black students, who typically bring more of life's struggles with them to college than their White peers. While there are exceptions to this rule across the race and ethnicity spectrum, these tendencies are indisputable. Leaving their homes and neighborhoods to attend college, many students of color find the same racial biases (if not outright racism) on campuses across America. Some students even find an increase in these experiences, as many leave majority-minority communities and enter predominantly White campuses. Black students report old stereotypes and bias across the academy. Black students commonly report microaggressions from some faculty and other students and acts of overt racism.

African American students often report a sense of isolation and cultural invisibility on campuses. This is especially true at institutions that have histories of exclusively White students, holding vestiges of whiteness embedded in the institution. African American students report being less likely than White students to be selected for positions of power and prominence in the student body. Black cultural markers are often not reflected in campus life, leaving many Black students feeling marginalized and longing for home. Like a long-term traveler or expatriate living in another culture, experiencing how other people live is interesting and educational, but it wears on a person over time. Most people need to touch on familiar values, norms, and customs of the environments they were raised in on a regular basis to feel a sense of place and belonging. This sense of cultural familiarity is especially true when feelings of vulnerability or uncertainty arise. When stress enters our lives, cultural touchstones are important coping resources—this is where the idea of "comfort food" comes from. Learning environments across higher education are intentionally designed to stretch, push, and expand students. This means they are constantly, by design, put in uncomfortable positions with a great deal of stress added to their lives. This is all done in an effort to help each student grow. The higher education learning environment is already difficult. For Black students (and many other students of color), the complexities of this environment are compounded with a range of additional issues they encounter on a daily basis.

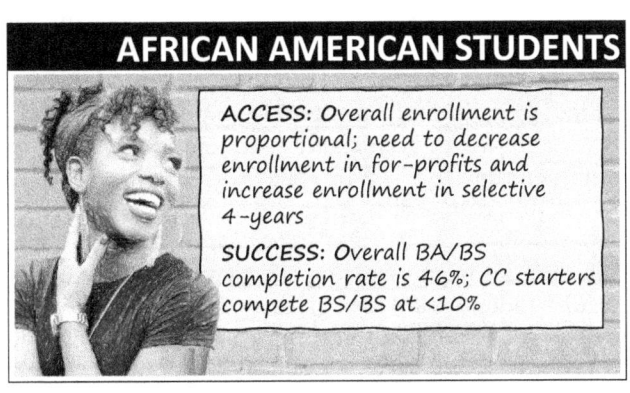

AFRICAN AMERICAN STUDENTS

ACCESS: Overall enrollment is proportional; need to decrease enrollment in for-profits and increase enrollment in selective 4-years

SUCCESS: Overall BA/BS completion rate is 46%; CC starters compete BS/BS at <10%

If we hope to graduate African American students at rates proportional to those of White students and place them in positions of influence in society at proportional rates, we need to increase both access and success. Regarding access to higher education, we have reached proportionality overall. The percentage of Black students attending higher education is approximately equal to the percentage of African American residents in the United States. However, the access patterns need to shift, by *decreasing* the number of students who attend for-profit institutions and *increasing* the number of Black students who attend selective universities. Regarding success in college, we need to see significant rate increases for BA/BS degree completion. Overall completion rates need to move from a six-year rate of 46 percent to something in the range of 70 percent. For Black students starting out in community colleges, we need to effect significant improvements if we hope to reach a success rate near 70 percent. Black students starting in community colleges have a six-year BA/BS completion rate at less than 10 percent. If we are able to achieve these outcomes nationally, we will be graduating a proportionate number of African Americans from colleges and universities.

Latinx Students

While the story of a Hispanic presence in American history can be traced to the early Portuguese and Spanish explorers, including initial Spanish territories south of the colonies, historians typically start the story of systematic discrimination against Latinx communities in America with the end of the Mexican-American War in 1848. The settlement after the war gave major portions of Mexican territory to the United States and granted U.S. citizenship to Mexicans living in that territory at the time. Overnight, the United States became a country with a significant Latinx population, and, almost immediately, many were treated with great bias. Regardless, immigration added numbers to Hispanic American communities over the years, and, like many immigrants or families with recent immigrant histories in America, Latinx communities experienced organized and open discrimination, especially during difficult economic times, when they became convenient scapegoats. These communities were subjected to a Jim Crow-like experience with segregation, exclusion from White-only establishments, state-sanctioned deportation of Latinx citizens (*repatriation*), violence, and even mob lynchings. Millions of Latinx citizens and residents in America were subjected to these abuses under legal and cultural structures that provided the authority, legitimacy, and even encouragement to the majority White population who perpetuated this treatment. During this history, discriminatory attitudes were baked into many of our public and private institutions, creating barriers that have not been fully removed and continue to be experienced by Latinx Americans today.

Like African Americans, Latinx communities have been fighting for education equality with regard to access and completion. The struggle to end segregated schools, for example, came to a head in 1946 with the *Mendez v. Westminster School District* case. This case required that district to end segregation for Latinx students and laid the groundwork for *Brown v. Board of Education* in 1954. After access started opening up, Latinx communities began tackling a hegemonic curriculum that devalued their cultural and linguistic identities. Through this curriculum, Latino children also were often viewed as intellectually and culturally inferior. During the civil rights era, as Hispanic communities started exercising greater political power, policy changes slowly began to appear and, throughout the late 20th century, especially in the Southwest, Hispanic leaders emerged, most importantly in local government. While there have been significant gains because of these ongoing efforts, Latinx students continue to experience unacceptable dropout rates, cultural segregation, language discrimination, less public funding for education, and more.

The fastest growing race/ethnicity group in American over the last half century have been Latinx Americans. Today, there are over 60 million Hispanics living in the United States. According to the U.S. Census Bureau, Hispanics have grown from approximately 3 percent of the population in 1960 to an estimate of 18.5 percent of the population in 2019 (U.S. Census Bureau, 2020). In 2018, educationdata.org looked at all undergraduates in the United States, with a particular eye to students of color. It found that 21.8 percent of U.S. undergrads are Hispanic (educationdata.org, 2020b). These data demonstrate significant progress with regard to access, with Latinx undergraduate percentages exceeding the overall Latinx population in the United States. Combining this finding with a similar finding for African Americans, we should take some pride in this increase in access. Latinx advocates in particular should stop from time to time to appreciate the impact their work has had.

Higher education now needs to address academic outcomes for Latinx students, which are similar to patterns seen for African American students. We need to help expand access for Hispanic communities to more selective institutions, decrease the disproportionate amount of debt Latinx students accumulate to fund their education, and improve their college completion rates. Latinx students are more likely to attend for-profit private institutions than White students. Attending these institutions contributes to higher debt and lower completion rates (Espinosa & Baum, 2019). According to Libassi, between 2013 and 2015, 25.2 percent of Hispanic students completed their programs (bachelor's degrees or certificates) from private for-profit institutions (Libassi, 2018). Regarding completion, Latinx students have a six-year completion rate of 56 percent (educationdata.org, 2020a). When Latinx students start at a community college, their six-year completion rate for a bachelor's degree drops to 13.8 percent (Community College Research Center, 2020a).

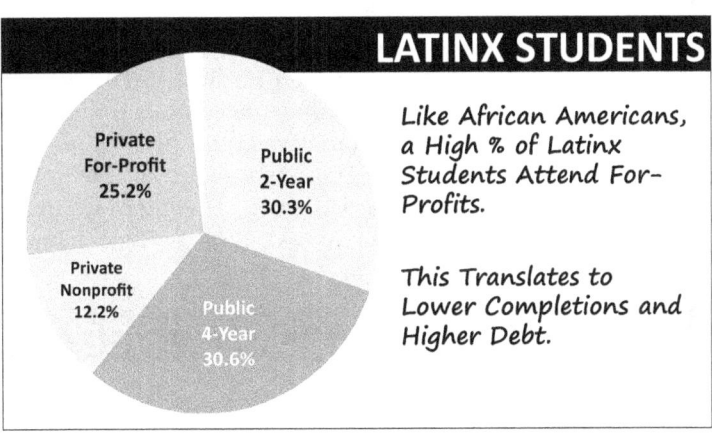

The pathway to a bachelor's degree for many students from Hispanic families starts at a community college. However, with only 13.8 percent of these students finishing the BA/BS journey, the community college system needs to make reforms that improve this percentage dramatically. We have addressed the access issue, but if we want to address the large inequities in society that exist for Latinx communities, we need to make sure they are graduating at rates similar to more successful population groups. This means that social and institutional barriers must be identified and mitigated, if not entirely eliminated.

Latinx students face many of the barriers discussed regarding African American students. Despite efforts towards cultural inclusiveness, deep-seated prejudice persists. They often must navigate more difficult circumstances. They encounter colleges and universities that have long histories and traditions built around majority White populations. They encounter persistent slights in and out of the classroom. They often experience few cultural references on campus, and consequently, they report feelings of isolation and cultural invisibility. These and many other challenges are piled on top of the significant academic challenges that all students face in college.

Some of the daily life pressures that many Latinx students face come from their association with immigration or recent immigration histories. Large portions of the American public have historically been cruel to recent immigrants. César Cuauhtémoc García Hernández points to a particularly negative part of this phenomenon, "crimmigration," by which immigrants are more likely than non-immigrants to be treated like criminals. While he mainly discusses contemporary immigration, the idea of associating new immigrants with criminality holds a long, uninterrupted history in the United States. The country has seen many immigration waves, including Irish, Italians, Jews, Eastern Europeans, Chinese, Vietnamese, Mexicans, Central and South Americans, and Middle Easterners. Through these waves, immigrants have routinely experienced scapegoating, with large segments of American society blaming new immigrants for war, social unrest, job losses, and many other problems. This blame is always difficult for new immigrant populations to counter, often struggling with English, uncertain how American institutions function, afraid of retribution, and typically in a powerless position until the second or third generation.

With over 40 million immigrants, the United States is the most diverse country in the world. The Pew Research Center recently assessed the state of immigration in the United States and found Hispanics make up 40–50 percent of individuals living in the United States who were born in another country (Radford, 2019), with half or more born in Mexico and the rest mostly born in Central or South America. Hispanics make up such a large portion of recent immigration in the United States that many Latinx students (including natural-born Latinx citizens) encounter some of the pejorative attitudes and treatments historically extended to immigrants in the United States.

A unique subset of the immigrant experience in the United States that many Latinx students encounter is known as Dreamers. Dreamers are unauthorized immigrants who came to the United States as minors. A typical Dreamer's immigration story involves illegal, or unauthorized, immigration by their parents. For example, if a father or mother enters the country outside of the immigration process and brings a child with them, the child has technically entered the country illegally; however, the child had no say in the matter and likely had no idea they were entering the country outside of the legally proscribed process.

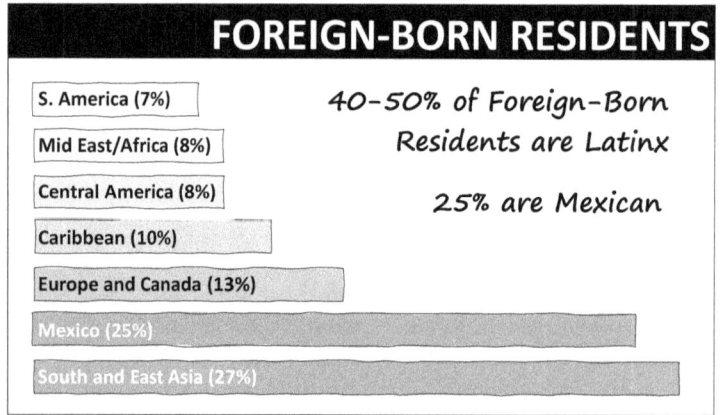

Many of these students came to the United States under these circumstances at a very young age and did not learn of their own uncertain citizenship status until they reached adolescence. This puts these individuals in a very precarious situation. They have tenuous legal status in the United States and often have zero ties with the country their parents came from.

DACA (Deferred Action for Childhood Arrivals) was written by the federal government to protect children brought to the country in the scenario described previously. The law allows these students to enjoy some U.S. benefits as if they entered the United States legally. During the Trump Administration, the president worked to eliminate or lessen DACA benefits, but the courts have opposed his efforts. Some states have also passed similar legislation to support DACA-like benefits.

While DACA residents in the United States come from many countries, the majority are Latinx. According to Pew, 92 percent of DACA residents are Latinx, and 79.4 percent come from Mexico. Nine of the top ten countries of origin for DACA residents are in Latin America (Lopez & Krogstad, Key Facts About Unauthorized Immigrants Enrolled in DACA, 2017). Many of these students attend college with tuition rates and financial aid awards that would not have been possible but for DACA and similar state laws. Like many students from families with recent immigrant histories, they can have highly complicated lives. These students often live in homes with multiple generations and family care responsibilities. They may struggle with English as a first language, and most DACA students are from families with limited resources to support their children in higher education.

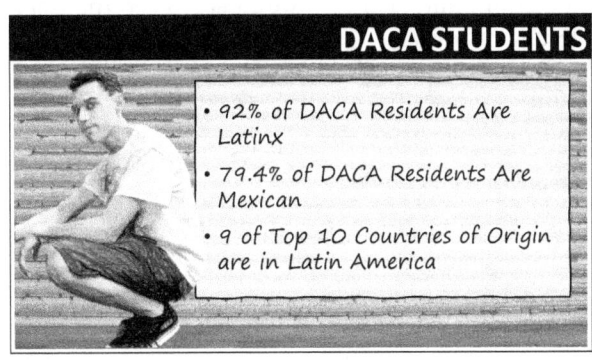

DACA STUDENTS
- 92% of DACA Residents Are Latinx
- 79.4% of DACA Residents Are Mexican
- 9 of Top 10 Countries of Origin are in Latin America

While institutional resources exist for most of these students, these students often do not take advantage of them. One reason, of course, is lack of knowledge about the resources, but another major reason is reluctance. With their citizenship status in somewhat of a gray area, many DACA students are reluctant to come out of the shadows for fear of deportation. In fact, many students who qualify as having DACA status have refused to register for the program under fear of President Trump's rhetoric about immigrants, especially Mexican immigrants. I saw this firsthand as president of Norco College. During the Trump presidential campaign and early in his administration, he frequently used language that expressed a tough stance on immigration. DACA students in particular felt the sting of this rhetoric. During this period, a few students came to my office legitimately fearful of possible deportation, looking for some kind of reassurance from me. While this rhetoric was particularly heated in 2016 and 2017, the fear this creates in DACA and DACA-eligible students keeps many of them from accessing resources that could otherwise help improve their academic success.

To establish a society in which Latinx students graduate from American colleges and universities at rates proportionate to the most successful group in higher education, we have work to do with regard to access and completion. Regarding access to higher education, we have reached proportionality overall for Latinx students. The percentage of students attending college is approximately equal to the percentage of Latinx residents. However, as with

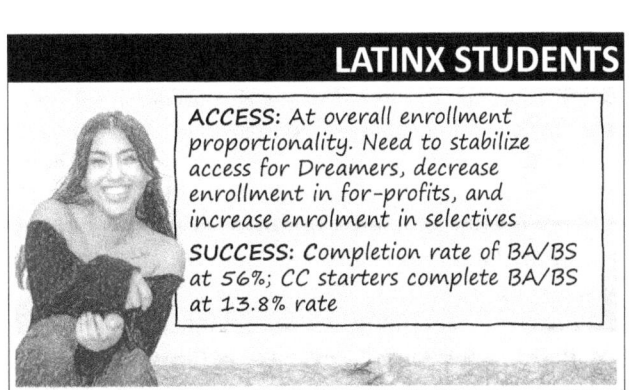

LATINX STUDENTS

ACCESS: At overall enrollment proportionality. Need to stabilize access for Dreamers, decrease enrollment in for-profits, and increase enrolment in selectives

SUCCESS: Completion rate of BA/BS at 56%; CC starters complete BA/BS at 13.8% rate

African American communities, the access patterns need to shift, by decreasing the number of students who attend for-profit institutions and increasing the number of Latinx students who attend selective universities. Dreamer students need their access guarantees to be secured with renewal and support of DACA and related state programs. Regarding success in college, we need to generate greater completion of BA and BS degrees. Overall completion rates need to move from a six-year rate of 56 percent to something in the range of 70 percent. For Latinx students starting their journey in a community college, we need to see their six-year BA/BS completion rates move significant distances, as they have a 13.8 percent completion rate. If we are able to nationally achieve these outcomes, we will be graduating a proportionate number of Latinx students from colleges and universities.

Southeast Asian Students

The history of discrimination against Asians in America starts with a significant rise of Chinese immigration in the mid-1800s. The Gold Rush and construction of the transcontinental railroad were the primary forces drawing Chinese immigrants to American ports on the West Coast. Almost immediately, Chinese immigrants reported the ugly encounters that so many immigrant groups have experienced in the United States. The swelling discrimination against Chinese eventually translated into official government-sponsored discrimination with the Chinese Exclusion Act, a piece of federal law that placed a ten-year moratorium on immigration from China. Similar treatment is recorded across several Asian communities as they immigrated to the United States, including Japanese, Vietnamese, Filipino, Korean, and a range of other Asian immigrants. For example, in the early 1900s, many Filipinos were ruled enemies of the state under laws written by the FDR administration. During World War II, the U.S. mass-incarcerated Japanese Americans in internment camps, treating them as possible threats to national security, while American of German descent suffered no such treatment. These and similar acts are part of the Asian-American experience that continues today. As recently as 2020, the American president fostered a documented rise in Asian discrimination with rhetoric blaming the COVID-19 international pandemic on China, often referring to it as the "Chinese Virus." His rhetoric corresponds with a reported increase of racial bias again Asian-Americans (Darling-Hammond, et al., 2020).

Despite a difficult history in the United States, Asians are often characterized as the "model minority." While there are problems associated with this characterization, Asian students succeed in impressive numbers. Asian students consistently perform at the highest levels with regard to SAT/ACT scores, selective college admissions, academic course performance, and higher education completion (Hsin & Xie, 2014). This level of achievement was underscored in recent legal actions that received national attention regarding Harvard's admissions policies. During the conflict, some claimed that Asians are overrepresented at the university, while others claimed that Asians were experiencing discrimination in admissions as the university sought to bring more demographic balance to the student body by reducing the number of Asian applicants with very high high school GPAs. Both arguments extend from the basis of Asian-Americans academically outperforming other groups in the United States.

The idea of the "model minority" is problematic in the sense that some communities within the larger population of Asians do not experience the same kind of academic success as other sub-groups. When the Asian population is disaggregated, it is clear that many Southeast Asian students are struggling. The Center for Southeast Asian Studies at Northern Illinois University defines the region as including 11 countries: Brunei, Burma (Myanmar), Cambodia, Timor-Leste, Indonesia, Laos, Malaysia, Philippines, Singapore, Thailand,

and Vietnam. Not all of these countries have large immigrant populations in the United States, but the populations that do exist in the United States often struggle with academic performance. For example, less than 38 percent of Hmong, Cambodian, Laotian, and Vietnamese American residents hold a high school diploma, and less than 26 percent hold bachelor's degrees. Less than 13 percent of Laotian residents have finished a four-year degree, whereas over 70 percent of Indians in the United States hold a BA/BS (Jaschik, The Deceptive Data on Asians, 2013). The "model minority" moniker generally applied to Asian Americans causes us to miss the struggle that several sub-groups, especially sub-groups from Southeast Asia, encounter as they move through (and all too often out of) higher education.

ASIAN SUB-GROUPS

	Hmong	Cambodian	Laotian	Vietnamese	Chinese	Thai	Bangladeshi	Pakistani	Indian	Korean	Filipino	Sri Lankan	Indonesian	Japanese	Taiwanese
No HS Degree	37.9	37.4	33.8	29.4	19.3	16.8	16.6	13.4	8.8	8.3	7.9	7.6	7.3	5.3	4.8
BA or Higher	14.7	14.1	12.4	25.8	51.5	43.8	49.9	53.9	71.1	52.7	48.1	57.4	48.7	47.7	74.1

Many Southeast Asian Students Struggle

In 2010, Asian immigration to the United States surpassed the volume of Hispanic immigration, establishing Asians as today's fastest-growing ethnicity/racial group in the United States. In 2017, Asians made up 37.4 percent of all immigrants to the United States, while Hispanics made up 26.6 percent (Jynnah Radford & Noe-Bustamante, 2019). According to the U.S. Census Bureau's 2019 population estimates, there are 19.3 million Asians living in the United States, making up 5.9 percent of the U.S. population (6.1 percent if Native Hawaiians and Pacific Islanders are included). Of all undergraduates throughout the United States, 7.35 percent are Asian/Pacific Islander (educationdata.org, 2020a). This number supports the "model minority" idea, with Asians exceeding their proportional representation in colleges and universities. However, when we look at college-going rates for Southeast Asians and Pacific Islanders, we see that underenrollment.

This same pattern appears to be present with regard to college completion data. Identifying college success rates for Southeast Asians is difficult because most data are collected at the aggregate level—all Asian groups are lumped into one data set. However, a few studies have looked at success rates through a disaggregated lens and find that Southeast Asian Americans and Pacific Islanders tend to have educational outcomes similar to African American and Latinx students (The Campaign for College Opportunity, 2015). For example, the Campaign for College Opportunity report found that less than half of Southeast Asians, Native Hawaiians, Guamanians or Chamorros, Laotians, and Samoans graduate from the California State University system within six years. This is very similar to Black and Latino students. These findings are important because in our current reporting of all

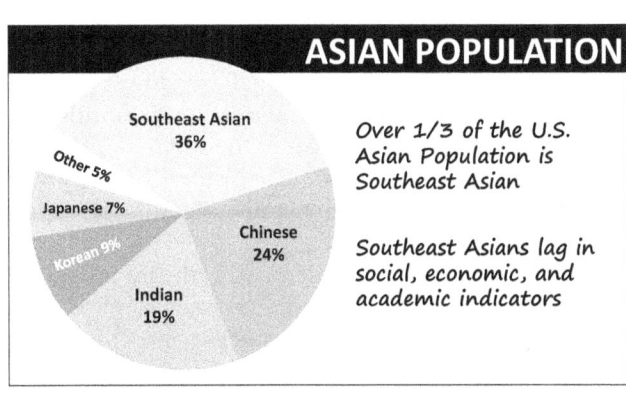

ASIAN POPULATION

Southeast Asian 36%
Other 5%
Japanese 7%
Korean 9%
Chinese 24%
Indian 19%

Over 1/3 of the U.S. Asian Population is Southeast Asian

Southeast Asians lag in social, economic, and academic indicators

Asians together, we often come to the conclusion that Asian communities are uniformly excelling. But in reality, Southeast Asians, Pacific Islanders, and to a certain extent Filipinos need to be brought into the same conversation we are having about Latinx and Black students.

The Asian population in the United States is large, and about 36 percent of this population is Southeast Asian (Lopez, Ruiz, & Patten, Key Facts About Asian Americans, a Diverse and Growing Population, 2017). With over half of Asian undergraduates starting at a community college and a likely higher percentage of Southeast Asians, Pacific Islanders, and Filipinos starting their undergraduate journeys at a community college (Ashford, 2019), we need to make sure these groups find greater access and greater success. One of the most significant ways higher education can help Southeast Asian communities is by successfully matriculating them through to BA and BS degrees at rates that are proportionate to their population. The first work that needs to be done for this community relates to data. These communities are lumped into other Asian groups, and their struggles are subsequently lost. Preliminary data suggest that their college-going rates are disproportionately low and need to be addressed with better recruitment. Given that their academic patterns appear to be similar to Latinx and African American students, they are likely attending for-profits at disproportionately high levels, and they are most certainly underrepresented at our most selective universities. Regarding success in college, we need to generate greater completion of BA and BS degrees for this community. Overall completion rates are reported below 50 percent for California universities. This is probably reflective of national trends. These completion rates need to be heightened to approximately 70 percent.

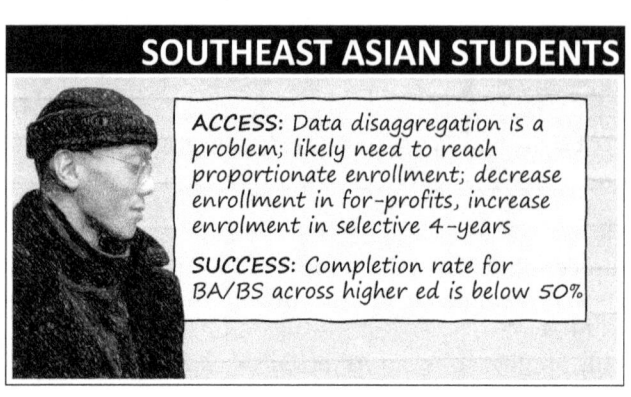

Indigenous Students

Indigenous peoples have played an integral part in the story of America, but not always in the way they would have wanted. Most often, they have been depicted in official narratives—the same ones taught in most U.S. schools—as obstacles and opponents to American nation-building and a policy of expansion and colonization whose ruthlessness was hidden behind the gilded phrase "manifest destiny."

While the historic struggles of Native Alaskans and Native Hawaiians to assert their rights to property and individual freedoms have been documented by historians—especially the interactions of Alaskan natives with Russian traders that resulted in their exploitation—the experiences of the American Indian especially epitomize the historical struggles of these peoples in U.S. history. Their plight sheds some necessary light on the particular challenges facing many Indigenous students in higher education and why they are still struggling today.

Ever since the late 16th century, with the arrival of the first European settlers in the New World, the American Indian population was subjected to what many historians call a centuries-long program of genocide and cultural erasure. Despite public expressions of sympathy and calls for understanding and support from various American presidents

(Monroe, Jackson, Grant, Cleveland, both Roosevelts, and Nixon among them), despite treaties with the federal government promising to provide tribal members with public services—including education—in perpetuity as a compensation for stripping them of their lands, the experience of Indigenous peoples in the United States has largely been characterized by federal policies and armed actions to either minimize them or eliminate them entirely. The list of tragic milestones in their history—including the Indian Removal Act of 1830, the forced relocation from ancestral lands known as "the Trail of Tears," the creation of reservations under various Indian Appropriations Acts, the Wounded Knee massacre in 1890—well exceeds the positive ones.

Though it had been in use in the 19th century, forced assimilation would eventually replace the policy of extermination in the 20th century, even though the goal was still the same: to wipe out Indigenous cultures and identities. The key to this strategy involved state-sponsored and faith-based schools, often in the form of boarding schools on and off reservations, that taught Indigenous children to view their native cultures as inferior to the American one. Children in these schools were punished for using their native languages and were forced to accept religious belief systems at odds with their own. Their hair was cut, their clothing replaced with uniforms, and their names westernized. These schools were clearly intended, as one Amnesty International report puts it, "to school, and sometimes beat, the Indian out of them." (For Alaskan natives, assimilation meant something different: To reduce hostilities between Russian traders and these various native communities, the tsarist government established a policy allowing for the marriage of traders with Indigenous women. The children resulting from these marriages became known as Creole peoples, who were Christianized by the Russian Orthodox Church and encouraged to be loyal to the Russian crown.)

Although it would evolve over time and there would be various attempts at reform made by agencies such as the Bureau of Indian Education, this dismal condition would last for much of the 20th century. The federal government passed several pieces of legislation—including the Higher Education Act of 1965 and the Indian Education Act of 1972—that sought to provide some remedies. The 1965 act addressed post-secondary education for Indigenous students, making possible the creation of tribe-controlled colleges and universities (the first one was established by the Navajo Nation in 1968). The 1972 act gave tribes more resources and support for educating their children. Other acts—along with efforts to collect and report educational data—soon followed, including the Tribally Controlled Community College Assistance Act in 1978, but even these measures weren't enough to make a difference. Still, there have been successes—like Hawaii's Kamehameha Schools, a well-endowed private institution that cultivates Indigenous students there with a pedagogy based on "native ways of knowing" (Wong, 2015)—but an across-the-board solution still hasn't been found. Poor academic outcomes in reservation and non-reservation schools, and their disastrous impact on post-secondary attendance, have continued for many reasons, most prominently continuing systemic discrimination and conflicts with state and local authorities over curriculum, funding and staffing, and the common problems affecting most educational institutions operating in isolated, rural areas (recruitment and retention being the most significant).

Today, the push for access to higher education and better treatment for Indigenous students continues. During the Obama administration, a listening tour across the country and up into Alaska studied the problems of Native education and set in motion initiatives including grants to improve working partnerships between tribes, state agencies, and school districts. The federal Every Student Succeeds Act (ESSA) called for states to consult with tribes about their educational plans, and the Obama administration issued a report calling for solutions to the "deeply troubling and destructive federal policies" that

INDIGENOUS PEOPLE GROUPS

- Blackfeet 105,304
- Apache 111,810
- Sioux 170,110
- Chippewa 170,742
- Mexican-Amer Indian 175,494
- Choctaw 195,764
- Navajo 332,129
- Native Hawaiian 527,007
- Cherokee 819,105

U.S. recognizes over 550 Indigenous people groups

2010 Census shows 9 groups with populations above 100,000

have smothered Native education for years. But during the Trump administration, little action was taken to respond to this report by his education secretary, Betsy DeVos.

Although completion rates for African American, Latinx, and Southeast Asian student populations need to be increased, these rates for the nation's Indigenous students remain at the very bottom.

According to the Census Bureau, in 2017, nearly 6.8 million people in the United States identified as American Indian or Alaskan Native, and 1.5 million identified as Native Hawaiian/Pacific Islander, which amounts to about 2.49 percent of the country's total population. Indigenous students (in particular American Indians and Alaska Natives) represent only 1 percent of the U.S. undergraduate population and less than 1 percent of the graduate population, according to the Postsecondary National Policy Institute (PNPI). Data for postsecondary attendance of Indigenous students are difficult to collect because these student numbers remain so low. Such small student population numbers create a kind of invisibility that the American Indian College Fund and other Indigenous advocacy groups point to as part of the access-and-success problem for Indigenous students in higher education today.

Available data are far from encouraging. In 2018, nearly 20 million students enrolled in American public and private post-secondary institutions. Of this figure, American Indian and Native Alaskan students numbered only 105,105 in public schools and 19,390 in private schools (Education Data, 2020), or about .06 percent of the entire enrollment group. Out of this small group, only 10 percent of Native students completed a bachelor's degree, while only 17 percent attained an associate degree (educationdata.org, 2020b). These low rates underscore a desperate need for more responsiveness to these students' particular situations. Other studies note that enrollment rates for Indigenous

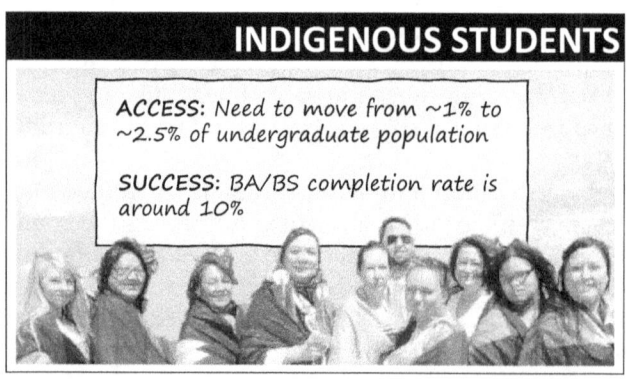

INDIGENOUS STUDENTS

ACCESS: Need to move from ~1% to ~2.5% of undergraduate population

SUCCESS: BA/BS completion rate is around 10%

students haven't changed in a measurably significant way in the last 20 years (Minthorn, Indigenous Perspectives on Native Student Challenges in Higher Education, 2020).

Such low participation and success numbers are not surprising. The heirs of a cultural heritage dismissed as primitive and backwards for generations, many of these students are first-generation college students without the benefit of support from family members who have gone on to a post-secondary education. Many have had so many negative experiences and poor results at the elementary and secondary school levels that they regard the country's educational system with suspicion and can't see the benefits of continuing. Studies and reports conducted by various institutes and media outlets describe the limited resources and physical squalor of dilapidated reservation schools, while those native students who attend their local school districts are subjected to experiences that emphasize discipline over learning or else get shunted off into remedial programs with little or no college preparation. For some of these students, a lack of interest on the part of school administrations—which contributes to the invisibility problem mentioned previously—along with the daily slights or microaggressions of offensive and culturally insensitive language and other instances too many to count and a sense of futility about their lives has led, tragically, to a high suicide rate for these young people (Green & Waldman, 2018).

Those who do go on to enroll at a community college or four-year institution continue to wrestle with their invisibility in society and bear the daily discriminatory experiences that reinforce the belief that they are undeserving of better treatment and should be kept separate from the mainstream. Native advocates argue that much of the systemic discrimination in the educational system today stems from a lack of understanding of who Indigenous groups really are (Minthorn, Indigenous Perspectives on Native Student Challenges in Higher Education, 2020). Rather than a recognition of the diversity and differences within Indigenous cultures, they are reduced to a single homogenous group, with a single ethnic label and identity, which couldn't be farther from reality. Today, according to the U.S. Census Bureau, there are more than 550 federally recognized and nearly 100 state-recognized American Indian tribes in the United States, with at least another 400 tribes that do not benefit from state or federal recognition but still exist as intact cultural groups. Each has a unique cultural identity and heritage. Though Alaska natives are identified with only three groups—Eskimo, Aleut, and American Indian—the same richness, diversity, and differences still exist, as these tribes embrace at least 11 distinct cultures and speak 20 different languages (Alaska Native Groups & Cultures, 2020).

But a recognition of this multiplicity of Indigenous cultures—which is equally true for Afro-centric, Hispanic, and Asian peoples—doesn't exist at the post-secondary level, and it shows in the numbers. Only 17 percent of Native American students continue their education after high school compared to 60 percent of the U.S. population (PNPI, 2020). Of that group, about 41 percent of BA/BS-seeking students graduate within six years, compared to nearly 63 percent of White students (educationdata.org, 2020b). At community colleges—which often draw the highest number of Indigenous students—in 2017, only 27 percent of Native Americans attained an associate degree or higher, compared to 54 percent of White students (PNPI, 2020).

Greater sensitivity to the complex backgrounds of these students—and the circumstances affecting so many of them—should influence the outreach of colleges. Helping them navigate the higher education landscape involves addressing historical obstacles that continue to present problems today and that are reflected by low completion rates. In terms of economics, colleges and universities—even public ones—are expensive, and it's difficult for many of these students to afford it. That's why about 85 percent of Native American students receive federal grant aid (compared with 69 percent of White students), and 62 percent of Native American students are forced to take out a federal student loan (compared to 56 percent of White students) (PNPI, 2020). All of these factors—historical, cultural, economic—create barriers to success for Indigenous students at the postsecondary level. Driving up their completion rates requires a concerted effort in all of these areas to achieve academic equity.

Working Adult Students/Nontraditional Students

Today many working adults in "old economy" jobs—which refers to industries that dominated the economy in the 20th century like steel, manufacturing, and agriculture—are experiencing hardship as high-tech or technology-supported industries have become the drivers of the global economy in the 21st century. U.S. jobs that require manual labor, low cognition, low skills, and repetitive tasks are declining. For those that remain, salaries are projected to stagnate. Some reports predict the United States and Europe will lose as many as 23 million jobs in these categories by 2030 (Woetzel, 2019). To transition to "new economy" jobs, working adults often turn to community colleges. While there are several good programs across the community college sector that place students directly into growing fields, working adults often return to the classroom with a range of hurdles that they confront as part of their academic journeys. Most of these students have full-time jobs with fairly conventional work hours. Many have spouses, children, mortgages/rent, and all the bills that come with adulthood. They often have not been in an educational setting for several years, maybe decades, and must acclimate to the college environment.

For these students, the traditional structures of higher education pose significant problems. Class schedules are primarily built to accommodate "traditional students" and faculty preferences for mid-morning and early afternoon classes. These scheduling priorities, of course, produce schedules that conflict with most work schedules. Adding to the problems facing working adult students, campuses are not kid friendly and have limited or no daycare services. The college experience on most campuses is built around the transition from high school to college and the development of 18- to 22-year-olds, not working adults. These challenges (and more) put working adults in a situation where success is often more difficult than it could be if our colleges were designed with more of their circumstances in mind.

Many of these people (though not all, of course) are frustrated with the way the economy has developed over their time and the toll it has taken on their work lives. Oftentimes, their jobs have the added meaning of representing family tradition, which adds additional frustration to their loss. For example, a coal miner who comes from a long family tradition of coal mining is struggling not only with his personal need to earn a living but also with a loss of tradition and in many ways a loss of identity as he tries to hold on to a dying career. Many people living in "Rust Belt" states like Ohio, Michigan, and Pennsylvania have been hit especially hard by economic downturns over the past 30 years. Several studies suggest that annual incomes in these regions have fallen as much as $75,000. A 2019 report on adult learners from Jobs for The Future (JFF) recently summarized this dilemma. It points out that there are approximately 29 million people in the United States lacking a high school equivalent education, trying to find jobs in an economy that gives nine out of ten jobs to applicants with degrees (Bragg, Endel, Anderson, Soricone, & Acevedo, 2019). The odds are clearly stacked against them, which is why a post-secondary education—especially the kind provided by U.S. community colleges—promises such a dramatic improvement of their circumstances.

While there are many who fall into this category across the Rust Belt, working adults are a diverse group spread throughout the entire country. And when these individuals transition into a college setting, we often refer to them as "nontraditional adult learners" (NALs). The Education Advisory Board (EAB) reports that these students are typically age 25 or older (but this term can also apply to those under 25 if they have adult responsibilities) and represent a wide range, including Baby Boomers, millennials, military veterans, parents, career changers, disaffected old economy workers, and more (EAB, 2019a).

Most nontraditional adult learners return to school to develop new economy skills, advance in their current careers, and acquire more skills and knowledge relevant to the changing needs of their industry. Others want to complete a degree now that other responsibilities in their lives—like raising a family or serving in the military—have been mostly fulfilled and they can focus on the next phase of their lives. The group's diversity is also true of its prior experience of post-secondary education: Though some have no higher education experience at all, others may have taken classes online or in person or even completed one (or more) degrees. Education, in fact, matters a great deal to this group. A 2018 study by Public Agenda and the Kresge Foundation found that 57 percent of adult learners surveyed said that a bachelor's degree is a worthy investment, while slightly less—about 47 percent—said the same thing about acquiring an associate degree or certificate.

The National Center for Education Statistics (NCES) reports that 2010 was a pivotal year for working adults/nontraditional students, with an acceleration in enrollment that put this population at their highest level of college enrollment with 8.9 million. That acceleration has continued with a growth rate of 35 percent, now reaching a total population of 12 million. NCES estimates that enrollments from this population will continue to grow

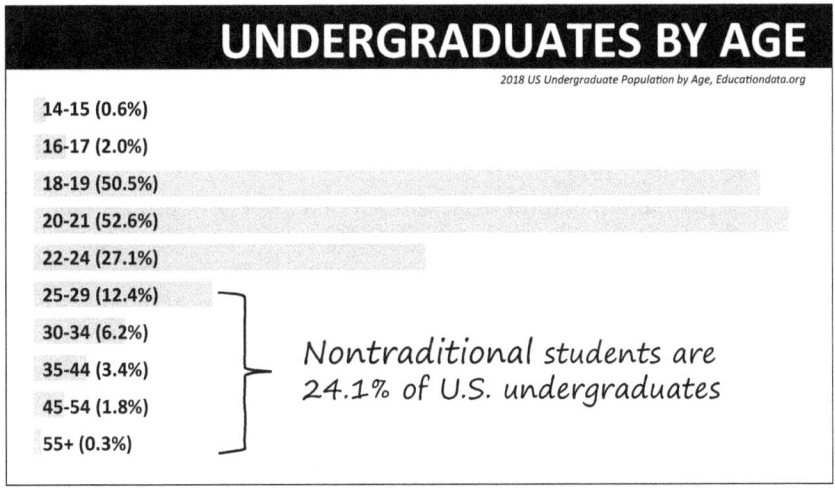

by another 11 percent to 13.3 million by 2026. With this growth, EducationData estimates that 24.1 percent of undergraduates are 25 years old or older, and this strength of enrollment is likely to continue for the next decade at least, given the economic changes that are under way. Extrapolating from a report released at the 2019 World Economic Forum in Switzerland, the United States and European economies are likely to lose 23 million "old economy jobs" and add 38 million "new economy" jobs by 2030 (Woetzel, 2019). The jobs projected to decline include those that require manual labor, low cognition, low skills, and repetitive tasks. Jobs that will be added require technological expertise, people and management skills, elevated levels of cognition and skills, and creativity. In other words, jobs that are predicated to grow will require technical degrees/certification (e.g., AS from community college) or BA/BS and above degrees. With an estimated 49.9%

JOB LOSSES AND GAINS

U.S. & Europe predicted to lose 23M "old economy" jobs and add 38M "new economy" jobs by 2030

Old Economy Skills	New Economy Skills
• Manual Labor	• Technology
• Low Cognition	• People Skills
• Repetitive Tasks	• High Cognition
• Low Skill	• High Skill
	• Creativity

of the 2016 workforce in "old economy jobs," we need to maintain and grow our pipeline to education for working adults.

The is a large cross-section of our community, and success is not only vital for each one individually, but their success is vital to overall economy. Like the other groups we have already discussed, completion rates are low for nontraditional adult learners. Because of their interest in attaining specific work-related skills or vocational training of some kind, many of these students tend to enroll in for-profit institutions (PNPI), and many start their journeys at a public two-year college. One of the challenges they face on this journey is the decision about whether to enroll full-time or part-time. Not surprisingly, because of competing demands in their lives, online options are a popular choice for this group: They are more likely to take advantage of online class options, with about 80 percent of students 25 years old or older enrolled in online programs (PNPI). The older the student, in fact, the more likely they are to attend school on a part-time, part-year basis.

Because of these issues, and more, degree completion remains low. Only about half of those who enroll in community colleges earn an associate degree; the other half leaves after three years without a degree. At four-year schools, the BA/BS completion rate number drops even lower to 15 percent. For those students starting out at a community college and intending to complete a bachelor's degree, only 23 percent reach this goal in eight years (EAB, 2019b).

Time is one of the factors behind these low success rates. Even in a home where the adult student has moved beyond the usual obligations, the necessary time required for study can discourage degree acquisition. Another struggle common among working students and other older NAL students is the "youth-centric" focus on many campuses that "can confirm their feelings of alienation and isolation as college students" (Chen, 2017). These students often feel that they hold secondary status with our undergraduate institutions more calibrated for traditional students.

The solutions to these problems are relatively simple to effect—unlike some of the considerable barriers facing other student populations described in this chapter. Working adults need a strong support structure. Offering evening hours for college counselors and administrative offices is one positive action that recognizes the circumstances of these students, who may not have the flexibility in their 9-to-5 work schedules to reach out during the day for assistance. Another effective solution is to create support groups for older students, which can create a more inclusive environment and sense of belonging and relevance for this often-neglected campus population (Chen J., 2017).

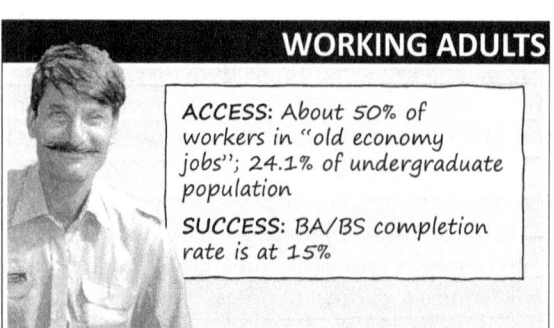

WORKING ADULTS

ACCESS: About 50% of workers in "old economy jobs"; 24.1% of undergraduate population

SUCCESS: BA/BS completion rate is at 15%

Two- and four-year institutions can offer cost-effective strategies to adult learners and help them as they seek better jobs and a better quality of life for their families. Recognizing the critical importance of creating pathways to and through postsecondary education for this group—that accommodate their backgrounds and the pressures of jobs and families—is a key strategy in transforming how we deliver education and equip this group with better skills in the workplace. The fact that completion rates remain low is a sign that an important message—that adults of all backgrounds should be able to succeed in postsecondary programs and improve their prospects in the job market—is not reaching enough of them.

LGBTQ+ Students

LGBTQ+ students are part of a community formed around sexuality and gender identity. The community includes students who identify as lesbian, gay, bisexual, transgender, transsexual, queer, intersexual, asexual, pansexual, agender, bigender, gender variant, pangender, and more. These groups have been part of the human experience throughout history; however, they have had to live in the shadows for most of this history, certainly for nearly all of U.S. history. Historians have started to shine a light on this long history, as demonstrated by a 2014 book examining the lives of two 19th-century Vermont women whose relationship functioned as a marriage even though they didn't have legal rights or the blessings of a church. Historians also have documented the covert efforts of organizations in the early years of the 20th century to improve the circumstances of gay and lesbian Americans, who lived under constant threat of arrest and the penalties of state sodomy laws. Some historians and cultural critics point to 1950 and the creation of the Mattachine Society, the first public organization of gay men, as a turning point for the nation's homosexual population (Kesslen, 2019).

But it wasn't until the turbulence of the 1960s—with protests on behalf of civil rights, feminists, the anti-war movement, and others—that activists for LGBTQ rights saw their cause within the greater context of social change taking place across the country. In the ensuing years, openly gay people would go on to hold public office, and consensual sexual relations in same-sex relationships would be decriminalized from state to state (but not immediately; such decriminalization would still take decades). The changes taking place in the second half of the 20th century marked an improvement but hardly signaled the end of the struggle for equal treatment under the law. Brutality continued for many openly LGBTQ+ people—the 1998 torture and murder of University of Wyoming student Matthew Shepard is a tragic, horrifying example—while during the Clinton administration, the military's long ban against openly homosexual members continued with the infamous Don't Ask, Don't Tell policy. George W. Bush's presidency was particularly difficult for the LGBTQ+ community, as Bush supported a constitutional amendment to ban same-sex marriages.

It seemed that a new day was dawning regarding LGBTQ+ rights, however, with the election of Barack Obama in 2008, but, even then, change didn't happen right away. You may recall that even Obama frustrated the Rainbow Community early on in his presidency when he would not take a firm stand in favor of gay marriage rights. As public opinion seemed to shift during his administration, his verbal support became more evident toward LGBTQ+ rights and issues. During this time, many states followed suit by recognizing gay marriage. Public figures began announcing their unconventional sexuality, and similar social markers pointed to an improving environment for LGBTQ+ students.

This attitudinal shift had a positive impact on higher education as well. Support for LGBTQ+ students began to rise, and recognition of the considerable challenges they face began to capture more dialogue in student success conversations. These changes are fairly recent and nowhere near complete. Many LGBTQ+ students report ongoing bias and outright discrimination off and on campus. Persistent religious doctrine, old policy biases, unintended lecture slights, and deeply held homophobia continue to add obstacles to our LGBTQ+ students' lives. These are areas that colleges and universities need to correct if they hope to help LGBTQ+ students find greater success.

According to a 2019 report by the Williams Institute at the UCLA School of Law (which analyzed the results of a recent Gallup survey), some 4.5 percent of the American population—or about 11.3 million adults—identify as lesbian, gay, bisexual, or transgender (Trotta, 2019). Many of these Americans live in urban areas: Though LGBTQ+ communities are spread out across the country, they typically are more concentrated in larger cities, which afford them more protections and opportunities than they can find elsewhere (The Williams Institute, UCLA School of Law, 2019).

As is true of Indigenous students, LGBTQ+ students are poorly represented in educational data, but for different reasons. Where Indigenous students have been largely overlooked and ignored due to their small numbers, LGBTQ+ students have often been reluctant to identify themselves in campus surveys and other reports out of concerns regarding a range of homophobic reactions they may experience from people in their private and academic lives. This leads to shortcomings in multiple data sets and limitations of our ability to generalize about their circumstances. For that reason, much of the data about LGBTQ+ students are incomplete and must come from a mix of sources. According to PNPI, in 2016, the American College Health Association found that in a sample of some 33,000 undergraduate students, 10 percent identified as gay, lesbian, bisexual, trans, asexual, pansexual, or questioning. This is more than double the number of the Williams Institute for the general population.

When it comes to BA/BS completion rates, a 2015 study showed that LGBTQ men are twice as likely as LGBTQ women to obtain a bachelor's degree. In fact, LGBTQ men are more likely to finish their bachelor's degrees than non-LGBTQ men. The probability of LGBTQ women completing a bachelor's degree is 25 percent, which is lower than the predicted probability of 34 percent for heterosexual women (Wade, 2015). Though the data are incomplete, it's also clear that LGBTQ+ students struggle against being stereotyped and treated as a single, homogenous group in academia in ways that are similar to what Indigenous groups experience. A 2013 Pew survey of LGBT Americans provides details that show this treatment isn't fair or accurate. Bisexuals, for instance, were found in the survey to be less likely to be college graduates than gay men or lesbians, leading to the conclusion that the relative younger age of bisexuals and their belonging to a generation that doesn't place a high value on traditional educational pathways may be factors in this lower result that aren't true for others in this population (Pew Research Center, 2013).

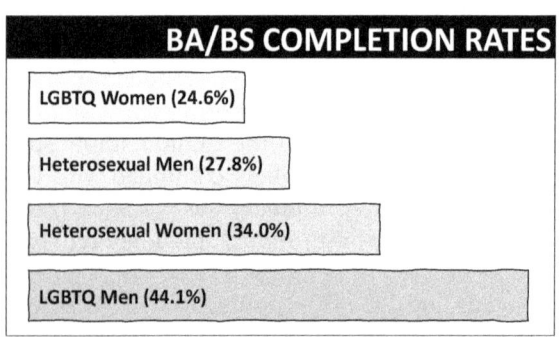

Improving outcomes for LGBTQ+ students at two-year and four-year institutions starts with the data. It needs to be vastly improved—and many gaps must be filled in—if we want a clearer understanding of how to improve completion rates and future outcomes for our LGBTQ+ students. This is not to suggest that there is a problem with survey strategies or sampling methodologies. It is not a technical issue in this case. The solution starts with fostering more trust and feelings of security in these students, who still largely fear harassment and discrimination and are unwilling to participate in the kinds of fact-gathering that will improve the data. Until they feel free to identify themselves without fear of punishment, the numbers will not change substantially. According to Campus Pride Index, these changes will require significant work across higher education, given that only 26 percent of college campuses in the United States prohibit discrimination based on sexual orientation and only 13 percent include gender identity expression as part of their policies. Many schools simply do not explicitly include LGBTQ+ students in their anti-discrimination policies and have applied to the U.S. Department of Education for a Title IX exemption in this regard. The exemption opens up avenues for discrimination against these students by groups who hold beliefs that oppose LGBTQ rights (Windmeyer S., 2016a).

MILLENNIAL ATTITUDES

- Ally-level support is declining with non-LGBTQ millennials
- Creates less supportive environment for LGBTQ community

Are you an LGBTQ Ally?

2018 (45% at Ally Level)
2017 (53% at Ally Level)
2016 (63% at Ally Level)

Work also needs to be done at the cultural level on campuses. According to a recent GLAAD/Harris poll (Ellis, 2019), young people are increasingly identifying as LGBTQ in surveys; however, there has also been a recent rise in push-back from millennials regarding acceptance of the LGBTQ community. Their poll finds that non-LGBTQs between the ages of 18 and 34 have recently swung from a majority holding opinions that they describe as "Allies" (strong support for LGBTQ) to a more recent majority they describe as "Detached Supporters" (varying support for LGBTQ). Because of a less supportive environment, many LGBTQ+ students report experiencing harassment based on their sexual identity and a "chilly" environment on college campuses that directly impacts their retention rates. One Campus Pride survey indicates that 33 percent of LGB and 38 percent of transgender students seriously consider leaving school because of insufficient on-campus support and the challenging atmosphere they must navigate (Windmeyer S., 2016b).

In approaching LGBTQ+ student populations, we need to remember that any student leaving home for college is entering a significant, and difficult, rite of passage on the way to adulthood. That rite is especially difficult for LGBTQ+ students because they face additional challenges related to a decision to *come out* that other students do not face. Feeling welcome and accepted are deep concerns, especially because the degree of security a student feels affects their decision to come out. Such concerns go hand in hand with fears of bullying and harassment and can lead to social isolation and even fear for their personal safety. According to research, as many as 60 percent of LGBTQ+ students feel unsafe at school because of their identity. That is why it is critical that our outreach to these students provide them with clear information and reliable resources to make their pathway to higher education less difficult.

The publication *Community College Review* outlines important critical features for LGBTQ+ students to consider before enrolling at any two- or four-year school. It must have

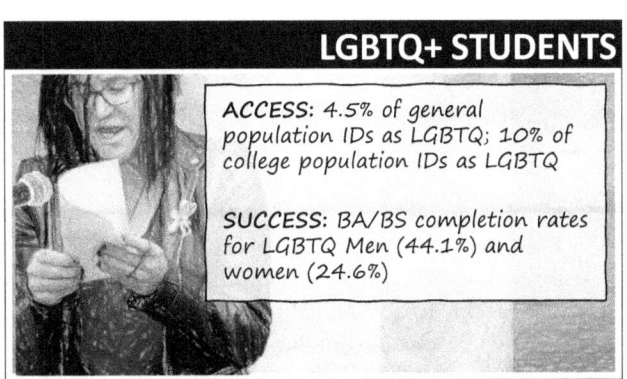

LGBTQ+ STUDENTS

ACCESS: 4.5% of general population IDs as LGBTQ; 10% of college population IDs as LGBTQ

SUCCESS: BA/BS completion rates for LGBTQ Men (44.1%) and women (24.6%)

an official policy on diversity and inclusion, for example, as well as focused counseling services, campus security trained in diversity, and student accommodations that are inclusive. Campus Explorer reports that more than 100 LGBT Centers exist on college campuses today across the nation—up from about 60 in 2006 (Henshaw, n.d.).

All educators at two-year or four-year institutions must realize that in their student population are students who remain silent today about who they are. Unfortunately, much of the responsibility for LGBTQ+ student success still rests on the students themselves. With much still unfinished regarding discrimination and their rights, it is up to each of these students to know their rights as much as possible before setting foot on any college campus. We can serve as mentors and guides to help them find the right resources to continue the journey and continue to change the environments. If we are to improve the completion numbers for this community, more of our country's public educational institutions need to establish policies that more overtly and comprehensively condemn discrimination against this population of students.

Foster Care Students

Foster care students may be the group of students with the most complicated lives. They have been raised with a shortage of love in their lives, with parents who have not been present on a consistent basis to guide them. They are the most likely group of students to experience housing and food insecurities, both of which create more anxiety than the pressures of homework or tests. These students come to our institutions with a lifetime of experience in which important people and important institutions have routinely disappointed them. For many of them, their negative experiences become their expectation. In many ways, our colleges are simply not prepared to help foster care students. For example, these students are most likely to start their education at a community college, but given the inadequate funding directed to most community colleges, we are least likely to have housing, adequate health services, or food support. Foster students need wraparound services in their lives that extend well beyond academic and learning support.

Exploring postsecondary options and figuring out the college application process are daunting challenges because many in foster care can't turn to parents for help, financial assistance, or the kinds of emotional support most students need as they face new academic demands and social challenges that are part of student life. They can't rely on the support of caseworkers, foster parents, or any other guardians in these areas, either. Several studies find that foster youth are so isolated with regard to support that they often don't realize their eligibility for state and federal financial aid or other kinds of scholarships, which could significantly improve their lives and increase their opportunities, and as a result *leave money on the table.*

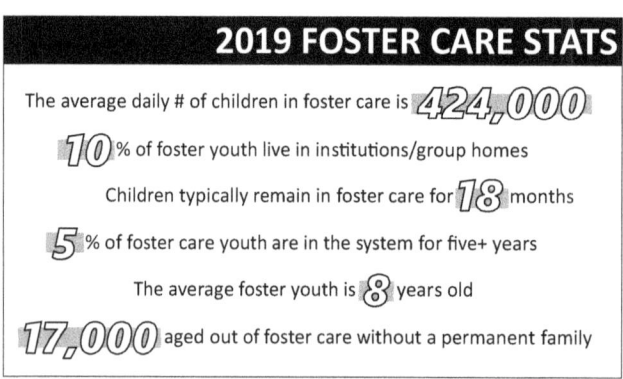

2019 FOSTER CARE STATS

The average daily # of children in foster care is 424,000

10% of foster youth live in institutions/group homes

Children typically remain in foster care for 18 months

5% of foster care youth are in the system for five+ years

The average foster youth is 8 years old

17,000 aged out of foster care without a permanent family

According to 2019 federal data, there are about 400,000 children in foster care, ranging from infants to age 21 (About the Children, n.d.). They enter the system most often because they have experienced abuse or been abandoned by their families. According to *AdoptUsKids*, about 20,000 youth *age out* of the foster care system on an annual basis when they turn 18 or 21 or because they've finished high school—the circumstances vary from state to state.

Aging out of the foster care system is a perilous time for many; they aren't prepared and don't have the skills to navigate the world as legal adults. The National Foster Youth Institute reports that only about half of those who age out of the system will find decent employment by the age of 24. About 20 percent of those who reach the age of 18 become instantly homeless; seven out of ten women in foster care become pregnant before reaching the age of 21. Many suffer long-term symptoms of post-traumatic stress disorder (PTSD) as a result of coming from violent homes, and this condition contributes to their chronic inability to find a secure, stabilizing environment (Sorrell, 2017).

Higher education often holds the only key to reversing the unhappy circumstances of their lives, but very few benefit from educational opportunities. About 50 percent of foster youth graduate high school by the age of 18, according to a 2014 report by the National Working Group on Foster Care and Education, and only about 20 percent of these graduates continue on into college—well below the national average—but their BA/BS completion rate for a bachelor's degree plummets to between 2 and 9 percent (National Working Group on Foster Care and Education, 2014). Too often, young people who've spent time in foster care lack not only the money to apply and pay for college but also the direction and support of adults to sustain their efforts and stay focused on their goals.

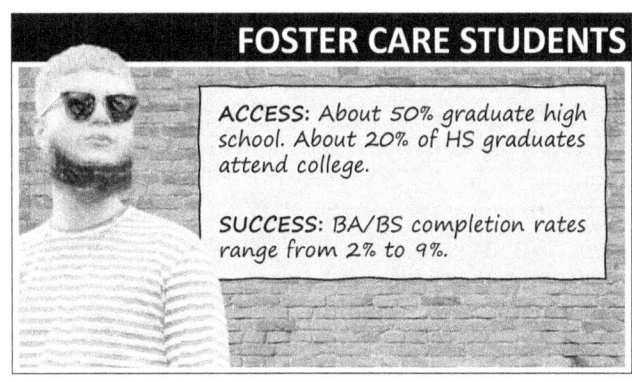

They don't have relationships with adults who can help them to fill out applications, secure financial aid, and choose a school. Many have bounced among homes and schools, leaving them unprepared academically. They may not have anywhere to stay during summers and other college breaks, either. They rarely have anyone they can turn to during an emergency, either (Smith-Barrow, 2018).

Kathi and I had a college student named Michael who had been in foster care most of his life live with us for a few months while he was trying to find housing. He was a big guy, probably six foot six and 250 pounds. One evening, I was sitting on the couch downstairs watching television, and Michael came downstairs to get something to eat. He surprised me a little when he walked around the corner and into the room. I can usually hear movement upstairs and certainly hear anyone walking down the stairs. But he moved silently through our house. He was like this in family conversations as well, often psychologically placing himself in the back of a conversation. I later learned this was something he had practiced nearly his entire life. Having moved in and out of more than ten foster homes during his life, he always tried to go unnoticed in these homes, hoping that they would keep him.

One evening, we were driving home from a family get-together with my in-laws. Michael, Kathi, Elizabeth (one of our daughters), and I were in the car. It was late. We were all quiet. Just to make conversation, I asked Michael what his plans were for the next day. He said he didn't know, adding that he typically wakes up each morning and works with whatever the day brings. He didn't say this as though it was a philosophical approach. It was more of a throw-away comment, describing what his typical morning is like. Later I thought back on that brief conversation and cried about it. Dreaming, planning, and aspiring have always been a part of my life that I love. I cherish this kind of thinking in my private and professional life. I love to dream big and develop plans to move in that direction. I can't imagine the development of my life without this. Michael was at the age when dreams should be boundless, imaging the possible life in front of him. Instead, his foster care experience had stolen these from him, leaving him accustomed to having no dreams for tomorrow.

Most students from foster care backgrounds have searing gaps in their lives that come to bear in their postsecondary experiences. Not surprisingly, it turns out that they do better—and seem more likely to experience better outcomes in school—when they receive regular adult engagement concerning their educational efforts. The low end of their BA/BS completion rate reflects an absence of accountability to older adults, but when regular follow-ups are added with a child-welfare agency, and when the students are age 25 or older, that completion rate increases. While one 2005 study showed that foster youth had a BA/BS completion rate of about 2 percent, those rates increased considerably when more accountability to older adults in the form of regular follow-ups was included. The completion rate increased to 10.8 percent when these students were regularly interacting with a voluntary child welfare agency about their efforts.

According to the National Association of Student Financial Aid Administrators, one early NCES post-secondary survey in 2001 found that foster youth seem to enroll in two- and four-year schools at much higher rates than other undergraduates, but they were only about half as likely (26 percent) to complete their programs after six years (Davis, 2006). One 2010 report showed that the college completion rate for foster youth varies between 1 and 11 percent compared to a 30 percent completion rate for all students ages 25 to 29 (Dworsky & Pérez, 2009).

Education advocates on behalf of foster youth say that finding permanent homes and contending with fewer placements—which disrupt normal routines and established relationships in a particular community—are significant factors in boosting the likelihood that these students will seek out a post-secondary education (Davis, 2006) and have the resources and commitment to stay and complete programs. Left without support, left without networks to advise and guide them through the academic landscape, the future for these students remains bleak.

Military Veteran Students

Veterans of the U.S. military have historically found the transition from their military lives to civilian lives to be difficult. This is not the case for every veteran, but it is for many. This includes transitioning into civilian education. While all vets have educational benefits provided to them by the federal government, many do not attend college because of the difficulty and discouragement they experience during the military-to-civilian transition. The highly structured lifestyle in the military and the mission-driven approach is wildly different from the unstructured environment in higher education. Active duty personnel are well trained to operate in a military environment, not an academic one that provides so many unclear choices. And the more combat a veteran has seen, the more likely they are to have very intense negative reactions to unstructured and individualistic environments. Vets with PTSD can have very negative reactions to an academic environment. This challenge is as old as the military itself in the United States.

The Pew Research Center finds that some veterans make the transition to civilian life with few problems. Typically, though, these veterans are either commissioned officers or have graduated from college; the higher education hurdle is already behind them. For the rest, other considerations in addition to moving from a structured to an unstructured world affects their decision to pursue a post-secondary education. Most are usually older

TRANSITIONING TO CIVILIAN LIFE

Likelihood of Successful Transitions to Civilian Life (Pew)

◄ More Difficult | Less Difficult ►

- -26% Experienced Trauma
- -19% Seriously Injured
- -15% Post-9/11 Vet Married While Serving
- -15% Post-9/11 Vet
- -7% Served in Combat
- -6% Knew Someone Killed/Injured

- College Graduate 5%
- Understood Missions 10%
- Officer 10%
- Religious Post-9/11 Vet 24%

than most other students and are more likely juggling college with family responsibilities, jobs, and service-related disabilities, and they often face significantly more red tape (Morin, 2011) before enrolling. Successfully living in war or preparation for war and successfully living in peace require two very different approaches for these students. Colleges and universities need to anticipate these differences on behalf of the men and women who have served and help them make this important transition successfully.

According to a recent report put out by the U.S. Census Bureau (Vespa, 2020), there are nearly 18 million veterans in the United States. This makes up about 7% of the adult population in the United States. Of this population, the largest group is Gulf War-era veterans, at about 7.5 million. These individuals served in the Gulf War era from the early 1990s to the present. The second largest share is the 6.3 million Vietnam veterans. As considerable as these numbers are, the share of the U.S. population with military experience is steadily declining. The Census Bureau reports a drop of more than half in the past 30 years, from about 18 percent in 1980 to 7 percent in 2016. Another changing characteristic of the veteran population is gender. Even though 91 percent of current veterans are male and 9 percent female, the Department of Veterans Affairs projects changes in the years ahead, with the numbers of female veterans expected to grow to 2.2 million by 2045. Age is another characteristic expected to change. The veteran population is expected to skew younger by 2045 as well: 33 percent of veterans will be younger than age 50 (as compared to 27 percent in 2016) even as the general population of the United States continues to age (Bialik, 2017). These estimates suggest we should anticipate expanding support for military veterans in higher education.

In one form or another, a government policy of helping veterans has existed for much of U.S.

MILITARY SERVICE PERIODS

Nearly 18 Million Vets in The U.S.

	All	Men	Women
All Service Periods	17,960	16,310	1,653
Post-9/11 (Sep 2001 or later)	3,764	3,132	632
Gulf War (Aug1990 to Aug 2001)	3,804	3,247	557
Vietnam Era (Aug 1964 to Apr 1975)	6,384	6,146	238
Korean War (Jul 1950 to Jan 1955)	1,306	1,268	38
World War II (Dec 1941 to Dec 1946)	485	463	22
Pre-World War II (Nov 1941 or earlier)	12	11	1
Peacetime only (Periods not above)	4,034	3,653	382

history, focused primarily on assistance with housing and medical treatment. The G.I. Bill's comprehensive approach changed that. Signed into law in 1944, the G.I. Bill has served as the centerpiece of the military-to-civilian transition since the end of World War II. It gives educational assistance to service members, veterans, and their dependents with support for tuition and other college- or trade-school-related expenses. By 2017, about 5.2 million veterans (28 percent of all veterans) over the age of 25 had completed a postsecondary degree or credential program of some kind (PNPI). Research also shows that these students don't move immediately from high school to college for an obvious reason: their military commitment. Instead, the average time between high school graduation and college enrollment for these students is about five years (PNPI, 2019a).

Understandably, many schools are eager to enroll veterans as students because of the $10.2 billion in annual G.I. Bill benefits that comes with them. With over 18 million veterans in the United States, there are many to recruit. Regardless, many vets do not take advantage of the benefits, with only 5 percent of undergraduate and graduate enrollment made up of veteran students (Hill, Kurzweil, Pisacreta, & Schwartz, 2019). And on top of low enrollments, many student-veterans don't complete degrees, according to data from the Departments of Defense, Education, and Veterans Affairs. In 2015, about 54 percent of student veterans were enrolled in associate degree or certificate programs, and 44 percent were enrolled in bachelor's degree programs (Marcus, 2017).

These enrollment figures may be comparable to other national averages, but the actual completion rates are far lower. A review of federal data in 2014 showed that only about 15 percent of full-time students receiving G.I. Bill money graduated from community colleges with a two-year degree. That percentage includes students who took three years to do it. According to the National Veteran Education Success Tracker, 53.6 percent of veterans using their G.I. Bill benefits graduate with a BA/BS within six years (Marcus, 2017). The fact that many students, not just military veteran students, take longer to finish points to a particular challenge for military veterans at our colleges. G.I. Bill benefits cover a maximum of about 36 months of school, which is enough to cover completion of a bachelor's degree for full-time students. But 36 months is also a fairly tight timeline for a military veteran student—especially if they are juggling a full-time job and a family (a situation similar to what most working adults face, mentioned in the previous section about nontraditional students). That leaves little room for unexpected emergencies or the chance the student might need to make an 11th-hour change to their course of study. These considerations may also explain why the completion rate for those attending community college on a part-time basis and who graduated within three years drops to 7 percent (Hill et al., 2019).

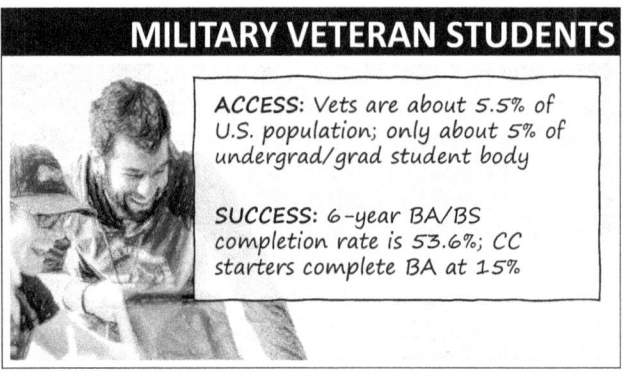

MILITARY VETERAN STUDENTS

ACCESS: Vets are about 5.5% of U.S. population; only about 5% of undergrad/grad student body

SUCCESS: 6-year BA/BS completion rate is 53.6%; CC starters complete BA at 15%

Still, one can't help asking, why? Why are completion rates for military veteran students so low? During their military careers, many of these student-veterans handled sophisticated, expensive equipment (not to mention the responsibility of protecting people's lives). When they return to civilian life, it isn't just the lack of structure that troubles them. When they go back to school, they often find that much of their specialized training gets thrown out the window and they have to start all over again. Many vets feel that they're wasting their time—and millions of dollars of government funds—on classes that they don't need because their military training already covered the material.

Consider a single financial fact: Helping just 6 percent of eligible vets—about 100,000—to receive one semester credit by recognizing their military training would translate into a savings of $1 billion for the government. In the end, though, many of these vets quit college and look for fields that don't require a degree—private security is a popular, and obvious, profession for many of them.

What military veteran students need is a better system that identifies their military training in some 25,000 courses offered by the military and translates this training to course work at colleges and universities. Even though the American Council of Education (ACE) already evaluates military transcripts to identify skills similar to college subject areas, this work is still too vague in many ways and doesn't come close to mapping military training onto existing college courses. Some states, like California, are leading the way with legislation to grant academic credits for prior military surface. In 2018, that state passed AB1786, which authorizes the state's community college system to grant academic credits for prior military service.

Even with such legislation, a bigger challenge remains in having public schools coordinate nationwide and finding ways to articulate military training and skills in terms of what one finds in community college course catalogs. Some schools have sought grants and nonprofit funding to help them develop online platforms for this purpose, but going their own way, one by one, provides only a partial solution. We still need coordination among schools nationwide, along with a national registry of veterans eligible for educational support. Such coordination and the creation of a registry would enable schools to quickly access and process military training records for some 1.6 million vets across the country who are in their 20s and eligible for educational benefits but don't know where to start.

In the shorter term, though, colleges and universities must address needs that veteran students have that are similar to what most working adults need—namely a greater sense of belonging and more visible support on campus. That translates into career and counseling services that take into account their special circumstances and challenges. It's also useful to establish a resource center—which some colleges have done—where veteran students can get together, chop it up about their days in the military, relax, and encourage each other. Many veteran students themselves believe that making such an effort to work out their educational pathways makes sense. After all, they have committed themselves to serving this country, even at the risk of losing their lives. Helping them to understand their educational benefits and finish college is an obvious way to show our commitment back to them.

Incarcerated and Formerly Incarcerated Students

Inmates and formerly incarcerated students bring a wide range of complications to their college pursuits that make success difficult. Learning successfully inside prisons is difficult for many inmates. Though they often have ample time to study and education is typically free, they have very strict controls over their time and highly complicated political environments that include an ever-present undercurrent of violence. They range in age anywhere from their early 20s to their 60s and have limited access to already-inadequate learning resources. Inside the prison classroom, many inmates experience a sense of hope, but once they leave that classroom, they are back in the prison world again, rarely treated as adults with anything of value to offer the world. A common misconception on the part of the public is that people in prison take classes because they have nothing else to do, but that's not the case. In fact, most incarcerated students already have assigned jobs, and there are limited private or quiet spaces for doing their classwork—and yet they manage to get the work done because they see value and opportunity in it.

Providing education for the incarcerated is not a recent idea. In the late 18th century, the Walnut Street jail in Philadelphia—one of the country's first "penitentiary houses"—instructed inmates in morality and religion with regular Bible readings, a practice that was soon copied by prisons in other states. By the early 20th century, prison reformers managed to get educational programs established for prison inmates, and the Higher Education Act of 1965 made them eligible to receive Pell Grants while in prison. College-in-prison programs thrived in the years that followed, but with the signing of the omnibus crime bill (known as the Violent Crime Control and Law Enforcement Act) into law in 1994, the incarcerated were made ineligible for those grants, and other withdrawals of public funding soon followed. By the early 2000s, the number of college programs in prison dwindled to just 12 across the country, according to American Public Media (Agarwal, 2018).

Formerly incarcerated students bring all their recent prison history with them—along with a complicated mix of new challenges—to their postsecondary educational careers. Most are unemployed, finding it very difficult to obtain jobs given their criminal records. It is easy for them to become discouraged, especially when their records decrease the chances of finding a job that pays a livable wage. The increasing importance in today's global, knowledge-based world of a college education makes this wage gap even harder to bear. As they attempt to rejoin society with all the good that was in their lives prior to serving time, they are also confronted with the bad. Under the pressure of economic survival, too many make the wrong decision to resume the lifestyle that led to their legal problems in the first place.

It is easy to see how these issues, swirling around incarcerated and formerly incarcerated students' lives, create distractions from learning. Setting aside the conversation about choices they have made that put them in this situation, colleges need to create environments that mitigate or eliminate the substantial hurdles that are in the lives of all students currently or formerly incarcerated.

According to the Bureau of Justice Statistics, the country's prison population has grown over the past 20 years. At the time of the passage of the omnibus crime bill in 1994—a bill whose harsh sentencing laws critics say exacerbated and increased the size of the incarcerated population—there were some 900,000 people in state and federal prison systems. That number has surged to just under 1.5 million in 2019, a slight drop (about 2.6 percent) from where it was in 2018. That number grows even larger if, in addition to state and federal prisons, we also include a variety of other forms of confinement, including juvenile correctional facilities, local jails, immigration detention centers, military prisons, and other facilities. The Prison Policy Initiative reports that the number of all confined people increased to a staggering 2.3 million in 2020 (Sawyer & Wagner, 2020; Mack, 2019).

Many consider the goal of reducing recidivism the most compelling reason for inmate education, since most agree that education is one of the best ways to lower recidivism rates. With an 83 percent rate of former inmates returning to prison, California is a good example of how severe this problem has become. To address this issue, the Bureau of Justice Statistics and Emory University's economics department conducted a study to see what significance education plays in lowering recidivism rates. This study found compelling results with a strong inverse correlation between recidivism and levels of education pursued while in prison. They found that inmates who pursue no education while in prison have a national recidivism rate of 76.6 percent. If an inmate pursues some high school education while in prison, their recidivism rate drops to 55.0 percent. Pursuing vocational training drops the rate to 30.0 percent. Achieving an AA degree drops the rate to 13.7 percent, while the completion of a bachelor's degree and master's degree drops the rates to 5.6 percent and 0 percent, respectively (Allen, 2006). Given the generally low education levels most inmates enter prison with, an AA degree is considered by many (including me) the sweet spot we should aim for in terms of prison education policy.

The recidivism-education connection is what led us at Norco College to lean into prison education heavily. We started a program in 2017 offering a few classes at a prison close to the college and quickly expanded the program into a full AA degree with a pathway to a bachelor's degree through a partnership with a local university. The program was enthusiastically supported by the prison warden and her education staff. It was also popular with many faculty at Norco College, finding the program to have a strong social justice element.

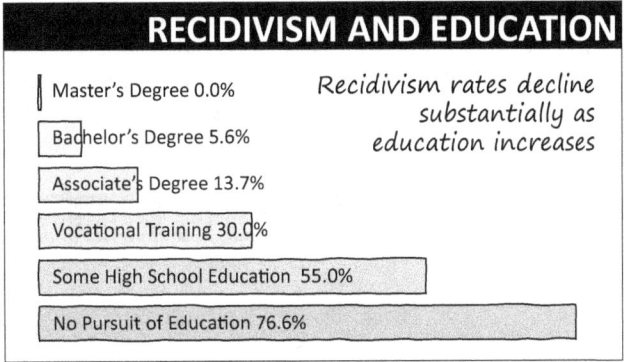

Faculty in this program commented on the quality of the teaching and learning environment. The physical learning environment was not ideal, with a prison check-in process that was sometimes complicated, inadequate classroom facilities, and limited office space. But the quality of academic engagement between faculty and students was so unexpectedly good that faculty repeatedly commented on how gratifying the experience was. I once gave a guest lecture in one of the English classes offered at the prison and can confirm the experience. Students were engaged, prepared, and curious. In addition, the student inmates brought to the conversation experiences that added a richness and depth to the teaching and learning. During this time with students, the guards standing outside, the noise seeping in from the yard, the creaking noise of the old wooden floor, and the uniforms each student wore faded as we engaged in a conversation of Nicole Gramsci, the *Prison Notebooks*, his concept of cultural hegemony, and how it is used by power structures to subtly yet effectively oppress targeted groups of people.

With such strong correlations between education and recidivism, several states are moving forward with prison education programs at the undergraduate level. Thirteen states in particular are pursuing this approach and combined serve about 86 percent of the nation's incarcerated undergraduate population (The Best Schools, 2019). In California, for example, 22 community colleges provided instruction and support to more than 7,000 students in the state's 35 prisons during 2017. While 13 states are moving in this direction, the other states and the federal prison system have been reluctant to offer educational services in prisons. Reports estimate that somewhere between 35 and 42 percent of correctional facilities offer college educational services. The federal government itself offers vocational training but does not offer associate or bachelor's degree education. All combined, this partial support of college programs for the incarcerated translates to an estimated 6 percent of

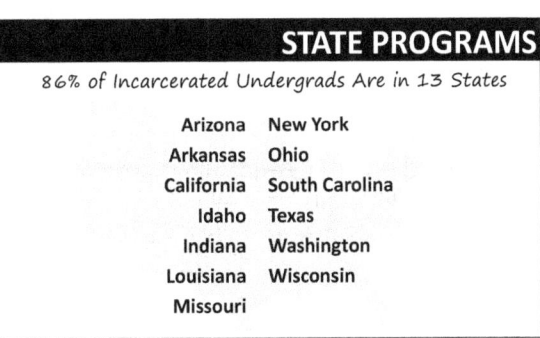

incarcerated individuals nationwide in college-level courses, requiring inmates to pay for their entire education. To make matters worse, many of the already limited number of inmates enrolled in college courses are not in programs that lead to degrees. It appears that roughly 71,000 of the two million plus inmates (about 3 percent) are enrolled in programs that lead to a degree (The Best Schools, 2019).

With all of the promise about the value of education and its positive impact on life after incarceration, prisoners who do find themselves in a prison that offers education are not finding the kind of success they and we hope for. Approximately 40 percent of inmates in state and federal prisons and jails do not have a high school diploma or GED (18 percent of the general population does not have a high school diploma or GED) (Contardo & Tolbert, n.d.). This means that many inmates start their educational journey by pursuing a GED. Of those who finish their GED, only about 10 percent go on to take college courses, and only 1 percent of them finish a degree. And when inmates are tracked beyond prison, as *formerly* incarcerated citizens, college completion rates do not fare much better. One study found that 55.4 percent of the general public has taken at least one college course, while only 23 percent of formerly incarcerated population has taken a college course. With regard to bachelor's degree completion, about 29 percent of the general population holds a degree, while less than 4 percent of formerly incarcerated individuals hold a bachelor's degree (Couloute, 2018).

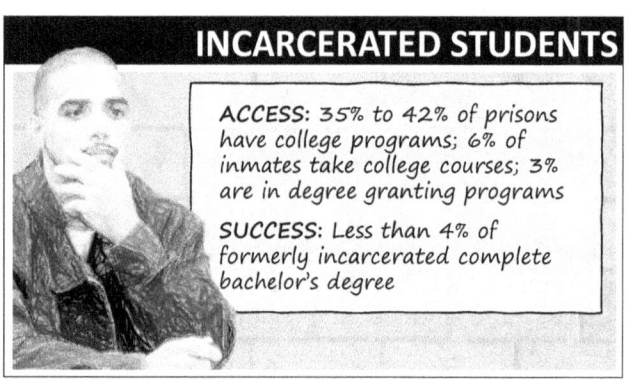

As mentioned previously, there are conspicuous obstacles for those who choose to pursue higher education in prison. Noise, a lack of current information or internet access, lost lessons and exams, miscommunications with academic advisers or professors, the stress and pitfalls of life on the inside, and more have made for an isolated learning experience. Prison staff can also be problematic and discouraging. These circumstances force these students to develop resilience they never experienced before.

For those who are able to persevere in these environments, the experience of higher education is a positive one. Some inmates who have been successful with in-prison education programs say that the program they took advantage of was far more effective than any others in addressing their criminality in a constructive way because it helped them to avoid a return to prison. Students learn critical thinking, communication and social skills, ethics, time management, goal setting, perspective taking, organization, and accountability for one's actions or inaction. This is different from basic adult education programs that are currently taught in most prisons. Inmates may train to become plumbers, mechanics, or carpenters, for instance, but that training still lacks the kind of decision-making skills that they will need outside of these occupations. This is why vocational training alone isn't enough; if it were, recidivism wouldn't still be a problem (May, 2020).

Not only are better educational programs in prisons better for the inmates, there are clear societal benefits, too. When any incarcerated student achieves a degree or certificate, they are instantly more likely to find work when they leave the prison. Many studies have argued persuasively that investing in their education creates reciprocal benefits for each individual and for society in general. In California, for instance, the annual cost of housing an inmate is about $75,000, which is more than the annual cost of attending

Stanford University. Seen in that light—prison costs versus educational costs—it makes more sense to invest in programs that will reduce these costs (and overall recidivism rates) and empower these individuals to become contributing members in their communities (Couloute, 2018). A recent policy analysis in the state of Washington found that for every dollar spent on education inside their prison system, the government saves about $19.74 (Coggeshall, Murke-Storer, Correa, & Tidd, 2019). Providing college education in prisons is good for inmates, it is good for society, and it is good for the taxpayer.

Poor and Low-Income Students

Students from backgrounds characterized as low income or beneath the poverty level bring the obvious stresses of limited resources to their postsecondary journeys. It is difficult for them to afford the basic requirements of school. They struggle to pay for books, tuition, and fees. Their transportation is often unreliable. Many are housing and food insecure. They struggle to pay for transfer applications, graduate and professional school exams, clothing for job interviews, and more. On top of these necessities, they often find it difficult to join important social activities given the assumptions that these activities make about access to money. For example, if a group of friends want to attend a concert or have dinner, poor students often must find a way to gracefully bow out because they simply do not have the funds. Along with the financial burdens, it is also likely that these students have emotional scars because of the strains that economic stress can put on family relationships and the public embarrassment and shame that poor people routinely encounter. Poor students have an experience that, in many ways, reflects the experiences of students of color. Academic culture reflects middle- and upper-middle class values and norms. Poor students don't see their experiences reflected in the fabric of higher education institutions and feel displaced, if not ignored. In patterns that mirror those of the student groups discussed previously, poor students encounter significant hurdles that they must clear in addition to the regular academic challenges of the learning process.

The U.S. Census reports that in 2018, there were 38.1 million residents in poverty. With 327.2 million living in the United States at the time, 11.6 percent of people in the United States struggle financially. The 2018 data were an improvement by 1.4 million people from 2017. That slight decline was received as positive news, and the improving U.S. economy seemed to account for that decline. And yet, though the 2018 report was encouraging, it showed that one in eight Americans still live below the poverty line—$25,465 for a family with two adults and two children. What that report also showed was that the number of people in the United States without health insurance grew from 25.6 million people in 2017 to 27.5 million in 2018, which included 4.3 million children. Income and poverty levels, as we've clearly seen during the global public health crisis that started in early 2020, can change dramatically. It remains to be seen what the figures for poor and low-income families will be when the final economic toll of the COVID-19 pandemic is taken both in the United States and worldwide.

INCOME DISTRIBUTIONS

Family Incomes in U.S. (Census 2019)

- Under $15,000 (9.1%)
- $15,000 to 24,999 (8.0%)
- $25,000 to 34,999 (8.3%)
- $35,000 to 49,999 (11.7%)
- $50,000 to 74,999 (16.5%)
- $75,000 to 99,999 (12.3%)
- $100,000 to 149,999 (15.5%)
- $150,000 to 199,999 (8.3%)
- $200,000 and over (10.3%)

Regardless of a country's overall distress—whether it's because of a global crisis or the regular fluctuations of its economy—the people falling below the poverty line remain one of our most vulnerable populations. Poor people are constantly under pressure to find food and housing (*safe* housing) without the predictability and comfort of a monthly paycheck to cover those needs. An unexpected windfall—a tax refund or side job—might ease the pressures of daily life, but only for a moment. "Being poor isn't the same as being broke," one commentator explains in the *Huffington Post*. "Broke is temporary; poverty becomes who you are." Poor families have to make choices that other families do not. They often must decide which bills will be paid and which will not. Do they pay the electricity bill or buy food? Do they make rent or purchase the prescription? These are impossible choices that millions of Americans (over 38 million) face on a monthly basis. They are choosing between hunger and cold, housing and health, and a range of other heartbreaking trade-offs—with little or no relief from these ongoing pressures (Tinson-Johnson, 2018).

The same disruptions and struggles experienced by any poor family are experienced by poor students on campus. Drawing on a sample of more than 33,000 students at 70 community colleges in 24 states, a 2017 study by the University of Wisconsin (Carapezza, 2017) found that one-third of community college students go hungry and 14 percent are homeless (Fry & Cilluffo, 2019). According to the lead researcher of the study, the problem of food and housing insecurity isn't unique to the community college system. The study found similar problems at some of the country's most expensive and most selective universities.

Despite facing many challenges, a rising number of students in poverty today are enrolling at two- and four-year institutions as compared to 20 years ago. The Pew Research Center reports that during the 2015–16 academic year, about 20 million students were enrolled in undergraduate education: 31 percent of the students were in poverty, which was up from about 21 percent during the mid-1990s (Fry & Cilluffo, 2019).

While enrollment rates may have gone up, completion rates haven't improved significantly. Research conducted in 2015 confirms that low-income students were less likely than economically more secure students to complete their college education despite recognizing the importance of receiving one. After graduating high school, only about 14 percent of poor students attained a BA/BS degree or higher institution within eight years, compared to 29 percent of students from middle-income backgrounds (College for America, 2017). And while these completion rates have slightly improved over the last three decades, the relative improvement of poor students to middle- and high-income students has been at a slower rate, meaning the success gap has widened over the last three decades (Pell Institute, n.d.).

BA/BS COMPLETION RATE

Poor and lower-middle income students are falling further behind

1970
- Poor 22%
- Lower-Middle 23%
- Upper-Middle 26%
- Wealthy 55%

2016
- Poor 25%
- Lower-Middle 33%
- Upper-Middle Income 59%
- Wealthy 75%

Many poor students in this group are more likely to start out at a community college and focus on a two-year degree because it seems more attainable—and affordable. For-profit schools are also a more likely destination for low-income students (PNPI, 2019b) than students from middle and upper incomes. That translates into about 42 percent in pursuit of an associate degree as compared with 32 percent for a bachelor's degree, according to data released in 2019 by the U.S. Department of Education's National Center for Education Statistics (Fain, 2019). The numbers for their peers from higher-income backgrounds are the opposite: 78 percent were more likely to seek out a four-year degree than a two-year degree (about 13 percent). Other numbers in the NCES data show that only 8 percent attend a four-year private institution, while about 13 percent enroll at a for-profit school (Chen & Nunnery, 2019).

NCES data show that even when poor and low-income students are academically proficient in high school and should thrive in college, their completion rates are not high. One obstacle the NCES data reveal about low-income students is related to information seeking. Students from low-income backgrounds are less likely to know where to find information about how to enroll in college or the benefits and aid that might be available to them (which echoes another group mentioned in this chapter, foster youth). Another challenge is posed by debt. Even when low-income students get loans or grants, they still struggle with debt that may force them to drop out entirely. A 2015 report by the public policy organization Demos noted that low-income students shoulder more student debt than other students, even if they receive Pell Grants. Because of this burden, about 38 percent of low-income students drop out under the weight of education-related debt (College for America, 2017).

The solution to this problem, and to helping improve completion rates, would seem to be obvious: more financial support for these students. But that's only the most obvious element of what these students need in order to complete their college educations. As is true of other groups described in this chapter, low-income and high-poverty students require a more structured social and academic support system as well. An oft-cited example of what that looks like is provided by the University of North Carolina at Chapel Hill, which established a special program combining  financial assistance with a support network that includes faculty mentoring, peer counseling, academic and career workshops, and social events. These students experience a greater sense of belonging and, thanks to such support networks, they learn invaluable skills that they wouldn't possess otherwise and that are crucial for student success: time management, for example, or note-taking and financial literacy.

In the real world, people who are ill equipped to take a journey in an unfamiliar place are more likely to lose their way. The same appears to be true of many subgroups within today's general student population. Much can be accomplished by someone who has resiliency and determination. This advice is a response often directed to poor students, suggesting that they are deficient in these areas. In reality, their capacity to persist often exceeds that of middle- and high-income students, but their reservoir of resiliency and determination is often depleted by their ongoing struggle for shelter, food, warmth, health, and safety.

The ten student groups discussed in this chapter each have unique histories that present ongoing challenges. As we develop solutions and services for these groups, we need to bring expertise to their specific needs. But one theme that holds most of the students from these disparate groups together is the idea of first generation to attend college. The vast majority of these students come from families where no one has attended college or no one has earned a bachelor's degree. They are part of families that do not have college-going traditions, and this lack of experience to draw on usually creates a set of hurdles in students' private lives that make academic success more difficult than for students who come from families with college-going traditions. First-generation students typically have different conversations around the dinner table than well-educated families. For example, while first-generation students have family members who love them dearly and hope for their success, they do not tell stories of going to college, or of their days in law school.

As a result, these students often do not grow up seeing themselves in situations related to higher education. They do not grow up learning all the unofficial rules associated with academic success. As they enter college, they are at an immediate disadvantage, wondering if they even belong in a place like college and knowing there is no one at home who can help them navigate the complexities surrounding matriculation. Many even report a kind of passive-aggressive attitude from family members who find the personal changes that a college student often makes as somehow behaving in a superior and conceited manner. Men in these environments often suggest that their masculinity is challenged by their families because of the college student's lifestyle. Women have raised complaints saying the family does not "understand" their career choices. All of these private life complications make success for first-generation students more difficult than for students from families with college-going traditions.

When considered as a whole, the individuals from these groups inherit a range of complications in their private lives that constitute extra weight that other students are not required to carry. As discussed for almost all ten groups, they have fewer resources, lacking money and the social/academic capitol needed to navigate much of higher education. They have less time to spend on education because of jobs and family commitments that are real demands in their lives. They are often less prepared, coming from under-resourced high schools and families that do not have basic knowledge about the college experience. They often lack confidence from long personal histories that include discrimination, marginalization, microaggressions, displacement, and injustice.

It is important to note that most of the hurdles that students face did not become part of their lives because of bad choices. Children don't choose the environment in which they are raised. They don't deserve the difficult environments they inherit any more than other children deserve the privileged environments they are born into. But these hurdles are real, they are present in our students' lives, and they make academic success—something that is already difficult—even more difficult. It is our job as academic professionals to recognize these hurdles, acknowledge them, and develop solutions that eliminate or mitigate them in our students' lives.

Recognizing the situation these students are in, understanding the disadvantaged start they have in college, and taking deliberate action to bridge these gaps is how we start to bring equity and social justice to their lives and our work. The most fundamental idea behind equity-mindedness is the recognition that some students have ample academic capital in their private lives, and other students have limited academic capital. Equity-minded strategies seek to identify the groups that have limited academic capital and augment this deficit in their private lives with public, government-funded resources.

The consequence of this approach usually leads to an unequal distribution of public resources in our attempt to establish equity. This inequality is commonly accepted, for example, in the distribution of financial aid. When I was in college, I was a Pell Grant recipient. This is a federal program for students with very low income—typically at or below the poverty line. Through this program, federal money is given to poor students and is *not* given to students from middle- or upper-income families. This is an unequal distribution of federal resources because we acknowledge that the students from poor families have fewer private resources available for education. This kind of calculus needs to be extended to all areas where historically underserved students lack resources. We need to identify the deficits in all forms of academic capital and augment them as much as possible with public/institutional resources. Much of this book is about presenting specific strategies that augment these deficits and, even better, eliminate or mitigate many of the barriers that cause these deficits in the first place.

Quantifying the Gaps

The students we serve experience an academic success gap, meaning they experience success less frequently than other groups. For many years, I have approached community college leadership with this understanding and have attempted to collectively apply strategies that demonstrate success for all, or at least some, of these groups. I was motivated by the idea that academic improvement for students of color, low-income students, other disadvantaged groups is the goal for academic reform. For example, aiming for year-over-year increases in graduation rates for military veterans or year-over-year enrollment rate increases for Indigenous students would set us on a course for meaningfully narrowing (and eventually closing) these equity gaps. But, there are two fundamental problems with this approach.

First, as we have already discussed in the book, there is a documented record of academic improvement over the last 50 years in higher education. More people are going to college, and nearly every group in the United States is adding higher levels of education to their communities. More poor and low-income students are going to college and completing their degrees than in previous decades. The rate of improvement has increased for both groups in a near linear fashion for five decades. But upper-middle income families and wealthy families have also shown academic improvements over the last 50 years, and their rate of improvement has been higher than for less-favored groups. As a result, while all economic groups have improved college attendance and completion rates over the years, poor and low-income students have fallen further behind because of their lower rates of improvement. We see this trend across nearly all the groups we have discussed in this chapter. If we want to secure equality in the United States, we need to stimulate accelerated academic improvement for the most disadvantaged groups. They need to experience improvement at faster rates if we hope to close these persistent academic gaps.

The second fundamental problem with a strategy that simply calls for improvement in academic outcomes for historically underserved students is connected to resources and expectations for change. I have stood in front of countless colleagues pointing to these inequities, calling for reform, and inviting others to engage in this effort. The response from the vast majority of my colleagues has always been positive and receptive. However, as I look back on these exchanges, we all had very different ideas about how much change should be made, and this in turn has a significant impact on the resources that are devoted to equity related efforts. For example, if you are aiming for a 2-percent increase in graduation rates for Latinx students, the strategy and supporting resources will be much different from a goal that aims for a 25-percent increase.

Committing to improving academic performance for students from disfavored communities is a first step, but the practical planning and collective action needed to effect change require specific targets. We need to know how much improvement we can reasonably expect or, in the context of this book, how much improvement we need to make in order to close the academic attainment gaps. We need to know how wide these gaps are. We have identified ten historically underserved communities and reviewed their academic experience. We have a good description of where they are. But for equality to reign on our academic institutions (and hopefully translate into American society as more students from disfavored communities graduate), we need to determine the distance between these groups and our most successful group(s). These data will quantify the distance we need to move each group in our goal for academic equality.

The most successful student groups in the United States tend to come from upper-income or wealthy White or Asian families. These groups have college attendance rates at 63% for the fourth-highest income quintile in the United States and 72% for the highest quintile (National Communication Association, 2019) and are consistently found to have bachelor's degree completion rates (many of the studies discussed in this book) from mid-60 to low 80 percentages (the average estimate looks to be around 70%). With these two parameters in mind (enrollment rates and completion rates), permit me to remind you of the overarching social justice strategy discussed throughout this book. The basic logic is as follows:

1. Social injustice exists in American society.
2. To address social injustice effectively, we need to put people from historically underserved communities into positions of prominence, power, and influence.
3. These positions need to be filled at percentages that are approximately proportionate to the populations these new leaders come from.
4. To deliver on this strategy, higher education must enroll and graduate students from these communities at proportionate levels.

Accepting these premises, the quantifiable targets we should shoot for are increases in college enrollments and degree attainments to match population percentages. To accomplish these two objectives, we need to build recruitment strategies that aim for enrollments to match population percentages and build academic success that brings all groups up to the completion rates of our most successful groups (about 70 percent completion rate) to make sure that the number of students from underserved groups walking across our commencement stages is proportionate to the number of people in the communities they represent.

Regarding enrollment, we are seeing some success with certain groups but still have work to do with others. Individuals from African American, Latinx, LGBTQ+, and poor communities are enrolling in college nationally at increasing rates. All four of these groups appear to have attained college enrollment percentages that exceed their percentages of the general population. In contrast, military veterans, working adults, Indigenous peoples, and Southeast Asians appear to be disproportionately under-enrolled relative to their numbers in the general U.S. population. The LGBTQ enrollment data should be taken with knowledge that not all LGBTQ+ individuals reveal this designation in polling data and other processes that

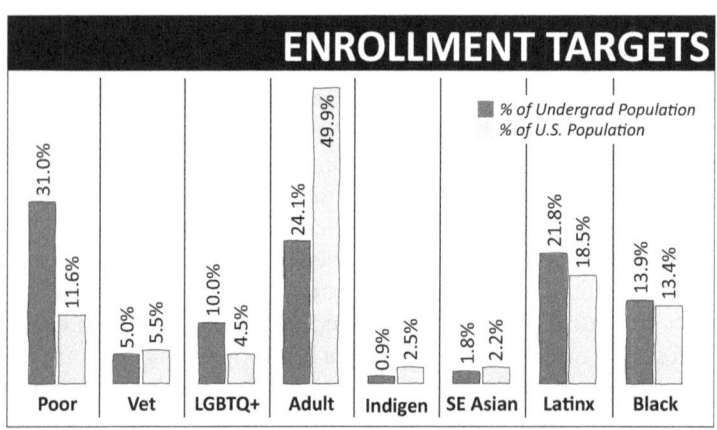

collect demographic data. The data regarding Southeast Asians are also a data set that is subject to margins of error because of how poorly we collect information for Asian subgroups in the United States. *Working adults* is also a data set that may have significant margins of error given how unsystematically some of these data are collected. Finally, foster care and incarcerated students were not included in the diagram because both have an extremely low *n*, but the two groups suffer from disproportionately low enrollments relative to their percentages in the population.

While some groups have proportionately exceeded the general population percentages with strong enrollment trends, it is important to note that there are other considerations that play into enrollment we need to consider. Nearly all of the groups discussed have higher enrollments in community colleges and for-profit institutions than in universities, with significantly lower enrollment in selective universities.

We also need to recognize the current discussion in literature about the kinds of majors that historically underserved students choose or are encouraged to choose. There appears to be a decided skew away from disciplines with higher earning potential. For example, engineering is a major that can lead to lucrative careers. As the field struggles with lower enrollments for women and students of color, some scholars point to possible sources of bias that cause this disproportionality in engineering. The type of institution students from historically underserved communities attend and the majors that they choose need to be considered in enrollment and access conversations. Regardless, looking at enrollment in college on a national basis, we have made strong achievements. We have a long way to go, but we are making substantial progress on behalf of disfavored communities and need to continue in this direction.

The story around completion data for students from disfavored communities is quite different from the enrollment and access story. While many groups are entering college at proportionate level, no one group is completing bachelor's degrees at levels that establish balance on our commencement stages. When measuring for BA/BS completion across a six-year time frame, Latinx students are doing best among the ten groups discussed in his chapter. They are completing at 56%; however, this is at least 14 percent below the top-performing groups (upper-income Asian and White students), 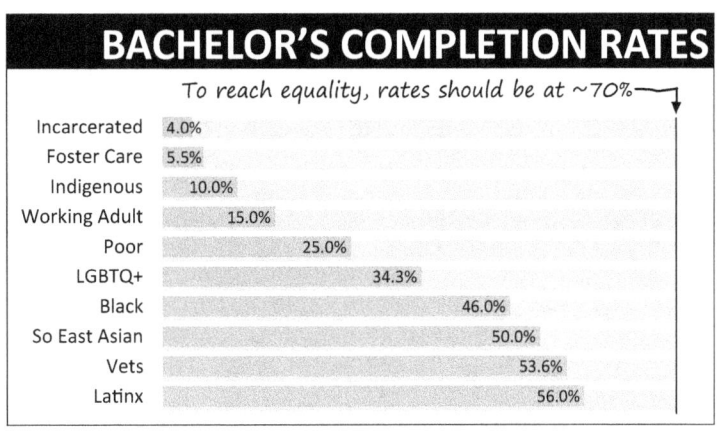 and when these students start out at a community college, the BA/BS completion rate drops below 14 percent. Military veterans and Southeast Asians appear to be completing degrees with fairly strong rates but still have considerable gaps to close, with 16.4 and 20.0 percent gaps, respectively. African American students are also grouped fairly close to the four top-performing groups but still have a 24 percentage point gap to close before they receive degrees with proportionality.

Starting with LGBTQ+ students, the completion gaps start to become larger. LGBTQ+ students have a 35.7 percent gap to close, poor students a 45 percent gap, working adults a 55 percent gap, and Indigenous students a 60 percent gap, while foster care students and incarcerated students have gaps of 64.5 and 66.0 percent. With all of these groups, the gaps are significantly wider when they begin their journey at a community college.

Over the years, it is clear that community college and higher education in general have made good progress with regard to enrollment and access for disfavored communities. But our work to increase rates of success for these students is in the early stages. There are substantial gaps in success rates that need to be closed. To make substantive progress with regard to gap closures, we will need to implement significant change.

In the next several chapters, we will discuss literature-based strategies that can be used to narrow (and eventually close) these enduring gaps. I have not been at an institution that has implemented all of the strategies that are discussed in the following chapters, but I have been involved with colleges where several of these strategies have been successfully implemented. When these practices are implemented well, they can create stress in the institution and certainly disruption, but they also generate significantly improved outcomes for students from disfavored communities. I have worked on initiatives at three colleges and have been able to narrow the equity gap at all three colleges.

Community colleges need passionate professionals who will make a commitment to implement many or most of these strategies. The strategies discussed will eliminate many hurdles in our students' lives, allowing them to spend more of their energy on achieving academic success. If implemented thoroughly, these strategies will create environments where more disfavored students find academic success and change the trajectory of their lives. If we are able to effect change at the magnitudes called for in this chapter, we will start seeing the equitable society we all want to live in. All of higher education needs to be engaged in this work, but the driving force behind the work will need to originate from community colleges. They are the institutions that serve the majority of disfavored students. They are, therefore, the institutions that create the foundation for establishing social justice in America.

4   Adding Academic Capital to Students' Lives

A few years ago, I had the privilege of getting to know a student named Brenda Lopez. Brenda was born in Mexico, and when she was six years old, her parents decided to move to Southern California. She attended elementary school, middle school, and high school in Corona, California. After graduating from high school, she enrolled in Norco College, where I was president at the time.

Brenda was raised by a family who loved her deeply and raised her in a very traditional social environment. She grew up with traditional views on gender roles: how they define our responsibilities in the family and the opportunities available to men and women in the workplace. These values and ideas were transmitted to her throughout her formative years by the most important people in her life. These were strongly held personal and family beliefs that Brenda brought with her when she enrolled in classes at Norco College. Like many first-generation students raised in traditional cultures, she started college with a limited view of who she might become and what the world had to offer her in terms of a career.

with Brenda Lopez

Brenda started taking general education classes at the college and quickly noticed that she was good with numbers and excelled in science courses. She heard about the STEM (science, technology, engineering, and math) Club at the college and decided to join. She very much enjoyed the club activities and social aspects and was soon deeply involved. She formed friendships with other STEM students. Two faculty members took a particular interest in her academic success, and through these exchanges, Brenda discovered engineering and declared it as her major.

I love the fact that she chose engineering. I remember talking to her about her choice, and she laughed, telling me she did not even know there was such a thing as engineering when she was growing up. In the circle of influential adults in her life, no one was an engineer, no one talked to her about engineering, and certainly no one ever encouraged her to pursue a career in engineering. This is not because Brenda was raised in a family who did not care for her. This did not come from a deep-seated dysfunction in or mistreatment by her family. She experienced love and the highest of hopes from her family. But no one in her family had completed college, let alone entered highly technical professions like engineering. Brenda was innocently unaware of engineering as a field of study and a professional career.

But her experiences at Norco College revealed such opportunities. During Brenda's first year in the STEM Club, she and a few of her classmates entered an engineering competition at UC Riverside. She enjoyed the preparation for the event and the competition itself so much that the following year, she applied for the competition again. This time she organized a team, coordinated the product design, and led her team through the competition. The competition required the development of a wind turbine, a small device that would allow blades to spin in the wind and generate an electrical current. Judges presented all turbines in the competition with the same amount of wind and measured which design generated the most electricity. Brenda's team developed a design with the use of powerful magnets, which lowered friction throughout the system and created the most efficient turbine in the competition. She and her team took first place. A group of students from a community college had taken first place in a university-level engineering competition. Brenda and her teammates became celebrities at Norco College.

I love this story because it is about a young woman with the courage to explore new ideas, work very hard, and take initiative. I also love this story because it is about the importance of faculty, staff, and other students coming together around an individual to help her succeed. Brenda has gone on to complete her degree through the Bourns School of Engineering at UC Riverside. Brenda has changed the trajectory of her life.

Socializing Agents

A major part of Brenda's story is about the transition she makes from the life that former voices in her head suggested to the life that new voices opened up. Students like Brenda often come to college with a limited view of what is available to them. This is largely due to the people who have been in their lives while growing up. We are all born into a trajectory for our lives that shapes the choices we make. We are born into a community of socializing agents who establish this trajectory and influence our choices throughout our formative years. Our family, friends, colleagues, neighbors, teachers, coaches, and religious leaders are present throughout our lives. In the day-to-day exchanges with these people, we come to understand who we are and who we think we can become. And because Americans tend to live in communities with similar socioeconomic status (SES), the messages we receive from these people are very consistent, setting us on paths or trajectories that suggest what we can offer the world and what the world has to offer us. This part of our socialization leads to a suggested set of skills to develop and a likely set of jobs to pursue. I am not saying that individuals have no control over the lives they choose, but I am saying these socializing agents have inexorable influence over us.

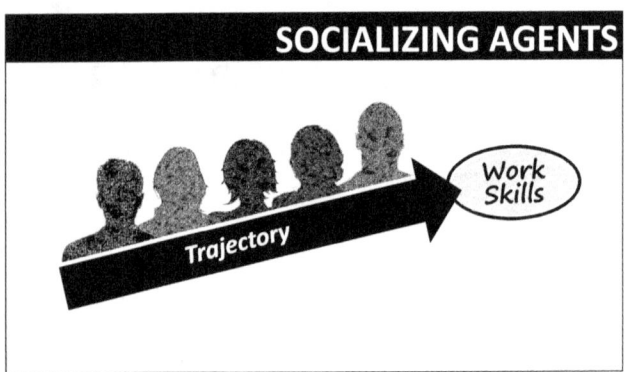

The absorption of expectations from our socializing agents can be obvious, like an explicit conversation from a parent or relative who is concerned about the choices you are making. In a family that values education highly, direct conversations will likely arise between parents and children relative to academic performance. Families that place a great deal of emphasis on the interdependence of individuals in the family will likely have explicit conversations if a member of the family is perceived to be spending too much time away from family. These are overt examples; however, there are millions of more subtle messages communicated to us during our formative years that are usually unrecognized. For example, a parent who gives their son construction tools as a gift and a parent who gives their son books as a gift are both making a gesture based in love. They are presenting a gift. But both gifts carry with them a suggestion to each boy. One says *I expect you to develop blue-collar-related skills* and the other *white-collar-related skills*. When a girl is encouraged to defer during moments of conflict, hold back during political discussions, or look for part-time work as a babysitter, these are all encouragements that point her in a particular direction, and when these suggestions come from the most important people in her life, from the people who love her and the people she in turn loves, she absorbs them at a very deep level. In this way, people close to her have a tremendous impact on what she thinks of herself and what she might be able to do professionally.

This process plays out all over the world, with some kids receiving millions of suggestions that will encourage them to move in the direction of academic success and growing career opportunities, while other kids receive millions of suggestions that encourage them to move in the direction of jobs that do not require college preparation and often lead to more difficult lives. Students from historically underserved communities overwhelmingly experience a socialization process that points them in a direction away from higher education and from careers that will lead to more prosperous lives.

This observation leads to one of the most important roles higher education can play in American society. If we hope to expand access to the American Dream for students from historically underserved communities, we need to find students who are on non-academic trajectories, leading to declining jobs, and change the trajectory of their lives by pointing them in the direction of jobs that are on the rise. We are trying to re-track their career goals to technical or professional trajectories. To do this, we must introduce new socializing agents into students' lives who are so influential that they are able to counter the weight of a student's socialization history and alter a lifetime of deeply established patterns.

This goal is challenging. A student who has been raised in a non-college-attending family often feels out of place in an academic environment. This feeling is something that I personally experienced during my early college years, and it is something that is repeated over and over during focus group meetings I have held with first-generation students. The feeling of being placed out of your environment is palpable, strong, and very difficult to overcome. People whose families have encouraged education and professional careers often do not understand this phenomenon and fail to give it the attention required for students who are experiencing it.

To capture a sense of this discomfort, imagine that a good friend invites you to a religious meeting that is extremely different from anything you are familiar with. For example, if you come from a Christian background, imagine your friend has invited you to a Hare Krishna, Wicca, or Hindu event. You agree to go because you do not want to offend your friend and you can tell that this is important to him or her. As part of this thought experiment, choose a specific religion and picture yourself actually going to the event with your friend. Imagine the people you will meet, how they may be dressed, the greetings that might be extended to you, the music and messages you might hear, the world and metaphysical view you will be presented with, the rituals you may be encouraged to participate in, and the invitation you might receive to join this religious community. You would probably feel very awkward and out of place. In fact, you would probably feel a strong desire to exit the environment as soon as possible. This is how many students from historically underserved communities feel when they initially enter an academic environment.

Let me turn the screw one more notch. Imagine that you return to this religious meeting a few more times and became convinced that you want to join because you truly believe you will become a better person as a result of joining the community. You change your hair style, your clothing, your beliefs, your language, your aspirations, your network of friends, and more. As this becomes evident in your life, how will your close friends and family react? Will they say you have "changed" with a derogatory tone? Will they treat you like you have made a mistake? Will some suggest you have been brainwashed? Will some try to get you to revert to your previous lifestyle? Will some stop associating with you all together? The unfortunate answer to these questions for most people is *yes*.

Such conflict describes what some of our first-generation students experience as they first enter the academic community. As they become college students, they start to entertain new ideas, they speak a little differently, they may start dressing in a new style, and they may change in many other ways. This is a normal part of development. However, as they make these changes, many first-generation students report that they receive discouragement from important people in their lives. People who love them more than anyone else make subtle and sometimes obvious statements belittling their efforts to grow. Male students often have men in their network of socializing agents challenge their masculinity as they pursue academic endeavors. Female students are often accused of deserting their families while they spend time in study groups. Students of color are accused of losing touch with their race or ethnicity. Students are subtly told they think they are better than everyone else when they express a new idea or speak with an expanded vocabulary. There are many more examples that students have revealed in focus groups of first-generation students. The salient point here is that college is hard enough with all the papers, exams, lectures, and required readings. Adding a set of socializing agents to the mix who actually add to the difficulty is overwhelming for many of these students. For this reason, students need to somehow incorporate new socializing agents into their lives.

We also must recognize that almost every student experiences a low point from time to time. This is completely normal. Regardless of family background, students will at times feel discouraged, low, disillusioned, lost, full of self-doubt, unsure, anxious, or overwhelmed. Some students have socializing agents that act as social capital during these times. Their socializing agents believe pursuing a college degree is important and will encourage the student to persevere. Other students—all too often students from historically underserved communities—have socializing agents who do not help in times like this. With love in their heart (truly), they see the student struggling at this low point and use their vulnerability as an opportunity to bring them back into the fold, pull them from the academic environment that they should "not have been part of in the first place." This pressure is a challenge that first-generation students are much more likely to face than students from families with college going histories.

One of the reasons Brenda was able to succeed was that she was able to establish new socializing agents in her life. However, her story is not a common experience in higher education for students with backgrounds like hers. Students from historically underserved communities attend colleges where it is difficult to find the support that Brenda received. It is difficult for them to establish new socializing agents, especially faculty members who will play this role. They typically attend colleges that are large commuter schools with high student-to-faculty ratios. For example, across the 115 California community colleges, 1,591,584 students took courses during the fall term of 2018. They were taught by 20,977 tenure-track faculty and 16,881.6 full-time equivalent adjunct faculty (California Community College Chancellor's Office, 2020a). This means that throughout the system, there are 42 students for every 1 full-time equivalent faculty member, or a 42:1 student-to-faculty ratio, and most of the faculty members are part-time faculty with limited availability to students. When I was a faculty member, I would typically have 800+ students per year. I taught especially large sections in political science because my high-attendance courses helped offset the more expensive courses at the college like nursing. Regardless, I found it impossible to develop a relationship with every student. Every term, I developed relationships with some students, got to know their personal situations, and tried to help them succeed. But it was impossible to build a relationship like that with 800+ students. This kind of learning environment is difficult for students. Many of them move through their academic journey in anonymity, with very few people around them who are tuned in to the challenges they face.

In contrast, students from affluent families often attend colleges and universities that boast student-to-faculty ratios that are very low, some of them as low as 6:1, meaning for every six students at the institution, there is one faculty member, and these institutions often have faculties in which over 90 percent are employed full-time, with lighter teaching loads than typical community college faculty. This creates an environment where faculty can know their students and participate in their lives accordingly. A number of years ago, I had a conversation with a colleague who was a tenured faculty member at an elite private university on the East coast while I was a tenured faculty member at a community college in Los Angeles County. We were trading classroom stories, and she told me that when she starts class, if she sees that one of her students is absent, she often picks up her phone, calls the student, and tells them to get into class. She taught one or two courses per semester (in addition to research responsibilities), with about 20 students in each class. In that environment, she could take a very active role in each student's life. I taught seven courses per semester with 50 to 65 students in each class. I remember thinking how impossible it would be for me to look out in the room, know who was absent, and make a phone call to each absent student. The reason for this difference, of course, is money. Colleges and universities with very low student-to-faculty ratios are expensive. One of the ways we keep expenses down for low- and moderate-income students is by having faculty teach many students, and while this practice addresses a significant financial hurdle, it creates severe disadvantages related to learning.

College students from historically underserved communities are typically on a journey with hundreds of hurdles in front of them, and they often walk down their paths with a great deal of anonymity. As first-generation students, they are likely to have no one at home who can help them navigate this path. And given the high student-to-faculty ratios at their colleges, there is likely no one on campus helping them navigate their path. This is one of the major reasons completion rates

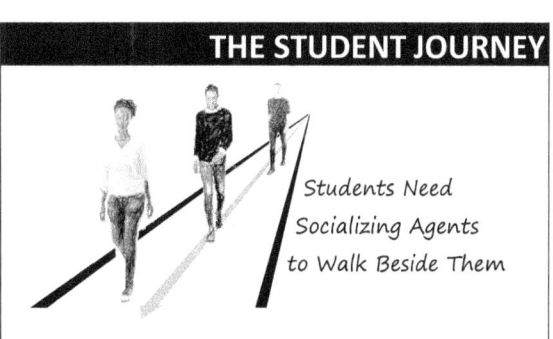

THE STUDENT JOURNEY

Students Need Socializing Agents to Walk Beside Them

for first-generation students are significantly lower than for other students. At community colleges, for example, the most positive national studies find that about half of their students finish and half fail to complete their AA degrees or certificates. Some studies put the completion rate as low as 25 percent.

If we agree that negative socialization influences and a lack of personal support on campuses present overwhelming barriers for first-generation students, then it seems clear that we must interrupt this sense of anonymity by leveraging new technologies, changing our service practices, and developing new resources.

Solutions and Strategies

The challenges discussed previously are largely private in nature, meaning the unique hurdles encountered by each group are typically not put in place by the colleges these students attend; rather, each hurdle originates from a force outside the college. These hurdles come from sociological constructs that have long histories and deep cultural roots, which make them difficult to address. These hurdles are not imagined or exaggerated. Because of these issues, students from historically underserved communities tend to have less time to study, they tend to have limited funds for educational expenses, and they tend to have insufficient preparedness for college. All these conditions are in place before these students step foot on college campuses. While these challenges are typically private in nature, colleges and universities can implement strategies proactively that address these issues and lighten, if not eliminate, the load.

Following are several strategies that will help build academic capital by facilitating the development of socializing agents in students' lives at the individual level.

Strategy #1: Develop Tracking Solution(s)

When I was president at Norco College, I had an office that looked out over the center of campus. From my office, I could watch students come and go, meet with friends, and study in the California sun. I would often comment to people in my office that if we randomly brought one of those students into my office, asked them for their name and ID number, and then tried to figure out where they are on their academic journey and how well they are doing, it would probably take us a good hour or more to figure it out. And this is the case on most community college and university campuses across the United States. We do not track our students very well. We put the burden on them.

For example, at all three colleges where I have held a leadership position, we had a large number of students dropping out. This is a problem across most community colleges (it may be all community colleges). Even though dropping out of school is a chronic problem and a likely life-changing decision for each student who decides to quit, most of our institutions do almost nothing proactively to intervene. When I was a faculty member, I was never notified when one of my students dropped my class. When I was dean, vice president, and president, I never received reports in real time or otherwise about students who had decided to quit. Part of this is my fault for not organizing these reports, but we are systemically not inclined to be proactive throughout the students' journey. Consequently, many students move through their journey by themselves.

To address this issue, we need to develop systems that tell us where each individual student is on their journey and the extent to which they are making progress. This is one of the main principles behind the guided pathways movement that has captured so much attention and is demonstrating significant promise. Students should be able to see their path through the institution with clarity, and we should know where each one is on the path so we can proactively guide them. But under our current systems, that degree of scrutiny would require us to meet with each student for an hour or more, on a frequent basis, to fully determine where they are in their journey. We will never be able to achieve this goal under current and anticipated future funding formulas. Instead, we need to leverage existing data and contemporary technology systems to make this a reality.

We already collect significant data about each student. We know when they register, how many units they are taking, whether their courses make progress toward program completion, when they should apply for transfer, their major, their GPA, their financial aid situation, their grades, their attendance, and more. However, these data are stored in dispersed data sets, in different systems, with different architectures. They are not collected or aggregated in any specific way, and too much of our student data are incomplete or inaccurate. As a college leader, I found it incredibly frustrating to know that these data were collected but, because of organization issues, nearly inaccessible. I know this is a problem in other industries as well. For example, public health records are so fragmented that we cannot fully leverage all the data we have collected as a society. Regardless, we need to address this issue with systems development that aggregates the data in a manner that can achieve the following characteristics.

The solution must *define all college pathways*. It is important that everyone (students, college personnel, community members, transfer partners, unified school districts) have the ability to see every program offered by a college and the required pathway to complete that program. These definitions need to be accurate and accommodate changes in real time or as close to real time as possible. The pathways need to be widely distributed, discussed, and assessed. Programs are the most important "products" a college offers to students, but they are all too often difficult to find. Can you imagine going to Ford Motor Company's website and finding all kinds of information about their customers, their employees, strategic documents they have written, processes they follow, committees with associated members and minutes, a history of the company, a company org chart, departments, and so on but very little about the their vehicles and little information about how to purchase one? This is what it is like at many college websites. Student have trouble finding the programs and what is involved to complete them. Although some colleges have this objective thoroughly nailed down, many others do not.

The solution must also *inform students of their individual progress*. Students need to know where they are on their journey and how well they are doing. A clear indication of progress is especially critical for students from historically underserved communities, who often do not have college completers in their personal lives to help with navigation. This is one of the functions that college counselors play; however, with many colleges at 700+:1 student-to-counselor ratios, too many students are moving through their college journey without ever seeing a counselor. We need systems that track progress along a chosen pathway that helps students see their progress. In addition to this, students need to receive constant feedback (at least weekly) from the college regarding their progress. Basic communications can come from an artificial intelligence (AI) engine that sends preprogrammed messages when students hit journey milestones. As discussed in Chapter 2, the feedback needs to come in an affirming and positive tone. If students do not respond to the AI communications, the system should then prompt personal interventions from identified college personnel. Counselors would respond to anyone in their caseload who is not responding, coaches to any team member, chairs to any student from their major, faculty to anyone in their classes, advisors to anyone in their club, and so on.

The solution must *inform college personnel of student progress*. As college personnel meet with students individually, they should be able to pull up a summary of the individual student's progress profile. This would be invaluable for counseling sessions and faculty office hours. For chairs, directors, coordinators, and other managers, the solution needs to flag students by group. The chair of the fine arts program should be able to track all majors in the department. The coordinator of the Umoja (an African American program on many campuses) should be able to track all African American students at the college. The transfer coordinator should be able to flag all students within range of transferring. In turn, personnel should be prompted to send out communications to individual students within their areas of responsibility.

The solution must *incorporate socializing agents* into the conversation. Socializing agents identified by each student (a parent, spouse, aunt, friend, faculty member, etc.) should be added to the system so they can participate in encouraging the student through their journey. By having the student identify the socializing agents in their lives and inviting them into this solution, we will be able to comply with FERPA (Family Educational Rights and Privacy Act) requirements for student privacy.

The solutions must be completely *integrated into mobile devices.* Cell phones are nearly ubiquitous on college campuses. A study by Ball State found that 99.8 percent of U.S. college students have phones (Ziegler, 2010) and over 94 percent of students want to use their phones in class (Kelly, 2017). The cell phone is clearly the preferred means of communication for college students and needs to be the primary way students receive pathway information.

Strategy #2: Incorporate Friends, Family, and Volunteers as New Socializing Agents

As discussed previously, first-generation students typically enter college with a limited academic social network. They enter college with socializing agents who, having never attended themselves, are limited in their abilities to assist them with college. One of the measures we can take to offset this deficiency is to introduce new socializing agents into their lives and incorporate them into the tracking/communications solution. I initiated a program like this when I was a dean at Cerritos College. Through the program, we asked selected students to nominate people from their private lives to become coaches or cheerleaders throughout their journey. Students nominated family members, spouses, siblings, former high school teachers, and more. We had very few problems attracting people to volunteer in this capacity. However, we had significant challenges related to training the volunteers. Most of them had no sense of an academic environment, and so the program was only marginally successful. What I learned from this experience was the need to bring these new socializing agents into a highly structured environment that requires very little time commitment. For example, my niece attended college recently. I always wanted to encourage her through her journey, but I had very little information about her progress and ended up being the uncle that gave general support over major holiday gatherings. Had I been in a system that gave me updates about her progress (finished her freshman year, made the dean's list, aced an exam), I would have been a better encourager in her life. Part of helping our students succeed includes helping them incorporate a few people into their lives as socializing agents and in turn helping the socializing agents communicate with their students easily, effectively, and consistently.

Strategy #3: Focusing on Students' Assets

Throughout higher education, some students are seen as having assets and others seen as having deficits. This divide breaks along historical lines, with many students of color, students from first-generation families, and students with low-income histories typically talked about as lacking the resources that are needed for success, while students from higher incomes are more frequently described as having the assets needed to succeed. These broad descriptions are to a large extent accurate. Early in the book, we talked about academic capital and the advantage it brings to a student. However, the constant framing and commentary around deficits, especially when it is communicated to students, can wear on a person in such a way that expectations of failure set in. When students of color, students with low income, or students from first-generation families are constantly reminded that the academic odds are stacked against them, they begin to believe us and see their own success as improbable (White, 2016). According to Byron White, communities that believe they lack agency and see themselves primarily as recipients of services struggle to improve.

To counter this negative approach, we need to work from an assets-based approach, where we look into students' lives, where we look into their cultures that have been historically marginalized and find assets that we verbally recognize as academic advantages. We need to look at African American communities and find traits that are assets. Look into recent immigrants' lives and see advantages that they uniquely bring. We need to look at poor students and find the assets they bring to our collective table. This is an assets-based approach to education. I am not saying that the professionals working in our colleges should ignore the hurdles in students' lives and stop trying to develop solutions to mitigate these hurdles. But I am saying that we need to consciously build confidence in our students by helping them see and leverage the assets they bring to the academy.

A friend of mine recently posted a video on social media of his four-year-old son learning to snowboard. If you watch the clip with the sound off, it is about 30 seconds of footage in which a young boy snowboards unsuccessfully. He probably falls ten times in the clip and never really stands with confidence. But watching the clip with the audio on is a lesson in great teaching. As his son tries to snowboard, the dad exclusively talks about the things his son is doing right, no matter how small. When his son falls, the dad comments on how long the boy was able to stand. When the boy falls again, his dad praises him for trying something a little difficult and how that caused him to fall. His dad praises him for getting up, praises him for sticking to it, celebrates every success he can find, all with the love and joy and enthusiasm of a parent. This is how we as human beings learn best. We need to feel the momentum of success when people point out our victories and progress, even if they are small. With an asset-based approach, we encourage our students by speaking to their agency and successes rather than focusing on their challenges and failures.

A report recently released by the Community College Research Center at Columbia University (Mayer et al., 2019) supports this point by indicating how negative messages discourage students even when intended to provide support. The Columbia research team found that the Gates-funded iPASS program was having neutral or negative impacts on students' success. The program uses technology to find at-risk students and provides them with early interventions by connecting them with campus-based resources that can help with whatever risk has been identified. If a student does poorly on a quiz, they may be quickly referred to tutoring. If they have excessive absences, they may be quickly notified to see a counselor. And so on. The basic problem with the program is that it is framed around a deficit model. The program keeps catching students when they make mistakes. Each time the program reaches out to a student, it is notifying the student of a small failure or deficit, and as these accumulate, the student begins to feel like they are not succeeding. The program is constantly reminding the student of how poorly they are doing. iPASS comes from a place of good intentions but makes many students feel like they are failures. If the program had been built to predominately capture moments of success and communicate these successes to students, with an occasional alert to risk-related behavior, students would feel a sense of success and momentum and therefore be more likely to continue their academic journey. If iPASS treated students like my friend treated his son, the program would have been much more effective.

This approach needs to be applied across our student body, especially with the students who are experiencing less academic success. We need to talk to Umoja students (an

African American program on many campuses) from the perspective of what they add to our community and how we need them to have a strong and pronounced presence because they add value to our institutions. We need to build systems that bring selected family members and friends into a dialogue about the student's journey, celebrating successes rather than constantly alerting students of their risks and deficits. Students who struggle with English as a second language need to be celebrated for being bilingual. Students with recent immigrant histories have made the very difficult transition of moving from one culture to another. They will have advantages as they move on to careers in an economy that is more globalized than any in human history. Students from low-income backgrounds will add much more empathy to the workplace because of their experience. Instead of looking for deficits, we need to find and celebrate assets that can be found in all our students' lives. There are substantial details that need to be addressed in any practical implementation of this idea, but the basic approach will help build a more affirming environment for students.

Strategy #4: Develop Hiring Practices That Increase Institutional Diversity

When students start college, it is critical for them to see themselves and their culture in the fabric of the institution. This can happen many ways, but the most important is by seeing students and employees who look like them and share similar experiences. This is especially important as students of color start college. Students of color who are first generation often feel displaced. They are often not confident they belong in higher education. Seeing themselves and cultural markers that they recognized in our institutions helps mitigate these feelings and gives them a greater sense of belonging. As students become comfortable with their place in the college, as they come to see the college as their home, they then need to start experiencing different cultures. They need to experience people who do not look like them and have lifestyles that are different than theirs. The world our students will enter when they leave college requires broad cultural literacy, and we need to prepare them for this milieu by creating college environments that reflect the cultures of the United States and the world. In this sense, the quality of our academic environment rises as the diversity of our employees increases.

With this in mind, institutional leaders should be strong proponents of hiring diverse candidates for faculty, staff, and management positions. To facilitate this approach, hiring practices should be redesigned with an emphasis on recruiting, interviewing, and hiring candidates with great equity skills. Equity-based skills should be something that are valued in the hiring process as much as other skills that we traditionally look for, and probing questions related to this skillset should be part of the job announcements and interviews. With this approach, I have found that candidates skew heavily toward candidates of color and as a result are more frequently selected. With that said, I have also been in interviews when the candidate with the highest skill set around equity-mindedness was White. Regardless, in all scenarios, the candidates to be selected should help add equity-minded expertise to the college.

Strategy #5: Expand Counseling Services

Academic counselors are important resources to students, especially students from historically underserved communities. Students from disfavored backgrounds often do not have someone at home who can advise them in academic and career preparation matters. Students have questions about majors and how they connect to careers, about transfer options, about course sequencing, about study techniques, and many other matters. Academic counselors serve as a primary source of advice for these students. However, like many resources in our students' lives, academic counseling services are insufficient—these students are once again underserved. For example, across the 115 California community colleges, 1,591,584 students took courses during the fall term of 2018. There were approximately 2,260 full-time equivalent counselors available to these students, with approximately 1,573 counselors in tenure-track faculty positions and about 687 full-time equivalent adjunct counselors (California Community College Chancellor's Office, 2020b). This puts the average student-to-counselor ratio at 704:1 in California's community colleges. The American School Counselor Association recommends a ratio of 250 students per counselor (Fuschillo, 2018). According to this recommendation, it is apparent that the 704 students who must share one full-time equivalent counselor are not getting the support they need. Students with questions that impact their academic and professional futures are often unable to see a counselor, and when they do, they are routinely required to address questions that have lifelong implications in a 20-minute session.

There are several steps we can take to address this issue. First, we need to continue making the case for more full-time counselors. This is obviously a resource issue that needs to be addressed at the legislative and institutional advancement levels. It is also an issue that needs to be balanced internally at institutions where resources and personnel are needed across many areas.

Second, we need to help counselors by taking routine and simple student questions off their plates. This will allow them to focus on student issues that require professional expertise. There are many process-oriented and simple-answer questions that counselors do not need to address. For example, we do not need professionals to be answering questions related to the registration process, logging in to the learning management system, applying for financial aid, and more. Our students desperately need counselors to help with their larger and more complicated questions like *How can I match a major to my strengths? Which transfer institutions should I consider?* and *What can I do to be more successful academically?* These are questions that need an engaged professional.

To pull the more routine questions from counselors, we need to turn to technology and paraprofessionals. We need to implement technology-based solutions that the private sector has already leveraged to address similar challenges. With effective artificial intelligence-based solutions, we can clear out much of the lower-level questions that counselors deal with. This can be done through a range of solutions. Some institutions are using a virtual counselor (think Apple's AI assistant, Siri) to interact with students. Others are using sophisticated customer relationship management (CRM) solutions that respond to students on behalf of counselors. In addition, we need to provide counselors with paraprofessional staff and student/peer assistants who can address many of these issues and do a lot of the clerical follow-up that currently takes counselors away from counseling. Finally, we need to incorporate faculty advising. Faculty have deep expertise in academic and professional areas, especially as they relate to their disciplines. Leveraging this expertise in a coordinated manner will help with the overall counseling load.

The third element we need to implement is a team-based caseload approach. In our current model of counseling at most institutions, students request an appointment through the counseling department and are assigned to a counselor at a specific time and date. This is the approach counseling professionals have been forced to take for efficiency. Since counselors work under more pressure than other faculty because of the student-to-counselor ratio imbalances, they have moved to this model. As we build out our capacity with the use of technology, paraprofessionals, and faculty advisors, we need to move away from this model and toward a more team-oriented approach around common disciplines and a caseload approach.

The caseload approach is important because students need to see the same counselor or same counseling team on a regular basis. This arrangement is what most of us expect in our personal lives when we seek professional advice. When we see a physician or a therapist, we expect to see the same person or at least a relatively small team on a consistent basis. We want to know them and want them to know us. Students need the same kind of continuity when they seek academic counseling. There is a strong body of literature that points to the need for "connectedness." Students, especially students from disfavored backgrounds, need to feel connected to the academy, and when they do, it has a particularly strong impact on retention (Gerda Hagenauer, 2014). We are much more likely to give students this sense of connectedness if they consistently see the same counselor or small counseling team. The team, of course, needs to be built around the resources that have been identified in the previous strategies. The team should consist of a counselor, with a paraprofessional or two, a group of faculty advisors, and a network for socializing agents wrapped around a set of students in a particular field or discipline. This approach can create a powerful sense of community for everyone involved and drive student success.

This work will be particularly challenging because it requires new technology solutions and operational practices. We will need to implement these carefully with the bargaining units, academic senates, and other constituent groups who engage in conversations related to working conditions and academic practices. We will also need to look for effective public-private partnerships in the development of solutions. But these changes are essential if we hope to expand the capacity of counseling in our institutions and the value of counseling in our students' lives.

Strategy #6: Nurture Faculty-Student Relationships

The faculty-student relationship is one of the most important in a student's academic life. It is an important relationship for all students, but the relationship yields particularly strong results for historically underserved students (Gerda Hagenauer, 2014). Given the importance of this relationship, we need to support it as much as possible. We need to make sure we are not pulling faculty from their students.

One important way we can support these relationships is by reducing non-professional and non-academic work in faculty members' lives. Having faculty attend to compliance work, clerical work, and related activities reduces the amount of time they have for students. A place where this often happens is around committee work. Faculty need to participate in the running of the college as part of collegial governance, but pulling faculty out of the classroom to do too much committee or conduct management work results in the reduction of time they can spend with students. Another area where this has crept into faculty members' lives is in a growing area of compliance-related work. Faculty are increasingly asked to enter large amounts of student performance data that are not always connected to course grading. This trend comes from well-intentioned legislatures, accrediting bodies, and managers who want to promote greater learning through accountability and data-driven decision-making. But the implementation of this approach has pushed a significant amount of data entry work into the lives of faculty, and every hour they spend at a keyboard punching in data is an hour taken away from their students. It is important for faculty to be involved in shared decision-making across campus, and we need to collect data on student learning, but institutions should be cautious about requiring too much work from faculty outside the classroom, because students can suffer from this overload.

Hiring greater proportions of full-time faculty, while expensive, is another area where we can improve the faculty-student relationship. Many higher education institutions, especially community colleges, use part-time, or adjunct, faculty to teach a significant percentage of classes. These faculty often teach at several institutions and typically do not have time to spend with students, and given the uncertain nature of their work, it is difficult for students to build long-term relationships with them. When institutions must employ part-time faculty to teach, it is important to provide them with the resources they need to build relationships with students (e.g., office space and paid office hours).

Strategy #7: Address Food, Housing, and Health Insecurities

The Hope Center at Temple University recently conducted a national survey of undergraduate students and found alarming rates of student food and housing insecurities. They found that 45 percent of respondents experienced food insecurities in the prior 30 days, 56 percent of respondents experienced housing insecurities in the previous 12 months, and 17 percent of respondents experienced homelessness in the previous 12 months. Rates were higher across nearly all measures for two-year college students and historically underserved students. Veterans, foster youth, and formerly incarcerated students also showed higher insecurity rates than others with regard to food and housing (Sara Goldrick-Rab, 2019).

Maslow's model of needs classifies food and shelter as basic needs that must be met before humans can develop psychologically or cognitively. In this sense, we have many students (approaching half at some institutions) who experience basic challenges that make learning nearly impossible. A cold, homeless, and hungry student is almost guaranteed to drop out of college. If we hope to position these students for academic success and in so doing change the trajectory of their lives, we must develop creative and collaborative solutions to mitigate these insecurities.

There are several solutions colleges and universities can pursue. Maximizing financial aid for these students is an obvious strategy that can help. Developing campus food pantries is a growing trend that allows students to find a convenient source of food. Job placement can help students find sources of income. Providing campus resources for homeless students like showers and lighted parking lots for students who occasionally sleep in cars can help. Partnering with government agencies to incorporate programs on campus can help bring resources to students. Examples include the Supplemental Nutrition Assistance Program (SNAP), which provides students with food stamps, and the VA, which provides veterans with a range of support services. On-campus or near-campus housing is a solution that would help many students as well.

To make all of these services part of the college experience, colleges must invest in hiring personnel who can develop and oversee these services. Public partnerships with local, state, and federal agencies that provide food and shelter services bring additional resources to the campus. Public-private partnerships can bring private revenue to contribute to solutions (e.g., housing) with agreements to share revenue on the back end. A culture of care should be established throughout campus to make sure all are looking for opportunities to help in these areas and people who need assistance with food and shelter do not have to live in the shadows.

Strategy #8: Create a Sticky Campus

Student engagement as an indicator for student success is approaching settled territory in education research. There are so much data supporting this correlation that there is little debate over the need for it, and much of the dialogue has shifted over the last decade to practical and effective ways to stimulate engagement. One of the ways to help generate greater student engagement is the "stickiness" of a college campus. Getting students to stay on campus (stickiness) is important because it makes them much more likely to build relationships with other students, faculty, staff, and managers. It puts them in a target-rich environment for meeting new socializing agents. It is literally the behavior that one must enact to join the college community.

There are several ways to increase stickiness. In the most general terms, we want to design our colleges in ways that encourage, tempt, or inspire students to come to and remain on campus. We need to abandon the architecture that encourages students to park their cars, walk directly to class, and walk immediately back to their cars when their classes end. This arrangement makes it easy to practice behavior counter to campus engagement. Staying on campus increases engagement. In this sense, residential campuses are at a tremendous advantage. They literally have students living on campus for an immersion experience. In contrast, community colleges, the schools that are more likely to serve historically marginalized students, are commuter schools. For students at these schools, engagement is more difficult. On these campuses, we need to be deliberate about creating meeting spaces, study spaces, tutoring spaces, hangout spaces, and more. We need to make these spaces inviting with food, drink, music, and energy. Our institutions need to be designed to bring people together, mix a range of cultures, and inspire students to both recognize their backgrounds in the institution and see other ways of living in the institution. Such communal experiences will inspire students to reach for something bigger than the aspirations of their youth. As a well-designed cathedral inspires many to look toward the heavens, the architecture of a college campus should inspire students and everyone who works at the institution to reach for growth around a celebration of ideas with the spirit of community.

The campus also needs to be as clean as possible if we hope for it to be sticky. Cleanliness is an important subconscious message that we send to students. In our private lives, most of us go to great lengths to clean our homes and yards before we have guests over. We not only clean, but we decorate, cook, and fill our homes with music to make our guests feel special. We want them to know we were anticipating their arrival and want them to have an enjoyable experience. The cleanliness of an institution makes the same statement. It says to our students we were anticipating their arrival, we want them to have a beautiful experience, we enjoy having them in our company.

Finally, great signage is something that can help students feel connected. Signage is how we make them feel comfortable by assisting them with navigation. If signage includes multiple languages (e.g., English, Spanish, and Mandarin), the feeling of connectedness can be extended. Multilingual signs are comforting to all students who speak other languages. They say openly that we are a community that embraces non-English speakers and say to all English language speakers that we expect them to be culturally fluent.

There are big issues associated with these solutions. Building and campus design are often very expensive. The design and construction are often things that take place over multiple leaderships and can lose a sense of direction and continuity as a result. Often there are legislative restrictions pressuring a minimalist approach out of concern for efficient use of tax dollars. Regardless, our physical spaces impact our students' sense of connectedness, bringing them

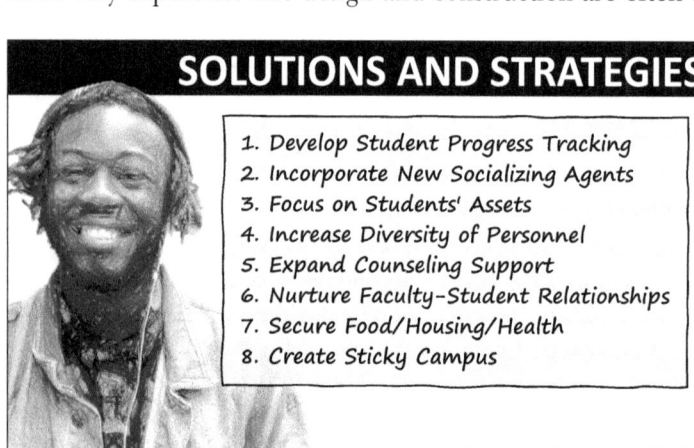

SOLUTIONS AND STRATEGIES

1. Develop Student Progress Tracking
2. Incorporate New Socializing Agents
3. Focus on Students' Assets
4. Increase Diversity of Personnel
5. Expand Counseling Support
6. Nurture Faculty-Student Relationships
7. Secure Food/Housing/Health
8. Create Sticky Campus

into a community that will place new socializing agents into their lives and improve their odds of success.

Conclusion

Students from historically underserved communities most often come from first-generation families. As a result, they do not have the social infrastructure, the social network of people in their lives that can help them navigate the complicated bureaucracies and academic requirements and standards of college. To counter this deficiency, to eliminate or mitigate these hurdles, we need to consciously and intentionally build environments that help our students establish new social networks with socializing agents that add academic capital and academic agency to their lives.

As professionals in the work of higher education, we need to be ready to support a revolutionary change in thinking about how to improve the lives of students from population groups that have been underserved throughout history if we are serious about using education as a vehicle of social justice. We need to move beyond the evolutionary approaches we have taken up to now and re-envision how we meet the needs of students in the 21st century.

5   Funding Higher Education Equitably

In early May of 2019, I received a phone call from the California Assembly office representing Norco College's service area. The chief of staff started by saying he had good news regarding funding for our Veterans Resource Center (VRC). The district and the college had been lobbying for an additional $1 million to finish the VRC, and our assemblywoman (Sabrina Cervantes) was successful in securing funding during the state budget development process. He then said he had more good news, indicating the assemblywoman had also secured an agreement for funding of a veterans and foster youth housing project in the amount of $24 million. The offer from the chief of staff was a great surprise because we had not specifically requested housing funds from her office; rather, I had been making general requests for housing support in several public settings over the course of 18 months, hoping that someone would respond. He was careful to indicate the budget process was not completed and asked if we were interested in the funding, knowing that there was a little more budget development to take place at the state level. I said "yes" without hesitation. He indicated he would need a short letter from me within the next 48 hours demonstrating our willingness to accept the funding.

In the California state budget development process, there is something called the *May Revise*. It is a time in the development process when the budget proposal for the state starts to solidify. The overall budget process begins with the governor's January proposal, an opening proposal for consideration. From January through May, the proposal is analyzed and modified by legislative committees and public advocates. In late April or early May, the governor meets with legislative leaders to consider ideas brought to light through the committee meetings and public advocacy to revise the proposal into the May Revise. In that brief period, when the governor is meeting with legislative leaders to solidify the May Revise, funding can pop. Proposals are suddenly agreed to or denied. Funding is suddenly cut or made available. Quick decisions with significant funding consequences are made in the final moments leading to the May Revise. Legislators and advocates who are nimble, aware,

With Assemblywoman Sabrina Cervantes

and prepared to act quickly during this time can benefit greatly. It was the hustle of Assemblywoman Sabrina Cervantes during the May Revise that created this opportunity.

After I hung up the phone with the chief of staff, I immediately contacted two vice presidents and consulted a few other college leaders in a collaborative effort to develop the required letter. We would need to move fast if we were going to get that funding. The VPs responded with a draft letter to me the next day. After a quick review, I forwarded it to my boss, the district chancellor, excited for him to see and approve the letter for submission to the assemblywoman.

What ensued was a back-and-forth that I never anticipated. The chancellor reacted to the opportunity with reservation. He was concerned about the need for a rapid response and how it might undercut our shared decision-making processes. He was also concerned about how the other colleges in the district might react to such a large amount of funding going to just one college. And he was concerned that this offer was not made directly through the Board or his office. These were all valid concerns, but in relation to the opportunity and the housing needs of veterans and foster youth students, I felt strongly that we should move forward with the letter and pursue the funding. He felt we should hold off. We had several private conversations over the course of three days that grew increasingly difficult as I tried to persuade the chancellor to submit the letter.

On Friday evening of that week, five days after Assemblywoman Cervantes' office called with the news, I made a call to the assemblywoman's office letting her know that we would not be submitting the letter and would not be able to accept the funds.

In the course of one work week, the leadership at Norco College and I went from the rush of excitement about a major gain to the onset of frustration about a major lost opportunity. That period was one of the most difficult in my entire professional career, but the individuals who felt the loss most were those associated with the Veterans Resource Center and the Foster Youth Program. A week or so after we passed on the funding, the district gathered for a regularly scheduled board meeting. As president of Norco College, I had a permanent seat at the Board table and provided an update to the chancellor and Board on major activities of the college as part of a standing presentation. I usually arrived at Board meetings with my comments prepared; however, coming into this meeting, I was not sure what to say. The loss of potential funds for our vets and foster youth had the college community upset, but my boss was clear on why he felt we needed to turn down this opportunity and had been clear over time about his disdain for public disagreements from any of his executive team members. As the meeting started, I was not sure if I would speak to the matter or simply remain silent about it and move on.

At the start of the meeting, several students and some staff pulled cards to speak in open session. Several veteran and foster youth students came to the public podium and spoke in protest of the decision. A few staff members did the same. One student had a particular impact on me that evening. She had come to us through the foster care system and spoke to the board about being homeless. She talked about sleeping in her car and occasionally on friends' couches. She gave a detailed account of how cold the winter evenings could be in her car and how she occasionally slept beside a pipe behind the campus because it was a little warmer there. She told her story with a subdued tone that reflected her expectation that significant adults in her life would let her down. I listened and felt like one of those adults in her life and in that moment decided to speak to the issue at the board meeting.

When my time arrived to give an update about Norco College, I was very brief. I said that I felt we had missed a major opportunity to direct funding toward students who need it most. I said because of this missed opportunity, the prior week had been one of the worst in my entire professional career and we needed to do a comprehensive debrief at the college and district to make sure this never happened again.

Rarely have I been in such a difficult professional dilemma. In the moment, I felt that silence from me would betray students. They needed to hear me say out loud that turning this money away was a mistake. I also knew my boss expected me, especially in public settings, to support his decisions, or at least never oppose him in public. My boss, the chancellor. allowed me to privately disagree with him but expected me to support him in public. This is a widely held and reasonable expectation. But the image of a student sleeping outside, by a pipe, in the back of the campus to stay warm overwhelmed my sense of prudence. I had made a moral commitment a long time ago to advocate for people in situations like this, and to say nothing felt more wrong than publicly opposing my boss.

I still feel conflicted as I write this paragraph. Both expectations are right, of course. Making my decision presented me with the kind of dilemma faculty confront students with in hypothetical classroom scenarios. I always enjoyed struggling with them as a student and enjoyed using them to teach my students as a faculty member. But facing such a dilemma in real life is anything but enjoyable. It was agonizing in the moment. It was agonizing in the fallout.

This story is an example of how we have ended up with systemically unequal funding in higher education. We have settled into a national framework, state by state, where public, nonprofit, and private funds for higher education are distributed in an inequitable manner, with disproportionately high levels of funding distributed to students from upper-middle- and upper-income families, while disproportionately low levels are distributed to students from moderate- and low-income families. The structures that keep these inequities in place are deeply established in our way of thinking about education resources for higher education. They are embedded in our official public policies and the philanthropic culture built up around higher education. These rules, laws, guidelines, and cultural norms that sustain this inequity have histories that are long, with justifications that have become unquestioned. Benefitting from this framework is a higher education power structure that may use very progressive language about equity but resist suggestions to restructure funding in a more equitable way and cling to traditional structures of power and influence. Powerful people benefit from the unequal distribution of funding, and the idea of altering the balance of power built up around these structures historically overpowers suggestions to more equitably distribute funding across higher education.

Understanding the Bias in Public Education Funding

Throughout most of American history, higher education has been very exclusive, with a small percentage of the population achieving a bachelor's degree. As late as 1920, less than 4% of Americans attended college (Education Encyclopedia, 2019). Since then, the number has exploded. In contemporary America, nearly 70 percent of high school graduates enroll in college (TED: The Economic Daily, 2017). The need for this higher level of education has been largely driven by our changing economy and the skills that are needed by employers. The implementation of this expansion has been driven by the growth of public colleges and universities.

In our drive to make college education as accessible as possible, we have developed a diverse system of colleges and universities. Our original universities (e.g., Harvard) started as private institutions, most often sponsored by religious organizations. These institutions dominated higher education throughout the 18th and 19th centuries in the United States. Over time, we have added institutions for women, African Americans, and Native Americans. We have added large publicly funded military academies, state universities, and community colleges. To a large extent, the growth of this system has been fueled by a desire to expand access to college and, by extension, to the American Dream.

A consequence of this history is that we have types of institutions with student bodies that tend to have different demographic characteristics. Obviously, our colleges for women, African Americans, Native Americans, and other defined groups have well-defined student populations. But beyond these institutions, we have four general types of higher education institutions in the United States with different characteristics regarding student populations. The four most common types of higher education institutions in the United States are: 1) public two-year colleges, also referred to as community colleges; 2) public four-year colleges and universities; 3) private nonprofit four-year universities and colleges; and 4) private for-profit four-year universities.

HIGHER EDUCATION

Community Colleges
- Miami Dade College
- Indian River State College
- Alamo Colleges District
- Pasadena City College

Private Non-Profit
- Princeton University
- University of Chicago
- Stanford University
- Amherst College

Public 4-Yr Universities
- U of California Berkeley
- University of Michigan
- University of Virginia
- University of Florida

Private For-Profit
- University of Phoenix
- Capella University
- National American University
- Grand Canyon University

Across these four types of higher education institutions in the United States, there are significant student population differences regarding income and ethnicity. In private nonprofit universities and colleges, we find students from families with relatively high incomes. The same is true for public four-year institutions. And when you isolate the most select institutions among these categories, the trend is even more pronounced. We see this trend when we analyze students in the nation's universities ranked highest by *U.S. News and World Report*, which uses a complex set of criteria to determine its rankings. We see significant differences in income when we assess students in the top ten universities in these rankings (all private nonprofits), the top ten liberal arts colleges (all private nonprofits), and the top ten public universities (U.S. News and World Report, 2019). A consistent finding across almost all of these institutions is a very low percentage of students from middle-, lower-middle- and low-income backgrounds. Princeton University, the university ranked highest, has a student body—a study body it carefully selected—in which only 13.6 percent come from the middle class or below. This small number, of course, means that 86.4 percent of their students are from upper-income and wealthy families. On average, the top ten national universities have student bodies with 18.8 percent from middle-income or lower families. The top ten liberal arts universities have student bodies with 17.9 percent from middle-income or lower families. And the top ten public universities—institutions funded to expand access—have student bodies with 27.8 percent from families in the middle-income or below category.

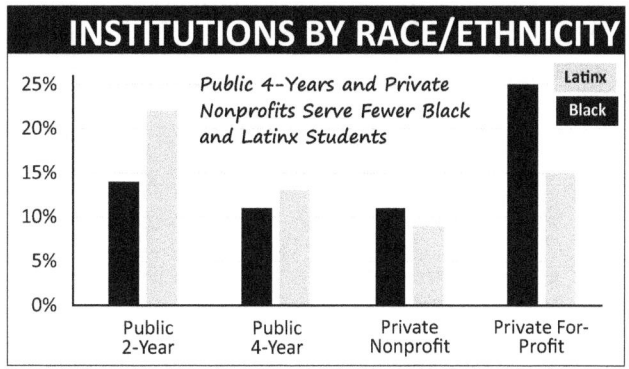

As we have mentioned elsewhere in this book, income and color have a close association in the United States, so it is not surprising to find that Black and Latinx students are also grouped disproportionately across institutions of higher education. Public four-year and

LOW-/MIDDLE-INCOME STUDENTS

Top 10 Universities

Institution	%
Princeton	13.6
Harvard	20.4
Columbia	21.1
MIT	23.4
Yale	16.3
Stanford	18.6
Chicago	24.5
Pennsylvania	16.5
Northwestern	16.8
Duke	16.5

Top 10 Liberal Arts

Institution	%
Williams	19.6
Amherst	24.4
Swarthmore	18.2
Wellesley	24.3
Pomona	21.8
Bowdoin	17.5
Carleton	15.5
Claremont McKenna	15.2
Middlebury	14.2
Washington and Lee	8.4

Top 10 Public Universities

Institution	%
UCLA	33.5
UC Berkeley	29.7
Michigan	16.5
U of Virginia	15.0
Georgia Tech	21.9
UNC Chapel Hill	20.7
UC Santa Barbara	33.1
U of Florida	30.1
UC Irvine	34.2
UC San Diego	43.0

Top 10 Community Colleges

Institution	%
Miami Dade	77.7
Indian River	63.4
Alamo	66.0
Broward	68.5
CUNY Kingsborough	NA
Mitchell Technical	56.4
Odessa	61.0
Pasadena City	66.1
Pierce (WA)	42.3
San Jacinto (TX)	56.6

INSTITUTIONS BY STUDENT INCOME

Public 4-years and private nonprofits skew toward upper-income students

(Bar chart showing income distribution across Public 2-Year, Public 4-Year, Private Nonprofit, and Private For-Profit institutions, with categories: <$30,000, $30,000-64,999, $65,000-99,9999, >$100,000)

private nonprofit institutions tend to have fewer Black and Latinx students than community colleges and for-profit institutions.

We see a clear trend relating this fact to historically underserved students. Community colleges and for-profits are carrying the heaviest load of historically underserved students. Public four-year universities are next in terms of their response to these students, and private nonprofits are the least likely to serve students from historically underserved communities. Finally, if we isolate for selectivity, the most selective public and private nonprofit institutions are the very lowest to admit students from historically underserved communities.

These demographic trends raise a concern that was addressed in 1954 under *Brown v. Board of Education*. Prior to 1954, public schools were segregated under the separate but equal doctrine (*Plessy v. Ferguson*). Brown argued that the separate but equal doctrine perpetuated inequality in the United States, and in a major break with precedent, the high court upheld their argument, setting the stage for desegregation in schools. While we do not have a segregated system in higher education, we do have a system that skews demographically along income, race, and ethnicity. This distinction leads us to this essential question: are institutions that disproportionately serve students from historically underserved communities providing the same quality education as institutions that serve predominantly White and upper-income students?

The direct answer to this question is *no*. I believe the quality of education has very little to do with the personnel who teach and serve in these institutions and much more to do with how much we invest in these institutions. According to a recent report from the Century Foundation (2019) on educational institutions throughout the United States, private four-year institutions spend an average of $72,000 per full-time equivalent student (FTES), public four-year institutions spend an average of $40,000 per FTES, and community colleges spend an average of $14,000 per FTES. It is true that many of the private and public four-year institutions have research as part of their mission, while community colleges do not. This naturally means they will cost more to run. But the study goes on to calculate spending per institution controlled for research costs and still finds that private four-year institutions spend three times more per student than community colleges, and public four-year institutions spend 60 percent more per student than community colleges.

Given that community colleges serve a much higher proportion of students from historically underserved communities, this disparity of public funding is nothing short of discrimination against these communities. California's public funding of education is a very good example of this biased practice. According to state-authorized public policy, K12 districts received $11,574 per FTE student in the academic year of 2018–19. In the same year, California State Universities (e.g., Long Beach State, San Francisco State, Cal State LA) received $17,784 per FTE student. University of California institutions (e.g., UCLA, UC Berkeley) received $32,593 per FTE student.

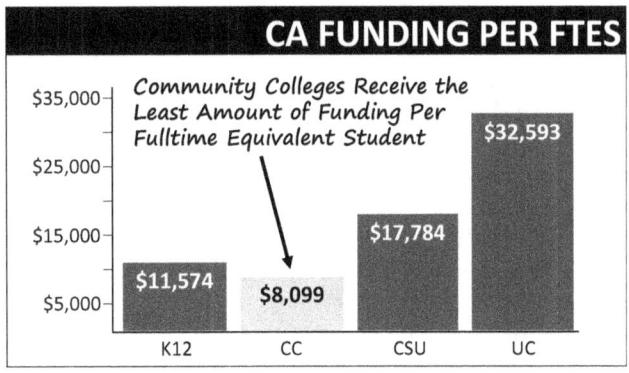

And California Community College districts received $8,099 per FTE student—the least amount of funding per student in the entire California education system (California Community College League, 2019). This funding gap in turn translates to a lower-quality educational environment by design. Because of this disparity, community colleges have student-to-employee ratios that are substantially higher than CSUs or UCs. They have a lower percentage of full-time faculty working at their institutions. Their educational facilities are less developed. Service levels for students are lower. Incredibly, what I am describing here is not a description of private funds and how they are biased against students from historically underserved communities. I am not describing a funding model from an earlier period in U.S. history. I am describing the contemporary distribution of *public funding* (from taxes) and how it has been codified by elected representatives to invest less in students of color, less in students from cycles of poverty or low income, and more in students who are predominantly White and predominately upper income.

Understanding the Bias in Nonprofit Funding

In the mid-2010s, some individuals and groups in philanthropy circles began to take notice of these inequities in public funding and initiated a dialogue shift. During this time, nonprofits began expressing some doubt in the institutions they had been funding by placing greater emphasis on the impact of their funding, especially on issues of social justice. They started shifting toward outcome expectations connected to their investments.

Rather than simply donating to an organization or a cause, as older approaches had emphasized, many philanthropists, especially large philanthropists, pivoted to a funding model that looked for opportunities to make structural and long-term change that would impact the social good and help advance social justice (Pechan, 2019).

Social justice work is directly tied to social mobility. As we have discussed at length throughout this book, individuals from historically underserved communities typically have odds stacked against them with regard to achieving the American Dream. It is routinely more difficult for them to move up socially, economically, or politically than individuals from more favored communities. Working to eliminate or mitigate these inequities is social justice work at its core. The primary distinction between older models of foundation giving and newer models is the recognition of social justice and promoting it. Older models made charitable donations to organizations or causes with a mission. Today's philanthropists often come with a social justice mission attached to their funding, and they select recipients most likely to deliver on the foundations' mission (Lawrence, 2009). It is as if the tables have turned. The newer model is often referred to as *mission-related investing*, *impact investing*, or *program-related investing*.

A good example of this approach can be found in a recent study by the Bridgespan Group (Bielak, Murphy, & Shelton, 2020). In its study, Bridgespan started with a straightforward and provocative question: "If we had a billion dollars to improve social mobility and expand access to economic opportunity for every American, what should we spend it on? Of all the initiatives and programs we could give our $1 billion to, which would have the most significant impact on social mobility?" To answer this question, Bridgespan applied the social genome model (SGM) in an assessment of program impacts on society over time. With this approach, it was able to calculate the return on investment for several programs/interventions. At the end of the analysis, Bridgespan concluded that six areas of emphasis could elicit significant mass impacts on social mobility if these six had a large investment to expand or increase their work. The areas were:

- Improving early childhood development
- Establishing viable pathways to careers
- Reducing unintended pregnancies
- Decreasing overcriminalization and overincarceration
- Creating place-based strategies to improve access to opportunity across regions
- Building capacity for continuous learning and improvement of social service programs and providers (Bielak et al., 2020).

These are the six areas it concluded would yield the best results if it "had a billion dollars to improve social mobility." All of these areas presume that the billion dollars of philanthropy would go toward structural change.

The Bridgespan study underscores an area where social justice work may be needed most—education. Of the six core areas, at least three are tied to education. "Establishing viable pathways to careers" is one structural change that we need to address. "Creating place-based strategies to improve access to opportunity across regions" is another change it calls for. "Building capacity for continuous learning and improvement of social service programs and providers" is a third

ADDRESSING SOCIAL MOBILITY

1. Improving early childhood development
→ 2. Establishing viable pathways to careers
3. Reducing unintended pregnancies
4. Decreasing overcriminalization and overincarceration
→ 5. Creating place-based strategies to improve access to opportunity across regions
→ 6. Building capacity for continuous learning and improvement of social service programs/providers

area that Bridgespan addresses. All three of these areas are found primarily in higher education.

With this approach, social justice philanthropists working on structural change are not trying to fix students; they are trying to fix or create institutions to do the structural work that is needed. They are trying to spend their money in ways that get to the root of the problems instead of addressing only the symptoms. As such, many new contributors act as partners more than benefactors. They often contribute money, time, knowledge, skills, and access. With their focus placed on systems/processes rather than individual students, charitable giving can effect change for many more individuals over the long run. Every student who experiences the reformed system will theoretically be impacted by the philanthropist who helped fund and support the change. With this model, philanthropists and nonprofits can make a one-time contribution to change structures and impact student success for as long as those changes endure. They do not have to commit to funding students year after year. They can commit to funding structural change once and then watch that new system impact students' lives year after year.

I believe the approach the new philanthropy community is taking, structural change for social justice, is spot on. As we have seen throughout the discussion in this book, inequity in higher education is tied to enduring structural problems. The lack of socializing agents, inequitable government funding, poor intersegmental coordination, a ranking system that creates perverse incentives, antiquated pedagogy, institutional structures that resist change, and more have created longstanding structures that work against students from historically underserved communities. Philanthropy that targets these root causes will go much further than spending money to reduce pain in the life of a single student who has been structurally and institutionally held down. In other words, philanthropy that fixes root problems will help many individual students.

With these changes, the work that community colleges do should attract the attention of these philanthropists. Community colleges are quintessential examples of social justice institutions. This is one of the major distinctions between community colleges and four-year institutions. As discussed previously in this chapter, many four-year institutions nearly ignore students from historically underserved communities. Their admissions skews disproportionately toward upper-middle- and upper-income families. The more celebrated the institution, the more likely they are to focus on students from families of privilege.

It is somewhat astounding how we collectively support this notion. We pile praise and admiration on institutions like Harvard, Yale, Stanford, and others that unapologetically focus primarily on students from very privileged backgrounds to make sure these students continue to stay in positions of power. These institutions are contributing to limited mobility in American society. While I am confident that my colleagues in these institutions do not intend to have this impact on society, they are in fact overserving students from privileged backgrounds and underserving students from marginalized backgrounds. In contrast, community colleges are often not celebrated regardless of the very important work they do with regard to social justice. Community colleges serve about 34 percent of all undergraduates and well over half of students from historically underserved communities. Community college admissions skew toward marginalized and disfavored communities, providing access to the American Dream for groups that have been historically held back. Doing work in a community college is doing work in social justice.

However, while social justice philanthropy has seen an increase in philanthropy circles, this funding community has almost completely missed the idea that community colleges are doing most of the social justice work in higher education. In 2017, for example, higher education institutions raised a total of $43.6 billion. Much of this funding comes from social justice-related sources, but only 1.5 percent of the funding raised went to two-year institutions (American Nonprofit Academy, 2020). Given the mission of social justice organizations and the mission of community colleges, the amount is staggering. How could well-intended money miss the mark so fundamentally?

Bias in Other Funding Sources

Another funding source that is disproportionately stacked against students from disfavored groups is private giving to colleges and universities. According to the Century Foundation, private giving to community colleges is at $149 per full-time student, while giving to private research universities is $39,323 per full-time student (Kahlenberg, 2015). Students from private research universities are getting 264 times more private funding than colleague students at community colleges.

To underscore this point, consider the top ten higher education endowments in the United States: Harvard, Yale, Stanford, Princeton, MIT, Penn, Texas A&M, Michigan, Notre Dame, and Columbia. Combined, the top ten universities hold nearly $200 billion. The largest endowment in the United States is held by Harvard University at $39.2 billion. On average, the top ten control about $20 billion each. The top ten community college endowments are quite different. Combined, they control $956 million. The largest community college endowment is with Miami Dade College at $486 million. On average, the top ten control about $96 million each. In this comparison, the top ten university endowments have received about 206 times more private funding than the top ten universities.

TOP 10 ENDOWMENTS (4-YEAR)

University	State	Endowment	Students' Median Family Income
Harvard University	MA	$39.2 Billion	$168,800
Yale University	CT	$29.4 Billion	$192,600
Stanford University	CA	$26.5 Billion	$167,500
Princeton University	NJ	$25.4 Billion	$186,100
Massachusetts Institute of Tech	MA	$16.4 Billion	$137,400
University of Pennsylvania	PA	$13.8 Billion	$195,500
Texas A&M, College Station	TX	$12.7 Billion	$130,900
University of Michigan, Ann Arbor	MI	$11.7 Billion	$154,000
University of Notre Dame	IN	$11.1 Billion	$191,400
Columbia University	NY	$10.9 Billion	$150,900

As we have indicated several times in this book, the significance in these differences is related to the kinds of students each institution serves. Harvard (with the highest university endowment) serves a student body who overwhelmingly come from privileged backgrounds. On average, families of their students earn $168,800 per year, and 67 percent of Harvard's students come from the 20th income percentile in the United States. Miami Dade (with the highest community college endowment) serves a student body who overwhelmingly come from disfavored backgrounds. On average, families of their students earn $31,600 per year, and 9 percent of Miami Dade's students come from the 20th income percentile in the United States (The New York Times, 2017). According to an *L.A. Times* survey, most Americans consider an annual income of $30,000 the poverty line for a families with two parents and two children (Doar, Bowman, & O'Neil, 2016). And when we compare the endowments of Harvard and Miami Dade, we see that institutions serving low-income students receive drastically less funding from private sources than institutions serving high-income and wealthy students. The bias in private giving is worse than the bias we find with regard to public funding. Students from highly privileged backgrounds with deep private resources attend institutions with much higher private gifts. And the students who need philanthropy to add resources to their lives get far less from private gift givers.

An area of financial benefit that is often ignored in conversations like this is related to tax incentives or tax shelters. Private colleges, including very wealthy colleges like Harvard and Stanford, are classified as nonprofits. As a result, they enjoy significant tax breaks. They are exempt from property and sales taxes. Individuals who make contributions to the university can deduct these donations from their tax liabilities, and expenses paid to the university for attending (e.g., tuition) can be used as tax deductions provided that the individual meets federal income requirements (single filers earning less than $80,000 or joint filers earning less than $160,000 can deduct the expenses). These incentives apply to all public and nonprofit institutions; however, the institutions who enjoy the largest endowments and the highest valued assets enjoy the most significant tax deductions and shelter benefits (Kahlenberg, 2015). These incentives are not trivial. Combined, they add up to $37 billion in tax credits, exemptions, or deductions, which exceeds the amount of federal funding spent on Pell Grants by nearly $7 billion (Kahlenberg, 2015). And this benefit once again stacks resources in favor of students from upper-middle- and upper-income families. According to a report by De Alva and Schneider, federal, state, and local tax incentives, combined with appropriations from the three levels of government, add up to $41,100 per full-time student at private high-endowment institutions, $15,300 per full-time students at public flagship institutions, $6,700 per full-time students at public regional institutions, and $5,100 per full-time students at community colleges (2015).

TOP 10 ENDOWMENTS (2-YEAR)

Community College	State	Endowment	Students' Median Family Income
Miami Dade College	FL	$486 Million	$31,600
Valencia College	FL	$74.3 Million	$43,600
College of Central Florida	CL	$71.7 Million	$44,500
Clark College	WA	$65.2 Million	$65,100
Broward College	FL	$63.9 Million	$41,100
Northampton Community College	PA	$51.9 Million	$62,300
Northwest College	WY	$39.6 Million	$66,900
Sinclair Community College	OH	$36.3 Million	$58,900
Cuesta College	CA	$33.9 Million	$78,300
SUNY Broome Community College	NY	$33.1 Million	$54,000

These inequities established by funding from government, nonprofit, and private institution sources present a moral dilemma for many in higher education. Universities across the United States are filled with faculty and administrators who strive to promote more equity in society. I have found them to be conscious of the histories that hold back population groups in America while others flourish. I find them to be passionate about doing social justice work to eliminate or mitigate these hurdles that students from disfavored communities face. Some of our best thinking on social justice and social mobility comes from our research institutions. But most of my colleagues in prestigious universities are either unaware of or quiet about the role their institutions play in perpetuating social stagnation in the United States.

For example, there are several academics I highly respect with regard to equity-based research who conduct their work from faculty positions in the most respected American universities. Much of the research I have relied on in this book comes from their work. They have generated impressive analysis related to the causes of inequality in the United States and the scope of its presence in society. They have done very impressive work assessing very large data sets, presenting their findings clearly and fearlessly in defense of disfavored communities. These scholars have committed their academic lives to exposing and addressing these issues, and they are having a profound impact. However, the institutions where they work are often the most egregious offenders of academic equality. Most (almost all) of our most prestigious universities have done very little to change the role they play in society. They primarily receive students from the most privileged families in the world and work with these students to make sure their families maintain that privilege. While they promote social justice through a range of programs, their admissions practices do not reflect the same commitment. These scholars are living a life of contradiction, with research that condemns inequality in society while taking the salaries and prestige that come from institutions that sustain the kind of behavior their research condemns.

I truly admire the research many of them conduct and believe society benefits from it. But their willingness to remain with institutions that promote the opposite of their professional convictions is problematic across academia. I attended USC for my BA, MA, and Ph.D. I was heavily influenced by several faculty members who helped me start on the path that has led to this book. I was academically challenged to look at inequality in the United States and encouraged to use my life to do something about it. These attitudes and beliefs were sincerely shared with me by faculty who worked for an institution that primarily serves students from upper-income families. USC's students come from families with a median income of $161,400. Sixty-three percent of USC students come from families in the top 20 percent of incomes. Over 14 percent of the students at USC come from families who earn more than $630,000 per year, and only 4.9 percent or this university's students come from families that earn $20,000 or less per year (The New York Times, 2017). I know USC worked with me and played a major role in changing the trajectory of my life. I attended USC as a Pell Grant recipient and am grateful to the investment they made in me. In many ways, I love the Trojan family. But with a student demographic that skews so significantly toward wealthy families and away from poor families, they statistically have more impact on preservation of wealth than they do on social mobility. And yet, passionate faculty call for social justice from the lecture halls of this university and 40 or 50 others like it, year after year with little of no mention of the irony.

When confronted on the issue of disproportionate funding, proponents of the status quo seem to rely on three general arguments. The first is based on expenses associated with research. Large research institutions are more expensive because they are required to create a teaching and learning environment as well as to conduct groundbreaking research. Community colleges are only required to provide teaching and learning services. This is a valid point, but when controlled for education spending, when research expenditures are removed from the calculation, the numbers still reflect an underinvestment in students from marginalized backgrounds. According to the Century Foundation, after research dollars are removed from government spending on higher education and we isolate for teaching/learning related funds, private research institutions receive about $35,000 per student, private bachelor's degreee institututions receive about $22,000 per student, public research institutions receive about $16,000 per student, and community colleges receive about $10,000 per student.

A second argument often offered is the notion that community colleges teach only the first two years of college, while four-year institutions are required to teach lower-division (freshman and sophomore) and upper-division courses (junior and senior). With estimates placing upper-division instruction at 1.5 times more expensive than lower-division expenses, the bias is still not eliminated from the public funding allocation.

Finally, community college students tend to pay much less in college fees and tuition. With families paying higher tuition rates and other four-year universities, this explains why these students receive more funding per student. This argument has also been explored and controlled for in several analyses. The bias of public funding against students from historically underserved communities remains (Kahlenberg, 2015), and we need to collectively do something to address these significant inequities.

Discussion of Solutions

The way we fund higher education is discriminatory and simply must change. The distribution of public, nonprofit, and private spending is grossly biased toward students who already have significant academic capital in their lives and away from the students who need these resources most. Students from historically underserved communities are underserved by the way we allocate education funding. If we were truly committed to equity, we would change funding and spending in favor of individuals from historically underserved populations; however, we are so far from this reality that such a change in direction feels almost hopeless. The people who "belong" to the institutions that receive disproportionate shares of education spending—the students, faculty, administrators, trustees, alumni, and community members—have always benefited from the current models of distribution, and many of them have significant influence. The current distribution models are codified in law with long histories and traditions. But we may be able to start chipping away at these inequities with the following strategies.

Strategy #9: Conduct and Maintain a National Audit

We need a national organization that will commit to detailed analysis of this issue. We need to know precisely how much money is spent, which institutions receive the funding, and the student groups positively and negatively impacted. This objective will require a highly complicated effort, with education funding so wildly dispersed. As discussed previously, funding comes from federal, state, and local governments as well as nonprofit organization grants and private gifts. The U.S. Department of Education should ideally lead this effort, but if it will not, a national organization should take up the banner. This would be an ideal project for an organization like the Association of Community College Trustees (ACCT), American Association of Community Colleges (AACC), or Community College Research Center (CCRC) at Columbia University. I suspect that community colleges would be willing to subsidize an ongoing audit of this nature if the goal of the program were to establish equitable funding across higher education.

This is the kind of project community college board members need to support and lead. It will require a collaborative effort across districts and state lines. Federal legislation will likely be needed to initiative the audit and will definitely be needed to implement recommendations that redistribute higher education funding in a more equitable manner.

Strategy #10: Restructure State Funding

Most funding for higher education comes through state government. Community colleges need to engage in the state funding process with the intention of establishing equity in funding. As discussed previously, we cannot have higher education systems like California's where California State Universities (e.g., Long Beach State, San Francisco State, Cal State LA) receive $17,784 per FTE student, University of California institutions (e.g., UCLA, UC Berkeley) receive $32,593 per FTE student, and California Community College districts receive $8,099 per FTE student. This is a model that promotes inequality in society. This is work that will need to be supported and led by community college board members in a collaborative effort with other districts and the state community college system leadership.

Establishing a more equitable funding model for post-secondary education is an especially important topic given that many states are moving community college funding models in the direction of performance-based funding. Legislators across the country have become frustrated with low completion rates in community colleges and responded with funding models tied to outcomes like graduation rates, transfer rates, employment rates, and similar performance measures. I am personally in favor of accountability and clear performance expectations, but we need to understand that we cannot expect the same success rates as those of four-year institutions at community colleges when we give them less funding. Doing so is inherently unfair and bad policy. If I expected two runners to achieve a certain time in an upcoming 10K run and gave one runner ample resources for coaching, training, and nutrition and gave the other runner limited resources for coaching, training, and nutrition, we could not reasonably expect the two runners to finish with similar times. I know there are more factors involved, but most of us would expect the athlete with more resources to finish with a better time.

Inequitable funding for education is one of the oldest forms of discrimination in our history. We isolate a group of people, usually based on race, ethnicity, income, or religion. We say to them that they are eligible to achieve what everyone else in society is eligible to achieve. And then we covertly limit the resources they have access to achieve their goals and blame their underperformance on lack of individual effort rather than attributing some or all of the underperformance to unequal resources.

Strategy #11: Maximize Financial Aid

After my sophomore year of college at Cal Poly San Luis Obispo, I decided to transfer to a larger and more urban university. I spent a fair amount of time going through possible institutions, applied to several, and ended up being accepted to three. One of those was the University of Southern California. I remember attending a meeting on campus with a small group of students who had also been accepted and were in the process of making a final decision. We met in a fairly formal conference room at the Widney Alumni House. The Alumni House was the first building erected at USC and claims to be the oldest university building in Southern California. It was built in 1880 and has been in continuous use since. The building holds a prominent place near the center of campus and a prominent place in the history of the university. I remember looking around the room and noticing how carefully the building had been restored and cared for. I felt out of place given the formality of the setting, but I also appreciated that they scheduled the meeting in such a place of honor. The location of the meeting felt like USC was saying to me, "We believe you are special; we believe you will do great things." A month or so later, after I accepted the offer, I found myself standing outside, in a very long line, waiting to talk to someone in the financial aid office. In line, I could see the Alumni House. I remember thinking how special I felt in that space and how different it now felt waiting in line to process my aid applications.

I am grateful that there was a financial aid office and a line I could stand in that ended with a competent person who helped me secure funding for college. I would not have completed my education without the assistance. The point I am trying to emphasize here is how bureaucratic and difficult we make the financial aid process. The university gave thought to the admissions process to make sure it was appealing to students but had not done the same with regard to financial aid. Many of our students come from first-generation families. These families love their children (our students), but they have no knowledge of how college works and how to navigate the matriculation process. This includes the financial aid process. They don't know how to apply, when to apply, what to apply for, what they are eligible for. They are in the dark in this area. What they do know is that college is expensive, and they are worried that they cannot afford it. The combination of a complicated and bureaucratic process with underinformed students leads to billions of dollars in financial aid being left on the table. According to a recent study, the class of 2018 left $2.6 billion in federal financial aid unclaimed by students simply not filing their FAFSA (Helhoski, 2018). A report released by UC Davis reveals that California's community college students enrolled in the fall semester of 2014 left $130 million in federal aid on the table because of difficulties with the application process (The Center for Community College Leadership, 2018).

We need to shift our cultures on campus to regard finding money for students the same as securing donations to the college. We need to celebrate our ability to secure funding for them and give positive recognition to the staff and managers who organize this effort. We should be deliberate about maximizing the amount of financial aid that our students receive from federal, state, nonprofit, and private sources.

Strategy #12: Build Alumni Connections

It's difficult for most community colleges to develop alumni organizations. With most of our students moving through a transfer sequence, their goal and their mindset is to complete a bachelor's degree or higher. In the United States, we typically celebrate the institution where we received our bachelor's degree. As a result, universities are able to develop alumni networks more successfully and raise funds from former students that go into their respective foundations. Community colleges typically lack this kind of organization. We need to counter this trend to bring our transfer students back into our institutions as active alumni and friends of the college. To do this, we need to remind them of the turning point, the inflection, that took place in their lives at their community college. Many of our successful students came from backgrounds where the odds of success were low. They often came to our community colleges with low expectations and even a sense of not belonging in a higher education institution. At our institutions, they turned a corner and developed a new sense of who they are, what they have to offer the world, and what the world may have to offer them. This inflection point in their life often happens at the community college. If we can remind them of this story, it will connect many of our alumni with one of the most exciting and important transitions in their lives. From this narrative, we invite them into our strategy (from the alumni perspective) and ask them to help us replicate that experience for other students who come from a similar background. This is a very powerful story and an equally powerful invitation that can be used to build large alumni networks that will volunteer time, facilitate partnerships, and contribute resources to our institutions.

Strategy #13: Pursue Federal Grants

The Pew Foundation recently published a report on funding for higher education. According to this report, the largest share of government funding comes from the states. In 2017, $87.1 billion in state funding was directed to higher education. The federal government, however, is not a small player in higher education funding. In 2017, 74.8 billion federal dollars went to higher education (Stauffer, 2019). These numbers do not include student loans or tax incentives. Almost $28 billion of the federal funding goes to Pell Grant students, about $14 billion for veterans' education benefits, and nearly $27 billion for research grants. About $7 billion is set aside for other grants and programs.

One reason federal money is disproportionately given to four-year institutions is the federal government's emphasis on research. Another reason is our less effective participation in the grant-seeking process. As a system, community colleges need to advocate for moving a greater percentage of this funding toward teaching and learning activities, especially programs that support social mobility. In addition, individual community colleges need to be more deliberate about competing for large federal grants. Both approaches can have the impact of bringing more balance to the distribution of federal funding for higher education.

Strategy #14: Redirect Social Justice Funding

Community colleges do the heavy lifting with regard to social mobility and social justice work in the United States, and while our most celebrated universities bring dialogue to this discussion, they do not collectively do serious work in this space. Regardless, very little social justice funding from the nonprofit community goes to community colleges. In 2017, for example, higher education institutions raised a total of $43.6 billion. A significant portion of that funding was directed at social justice issues, but less than 2 percent of that funding ended up in the hands of community colleges (American Nonprofit Academy, 2020). With community colleges carrying the majority load of social mobility and social justice responsibilities in society, the nonprofit organizations committed to addressing these issues are clearly missing a major opportunity. We need to redirect this funding by telling our story in a more compelling way.

SOCIAL JUSTICE FOUNDATIONS
Top 10 for Social Justice Spending from 2003-13

Bill & Melinda Gates Foundation	WA	$1,878,479,380
Ford Foundation	NY	$1,435,363,555
Robert Wood Johnson Foundation	NJ	$1,107,246,658
W. K. Kellogg Foundation	MI	$909,208,269
Open Society Foundations	NY	$706,622,723
California Endowment	CA	$443,535,694
William and Flora Hewlett Foundation	CA	$416,194,831
Annenberg Foundation	CA	$381,569,764
Carnegie Corp of New York	NY	$368,344,700
John S. and James L. Knight Foundation	FL	$368,164,161

SOCIAL JUSTICE FOUNDATIONS
Top 11-20 for Social Justice Spending from 2003-13

Lilly Endowment Inc.	IN	$367,826,803
John D. and Catherine T. MacArthur Fndn	IL	$332,655,776
James Irvine Foundation	CA	$310,443,284
David and Lucile Packard Foundation	CA	$293,882,675
Wallace Foundation	NY	$286,134,944
Susan Thompson Buffett Foundation	NE	$282,475,087
Walton Family Foundation	AR	$274,837,252
Kresge Foundation	MI	$247,691,881
Annie E. Casey Foundation	MD	$212,241,962
Charles Stewart Mott Foundation	MI	$201,847,470

As a college president, I have spent a lot of time with regional, state, and federal leaders. I cannot think of a time when I told our story and it was not received well. In my experience, when people hear about our work to build capacity in students' lives, especially students from disfavored backgrounds, they almost always want to help. Somehow, our story is not getting through to the philanthropists who control nonprofit spending on social justice issues. From 2003 to 2013, 20 foundations spent almost $11 billion on social justice issues. I believe that if they had heard our story, a much higher percentage of that funding would have ended up in community colleges, helping implement programs that change the trajectory of students' lives. We need to engage in a campaign to redirect social justice funding from foundations toward community colleges. We need to do this as individual colleges and collaboratively as a system.

Strategy #15: Alter Tax Status of Institutions That Underserve Marginalized Students

Throughout the country, institutions of higher education maintain foundations to help organize giving to the institution(s) they represent. They operate as nonprofit entities and are given special tax privileges. They are given nonprofit status because they are seen as providing a social benefit and therefore exempt from many of the taxation rules that for-profit institutions live under. However, many of our largest foundations and related nonprofit entities that manage college and university endowments are, in fact, supporting institutions that support institutional admissions biases against student from disfavored communities. I won't go through the details of this institutional bias again (we discussed this issue thoroughly in this chapter previously). What we should do in these cases is alter their nonprofit status somehow. I don't know that we should reject it outright (although I am open to this discussion), but while these institutions practice such bias, we should tax their endowments and use these revenues to invest in community colleges—the institutions that are doing the country's most serious work with regard to social justice and social mobility for students from historically underserved communities.

I know this is a somewhat extreme suggestion and for that reason alone would need to be implemented with restraint. With that in mind, we could consider imposing a tax on all endowment money over $1 billion from colleges/universities that have biased enrollments—enrollments that disproportionately exclude students from historically underserved communities. This approach would impact about 100 universities in the United States. In other words, there are only about 100 universities that have endowments over $1 billion and show signs of enrollment bias. If we were to keep their first billion untaxed and tax anything over $1 billion in their endowments, this could generate significant funding for community colleges. Combined, these universities hold $462.6 billion in their endowments. If you count only the dollars accumulated after each institution's first $1 billion, this adds up to $362.6 billion (Barham, 2019). If we were to tax the $363.6 billion at 5 percent, it would generate $18.2 billion annually for community colleges. If we were to tax the $363.6 billion at 1 percent, it would generate $3.6 billion annually for community colleges. I am not saying that these are the exclusive or best options. But these examples provide a snapshot of how many universities would be impacted by a tax of this nature and how much funding could be redistributed in a more equitable manner.

SOLUTIONS AND STRATEGIES

9. Conduct National Audit
10. Restructure State Funding
11. Maximize Student Financial Aid
12. Build Alumni Connections
13. Pursue Federal Grants
14. Redirect Social Justice Funding
15. Alter Tax Status for Institutions That Discriminate

Conclusion

Writing this chapter was an exercise in frustration. I have spent decades working in higher education, and I am proud to be consistently around people who care about eliminating inequality in the United States and how education can play a significant role through social justice work. This was something that impressed me about academia as an undergraduate. It is one of the reasons I chose political science as a major. It is why I wanted to attend graduate school and why I have pursued a life-long career in community college work. I have enjoyed deep, meaningful conversations with colleagues across the two-year and four-year spectrum about these issues. I found this chapter frustrating because while I started the chapter with the basic idea that the funding was biased against students from disfavored groups, I had no idea how severely slanted it was.

I have been in student success conversations for 30 years. These conversations routinely are about pedagogy, services, student preparedness, prerequisites, and a range of other issues. And while I know this topic of unequal distribution of education funding has been written about for a number of years, I am baffled about why it is not a core topic in professional circles. How have so many of us committed to social justice work relegated this important issue to the back burner of policy considerations? This is an area that needs bold and unapologetic leadership on behalf of our students.

6   Establishing Best Practices

I started as a faculty member at Cerritos College after serving as a teaching assistant in graduate school for two years and one year of teaching as an adjunct instructor at several colleges in Southern California. As a young assistant professor, I was eager to develop strong teaching skills and looked for opportunities on and off campus to learn effective practices. I attended professional development activities, invited in-class evaluations, attended teaching-oriented conferences, took a course on pedagogy at a local university, and tried to talk to as many senior and respected faculty as possible about effective teaching techniques. As I moved through the college asking people to recommend faculty members I should watch, the individual who was recommended over and over again was Howard Taslitz.

Howard's Last Photo

Howard taught history at Cerritos College and was one of the most respected individuals on its faculty. He spent over 30 years in the classroom, starting as a faculty member in the early 60s and continuing through the mid-1990s. He was the kind of person who reached out to me as a new faculty member from the moment I set foot on campus, regardless of the prominent positions he held on campus. He was the commencement speaker on two different occasions. He served as chair of the social science, economics, history, and political science departments. He held the position of faculty senate president for ten years. He was a the most voracious reader I have ever met, the kind of person with stacks of books scattered through his home, having long run out of space on bookshelves. He was outspoken and opinionated but civil and curious about other views. He was the kind of faculty member who built community and held colleagues together while encouraging rigorous intellectual disagreement. And when he taught, he was the kind of professor who kept a lecture hall filled with engaged and attentive students. An old-school "chalk-and-talk" lecturer, he did not use technology or collaborative learning techniques. For over three decades, he used oration and storytelling to capture the imagination of his students. I remember walking by his classroom a number of times and hearing his booming voice carry outside the classroom filled with students. His courses were always first to fill and had the longest wait lists. He could literally lecture for three hours and hold an entire class's attention. I have been told he spent days going over his lecture materials, preparing notes and doing research.

I eventually got around to asking him if I could come into his classroom to observe him, and he quickly agreed. I remember sitting in the back of his classroom tying to blend in with the students and thinking to myself, this is how I want to teach. In many ways, Howard was the example of how I wanted to move through academia as a professional. I spent as much time around him as I could before he retired. I sought his advice, watched him manage meetings, listened to him debate, and experienced his sense of community. Howard retired after my third or fourth year as a faculty member. I called him a few years into his retirement to check in on him and invite him into some work I was doing. We had a nice chat. He politely declined the work, telling me he had been sick and did not feel up to the challenge. A year later he passed, losing a battle to cancer.

Howard spent 30-plus years developing a teaching style and technique, a pedagogical method that was refined to the highest level of expertise. He was a master. His students benefitted from this greatly, and a few of us who had the chance to witness him in the classroom were able to capture some of it. But largely, his technique was lost with his passing. We did not document his teaching. We didn't analyze his methods. We have oral history from the few that knew him, but nearly all of them are gone. After he retired, we hired a new historian to replace him. I was on the committee and remember her interviews. She was smart, talented, and filled with potential. But she had to start at square one, the same place where Howard started, and she would need to invest decades before she reached the same level of talent he had achieved toward the end of his career.

This happens year after year in higher education as great teaching faculty retire and take their techniques with them. We have become so accustomed to it that we are collectively ambivalent about this loss of intellectual capital with every generation that retires. It speaks to a cycle of development and loss, development and loss, development and loss. . . . This cycle occurs in our teaching practices and the other core skillsets in services, management, and institutional leadership. In all of these areas across higher education, individuals develop skills to very high levels and then retire, leaving their institution to bring in new people who have little or no knowledge of the best practices that came before them. As a result of this approach, we are not building on our own histories of best practices development across the academy.

One of the reasons for this loss is our reluctance to extend meaningful peer review to pedagogy, services, management, and institutional leadership. We practice these skills with a fair degree of privacy and often receive very little critique from peers. Compare these activities, for example, to another major activity professors engage in—research. We have a completely different tradition when it comes to research-based activity. Research is initially done in private. It may be done with a small team, but it usually starts as a private and rather concealed process until it is ready for review. At that point, findings are collected and presented for peer review. In the write-up that is submitted for peer review, we typically require that the author(s) spend some time reviewing literature to demonstrate how the submitted research adds to the previous findings and work from previous thinkers. If our peers are convinced that the findings add to the field and the methods used to draw conclusions and present findings are solid, the paper or manuscript is normally moved on for publication. If you have ever been involved in this process, you know that the peer review process is rigorous, nothing close to a rubber stamp. The requirement to add new findings to the field is a serious hurdle that the author is expected to clear.

We do not generally participate in a similar process with our teaching methods. We let (or require) each faculty member find their own way in the classroom. We do not take the best practices from one generation and expect the next generation to master those techniques and then add new techniques in a formal peer-reviewed process. Most institutions have some kind of evaluation process where peers are asked to evaluate the practices of their colleagues, but this activity generally lacks rigor. Colleagues and managers who try to insert themselves into the development of pedagogy in a serious way are often rebuffed and accused of interfering with academic freedom. There are faculty who welcome constructive criticism in the spirit of suggested improvements, but such an attitude is not a professional expectation of all faculty and others as it is with research.

Part of our reluctance to apply rigorous evaluation stems from the multivariate nature of teaching (this also applies to services and management). To evaluate teaching effectively, we need to look at the intended outcome of good teaching—learning. Great teaching is presumed to elicit deep learning, and the further a faculty member strays from best practices, the less likely a student is to learn. However, the connection between learning and teaching is not that simple. There are many other variables that impact a student's learning experience. The quality of institutional support, private resources, students' effort, previous learning, and other variables combine with the

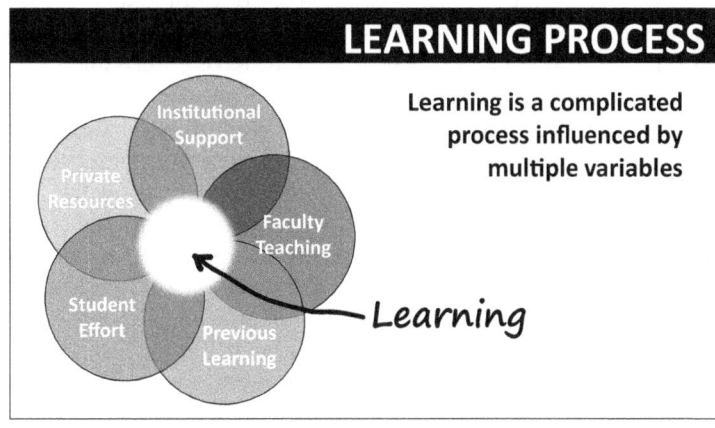

quality of faculty teaching to create the overall learning environment. For this reason, the most sincere faculty, the most self-critical faculty are right to be skeptical about evaluations. For example, it is possible for a faculty member to deliver excellence in pedagogy and watch students struggle with learning given substantive shortages of the other variables needed for learning.

When I was a new dean, one of my areas of responsibility was to administer the student evaluation of teachers. The process had a long history to it, with about 12 questions on a form that was administered to students at the end of the semester. The faculty member would select a student to administer the 15-minute evaluation and excuse him- or herself from the classroom to allow students the freedom to fill out the evaluation without the intimidation some might feel with their instructor in the room. The process had been conducted in this manner for decades. As a former faculty member and former faculty senate president, I felt strongly that the quality of teaching mattered in the success of students, so I wanted to collect all the teaching evaluation data to see what our collective pedagogical strengths and weaknesses were according to years of student evaluations.

As I started down this path, I encountered significant push-back from faculty leaders and managers, insinuating that I was somehow up to something sinister. Several individuals suggested that I should not collect and assess the data in aggregate form. Union agreements, academic freedom traditions, privacy rights, and more were brought into the conversation to stop the process.

Can you image the same kind of pushback happening in research? If a faculty member used the same arguments to thwart peer evaluation of their research, academics would condemn the individual. Research is to be poked, prodded, discussed, evaluated, and critiqued in a public effort to create the highest-quality and most reliable findings. We need to establish similar environments around the development of our pedagogy. Otherwise, we will have only anecdotal means of identifying the most effective teaching. The result: faculty members like Howard will come and go, and no one will be able to extend their work by standing on their shoulders.

Another reason pedagogy does not reach the same standards as research has to do with the diminished importance we place on teaching versus research. When I was in graduate school, every course I took revolved around learning the development of ideas in subfields of political science and how new research might move the field forward. We talked about previous research, looked at emerging research, discussed needed research, reviewed research techniques, and received encouragement from our mentors to enter a life of research. En route to my Ph.D., I did not take a single course on teaching political science and cannot recall one formal moment of instruction about pedagogy. This emphasis is pretty incredible given that most of my classmates who pursued academic jobs took positions that require much more emphasis on teaching than research.

This imbalance has carried over into the university tenure process. Nearly all universities require scholarship en route to tenure, with very specific research criteria laid out in the guidelines for tenure held by senior administrators. In contrast, while teaching criteria are often included in the guidelines, they are usually classified as recommendations rather than requirements and therefore are not subject to the same kind of intensive peer-review process that is associated with research (see Columbia University Guidelines for Tenure as an example). As a result, university faculty, especially those at top-rated research institutions (often referred to as R-1 institutions), spend much more time and energy on developing research than they do on develop teaching practices and in my experience do not always have a clear understanding of pedagogical science and how it relates to their own work in the classroom.

I recently had lunch with a faculty member at a high-ranking R-1 university. We met to discuss the disproportionately low number of students from lower-middle- and low-income families at her university and specifically in her program. Having recognized this problem, she was leading an effort on her campus aimed at solving it. In this capacity, she had recently attended a gathering of students from historically underserved communities where students told very personal stories about their struggles in making the transition from families with deeply held suspicions about higher education. I was one of the speakers at this meeting, so she and I got together over lunch at the faculty center to debrief. We talked about the students and their stories. She was particularly struck by the lack of support the students had from their families. This theme cut through all the stories students had told and struck a particularly deep chord with her.

I asked her how hearing those stories might change her approach to teaching. She paused with a puzzled look and said it would not change how she teaches. "The subject matter is the subject matter," she said. She strongly suggested it would inform and change how she works with students outside the classroom, but she saw no reason to make changes in the classroom.

As I reflected on her response after our exchange of ideas, I found it discouraging. She was a faculty member who was clearly committed to teaching. She never expressed the idea that teaching gets in the way of research. She is clearly bright and intelligent. She clearly wants to effect positive change in the lives of historically underserved students. She clearly was impacted at the emotional and intellectual level by these students' stories. And still, she saw no connection between these students' lives and her pedagogy. She is the "low-hanging fruit" for the changes called for in this book. She is supposed to be on board already. And there she was at one of the most celebrated universities in the United States, making no connection between what she does in the classroom and the success of the students she wants to help.

One of the reasons I have been drawn to community college work for my entire career has been the focus on teaching. I know research is important work and needed to solve some major problems we face. However, I believe we need more people *doing* the work of social justice. We have a well-developed understanding of the history, culture, and sociological constructs that feed inequality in American society. What we need are people who will make life-long commitments to implementing theory that will dismantle the structures that hold inequality in place. Teaching at institutions that primarily serve students from historically underserved backgrounds is one of the ways faculty can do significant social justice work.

To receive tenure at a community college, faculty are primarily expected to teach well. Most processes at community colleges include a fairly rigorous evaluation of teaching prior to granting tenure. As R-1 universities place emphasis on research for tenure consideration, community colleges emphasize teaching. However, clear definitions regarding what excellence in teaching looks like are rarely given. While many universities have adopted scoring or points-based systems for measuring research, the same can rarely be said for pedagogy. After tenure is granted, ongoing evaluations take place at nearly all institutions of higher education; however, the level of scrutiny typically declines significantly. At all three institutions where I have held leadership positions, the bar for receiving tenure was much higher than the bar for a satisfactory rating from peer-based evaluations after tenure. The evaluation process at community colleges still places a premium on teaching practices; however, the process is often conducted by colleagues and usually is heavy on the praise and light on the criticism.

While most community colleges place a premium on the evaluation of teaching practices, there are institutional hurdles that keep us from collectively pushing for excellence and the full implementation of best practices. These structures come from a place of good intentions and have had overall positive impacts on academia, but they have also had the unintended consequence of making the pursuit of best practices difficult.

Collective bargaining in higher education is an area that makes the pursuit of best practices difficult. I say this with full knowledge of the benefits that unions bring to the academy (Schmidt, 2015). I served as an executive on the union board as a faculty member and have had positive relationships with union members throughout my tenure as an administrator. Faculty unions in particular have had positive impacts on higher education. A recent study looking at the causal effects of faculty unions on public colleges and universities found a significant and positive impact on faculty participation six areas. Institutions with a faculty union tend to have higher levels of faculty participation with regard to overall institutional decision-making, college-wide salary scale development, faculty salaries, appointment of department chairs, assignment of teaching loads, and curriculum design/development (Porter & Stephens, 2010).

These gains have all had positive impacts on our institutions and largely explain why unionization in public education has thrived while union membership in the private sector has been in a 50-year decline (Wachter, 2007). Approximately

> **CAUSAL EFFECT OF FACULTY UNIONS**
>
> *Public institutions with unionized faculty have higher levels of faculty participation in . . .*
>
> - Overall institutional decision-making
> - College-wide salary scale development
> - Faculty salaries
> - Appointment of department chairs
> - Teaching loads
> - Curriculum design/development
>
>
> ORGANIZE

50 percent of public-sector employees are represented by unions compared to only 7 percent of private-sector employees belonging to a union (Edwards, 2010). Numbers of union participation at public colleges would be even higher if 23 states had not legislated that public employees cannot have union representation. Education is one of the more unionized sectors, with about 21 percent of private institutions in higher education and about 35 percent of public institutions in higher education unionized (Gier, 2018).

With all of the benefits unions bring, managers and union leaders need to continue working out agreements that build pedagogical best practices development into our evaluations. And we need to evaluate teaching techniques from an affirming professional development model rather than a punitive evaluation model.

Academic freedom is also a feature of higher education that can have the unintended effect of deterring the pursuit of excellence in pedagogy. Academic freedom is one of the most celebrated concepts in higher education, with roots that extend back to an academic charter in the 1100s developed by the University of Bologna. The document is so celebrated in higher education that in 1988, 430 university leaders signed the *Magna Charta Universitatum* to mark the 900th anniversary of Bologna's founding (Moore, 2019). The basic idea of academic freedom is unfettered pursuit of truth. Those who support academic freedom work to establish an environment where academics can pursue ideas without fear of reprisal from their institutions. With a history of examples where politics have interfered with science, this fundamental idea is extremely important.

In the United States, the torchbearer of academic freedom for the last 100 years has been the American Association of University Professors (AAUP). Since 1915, AAUP has maintained and updated a set of professional principles defining faculty rights and responsibilities that give shape and meaning to this concept. However, it is not always an easy idea to apply. For example, it is held that faculty have significant latitude with regard to pedagogy under academic freedom. How to teach a course is up to the faculty member. At the same time, academic freedom acknowledges that incompetent teaching is not a right and is not protected under academic freedom (Nelson, 2010). These two statements can be contradictory in their implementation. On the one hand, suggesting pedagogy improvements can be seen as interfering with academic freedom. Such a charge can pose a problem for academic leaders (faculty and administration) trying to enhance the quality of teaching at their institutions. On the other hand, allowing ineffective teaching to remain because of academic freedom has the consequence of hurting students. This conflict puts all of us who strive for excellent in teaching in a difficult situation at times.

Peer review is another important concept in academia. It has a long tradition, with the first recorded article published after peer review in 1731 by the Royal Society of Edinburgh (Shema, 2014). The idea acknowledges egalitarianism and collective expertise. Submitting work to our peers for review is an acknowledgement that our colleagues are the best instrument for measuring excellence. Peer review is most rigorously used in assessment of research with the use of single- or double-blind reviews. In a single-blind approach, the author's identity is revealed to the reviewers, but the reviewers' identities are not revealed to the author. This is the most common approach. In the double-blind peer-review model, anonymity cuts both ways. The reviewers do not know who conducted the research, and the authors do not know the identities of the reviewers. The double-blind approach removes more bias from the process because the author's reputation cannot be factored into the evaluation (Shema, 2014). These two approaches have been used to consistently produce some of the most prolific and influential research in the world.

Most colleges and universities also use peer review for assessment of teaching practices. This is applied during the tenure evaluation process and ongoing evaluations throughout a faculty member's career. However, the peer-review approach typically used is a "zero-blind" approach. The faculty member's teaching practices are most often reviewed by colleagues who are known to the individual being reviewed.

I have personally experienced both processes. I have submitted academic work for peer review in a single-blind model. I have had my teaching practices evaluated by a group of peers in a zero-blind model. And I have evaluated other faculty members' teaching practices in a zero-blind model. In my experience, the zero-blind model is fraught with problems of bias. When I was a faculty member, I was allowed to suggest who would serve on my evaluation team. I always wanted to improve, so I tried to select individuals who would give me good feedback, but I also tried to pick people I already had a positive relationship with to make sure the overall process went well. When I served on evaluation teams, I always knew the person I was evaluating on a professional level and was very much aware of the idea that a negative evaluation had the potential of damaging our relationship, while a positive evaluation could enhance the relationship. As an evaluator, I tried to keep these complications at bay, but they are political realities that are difficult to ignore.

The bias enters with regard to incentives. When the person being evaluated knows the evaluators, the evaluators are incentivized to offer a positive evaluation and disincentivized to offer a negative evaluation in order to maintain good relations. This is not a sign of insufficient professionalism; it is an acknowledgement of our humanity. Most of us want to build good relationships. We want to work in an environment that is supportive and uplifting. Evaluating our peers in a zero-blind model can pose a threat to this environment if we choose to critique a colleague's pedagogy.

Shortly after I left my position as a faculty member to become a dean, I was asked by colleagues I had known for many years to participate in an evaluation process. A faculty member I had known for decades was struggling in the classroom, student learning appeared to be suffering because of his performance, and his colleagues decided they would like to intervene through the evaluation process. The goal was to use the process to evaluate his teaching, identify the problems, call these issues to his attention, and address them with an improvement plan. When the assessment was completed by the evaluation team and the findings presented to the faculty member, a number of complications emerged related to collective bargaining, academic freedom, and peer review. The evaluation went down a dark path for several reasons.

First, the college had never defined the characteristics of teaching excellence and therefore had no agreed-upon any basis for measurement. Definitions of excellence in pedagogy were not addressed in any academic senate or collective bargaining documents. As a result, the faculty member was able to argue that teaching excellence was a vague idea and the conclusion from the evaluation team was arbitrary if not political. Second, he made the argument that his teaching methods were protected under academic freedom and not wrong, just misunderstood because of their creativity. Finally, he presented previous evaluations conducted through peer review that had all indicated his performance was good if not excellent. Ironically, I was one of the former evaluators who had done a light evaluation under the pressures associated with zero-blind peer review. In the end, his evaluation techniques were not sufficiently corrected and relationships were damaged greatly.

Not all evaluations end this way. This one was one of the more extreme I have encountered. Other, more objective, measures can be introduced into the evaluation process. For example, single-blind student evaluations are common at college and universities. Also, we can use quantitative data like retention and completion rates in the process. However, interpretation of these data is subject to all the biases discussed previously. For us to collectively bring pedagogical development to the same level as research development, we need to address these institutional hurdles.

Other Skill Sets: Services, Management, and Leadership

We have spent most of this chapter discussing faculty and pedagogy. But the structures that often hold us back from achieving excellence in pedagogy also apply to the other major skills in higher education: services, management, and leadership. Staff and some faculty (e.g., counselors) move through their day providing services to students. While most staff are not subject to tenure, they are included in evaluation processes throughout their careers. Administrators manage our colleges and universities on a daily basis, and many people across all constituent groups are involved in leadership. Like pedagogy, these functions rely on skill sets that require years to master, and the collective development of these skills encounters many of the same challenges that pedagogy development encounters. We lose institutional capital in these areas with each generation because we are not formally collecting, identifying, and passing on the expertise that individuals develop. We do not require a "literature review" approach where employees are expected to master the skill developments that came before them. We are not defining excellence through our collective bargaining and representative groups. We often use zero-blind peer assessment, introducing significant bias into our practices. All of these missing elements create an environment that may be a little more relaxed and less stressful than environments that are designed to push each other toward excellence against standards that are clearly defined, but such an environment also encourages practices that are not at the highest levels. Many, many employees across higher education move toward best practices as a matter of personal and professional pride. But for us to create environments where most are performing at the highest levels, we need to build structures that not only allow us to pursue excellence as individuals but institutionalize these expectations.

Discussion of Solutions

The work we do in higher education makes a difference in the success of our students. Teaching, serving, leading, and managing have direct and indirect impacts on students, and the importance of this impact is profound at institutions that serve high concentrations of first-generation students. First-generation students often have limited academic support in their private lives, so for them, our work takes on heightened importance. In other words, if you consider yourself committed to the success of students from historically underserved communities, you must find a way to be committed to pursuing best practices across the institution. Creating policies that allow us to achieve or settle into OK practices without consequence may establish a less stressful work environment for individuals who are comfortable working at these levels, but it creates a learning environment where fewer students will succeed. The connection between excellence in our practices and student success is real, but the challenges of creating an environment that substantially increases student success are also real and therefore difficult to implement.

Strategy #16: Implement Best Practices for Pedagogy, Service, Management, and Leadership

The four main skill sets in community college work include teaching, serving, managing, and leading. There is a deep and mature literature discussing best practices in all four areas. Combined, this body of research constitutes a compelling amount of thought. As such, the challenge is not figuring out what we need to do in terms of best practices. The challenge is creating a workplace environment that is serious about embedding the expectation of excellence in the culture and practices of the institution.

I have spent 30 years in community college education. I have worked at three major colleges and consider myself a student of community college systems/management. I have taught, I have been the dean over academic services, I have held several leadership positions, and I have managed in several capacities. Over three decades, I have been surrounded by individuals who encourage me to do great work, but none of these institutions have defined what *great* looks like. I was never given a rubric of teaching characteristics that define what excellence looks like. I was never handed a set of criteria that define what excellent services look like. Great management and leadership have never been enumerated for me. There is good thinking scholarship around this idea by our colleagues, but, in my experience, defining excellence inside our institutions is lacking. The thought of this is intriguing. It would have provided significant clarity to my own development over the years, and I know several colleagues who have expressed a desire for this kind of clarity.

The best practices literature in all four areas is very diverse. It needs to be reviewed and assessed by each institution with the goal of finding an approach that fits the college culture and history. After a review of this nature, we can establish definitions of excellence. However, completing such a task could take a long time and would most likely require considerable deliberation. However, a pathway institution could get the conversation started immediately by leveraging the set of values already adopted by that college. Initial definitions of excellence in all four areas (teaching, serving, managing, and leading) can be pulled from the values that are most important to the college. These values are typically already established and have usually been officially articulated. They have been adopted through an official process, embedded into foundational documents (mission, vision, and values statements), and published for all to see. One way to start creating definitions of excellence across all four skill sets is to use these values as a framework.

For example, *student centeredness* is often identified as a core institutional value. This is the idea that we need to make decisions about the institution and about our own personal work with students at the center of our thought process. We need to shape our work in ways that move students forward. While this is an obvious value that colleges should embrace, it is not an obvious value in the work of every employee on campus. The further an employee is removed from regular contact with students, the more difficult it is to make this value a meaningful part of day-to-day work.

This distance from student success was apparent when I was a dean and supervised a graphics designer. She was very pleasant to be around and highly talented, but she was unreliable. She chronically came to work late, had excessive absences, and often missed important deadlines. Her previous managers had turned a blind eye to this behavior, and it had set in as habitual for her over the years. Early on I approached her about her reliability problems and asked her to correct the behavior. This request, of course, involved a long process that created a fair amount of stress for both of us. The turning point in this process came during a difficult conversation in my office. In the conversation, she asked me in a very respectful way why I was being such a stickler on her work habits. She could not see how her behavior was really hurting me or anyone around her. To answer her question, I talked about our students and how they come from backgrounds where the academic odds are stacked against them. I talked to her about the transformation that happens in these students' lives when they experience academic success. And then we talked about her work and how it is connected our students. I tried to help her see how her work helps students find success.

This explanation was a turning point for her and how she perceived her value, how she perceived her contribution to the larger mission of the college. It still took a while for her to improve, but the turning happened when she could see how her work was connected to students.

So many people in our institutions are caught in the same situation as that graphic design artist. Grounds keepers, electricians, janitors, accountants, administrative services personnel, and many others find it difficult to see how their work is connected to students. This is a failure of management or leadership in our colleges. They must understand how every job is connected to students and help those who carry out those jobs see the connection as well. These connections are foundational to the success of the college and the pursuit of excellence. When you can see how your work is connected to students and their success—when you are *student centered*—it is difficult to argue that half-hearted levels of work are good enough.

Another value that nearly all colleges embrace is *inclusion*. Inclusion is typically enumerated and defined in the foundational documents of our institutions. We recognize that we serve diverse students and publicly acknowledge the importance of this. But we do not always insist that it be a core element of our practices. I have heard faculty suggest that "content is content" in their classrooms and thinking about diversity around the presentation of content is not necessary. A chemistry professor might say, "The periodic table is the periodic table." This implies that teaching general chemistry is inherently unbiased and neutral. But *how* we teach, the methods we use, the examples we choose, the delivery systems we employ make learning more and less approachable for different groups. The same applies to how we deliver our services and how we manage our organizations. The practices we adopt matter and must be adopted with conscious discussions of how they impact all our students. This means we need to move away from the Darwinist approaches, looking to eliminate the weak students and advance the strong. If we value inclusion, our roles should be to deliberately include as many as possible and help as many as possible find success. This is a value that should be added to our expectations for excellence with clearly defined applications that we can integrate into skills of all employees at our colleges.

Another value higher education generally embraces is *community*. This cohesiveness we try to build into our institutions should be a value that cuts through our teaching, service, and management/leadership practices. This sense of community is especially important for institutions that serve students who come from families that do not have college-going traditions. These students enter college feeling displaced and therefore need to encounter practices that draw them into the college community. Literature is especially clear on the need for students to build relationships with other students and a few faculty members. Teaching practices should consciously help students connect with other students. Services need to bring students together in environments where they help each other and find community. Management needs to embody this approach and teach those they manage how to build skills that yield such results. This value can be integrated into a definition of excellence for the institution.

An affirming educational environment is another common value embraced by the academy. In an affirming environment, people feel supported and lifted up. They tend to feel good about themselves and their work in these environments. Embedding positive influence into our practices starts with the understanding that students from disfavored communities often enter our colleges within a frame of deficits. They are constantly told that they have problems to address. As professionals in their lives, we need to be fully conscious of the hurdles they face and do work to mitigate or eliminate these hurdles. But in our direct work with students, we need to look for ways to flip their deficits into assets as part of our conscious practices. Students who speak multiple languages, navigate between multiple cultures, and come from families with recent immigrant histories as a result have assets and strengths that other students do not have. Our practices in the classroom, over the counter, and in meetings need to recognize these assets in meaningful ways. An affirming approach should carry over to all our interactions with students. We need to catch them performing successful actions and express favorable recognition much more often than catching them performing incorrectly and calling them out. This is another value that we can articulate with specific actions that help us know what excellence looks like.

There are many more examples that we can draw from common values embraced by higher education. Each one represents a good starting point for defining excellence. With that said, I don't think the big challenge is defining excellence. The big challenge, the idea that kept me a little anxious as I wrote this section, is entering into the conversation. Just thinking about this and the realities associated with holding each other to high standards can induce anxiety. Clearly defined expectations and standards of excellence translate into accountability. This is the palpable undercurrent that so often shapes and even more often derails these conversations. Implementing this solution strategy will take great leadership from individuals across the entire institution. If leadership inside the three core constituent groups—faculty, staff, and management—can agree on making their college a place where excellence is the driver of all parts of their mission, then we can at least start this conversation agreeing on the foundational idea.

Strategy #17: Implement Standards of Excellence for Programs

I think of programs as our primary products or services. The most obvious programs are our academic programs, often referred to as *majors*. We design our academic programs to give students a base of knowledge, introduce them to an area of expertise, connect them with other students in the field who may become life-long colleagues, and provide them with mentors (e.g., faculty) who can help them navigate the academic and professional challenges in the student's major field. Our service programs are established to help students move through the institution successfully. These include services like admissions and records, counseling, financial aid, tutoring, library services, and job placement. We need to know all our services and assess each one against defined standards of excellence with support structures that continually move each program toward these best practices.

When I was a dean, one of my areas of responsibility was institutional effectiveness. In this role, I worked with a team that decided that to start measuring academic program success. We spent a significant amount of time thinking through how we would measure program quality and settled on two indicators: 1) program course success and 2) program course retention. There are other measures that can be used (e.g., program completion and student evaluations), but these were the two measures we decided to start with.

We had been conducting program review for several years at the college, but the measurements used in program review were chosen by each department, and data to support the measures were equally diverse. As a result, we had no consistent means of comparing departments. The process was so muddy that it had turned into a compliance exercise and received very little attention from senior leadership. The institution did not use program review to evaluate and improve programs. In response, we wanted to develop a process that would allow us to compare success rates across the college, use these data to measure quality, and spark an institutional discussion around program improvement.

The initial idea of publicly discussing program success and doing so using comparisons between programs was controversial. People were understandably nervous. Throughout my experience in higher education, I have noticed that there is often push-back and fear about accountability measures. I know some of this resistance comes from individuals who are underperforming and want to remain in the shadows, but most of the push-back comes from individuals who are concerned that transparent evaluation and scrutiny of their work will be used in a punitive manner by leaders or managers who have bad intentions. There are histories of such at many institutions, and these need to be factored into the conversation. But, once we moved past the initial fear and focused the dialogue on improvement, the program evaluation process was generally well received and generated positive dialogue.

Conducting program assessment is difficult on two levels. First, measuring success is complicated. These are large programs with multiple variables contributing to program outcomes, and nearly all of these variables have some kind of human element involved, giving everything a degree of unpredictability. Measuring programs is not like measuring a phenomenon in natural science or engineering, where we isolate precise variables and measure them with high levels of confidence in the results. Instead, assessing programs is an exercise in social science research, and, like all social science measurements, we must determine the most significant indicators of success, choose those that have existing data available or data that can be collected fairly easily, and understand that because of the human element, our measures will have relatively low levels of reliability. For this reason, it is very important to have a comprehensive conversation about program measures before applying a methodology.

The second area that is difficult is determining corrective actions at the end of the review. When data suggest that a program is struggling, it is not always clear what needs to be done to improve conditions. As a VP of academic affairs, I sat on the program review committee. In this role, I read through self-evaluations conducted by programs and listened to oral presentations made by the leadership from each program. I recall one of these oral presentations by our business department that reflected this problem. We settled on a conversation around the success of different student populations. In particular, Latinx students were struggling in the program. We brought their lack of success to the attention of the department chair, and he acknowledged the problem. But that was about all he said. I remember being concerned about his response and later followed up with him about his lack of further input. He explained that his response was brief because he honestly felt that there are issues in students' lives that tend to break down along lines of race, ethnicity, and income. These issues, he felt, make it more difficult for some to succeed. He understood the academic struggle of Latinx students in his program as a larger social and cultural issue, not as a program-related issue that he or his colleagues could address.

My point with this story is that data (e.g., Latinx students are not succeeding in your program) do not necessarily guide us in a common direction unless they are tied to a larger, agreed-upon philosophy or perspective. We had not established at that institution that our job as professional educators was to counter the academic inequities in students' private lives, and as a result, the data that demonstrated inequitable performance in his program elicited very different suggestions for solving the problem. This difference in how we view our work is a critical point that we all need to think through extensively before we can suggest program corrections that we agree to implement.

The conversation I had with the chair of the business department brings to light a fundamental idea this book is trying to establish. There are many groups in higher education that experience less academic success because of issues in their private lives. For example, many Latinx students come to our colleges having lived through a range of experiences that make their success in college less likely. We have discussed many of them already in the book (see Chapter 3). These issues are heavily documented in literature. The core questions that we need to confront as educators is, *Are we going to do anything about it? Can we do anything about it?* The business department chairperson came from the perspective that these were large cultural and sociological issues that were beyond the reach of his classroom, his department, his college. He held empathy for all students who came from backgrounds like this but did not see how he could address or counter these issues. As a result, when confronted with the knowledge that Latinx students were systematically performing worse in his program, he agreed but did not feel any sense of responsibility for the disparate success.

To end equity gaps in the United States, higher education professionals need to agree that we are in the business of creatively undoing the disadvantages that so many of our students have experienced before they came to us. From this approach, we can approach the problem by exploring ways we can change and the steps needed to correct these problems. Is it that teaching practices need to change? Are the GE courses that support the program the problem? Is poor leadership from the chair or dean the problem? Is the outside economy placing some kind of squeeze on the program? Are the strategic documents of the institution creating problems? Is the program underfunded and therefore in need of resources? These and more are possible factors that can take prescriptive actions in a range of different directions.

With effective program assessment, we can identify best practices that exist in our own institutions and use them to help struggling programs. This is a process that needs effective leadership, but it puts the people inside these programs in a vulnerable situation. For this reason, we need to generate an institutional commitment to a student-centered approach and what that means for the work of the institution.

Strategy #18: Categorize Every Institutional Activity Under a Program

Many individuals working in our institutions do not think of themselves as belonging to a program at the college. They think of themselves as helping to run the institution, not a particular program. Because a program typically has a mission tied to the mission of the college and because just about all college mission statements include a commitment to student success, these employees perform their tasks without thinking about contributing to student success. We need to think through the idea of reconceiving of them as members of programs and bringing them into program review and assessment tied to the college mission.

For example, staff who work on our facilities and grounds do not typically think of themselves as providing a service for student success. We need to rethink how such employees regard their work and reframe it so that it is connected to success. We could recognize how architects have known for centuries that the spaces we move through impact our behavior. In this sense, the people who design and maintain our facilities are influencing student behavior. This work can be done in a way that enhances student success or deters from it. For example, designing and maintaining beautiful study spaces inspires students to study, whereas dirty and poorly designed study spaces turn students away from studying. Framing their work in this light gives it a more programmatic feel and helps connect employees to the core mission of the college. This example can extend to many employees in our institution who do not typically see themselves as providing services to students.

Strategy #19: Build Visual and Physical Surroundings That Support Equity

When we design academic spaces, whether they are large or small, we need to be asking ourselves, "Are we trying to build Pebble Beach or are we trying to build Central Park?" Both are iconic and beautiful, but they create entirely different experiences. Pebble Beach is an exclusive golf course and club overlooking Carmel Bay in California. Many consider it the most beautiful golf course in the world. It is part of the PGA tour and a bucket-list experience for many golfers and vacationers throughout the word. Central Park is an 843-acre park located in the middle of New York City, between the Upper East and Upper West sides of Manhattan. It is said to be the most filmed location in the world and is visited by nearly 40 million each year. Both are among the most beautiful properties in the world. However, the experiences are vastly different. Pebble Beach is exclusive, with grounds that are tightly controlled, and playing a round of golf there is absurdly expensive. A caddied round of golf costs close to $700 (not including the tip). On the other hand, Central Park is open to the public, with open access park entrances surrounding its perimeter. While there are vendors inside the park, the park itself is free to the public. One is deliberately *exclusive*, the other deliberately *inclusive*.

Our college properties send similar messages. I recently had a meeting at a selective private university located in an urban area that has literally built a wall around the perimeter of its campus. I counted about ten entrances to the campus, each guarded by a staff kiosk. The message at this university is clear: *We need make sure you are permitted to come on this campus.* In contrast, I have been to other colleges and universities that are wide open, as if to say, *please come in and be part of our community.* Architecture matters and needs to reflect the values of inclusion.

A few years ago, I was working on a facilities master plan. As president of the college, I wanted to make sure everyone had positive reactions to the new aesthetic being proposed in the plan, so I met with a wide range of groups. One of the meetings was with Umoja, a support group for African American students. A dozen or more Umoja members and their advisor came to my office to discuss the plan. We looked at several mock-ups of the proposed aesthetic. I asked them what they thought. After some initial hesitation to see if criticism was safe, they let me know definitively, but still respectfully, that they did not care for the look and feel. Their response prompted a long conversation about design of a campus. I particularly remember a few students telling me about universities they had visited to consider for transfer. On some campuses, they immediately felt at home. On other campuses, they felt out of place. As we discussed this, it became clear that the sense of belonging to a campus came from tangible markers that indicate the campus embraces recognizable elements of their culture. The best way to create a welcoming atmosphere is to have people from all cultures on campus, but we can also be create a positive environment through architecture, graphic design, posters, music, and more that speak to all groups, but especially historically underserved populations.

The first full-time dean's position I had was as supervisor over a number of academic support services. The college president asked me to lead a complete transformation of skill development centers by combining them into one coordinated success center that would help students develop skills in math, English, reading, foreign languages, study skills, and other content areas. During the transformation, one of the things I was deliberate about doing was to break up the study environments that encourage quiet isolation and move toward an environment that encouraged more collaboration. I wanted the Math Success Center to have the ambient noise of a restaurant. To establish this environment, we arranged tables in a manner that would encourage students to sit together and help each other with homework. Soon there was a low buzz of conversation in the room most of the time. I will admit this was an intuitive decision, but later I found several articles discussing cultural learning patterns and how some cultures teach children to learn as individuals in disciplined silence, while other cultures encourage children to learn together in groups and embrace the energy of collaboration. When we build study areas that require students to sit in isolated cubicles, we are preferencing certain cultures over others, creating hurdles and disadvantages for students who were raised in cultures that encourage collaborative learning. Design has an impact on learning. We need to make sure our design is as inclusive as possible, if not slanted in favor of historically underserved communities.

Strategy #20: Expand Professional Development

Have you ever wondered about the following puzzle? No one wants the equity gap in student success to exist on our campuses. I have literally never met a person who is happy with the existence of this gap. Yet it persists. I believe one of the main reasons for gaps that persist is that we collectively have low equity skills. I believe professional development should be largely (maybe exclusively) devoted to improving equity skills across the campus. If we hope to close the equity gap, we all need to become better at what we do through a lens of equity-mindedness. From the president's office down, colleges need to develop this important skill set and continually expand its application. We need to collectively develop equity-based standards for teaching and manifest the courage to implement them.

Although doing so presents challenges for academic freedom and union contracts, we will never close this gap if we do not address perhaps the most influential relationship on campus, the faculty-student relationship. Equity-mindedness should also extend to how we deliver services and lead/manage. Developing the highest expectations for our services and leadership/management and measuring these standards for effective implementation is essential to closing the gap.

Strategy #21: Establish Support Services to Disproportionately Impacted Groups

There are several boutique programs at colleges across the country that provide assistance to groups who often struggle academically. The success with most of these programs comes from the community they establish and the support services they wrap around their students' academic lives. Running several of these programs at Norco, I have been impressed with their success but am frustrated with their inability to scale because of programmatic expenses. For example, the services provided to 60 students enrolled in the Puente program (program for Latinx students) at one college I managed included a dedicated counselor, a faculty member, a meeting space and a modest budget for group activities. There is no way this level of

> **SOLUTIONS AND STRATEGIES**
>
> 16. Implement Best Practices for Core Competencies
> 17. Implement Programmatic Standards of Excellence
> 18. Categorize All Activities under Programs
> 19. Build Physical Spaces to Support Equity
> 20. Expand Professional Development
> 21. Establish Targeted Support Services

service could have been scaled to the 6,000+ Latinx students who were enrolled at the college but not engaged with the Puente program. This same dilemma exists around Umoja (African American students), DACA, LGBTQ+, men of color, veterans, the formerly incarcerated, foster youth, and other programs.

To scale these services, we need to implement a few basic changes. First, we need to move to a model of counseling teams and caseload management. Through this approach, teams made up of counselors, paraprofessionals, and faculty advisors are assigned a group of students to track through the entire life cycle of the student experience. These teams are empowered to intervene rather than passively waiting for students to contact them. This change in operation requires a powerful CRM solution for tracking and communicating with students. This approach is somewhat disruptive to the way services are currently offered to students at most colleges and needs to be carefully coordinated with bargaining units or related groups representing college constituent groups. Regardless, it is the only way we will be able to scale up these services that are so important and effective in students' lives.

Conclusion

Community colleges serve many students from historically underserved communities. The three colleges where I have taught and managed have student populations where the majority of students come from this background. By definition, these communities receive fewer and lower-quality services across the public and private spectrum. This is all the more reason we need to be intentional about institutionalizing the pursuit of best practices. We need to move beyond this commitment at the individual level and into environments where institutions commit to the ongoing development of best practices across our pedagogy, services, management, and leadership. This emphasis will take great work from leadership across all constituent groups.

As leaders, we need to approach this with great enthusiasm and from an affirming frame of mind that constantly explains these goals from the perspective of student success. We need to hold each other to excellence, because this is what it will take for students to be successful, especially students from historically underserved communities. There will be issues of trust surrounding this approach. Too many people have experienced standards of excellence in punitive and "gotcha" environments that create a sense of negativity. We will never achieve these aspirations from a punitive approach. We must approach this from our mutual desire to see all student groups enjoy academic success and from our shared understanding that it will take excellence across our institutions to break these long and deep historical patterns that continue to hold whole communities back.

7 Creating Intuitive and Supportive Transitions

A few years ago, my wife, Kathi, and I had a student as a long-term house guest. We met Tyreese through one of our daughters during the summer of 2016. He was in the circle of her high school friends, and all of them had just completed their junior or senior years of high school. My daughter (our youngest) was one of the graduating seniors and was getting ready for college, while Kathi and I prepared for our first year as empty nesters. Tyreese had just finished his junior year of high school and was around our house a lot during the summer as our daughter's circle of friends got together occasionally to hang out around the fire ring in our back yard, around the pool, and in the loft upstairs. Several times over that summer, Tyreese ended up sleeping over on the couch in the loft.

Kathi, Tyreese & Erika

Tyreese played defensive end for the Vista Murrieta High School football team. He was a big, athletic, likeable young man. He was curious and enjoyed talking to all kinds of people, including Kathi and me. During the course of several conversations that summer, we learned that he lived a considerable distance from the high school and was making the drive because his local high school did not have a football team that played at the same level as Vista's. We learned he did not have reliable transportation to the high school and did not always have enough money for gas to make the drive. We learned that his mom and dad were somewhat present in his life but not always able to provide for his basic needs. So, toward the end of the summer, we offered one of our bedrooms and anything in our refrigerator to Tyreese, and he accepted.

At the beginning of his senior year, Tyreese's dad gave him an old, beat-up truck to drive back and forth from our house to school. I wasn't sure if it was properly registered, but I knew he did not have a driver's license. He was 16 years old, so Kathi and I encouraged him to get a driver's permit, offering to pay the fees and help him through the process. But he was "politely stubborn" about not accepting our offer. I was initially puzzled by this but eventually landed on the assumption (right or wrong) that he didn't want to go through a permitting process that would involve his parents. And given that we were not official guardians in any capacity, we had very little leverage on insisting he complete the permitting process. So, after several attempts to get him legally permitted, we gave in and waited about a year and half for him to turn 18 (he drove illegally that entire time). Right after his 18th birthday, I took him to the Department of Motor Vehicles (DMV) to go through the process of becoming a legally licensed driver.

Tyreese had been living with us his entire senior year of high school and was still living with us during his first semester of community college as we headed to the DMV. We had scheduled the appointment together online. He had studied a week prior for the test, and he had 18 months of driving experience, so he was well prepared. The online application materials indicated that he had to bring two pieces of evidence confirming his address. A phone bill and a utility bill were suggested, but he did not have anything like that, so we went through a drawer full of letters that had been sent to him by college football recruiters and selected three that were still in envelopes with his name and address clearly printed on them.

We arrived at the DMV early, knowing they have chronically long lines and brutal wait times. We eventually made it to the head of the line. As he approached the clerk, I stood closely behind him to make sure I could hear everything. He indicated that he was there to take the driver's test. When the clerk asked for proof of residency, he presented the recruitment letters. With an endless line to process throughout the day, she quickly indicated to him that recruitment letters of this sort where not allowed as proof and reiterated that he must provide something like a phone bill or utility bill. She dismissed him and told him to return with the required documents. Standing behind him, I had heard the entire conversation and watched his shoulders hunch in defeat. In that moment, his six-foot-four athletic body took the demeanor of a little boy accustomed to experiencing rejection.

I stepped in, asked Tyreese to sit off to the side (far enough to not hear the conversation) and spoke with the clerk. She had not been rude, but she had been curt, lacked empathy, and generally projected the stereotypical demeanor of a state bureaucrat. I quickly told her his story. I told her he was basically a foster-care kid, but unofficially, and that I did not have a shred of paperwork from any agency to substantiate that we were taking care of him. I told her about his parents going in and out of his life. I remember saying to her, "He doesn't have shit, not to mention a phone bill or utility bill in his name." I did not say this to her in anger, but I did say it with resolve. I could tell she was listening. I asked her to tell me what I could do to help. She explained that I should go to his high school, get a print-out of his transcripts with his address, and go online to his community college site and get his registration information with his address and bring them directly back to her. These options were not on the DMV site we had reviewed days before. She presented this information to me as if she were revealing a secret. In that moment, we connected with a shared interest to help Tyreese.

As we left the DMV, I told him about the work-around and how we could get the required documents. I told him we were going to complete the process that day. I also made a point of talking to him about bureaucracy and how our experience that day was unfortunately common in bureaucratic processes. They are often bumpy and the key is to openly communicate, search for creative solutions, and—above all else—persist. It took a few hours to collect the documents, after which we returned to the DMV and handed them directly to the woman we had spoken with in the morning. She processed his paperwork and directed him to where he would complete the written exam and take a driving test. After successfully completing these and shortly after his 18th birthday, Tyreese was a licensed driver.

Like most adults, I have been through bureaucratic processes like this before and I understand how to work a complicated process when I encounter hurdles. I understand how to keep moving forward until the task is completed. Tyreese, however, had never been through a process like this, and the moment he was told his recruitment letters were not sufficient, he felt he was at a dead end. He was not quitting. He did not lack resolve or grit. What he lacked was the skill set to move through a bureaucracy, and without an advocate in his corner, he may still be driving illegally today.

This is how many first-generation students feel as they attempt to navigate the bureaucracy from high school through college and into careers. They encounter overly complicated bureaucratic processes when they try to register in community college, navigate through the community college, transfer to the university, move through the university, and apply for jobs after college. Over the years, I have had several faculty members (individuals with higher education experience and Ph.D.s) come to me with complaints about the onboarding process. In all of these circumstances, the faculty member was trying to help a student (often their own child) register for classes and grew so frustrated with the process that they made a point of coming to my office to voice their frustration.

One of the reasons historically underserved students complete college at lower rates is bureaucracy. We have built cumbersome, dense, non-intuitive processes that they must navigate, and most of them are first-generation students, which means they will encounter these processes with no family member to help them. They usually have no one in their lives with higher education experience and all too often end up feeling like Tyreese, proudly handing his recruitment letters to a clerk at the DMV only to be shut down by unyielding rules. We must change this.

Students from historically underserved communities pursuing a career path encounter transition processes from high school to community college, then to the university, to their first career-related job, and beyond. Sometimes they move from high school to the military and then enter the pathway through in community college. Sometimes they move from high school to jobs and then enter a career pathway through a community college. The point here is that the most common route for historically underserved students trying to build a career is through a community college as part of sequence.

Students from families with college-going traditions follow a similar path, although often it does not include community college in the sequence. Both sets of students

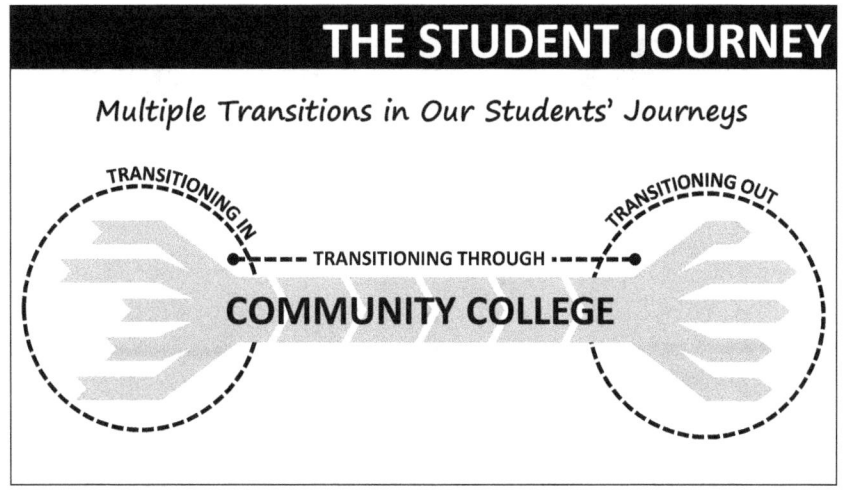

(first-generation students and students from families with college-going histories) move through these transitions with some difficulty, but the students from families with college-going histories experience much greater success. This is largely due to their social capital. They have relatives and close family friends who have successfully navigated these waters. They have socializing agents in their life who help navigate these transitions and consequently arrive at each transition point with a significant advantage. In contrast, historically underserved students typically lack people like this in their families. They have family members who love them dearly but most often did not attend college and have no knowledge of how to navigate these difficult transitions. This often leaves first-generation students to navigate these transitions by themselves, stacking the odds of success against them. Our job as community college professionals is to mitigate or eliminate these hurdles by making each transition less complicated.

Transitioning IN

Students entering the community college system start from several different places. Most students transition directly out of high school. They are what we think of as traditional students. In addition to this traditional starting point, many incoming students have jobs and desire to improve their job skills or prepare for new career opportunities. Many other students enter community college after a period of time in the military. Increasingly, international students are looking to start their American higher education experience at a community college. Finally, some students come from state or federal government programs. These include foster care and formerly incarcerated students. All of these groups share some common onboarding transitions they must address, but each group also brings a set of unique challenges.

Onboarding involves a set of hurdles each student must clear before they are allowed to begin classes. In California, for example, while all community colleges are open-enrollment institutions (everyone gets in), there are processes that act as de-facto gatekeepers, preventing many students from enrolling. Onboarding starts with students seeking information about the community college(s) they wish to attend. Once they have made a decision, they go through an online application process controlled by the state. After they have been accepted, students are assessed for placement, participate in orientation, attend a counseling session, and develop an initial education plan. These are often separate

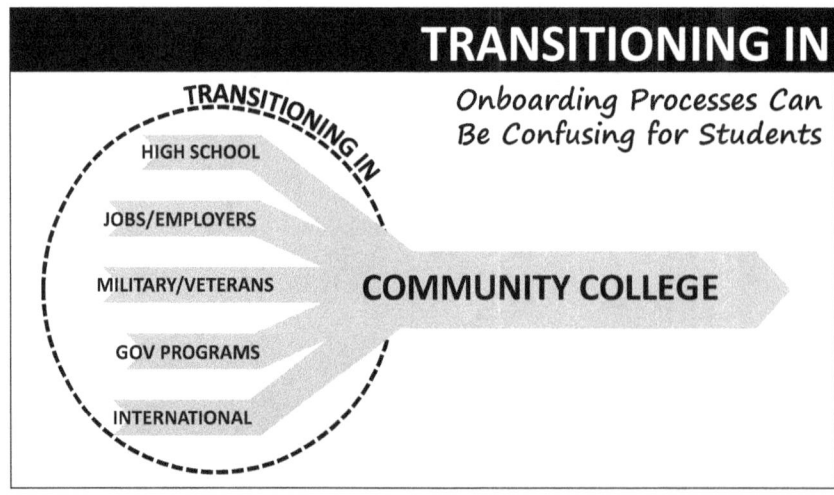

processes done in different offices spread across the campus. Sometimes they can be done online. Other times they are required to be done in person. After students have completed these steps, they are cleared for registration and can select courses to take and finally register for open courses.

CA CC ONBOARDING: Interest/Research → Application → Assessment → Orientation → Counseling → Ed Planning → Course Selection → Registration

The initial steps in the onboarding process are free until registration, where fees are assessed; however, the registration fees are very low for in-state residents and routinely waived for low-income students. Despite the affordability, the hurdles along the onboarding process deter as many as half the students who initially express an interest in enrolling. At the college where I have worked, only about half the students who start the application process actually end up in class. This low percentage suggests that the onboarding process is daunting. It is *not* too expensive; it is too complicated.

Transitioning From High School to Community College

In addition to the complications mentioned previously, the transition from high school to community college adds a layer of confusion. For one, we do not share data with local high schools and therefore have to collect it during application. This is an added layer of process that would not exist if we shared data. Second, assessment has been heavy over the years because community colleges have historically not trusted what high school transcripts indicate about a student's learning. This lack of trust has started to shift in California and other states where high school transcripts are now recognized as accurately reflecting learning outcomes. Also, orientation is generally inadequate. While orientation is meant to help students with initial planning, especially course planning, the counselor-to-student ratios are insufficient at most community colleges, making orientation sessions difficult to arrange and often too brief to provide comprehensive support. Finally, the registration process is a hurdle. The interface students must use to register for classes and complete other essential processes is rarely intuitive and often outdated for contemporary students. These hurdles (and others like them) are largely in place because of poor coordination between local high schools and their community college partners.

Transition From Workplace to Community College

While most students come to the community college directly out of high school, a significant number come directly out of the labor market. With over 60 percent of adults who have not completed college indicating they have thought about returning to college (EAB, 2019a), there is a potential for a large increase in this population at the community college doors. Often referred to as adult learners, these students return for a range of reasons, but most come to either change careers or develop skills that can help advance their existing careers.

For this transition to be successful, community colleges have developed career technical programs and workforce development programs designed to meet industry needs. These programs try to remain tied directly to local/regional economic needs and create onramps to contemporary businesses. Achieving this objective is often difficult, however, because business development, especially in entrepreneurial sectors, changes rapidly, while education moves at a much slower pace given structural and procedural constructs inside academia. Many colleges try to address this discrepancy by wrapping advisory boards or committees around specific programs. Regardless, annual budgeting cycles, long curriculum development and approval cycles, and related traditions make response time from higher education frustrating to many of our regional business partners.

People transitioning from work to college would benefit from having their relevant work experience recognized and credited academically. Skills learned on the job should be mapped to college curriculum and recognized for credit. For example, a person who has worked in a programming environment for a number of years and decided to return to college to complete their degree in computer science is typically required to take the full computer science curriculum before the degree is conferred. There is no formal mechanism or agreed-upon best practice across higher education to recognize the programming skills and knowledge the employee has learned over those years and therefore no elegant way to grant credit for this learning. There are exams students can take for course credit or to opt out of course requirements, but they are time consuming, require faculty participation, and are administered one student at a time. This is not a model that we can scale to deliver expanded benefits to returning students who deserve some kind of credit for years of work that may be applicable to their future degree.

Returning students usually have more complicated lives than traditional students. They often have spouses, children, bills, jobs, and related responsibilities that make their lives less flexible and almost always incompatible with the schedule of traditional students. Current trends that appear to respond to many of these challenges include compressed coursework offered in six- and eight-week formats and online education. These two approaches allow for high-quality learning in a format that gives returning students the flexibility they need to succeed.

The institutions that have been most responsive and creative in adopting these models are the for-profit institutions. They do not have the same structural parameters as public institutions that make innovation difficult, and they are often working with a model where they are almost exclusively targeting returning adults. The downside is the cost of these institutions. They operate under private college tuition rates, alluring returning students with flexible models but sticking them with significant debt through the student loans needed to pay high tuition.

Finally, the coordination between regional employers and community college educators leaves much room for improvement. And while we wait for these improvements to be identified and implemented, many returning students struggle in the transition between work and starting or returning to college.

Transition From Military to Community College

Since the establishment of the G.I. Bill in 1944, 5.2 million veterans have received degrees (The Postsecondary National Policy Institute, 2018). The G.I. Bill is among the more successful higher education assistance programs in the United States for students from historically underserved backgrounds. With the passage of the Post 9–11 G.I. Bill, this program has continued to support veterans in their transition from service to higher education. Like first-generation students moving directly out of high school, the majority of veterans entering higher education start their journey in community college (The Postsecondary National Policy Institute, 2018).

Many veterans have struggled with their transition into civilian life, and their difficulties are mirrored in their transition to higher education. While all veterans completed rigorous training and coursework in the military to establish a military occupation specialization (MOS), the two educational environments are very different. Higher education has done a poor job of recognizing military training with articulated units of credit.

I first became aware of this when I was vice president of instruction at Crafton Hills College (CHC). CHC has a well-respected and long-standing fire training program. The program includes courses in fire science and public safety related to fire service, a state-of-the-art training facility complete with three engines, and an accredited fire academy. The academy accepts and trains new cadets twice a year, and on a fairly regular basis, veteran marines from Camp Pendleton who served as fire fighters in the Marines join the CHC Fire Academy to transition from military to civilian fire fighter.

When I spoke with the CHC fire captain about this phenomenon and asked him if the training was redundant for the veterans, he indicated with concern that there was substantial overlap. In fact, we were taking marines who had been trained fire fighters and requiring that they take all the basic training again, teaching them such things as how to enter buildings safely, deploy ladders, ventilate, and operate a hose. These veterans probably knew 80 percent of the curriculum already and only needed 20 percent to make the civilian transition; however, we were requiring them to complete the full program.

This problem plays out for veteran after veteran across the United States. As they transition into colleges, higher education articulation officials fail to recognize the training (the education) they have done in one or more of the branches and typically end up granting little more than a minimal amount of physical education credit. While many veterans receive significant training in foreign languages, geopolitics, computer coding, engineering, advanced math, welding, culinary arts, auto mechanics, and much, much more, higher education routinely ignores this education and requires our veterans to nearly start from scratch. We need to give them the credit they deserve.

There are over 25,000 occupational specialties and 25,000 different trainings and courses offered by the five branches of our armed forces (Army, Navy, Air Force, Marines, Coast Guard) and more than 5,000 U.S. colleges and universities, each with hundreds of courses, and each course needs to be matched as equivalent (articulated) by faculty with each of the 25K military occupational specialties and 25K military courses. The American Council on Education has evaluated thousands of MOSs and made recommendations for college course credit. These are valuable but general (e.g., three units of computer science) and not specific (e.g., CSC 1A at Norco College). To be awarded college credit, currently each veteran must first apply to a college, then meet with a counselor to evaluate their Joint Services Transcript (JST) and make their case. The counselor then confers with discipline faculty and then communicates the result to the veteran, usually several days or weeks later. This time-consuming, confusing, and inconsistent process is repeated with every vet, every course, at every college.

In addition to the educational matriculation problems veterans face, higher education does not provide adequate services to veterans who have advising issues, career placement considerations, financial packages, and often health-related issues that are often quite different from those of the traditional students.

Moving from the military to education is a complicated transition. It is less than ideal, and given that more than two-thirds of our veterans are first-generation students, they do not have the social capital needed to assist with this transition. This is one of the major reasons that while an education is offered for free to U.S. veterans, less than one-third have completed their college degrees (The Postsecondary National Policy Institute, 2018).

Transitioning From Government Programs to Community College

There are several other special populations that come to the community college through a range of federal or state government programs. I have had significant experience with foster care students, incarcerated students, and formerly incarcerated students. All three of these populations skew heavily toward disfavored communities and carry all the challenges associated with these communities when it comes to onboarding through a bureaucracy. On top of this, they are often caught in their own bureaucracy connected to the county or the state and encounter particular problems in trying to get one bureaucracy to cooperate with another. Caseload counselors, parole officers, county assistance, group homes, and more carry their own layers of government process that do not function smoothly with the bureaucracies of our colleges. These challenges create an added layer of difficulty in the onboarding process for groups of students who already face a wide range of challenges.

Transitioning *through*

After a student completes the process of transitioning *in*, they start on the process of transitioning *through* their academic program. Moving *through* is the longest and most difficult part of the student journey. Through this part of the journey, students must enroll in initial courses, learn how to study at a college level, select a major, develop an education plan that prepares them for multiple exit options, secure financial aid, purchase books and supplies, join the academic community, and much more. I have been in leadership positions at three community colleges, and at all three, only 20 to 25 percent of students typically completed the entire process. Most community colleges have similar rates because of hurdles students encounter as they attempt to transition *through* their academic programs.

There are many ways to look at this part of the student journey. I find the Guided Pathways (GP) framework very helpful. Guided Pathways is an approach to supporting students as they move through their program. It is an approach that is used by many two- and four-year institutions. With a holistic perspective, GP integrates support services and academic programs with clearly defined pathways that help students move through the entire college experience successfully.

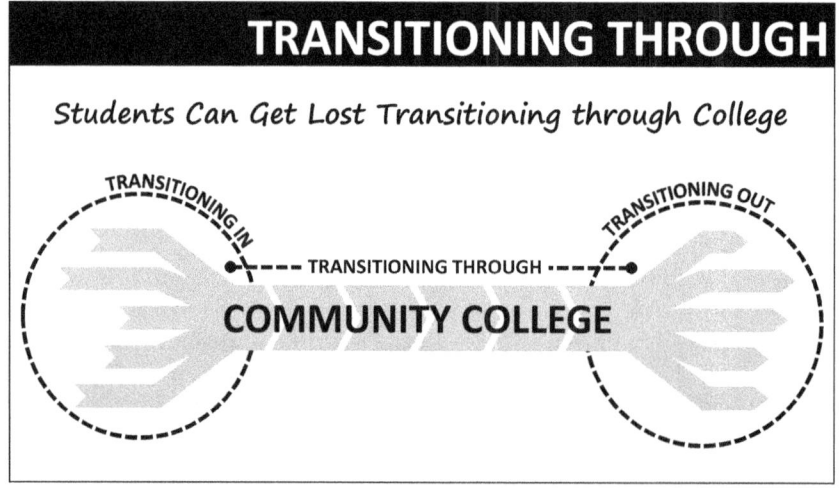

The Guided Pathways framework has been in development for several years. The first expression of GP started in 2004 with a program known as Achieving the Dream (ATD). Funded initially by the Lumina Foundation, the program addressed some of the issues that have become center pieces of GP work, including completion, equity, and overall college performance. By 2009, the Bill & Melinda Gates Foundation was involved with ATD and began adding components that became collectively known as the Developmental Education Initiative (DEI). DEI added a focus on developmental education reform. Throughout these developments, the Community College Research Center at Columbia University was involved on the research side, helping assess the effectiveness of these efforts. With their findings and additional funding from the Bill and Melinda Gates Foundation, the Completion by Design (CBD) initiative was launched in 2011. This program pushed deeper into college design work for greater student improvement. By 2015, the three programs amounted to a grand experiment in community college education techniques, generating significant findings that led to an important study, by Bailey, Jaggars, and Jenkins, called *Redesigning America's Community Colleges*. This is the book that brought us the Guided Pathways framework (Community College Research Center, 2015).

Guided Pathways presents an overarching strategy that attempts to fix what Bailey, Jaggars, and Jenkins call the "cafeteria model" of education. They claim that community colleges and many large state colleges used this model from the 1960s through 1990s to increase college-going rates (access) as a primary goal. To get people in the door, a large menu of flexible courses and programs were offered in an attempt meet any need (the cafeteria model). These models were developed with so much flexibility that they eventually became confusing. As a result, we ended up with colleges that are much better at bringing students into the institution than they are at getting students through the institution. Today, most students in cafeteria-model schools find it difficult to navigate through their colleges effectively. This is especially true for first-generation students. GP calls for colleges to reengineer the loose collections of courses and programs into tight, clear pathways that narrow student options but improve clarity and completion success.

The GP approach is often explained using four *pillars* that correspond with four big challenges students face when trying to move *through* our institutions. First, students find it difficult to see the entire path that they must follow. They need to see what is required of them from the first class to the last class and how they are going to build a coherent plan over a few years to complete that path in a timely fashion. There are several reasons such a path is cloudy at so many institutions. First, we do not do multi-year scheduling at the vast majority of colleges. In fact, I do not know of one community college that does this. We are just now moving in the direction of some colleges offering a one-year schedule, which is a step in the right direction. This means that students can build a two- or three-year plan to follow. In our current approach to scheduling, students select courses one semester or term at a time and hope their program's requirements will line up in a coherent way as they move forward. On top of this, schedules are frequently built around faculty preferences rather than students' needs. This practice commonly results in schedules where classes are piled up in *prime time* slots, limiting the ability for students to take all the courses they need. The result is semesters added to the two-year certificate or degree program.

More time is often lost in completing basic skills requirements in states with large basic skills requirements, with many students assessed into very low levels of math and English. This placement practice turns the two-year college into a four- or five-year experience, stacking years of basic skills education in front of students and creating a sense of discouragement from the outset.

On the curriculum and program development side, university and community college independence has been great for institutions and faculty who develop programs, but this independence has created tremendous confusion for students trying to develop a course sequence plan at their community college that matches all the different four-year transfer requirements that have evolved because of institutional autonomy.

During lean budget times—community colleges are chronically lean—we often schedule classes that do not have enough seats to accommodate all the students who what to enroll, as we must limit the number of classes the college can afford under its reduced budget. Also, unit requirement bloat in community college programs has allowed for more nuanced courses that enrich student learning, but this phenomenon has added more unit requirements to the student journey than is necessary and literally made it harder for students to move through our colleges. Add to all of this anachronistic technology that students do not recognize, and it is not difficult to see why so many student struggle to get *through* our colleges.

The second major challenge students face as they try to transition *through* our colleges is selecting a pathway. This is often referred to as *selecting a major*. The sooner this can be done, the more likely students are to make practical progress toward completion. There are several reasons this challenge exists. For one, first-generation students typically do not have knowledge of professions, and nearly all students lack awareness of emerging technical skill trades. First-generation students usually come from families and communities with few adults that have professional careers. Consequently, as these students move through their formative years, they do not see engineers, attorneys, physicians, CPAs, legislators, and similar professions inside their families. This makes it difficult for many of them to have a personal affinity with these careers and certainly obscures the routes to achieving them. With regard to emerging technical fields, these are unknown to many of us, let alone students. For this reason, choosing majors that prepare for these fields is particularly difficult. In the classroom of our traditional academic programs (social sciences, humanities, natural sciences, etc.), we are not making the employment connections to our disciplines effectively enough.

Some argue correctly that requiring students in their late teens to select majors that determine their professional careers is not consistent with human development. When I was in my late teens and exploring majors, I was completely unaware of my intellectual strengths and weaknesses and not ready to make effective decisions along those lines, and many freshmen and sophomores are in the same boat. This has led to criticism of our specific majors at the community college and a movement toward meta-majors that get students to select programs in more general directions rather than detailed career commitments. To accommodate these challenges, students would benefit greatly from career-based counseling, but the student-to-counselor ratios at community colleges have made this objective impossible to scale across the student body. These and other issues have created an environment that makes the important decision of which path to enter a difficult one for students.

Third, students who have selected and started down a path often deviate from it. A change in a student's educational goal can derail completion entirely but at a minimum will lengthen the time it takes to move *through*. Deviation from the path that leads to our goals is not unique to college students. It is a struggle we all face throughout our lives. Nonetheless, we need to help students keep to their plan to move *through* and need to be particularly attentive to first-generation students who have limited academic capital in their private lives playing this role. One of the reasons so many students get off track is our tracking systems. We are not doing a very good job of aggregating our data about student progress and leveraging them to know where students are on their journeys. On top of that, our student-to-counselor ratios are so high that we don't have enough counselors to do the tracking or intervene in meaningful ways with all the students who are struggling to progress through a pathway. With a greater number of counselors, or more efficient systems, we could enact a more intrusive counseling model, but without the capacity, we must move toward a passive model where we wait for students to come to us. Without this intrusion, students often make pathway progress decisions on their own. If they can't find a course they need, they look for alternatives that often do not satisfy their degree or certificate requirements. Many of the problems discussed previously (inconvenient schedules, insufficient courses) exacerbate these trends, leaving too many of our students off path and meandering toward completion.

Finally, too many students move *through* the path but go through the motions in such a way that they complete courses without learning sufficiently. As a former faculty member, I find this failing frustrating. Faculty spend hours preparing materials for the classroom, and to have students receive the content in a merely transactional manner, for only performance on an exam, can be discouraging. At the same time, I understand that imperfect learning is part of the development process. Many students (especially younger students) do not understand the intrinsic value of learning and often do not see the competitive necessity that deeper learning will bring to their future job search.

One of my daughters struggled with this casual attitude towards learning for a while. She found the learning process stale and boring, characterizing it as a series of assignments and requirements she needed to complete to reach her degree. She, like me, needed a few years of college-going experience to discovery the discipline that ignited her joy of learning. Helping students learn more deeply is essential to moving students *through* our colleges. We do not want to incentivize faculty and support staff to lower the learning requirements as a strategy for generating greater success. That would be a highly irresponsible. Instead, we need to make sure deep learning is a goal and be sensitive to all the issues in students' lives that keep them from learning effectively. Study habits, complicated personal lives, difficulty seeing the *learning-to-earning* connection, poor high school preparation, and financial burdens with purchasing books are real hurdles in students' lives that inhibit learning. We need to be fully conscious of these and more as we look to construct solutions that mitigate, if not eliminate, these challenges.

Transitioning OUT

Transitioning out of the community college, completing community college work, can be confusing for students. Most students attending community college intend to transfer to a four-year institution. As they prepare for this tranition, they are presented with a range

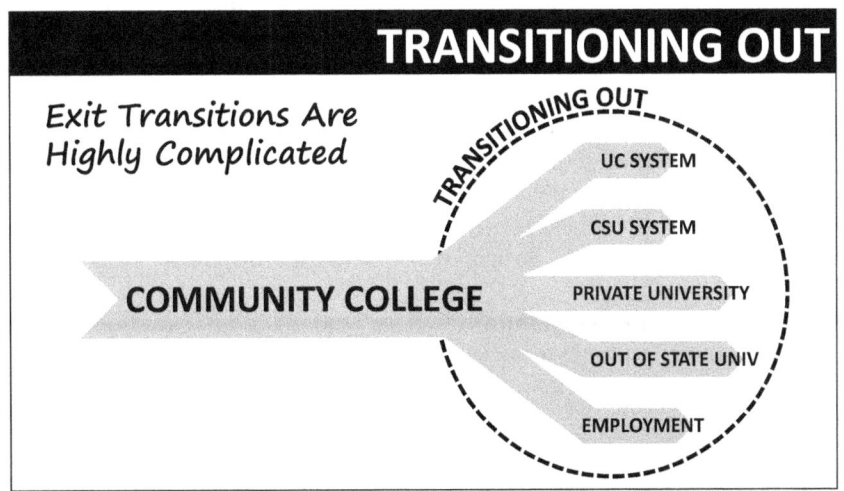

of options. At a few community colleges in the country, students can continue at their community college to finish a handful of bachelor's degrees, but most students must decide on whether they want to transfer to a public institution inside the state, a public institution outside of the state, or a private institution anywhere in the United States. As students prepare, they are confronted with a range of conflicting requirements and different bureaucratic processes required for entry into these institutions. A smaller group of community college students, but still a significant proportion, are focused on completing a degree or certificate that will lead directly to employment. These students are then faced with the same transitional struggles that bachelor's degree and graduate degree students face upon graduation. They must figure out how to move into the job market.

Transitioning From Community College to University

In 2015–16, 2,355,350 students enrolled in the 115 California community colleges (California Community College Chancellor's Office, 2020c). Three years later, in the 2017–18 academic year, 160,823 students completed an associate degree and, based on my experience at three community colleges in California, certainly tens of thousands achieved transfer readiness with regard to units completed (data on transfer readiness are not readily available at the California State data mart).[1] Given these numbers, I estimate that in 2017–18, over 200,000 students reached eligibility for transfer to four-year institutions, having completed associate degrees or accumulated enough units to transfer. But only 93,934 transferred.

TRANSFER

In 2018, nearly 94,000 CA community college students transferred to 4-institutions

	2017-18
University of California (e.g., UCLA)	18,703
California State University (e.g., San Jose State)	49,910
In-State Private (e.g., Stanford)	9,590
Out-of-State Public or Private (e.g., NYU)	15,731
Total Transfers	93,934

My experience at previous community colleges suggests that about half of students who are eligible to transfer from a two-year institution to a four-year institution actually complete the process, and the CA Chancellor's Data Mart numbers appear to readily match this rate for the entire state.

It is true that some community college students intend to complete their education with a terminal associate degree and move directly into the workforce. For example, many fire fighters hold only AA/AS degrees in addition to completing their fire academy training. But students who plan to end their education with an AA (or certificate) are in the minority. At most community colleges in California, they make up about 15% to 20% of the student population, with the rest (80% to 85%) indicating the intention to complete a bachelor's degree or higher. So why do so few students transfer once they become eligible?

There are several reasons community college students do not transfer at higher rates. One of them is the complications associated with unit and program planning. Students

---

1. The California Community College Chancellors Office Data Mart offers a range of data for the state community college system. It can be found at https://datamart.cccco.edu/datamart.aspx.

who start at a four-year institution have much fewer complications. When they declare a major, they are presented with a single clear and sequenced set of courses required to complete that major. For example, a student at San Diego State University who declares a psychology major must complete the program requirements for San Diego State, and that is all. She does not need to consider the requirements at other institutions.

Students at community colleges, on the other hand, are caught in a much more complicated web. For example, a student at Norco College (a two-year community college in California) who declares a psychology major needs to plan on several different program options because, while she knows her major, she does not know which university will accept her for transfer. Consequently, she needs to prepare for several schools. With this in mind, students often prepare plans for transfer to schools in the California State University system, schools in the University of California system, and maybe a few private universities, or out-of-state schools. This community college student prepares one plan for transfer to the CSUs because they have moved toward system-wide agreement on the most popular programs. But for the UC system schools, the private schools, and the out-of-state schools, this student must complete slightly different course requirements for each because these institutions have not agreed upon a common transfer package.

TRANSFER PLAN EXAMPLE

Cal State San Bernardino (CSU System)	1st Program Plan
Cal State LA (CSU System)	
Fullerton State (CSU System)	
Long Beach State (CSU System)	
CSU San Marcos (CSU System)	
UCLA (UC System)	2nd Program Plan
UC Riverside (UC System)	3rd Program Plan
UC Santa Barbara (UC System)	4th Program Plan
USC (Private)	5th Program Plan
University of Redlands (Private)	6th Program Plan
Occidental College (Private)	7th Program Plan
Arizona State University (Out-of State)	8th Program Plan

With this approach, we have literally made it easier to complete college at institutions that tend to serve students who are disproportionately White and from higher-income families. In contrast, we have made it more difficult to complete college at institutions that disproportionately serve students from disfavored communities. This is a classic example of institutional bias. It is education policy that discriminates against students of color and lower-income students. I firmly believe nearly all of the decision-makers involved in establishing such policy are not racist; however, they have collectively made a decision that generates racial and class bias.

Some states are trying to eliminate such bias. As mentioned previously, California has made some progress with the CSU transfer process through legislation. Connecticut has done some legislative work in this area, and so has Texas, but both states are still working on implementation details and facing some pushback from select four-year institutions. The state that appears to be furthest along is Florida. Through legislative leadership, the state has developed a common course numbering system and has required a number of measures that simplify the transfer process. These changes appears to be working. Over the last ten years, significantly more Aspen Award community colleges have come from the state of Florida than any other state.

Complications relating to transfer are not only confusing, but they result in loss of time and momentum for community college students (our most at-risk students in higher education), as they are required to take more units during their freshman and sophomore years than their colleague students at four-year institutions. When a recent study at Gateway Community College in New Haven, Connecticut, tracked 479 of its students who transferred from Connecticut community colleges to the University of Connecticut, it found that these students had spent time accumulating significantly more credit units than they needed. On average, the students completed 54.17 credits at their respective community colleges. Upon transferring, the University of Connecticut recognized an average of only 42.57 credits per student, applying the units toward GE or major credit. In Texas, a similar study found that students transfer after completing 80 to 90 credits, while only 45 were required by the four-year institution they transferred to (Smith, 2015).

Adding additional units to the community college experience can create another complication. It can push a student's completion timeline out of sequence with many of the universities. In California, for example, most of the UCs and CSUs accept transfers only for the fall term. Many students end up finishing their community college coursework in December because of the additional unit requirements and are subsequently forced to wait an additional eight or nine months before the fall transfer window opens. One of my daughters ran into this situation, having to push back transfer to a five-year institution by eight months because she was one course short of the requirements.

The lack of coordination between community colleges and four-year institutions has a range of reasons related to different missions, misaligned traditions, dispersed governing bodies, academic freedom, and others. Regardless of the reason, this fundamental breakdown is hurting community college students.

Transitioning From Community College to Jobs

I was a faculty member in the political science department for 19 years. My expertise was at the intersection of governance and technology. My dissertation was on this topic. I published a few papers on this topic, did a significant amount of consulting in the area, and was a speaker on the topic at a number of regional and national meetings. As a community college professor, however, my teaching focused mostly on introduction to American government courses and a few other introductory subjects. These courses did not give me a chance to teach deeply in my area of expertise, so I eventually developed a course on governance and technology. The course focused on strategic issues government employees should consider in deploying technology to deliver government services and expand civic engagement. The course was timely in the sense that the internet was emerging, but government agencies did not uniformly understand its best applications. I decided to offer the course exclusively online and marketed it to cities, counties, special districts, tribal governments, and federal and state agencies.

Given the timeliness of the topic and the applied approach, I soon had a full class, with students from all over the country, even a few employees from foreign governments. The program grew, receiving more and more attention from government employees and career-technical educators. Because of the success, I was eventually named California Educator of the Year by the California Community College Association for Occupational Education. This award helped create buzz around the program off and on campus.

Around this time, I had a surprising encounter with a fellow faculty member. I was getting a bite to eat and a cup of coffee in the break room when a colleague came in to do the same. She was an historian I had known for a while. I was on her hiring committee, shared an office with her for one year, enjoyed her company, and respected her contribution to the college. She was someone I would describe as thoughtful, intelligent, and kind. After she collected her food from the refrigerator, she turned to me and said, "You know the technology course that you developed and have been teaching?" I said, "Yes," thinking she was going to offer something constructive or maybe even complementary. She went on, "CTE [career technical education] courses like this one lower the quality of our academic program and I think you should reconsider offering the course." I was truly surprised. The course and everything involved with developing it had taken an enormous amount of energy. I didn't know how to respond. She left. I was irritated—it still irritates me as I write this.

I have been doing community college work for 30 years, watching CTE programs generally outperform the more traditional academic programs. CTE programs typically have better retention rates, better completion and graduation rates, better job placement rates, and eventually higher salary rates than other programs. In spite of this, they continue to be placed in some kind of second-tier citizen category at our institutions. They are considered by many personnel less academically rigorous and therefore less important to the academy. And because they tend to be more expensive (e.g., nursing instruction is much more expensive than sociology instruction), there tends to be fewer CTE faculty on campus. For these reasons, CTE does not get the kind of attention on our campuses that it should. I will admit to being in this opposing camp for a long time. It took me several years to see the value these programs offer our students.

It is predicted that by 2030, 1.9 million new job openings in California will require CTE skills at the certificate or AA degree level. In other words, 30% of all California job openings in 2030 will need applicants with technical training that exceeds the high school diploma but does not require a bachelor's degree. Our middle skills training infrastructure is primarily supported by community colleges and currently does not have enough capacity to deliver on this need (DeVol, 2016). CTE program development and enrollment in these programs is critical to our economy, and because there will be so many jobs in these areas, we need to do a better job of both expanding our CTE capacity and encouraging more students to move in these directions.

Career technical education is one of the important functions of community colleges in American society. Nearly all community colleges in the country include this branch of education in their mission. CTE programs are state and federally funded programs that focus on occupational skill development through certificate or AA/AS degree completions. Federally recognized CTE sectors are funded primarily through the Perkins program and include 16 industry clusters (or sectors): health science, business, sales, finance, IT, STEM, manufacturing, logistics, hospitality, government, law, agriculture, human services, construction, training, and the arts (Applied Educational Systems, 2019). Many state-funded programs also recognize similar sector categories with emphasis placed on industries that are prominent in their states. There are many CTE programs spread across community colleges. Among the most familiar examples are nursing, automotive, police academy, fire academy, allied health specialties, and logistics. Community colleges tend to develop programs that fit their regional economy. Through this approach, college personnel are able to build relationships with regional employers, build programs that meet the needs of these employers, and place students into these jobs.

CTE education has some very strong indicators of success. According to Applied Educational Systems, with CTE institutions on the rise and CTE graduates increasing, the United States now has over four million post-secondary students studying or interested in studying CTE disciplines. This is a national phenomenon, with the highest number of CTE degrees coming out of California, Florida, Texas, New York, and Illinois. Job opportunities are increasing in these fields, and students who enter these jobs experience significant pay increases. In fact, students who earn CTE certificates or complete training of between 7 and 17 credit units increase their earnings on average by about 14 percent, while students who earn CTE-related AA degrees at 60 or more credit units increase their earnings by about 45 percent (Stevens, Kurlaender, & Grosz, 2018).

This book has focused on many challenges that historically underserved students face. CTE education may be one of the areas where we are finding success nationwide. CTE education is a pathway that is growing and helping students successfully transition from *learning to earning*. There are many reasons for this increased success. Several scholars in higher education have called for a focus on how education connects to jobs. Also, the call from industry for more trained technical workers is driving a better connection between educators and employers. On campuses, tight cohort models used in many CTE programs keeps completion rates very high. For students, the focus on finding employment rather than learning a discipline helps them develop usable skills that lead to jobs. In addition, student-to-faculty ratios are often more ideal in CTE programs. And there are other reasons for the success of CTE programs.

Because CTE programs in our community colleges are generally more successful with students than the traditional academic disciplines, we need to look to them as models of expertise and best practices, extending their approaches across disciplines that struggle to help students from historically underserved communities.

Discussion of Solutions

Students encounter a range of confusing processes as they move through their journey. Transitioning *in, through*, and *out* presents a set of challenges that often disrupt their journeys, leaving too many students with incomplete experiences. The strategies discussed in the following help students—especially students from disfavored communities—complete their journeys with greater success.

Strategy #22: Implement Guided Pathways

To reduce the confusion in our open-ended, option-heavy, self-directed educational systems, Guided Pathways has emerged as an important framework. The framework suggests an important philosophical shift, away from "preparing students for college" and toward "preparing colleges for students." GP asks us to shift from the idea that college is complicated and only the hardest-working and most resolved students survive to an attitude that says we need to make the processes associated with moving through college more intuitive for all students.

According to EAB (EAB.org), the work of making our colleges more intuitive usually requires significant institutional change around eight core areas:

- Onboarding Guidance is critical because of the considerable confusion our students face with a mix or uncoordinated processes currently required to start college. To help them through these processes, they need significant guidance.
- Progress Tracking helps students know where they are as they move through our institutions and helps us know where they are along their pathway so we can intervene.
- Meta-Majors are broad majors like humanities, social sciences, and natural sciences. Meta-majors give students a chance to declare a major (this helps with tracking) without requiring students to know exactly what they want to do with their lives. Young students in particular need time to think about what they might want to major in, and meta-majors provide a nice compromise between structure and flexibility.
- Degree Maps provide students with clear courses and sequences that are required to compete their majors. The maps must focus on the minimum number of required units and resist unit bloat.
- Proactive Advising is an approach where counselors go to students when they are needed rather than the more typical passive advising approach where counselors wait for students to come to them.
- Relevant Resources must be personalized for students. Our colleges are filled with a range of programs, services, clubs, organizations, and so on. We must do a better

job of directing these resources to our students based on relevancy. For example, we do not need to pound every student with an invitation to the Transfer Center. Only transfer-intended students and students nearing transfer need to be alerted to this service. Telling every student about every service and requiring every student to discover every service are both bad strategies.

- <u>Course Milestones</u> help us track students while they are completing the work of the term. Without these measures, we often do not know about student struggles until it is too late.
- <u>Optimized Schedules</u> are schedules built around students' needs rather than faculty preferences. Optimized schedules maximize the odds of a student's ability to find the classes they need to complete their programs on time.

These eight characteristics have demonstrated observable success through a range of strategies across the country at two-year and four-year institutions. GP has a growing body of evidence demonstrating success for students and has generated impressive results for institutions that have implemented the strategy at scale. Florida State University and Georgia State University, City Colleges of Chicago, CUNY's Guttman College, and Miami Dade College are some of the colleges that have seen impressive results. With documented implementation in Tennessee, Indiana, Georgia, Arkansas, Florida, Massachusetts, Michigan, New Jersey, Texas, California, and Washington (Community College Research Center, 2015), GP is a strategy to seriously consider.

Strategy #23: Develop Intuitive Systems

A major challenge associated with each transition is systems development. With elegant systems in place, completing processes necessary for transitions can be more intuitive and generate greater success for students. There are three primary challenges associated with systems development for these transitions:

- Data collection, integration, and coordination
- Turning data into usable information that helps track/nudge students through the transition is critical
- Packaging the information in a usable interface that maximizes communication with students.

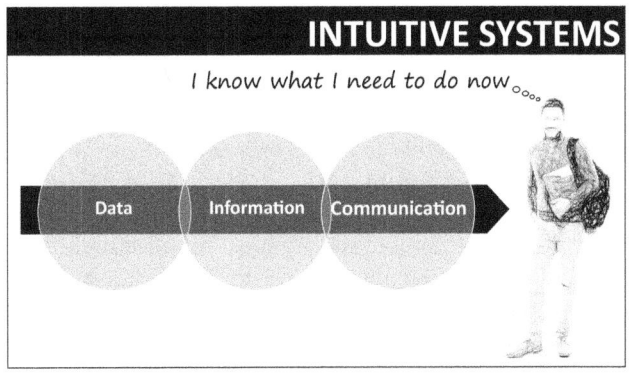

Leveraging large data sets ("Big Data") to create information about customers has been a corporate staple for at least a decade. Higher education recognizes the potential benefits of this strategy with regard to student success, but institutions struggle with effective implementation. There are at least five significant hurdles standing in the way of intersegmental data sharing: 1) privacy concerns, 2) historic misuse of data, 3) dirty data, 4) dispersed data ownership, and 5) technical challenges.

The goal is to capture student-related data, drop them into some kind of data mart, analyze the data, and turn them into information that helps the student understand how to be more successful and helps the institution understand how to intervene in ways that elicit greater success. The data exist in our student information systems (SIS), financial aid and data systems, learning management tools, personnel files, contact data sets, and a range of other large and similar systems that contain information about students. For some reason, we are comfortable about collecting student information in these individual systems; however, when discussions turn to connecting systems for a more holistic view of students, privacy concerns are often raised. This usually occurs under the umbrella of FERPA (1974), and is often used to shut down further discussion of data integration. It is important to acknowledge that FERPA is intended to protect the privacy of students, but the act and subsequent rulings on the act have clarified how institutions can integrate data systems and who can be classified by the institution as "school officials" with legal access to student information under the guidelines of FERPA. In other words, there is a clear pathway institutions can take to comply with FERPA and integrate students' data for the purposes of improving student success.

Another inhibitor to aggregating data is the fear that they will be used in a punitive manner. Higher education has a long history of weaponizing data as a disciplinary tool against faculty. This fear causes so many faculty unions to be wary about supporting the practice. Student success data mapped to the division, department, program, or individual faculty member can be used one of two ways. They can be used in a punitive manner to go after low performers, or they can be used as a resource to provide individuals/programs/departments with information that enlightens and helps improve practices. The potential for data to be used against faculty is often a cultural issue in institutions. Like all practices that can be harmful to any campus group, it comes from a history with a set of unofficial rules that guides practice. Moving from a "data as punishment" culture to a "data as resource" culture can be difficult, but this change must be initiated to ensure the collaboration needed in any data integration effort.

Dirty data have been another problem I have encountered in many data integration projects. When I was vice president of academic affairs, one of the projects I was working on was the organization and integration of our curriculum data. Like many colleges, we had cobbled together disparate processes over the years and ended up with a system where curriculum data were hand-entered into five different systems. Instead of entering data once into one system that was shared with all the others, the data were hand-entered each time. With data entry, human error is inevitably a problem. When the process is repeated five times, the probable number of errors is increased by five times, and the amount of time it takes to clean the data is correspondingly increased by five times (at least). This problem is a quality issue shared across higher education and most often revealed during data integration projects.

All of the systems spread across these segments that need to be integrated are often controlled by different authorities within each organization and across segments and ultimately by competing governing boards of each institution. Within an organization, one group may control the student financial data, another the student contact information. A range of faculty control mid-semester academic information, while admissions and records controls transcript information, and so on. With regard to interagency coordination, high school data are ultimately controlled by the unified school district, military education information is partly controlled by the Department of Defense and partly by Veterans Affairs, industry information is controlled by the employers, community college information is controlled by the Board of Trustees, and four-year institution data are controlled by the Board of Regents or Trustees. This makes for a very difficult logistics and political challenge.

Once we have met the considerable challenge of integrating data, once we have integrated databases with custom architectures, different programming languages, unique nomenclatures, varying storage strategies, contractual limitations on sharing, and more, we still have the challenge of turning the data into usable information, information that nudges students forward and supports them through their transitions. Dumping all these data into what Kenneth Green calls a "Data Gumbo" allows us to analyze these data and turn them into consumable information for students. But while this concept is easy to understand, it is very difficult to actually do (Green, 2018).

This challenge is critical. While a "Data Gumbo" is a necessary first step, it is difficult to use. Data analysts who have specific skills are typically needed to pull information from large data sets of this nature. An integrated data set of this nature is useful to researchers; however, we need to turn the data into information that students and support staff can easily use. We need these systems to readily identify where students are in their journeys, where they are in these transitions, and intervene accordingly. This challenge calls for great user interface design.

We need to make relevant data easily available to end users. When I was in college, personal computing was emerging, so I decided to take a course to see if I could learn how to use one. The course was basically an introduction to DOS (disc operating system). DOS was the interface that Microsoft licensed to IBM to control its machines. DOS was very confusing. It required the user to learn a wide range of commands to instruct the computer to carry out a series of functions. In the class, I felt like I was learning a new language, I struggled early on and ended up dropping the course.

A few years later, a friend of mine started talking to me about a new Mac Lab that had been opened up on campus and kept encouraging me to go to the lab with him. I was initially reluctant to go, with the DOS experience still fresh in my mind. One day he nearly forced me to go with him. I agreed and found myself hooked from the moment I turned the machine on. With only a little help from my friend and no instructor, I found the interface so intuitive I was able to use the machine almost effortlessly. To delete a file, all you needed to do was *drag* it to a trash can. To turn text into bold, all you had to do was highlight and click on the *bold* icon. This simplification was from the genius of Steve Jobs. One of the great skills attributed to Jobs was his recognition of the user experience and how important it was to the success of computer usage. His ability to understand the user experience changed personal computing forever with the development of GUI (graphical user interface), making personal computing accessible to mass audiences.

Steve Jobs was not a pleasant person to work for as the GUI was developed for the Mac. Taking something very complicated (personal computer) and making it simple to use (GUI) is difficult work. But this work and attention to the user experience made all the difference. This is what we need to do with the data we collect on behalf of students. We need to take a pile of information that is stored in complex ways and turn into something very easy for students and college personnel to use. We need to do this with the understanding that it is easy to make things difficult and difficult to make things easy.

Strategy #24: Establish High School Partnerships

One of the most important transitions to get right is the high school to community college transition. Most students entering community college come directly out of high school. Active partnerships with local high schools and local unified school districts (USDs) are critical to engineering a better transition. Our goal should be to create a transition process that is as smooth as moving from middle school to high school. This process should be assumed as a service to most graduating students and supported at a very high level.

Most community colleges have a presence on their area high school campuses throughout the year, especially toward the end of spring, as graduating students need to start thinking about college registration. Our presence is usually represented by outreach and admissions personnel looking to promote the college and encourage applications. Sometimes the presence is extended to counseling staff, who can help with onboarding requirements such as assessment testing and initial schedule planning. An area where we need to start doing more systematic work is with regard to data sharing. One of the reasons the middle school to high school transition is seamless is data sharing. Having all students in the same USD means that all the student data are in one data set and easy to move from one institution to the next. Data sharing agreements can help establish a similar connection between the high school and the community college. I have helped organize such agreements, and they were not that difficult to establish. High school leaders want more students to attend college, and as long as there is room to grow, community colleges want more students. Automatically enrolling students through shared data is a way to make the process extremely easy for graduating high schoolers.

Some states have already taken steps in this direction, as a trend in high school and community college partnerships is taking place to offer dual enrollment. Through dual enrollment, colleges are able to offer college-level (i.e., transferrable) courses on high school campuses, and students can take one (or more) of these courses (often free of charge) to receive both high school and college credit. This is a strategy that helps lower the intimidation factor of college for many high school students, helps lower the cost of college, and shortens the amount of time needed to complete college for many. Through dual enrollment programs, it is not uncommon for high school students to complete a semester of college work while they are in high school. This is a great way to build the relationship and improve the transition from high school to community college. Dual-enrolled students receive support from high school staff and college staff, the staff members build better relationships, and the college is able to expand outreach by being on high school campuses. This partnership is an approach where everyone wins.

Middle colleges are also an increasing phenomenon in the relationship between high schools and community colleges. Middle colleges take dual enrollment to the next level by establishing an actual high school that partners with the college to offer a significant amount of the college curriculum as part of the high school experience. While president of Norco College, I had the privilege of co-managing JFK High School, the largest middle college in California, with 600 students enrolled from 9th through 12th grade. The high school is located on college property, although separated from the main campus by a large parking lot. Students spend most of their day together on the JFK campus, taught by faculty who are employed by the local unified school district. Throughout the day, students are able to take some of their classes at Norco College. When they do this, they walk across the parking lot and sit in college classes with college students.

JFK started in 2006–2007 under a swirl of controversies and concerns expressed by the college faculty, many of whom feared that this program would lower the intellectual rigor in their courses and bring the overall emotional/development levels down in a manner that would negatively impact the college experience for other students. Now, more than a decade into this partnership, the contrary has become clear. With a long waiting list of families trying to enter JFK, their students are consistently among the higher performing at the college. Faculty speak fondly of having them in class, and the results are difficult to deny. The 2019 graduating class at JFK had 179 graduates walk across stage to receive their high school diplomas, and 172 of these students completed at least one college course while they were in high school. Sixty-four completed the equivalent of their freshman year of college (30 semester units) while in high school. And 21 completed an AA degree, making them eligible to enter college as juniors. Middle colleges are wonderful.

Strategy #25: Develop Solutions for Military Training Articulation

There are over 25,000 occupational specialties with corresponding trainings/courses offered by the five branches of the military service. We need a national solution that will map the training of sailors, soldiers, marines, and airmen to the academic curriculum of our community colleges. Military personnel complete rigorous training and coursework for their military specializations. In the Navy, for example, these are referred to as Navy Enlisted Classifications (NECs); in the Marine Corp, they are referred to as military occupational specialties. Training and courses for these specialties are at very high levels, equal to or exceeding many college courses. But when our active duty personnel (and vets) enroll in college, they usually get credit for just one physical education course. This practice does not give our men and women in uniform the credit they deserve, and it prolongs their time to graduation, which is not only a waste of time but of money.

As discussed earlier in this chapter, I first became aware of this problem when I was vice president of instruction at Crafton Hills College through the fire academy. The process that most colleges use to grant credit to men and women in uniform is highly ineffective. The American Council on Education has evaluated thousands of military occupation specialties and has made recommendations for college course credit. These recommendations are the result of painstaking work and have some value, but, as stated previously, they are general (e.g., three units of computer science), and not specific (e.g., CSC 1A at a specific college). To be awarded college credit, currently each active duty or veteran student must first apply to a college, then meet with a counselor to evaluate their Joint Services Transcript and make their case for articulation. The counselor then confers with discipline faculty and communicates the result to the student several days or weeks later. This time-consuming, confusing, and inconsistent process is repeated with every active duty or veteran applicant, for every course, at every college.

When I became president of Norco College, I was eager to address this challenge. For two years, we worked on the development of a program to map NEC and MOS training to college curriculum through a solution we eventually named MAP (Military Articulation Program). MAP takes the 25,000+ occupational specialties and related training/courses offered by the five branches and matches each to college courses. MAP does this by connecting ACE recommendations with college course catalogs over an intuitive user interface that allows faculty to easily evaluate a student's military training and grant credit for specific courses. These articulations are stored and shared with other MAP-enabled colleges. Faculty can adopt articulations from other colleges with similar courses and automatically send tailored offer letters to active-duty men and women or vets based on program, zip code, and NEC/MOS.

MAP is slowly emerging with a handful of colleges and needs to be accelerated as a nation-wide solution so we can collectively give our veterans the credit they deserve.

Strategy #26: Connect Careers to Learning

One of the ways we make transitioning to community college easier for working adults and many high school students is with programs that are tied to jobs in our regional economy. In Chapter 1, we discussed the changing economy. Led by globalization and digital technology, jobs have evolved dramatically in the last few decades, and the skill sets employers are looking for in their employees have changed accordingly. Today there are "20th century jobs" that remain, but they have flat wages and declining opportunities, whereas the "21st century jobs" are expanding with regard to wages and opportunity.

These changes need an urgent response from community colleges. There are tens of millions of working adults in these old economy jobs. We need to lure them into programs (community college workforce development programs) that help them retrain and reposition into careers with the promise of growth. We also need to attract the 30 to 35 percent of recent high school graduates nation-wide who do not attend college (Education Data, 2020). Without some kind of certification related to skills in the new economy, these students will struggle. Elegant workforce development programs and integration of *learning to earning* across our curriculum will help these two large populations transition more successfully into community colleges and into jobs with sustainable incomes.

Understanding the general strategy behind workforce development starts with understanding the significance of being a *community* college. One of the critical distinguishers between a community college and a four-year college or university is in the word *community*. Community colleges serve a region, and part of that service must be toward economic development, usually expressed as workforce development. In every region, there are industries that can be classified in three ways related to promise for students: 1) declining industries with substandard wages, 2) stable industries that continue to grow and provide livable wages, and 3) emerging industries that show significant promise for growth and sustainable jobs. Community colleges need to have a close relationship with all the stable and emerging industries in their region that offer jobs to individuals with technical training at the certificate or AA/AS degree levels. A comprehensive community college should offer AA/AS or certificate-level training for each of these industries as a workforce development solution for the region. Through these programs, we prepare new students and working adults for the entry-level jobs in these industries. The larger goal associated with this effort for a community college is to become *the* primary source of new hires in the stable and emerging industries across the college's service area.

Establishing strategic industry partnerships in the college's service is critical to success and of course aligned with the mission of most community colleges. The entire workforce development leadership team needs to build workforce-related partnerships in our communities. This objective includes community outreach to targeted industries and their respective leaders by working directly with businesses or indirectly with each business through affiliate organizations such as the chamber of commerce. With business partners on board, programs can be developed.

The most common type of workforce development program provides instruction toward a certificate or AA/AS degree. In developing these programs, the community college must develop programs that are in alignment with stable and emerging industries in its service area. In this sense, the college needs to think of itself as continually developing industry sector expertise. Most regions have industry sectors that are prominent or projected to grow. The mix of sectors in each college's services area is unique, so there is no set curriculum that every community college should adopt. Leadership at the college should know these sectors and the most prominent people in these sectors. Through relationships with regional business and industry, the college can make sure that regional sector needs and academic programs are aligned. Community colleges should have the highest level of expertise in training students for the jobs that are in these sectors. The community college should be seen as the primary source of early career technical talent for the prominent and emerging sectors in the region.

A growing programmatic area that should be considered by community colleges is apprenticeship education. This is an area that has great promise for workforce development and can only be developed in tight partnership with industry. Education through apprenticeships has a successful history in Europe and has seen pockets of success in the building trades in the United States. We need to expand this model to other industries, and community colleges should take the lead in this effort. California is now engaged an effort to grow community college apprentices from 50,000 to 5000,000, and several other states are moving in similar directions. Community colleges should be at the center of these programs as they are developed.

The basic idea behind apprenticeship education is that students should gain work experience while they are learning. In most apprenticeship models, students are employed (and paid) full-time under some kind of "tutor" at the worksite. Under this person's supervision, the student learns skills on the job. After work, the student then studies to learn additional information or practice skills that they will need to move beyond the level of apprentice. As regional economies change, the skills employees need change as well. Apprenticeship education is one way to address this skills gap between traditional and new or emerging skill sets.

We should also explore other areas where community colleges can contribute to workforce development. Contract education is a model some colleges use to design custom education packages for businesses or agencies in their regions. In exchange for the development of customized courses and often reduced class sized, the costs for the program tend to be much higher. Technology transfer is another area where community colleges may become involved. This is typically found at major universities (R1 universities), where the university tries to monetize its research by transferring discoveries into the marketplace. Under the Obama administration, laws were put in place allowing for and encouraging the release of military technology development. Community colleges can enter the process of helping transfer military technology to industry. For example, as incubators and accelerators are increasingly being introduced at community colleges in an effort to support and launch entrepreneurs, community colleges can add value by helping new businesses learn about publicly released military technology/solutions that can be modified for commercial purposes. Finally, granting credit for prior learning is an enticement some colleges are using to bring students into workforce development programs. With the promise of being granted college credit for learning that took place on the job or in the military, adults are more likely to enroll in career technical programs.

One of the problems many community colleges have with workforce training for new economy jobs is the lack of basic public awareness. When I was president at Norco College, we had a program that led directly to sustainable jobs in logistics. Graduates from the program had an employment rate in the high 90 percent range. Some graduating classes had a 100 percent employment rate. This success was partly due to the college being located in the Inland Empire, which has one of the largest logistics industries in the world. Because of this proximity, we had developed strong industry partnerships with the business leaders in logistics and supply chain-related industries. We had also invested significantly in instructional resources for the program. In all, it was a signature program; however, every semester, enrollment struggled. I remember thinking, "Why isn't there a registration line wrapping around the building?"

I believe the answer to this is related to the shift from old economy jobs to new economy jobs. The shift we have been making over the last few decades is hitting working-class and working poor families in particular because many of the jobs do not transfer very well. Professional class jobs have transferred over easily. For example, doing legal work or being an engineer in the old economy looks a lot like doing the same work in the new economy. There are obvious changes that the attorney and engineer have had to make, but their profession and basic practices in that profession remain. In contrast, the working class has had to transition to jobs that seem foreign to them and have no historic place in the traditions of their family. For example, coal mining is in decline, and renewable energy is on the rise. And while line workers in both fields are working in the energy business, the skill sets are widely divergent. As such, we have technical fields and blue-collar positions with openings in today's economy, but many of the families who traditionally work in these jobs from generation to generation do not recognize them, so they do not channel their children in these directions. This means as we develop technical and hands-on job training for new economy jobs, we need to communicate more clearly with the families who traditionally build careers in these areas.

As these programs are developed across campus, program expenses need to be factored into the larger campus dialogue, and budget priorities can be a difficult topic of conversation. Workforce development programs are typically expensive when compared to many of the traditional instruction courses offered on campus. For example, I taught political science for 19 years. To have an ideal teaching and learning experience in my classroom: I needed a white board, a computer with internet access, a projector or large digital screen, and moveable chairs for student collaboration. My colleagues who taught in the fire academy needed fire engines, ladders, hoses, breathing equipment, dummies, spray walls, and much more. The fire program cost significantly more than the political science program. The larger campus community must understand such resource needs as it considers the value programs provided for the community it serves.

Strategy #27: Establish Common Course Numbering and Shared GE Packages

Common course numbering could establish common course designations across higher education so students moving throughout the system (e.g., community college students transferring to a university) are able to move more intuitively and more efficiently. I spent most of my career in a state (California) with no common course numbering. As a result, I watched my students struggle through the transfer process, having to build crosswalks between the courses they took at the community college and the individual program requirements at each four-year institution they planned to transfer to. For years in California, this meant a unique crosswalk and unique set of requirements for every four-year institution, even though most of the universities were in the same system (California State University system or University of California system). As of 2018, 33 states still have confusing systems like this (Education Commission of the States, 2018). California took a step toward the other 16 states that have adopted common course numbering with the development of the ADT (Associate Degree for Transfer) program, requiring community colleges and colleges in the CSU system to recognize common course requirements by discipline. The CSUs and California Community Colleges now recognize course requirements for years one and two across multiple programs (approximately 40). With this agreement, students are able to complete 60 semester units (or 90 quarter units) at their community college and transfer to a CSU as a junior. This agreement has been very successful, as have other such agreements in the other 16 states that have adopted such practices.

Adoption of common course numbering and the subsequent GE packages that go along with this approach typically require legislation or administrative policy development. What we have not seen is grassroots recognition from faculty, departments, and collective colleges that this standardization works and therefore needs implementation. More typically, a strong legislative or other policy-making body needs to impose this standardization on the system before these autonomous and independent institutions of higher education find common and intuitive pathways for the students who must navigate these otherwise confusing transitions. With that said, this work typically needs to be sponsored by institutional leaders, board members, regents, and elected officials.

Strategy #28: Build Student-Centered Schedules

Most undergraduate students attend college with complicated private commitments in their lives making traditional college schedules difficult. Approximately 22 percent of undergraduates have children. Roughly 70 percent of these students are mothers, approximately 30 percent are fathers, and the majority of these individuals are raising their kids as single parents (Cause, Holtzman, Gault, Croom, & Polk, 2019). In addition, about 40 percent of all undergraduate students work at least 30 hours per week, and one-quarter are employed full-time (Carnevale, Smith, Melton, & Price, 2015). The full-time college student with parental funding to cover all expenses and ample time to enjoy a residential, on-campus experience is nowhere near the average experience for most college students in contemporary higher education. Most students are hustling with complicated and complex lives.

In the midst of these challenges, many colleges continue to build schedules that do not accommodate students. This problem is often caused by faculty choosing schedules that are convenient for their lives and chairs or managers who do not facilitate more collaborative and more information schedule development processes that bring students needs to the forefront. This failing often ends up lengthening the amount of time students spend in college because classes they need to graduate are not offered at times that accommodate students' complicated lives. A solution for this problem is to develop schedules built around students' needs rather than around college and university employee preferences.

When I was a faculty member, the chair of the political science department would come to me each semester with a slate of possible course offerings and ask me which I would prefer. In the early years of my career, the options were slim, as I had no seniority. As my seniority increased, my options increased. Once I became the most senior faculty member in the department, I was able to build the ideal schedule around my life. I built it around traffic, my wife's work schedule, and our kids' schedules to make our family commitments as convenient as possible. In 19 years as a faculty member, I was asked to bend my schedule around students' needs only a handful of times. When I became dean and vice president of academic affairs, I continued this practice. It was part of the tradition and kept schedule development as smooth as possible.

A few years ago, a number of faculty and managers set aside a two-day retreat to look deeply at our scheduling practices. I was president of the college and encouraged them to do this work because, while our enrollment was growing, our physical capacity for adding classes was not. We were running out of room and needed to start thinking creatively. At the retreat, we put the entire schedule on a wall. It included all the buildings, classes, times, courses, and faculty mapped out for all to see. The retreat was a success in the sense that participants figured out a way to squeeze more classes onto campus, but the big take-away from that retreat that several faculty and managers brought back was how inconvenient these schedules were for students. Many courses were piled up at the same times and on the same days, making it nearly impossible for students to take all the classes they needed efficiently. The schedule they observed was particularly difficult for students with work and family lives.

Most colleges have scheduling practices that are anachronistic and visible only from the faculty member's or the department chair's perspective. We do not have major systems in place that allow us to see the entire schedule from a student's perspective over multiple years. As a result, we build schedules that do not accommodate students' complicated lives. In this sense, we are building one of the hurdles that students must overcome to be successful. Schedule development software is emerging that helps gather student time restrictions and preferences; however, many is in early phases of development.

Strategy #29: Offer Online Courses and Services

One of the ways that we can overcome these scheduling challenges is with an expansion of online education; however, at many institutions, our traditional brick-and-mortar approach to education has created a drag on the development of these courses. They are perceived by many as less rigorous and less academic. As a result, the power structures within our institutions have not developed programs using this modality with a sense of urgency.

On the other hand, the Covid-19 pandemic forced higher education to move in this direction turning on a dime in the spring of 2020. Instruction, services, and management moved to digital environments out of public health necessities. As our institutions come back into balance, some of this learning and provision of support services will remain. College leaders need to leverage these innovations for the benefit of our students.

There are colleges that successfully moved in this direction before the pandemic. Arizona State University, for example, grew online enrollment by 600% between 2012 and 2018 (Levine, 2019). This growth was not an accident. It happened through serious academic planning, development, and management to build out online offerings that match the quality of the university's traditional offerings. As the demand for online instruction from our students expands, we need to respond with development of high-quality learning experiences that are delivered online. When substantive online learning is added to a more student-centered scheduling process, we will have lowered one of the major hurdles for students with complicated private lives.

SOLUTIONS AND STRATEGIES

22. Implement Guided Pathways
23. Develop Intuitive Systems
24. Establish High School Partnerships
25. Articulate Military Training
26. Connect Careers to Learning
27. Establish Common Course Numbers
28. Build Student-Centered Schedules
29. Offer Online Courses/Services

Conclusion

Students from historically underserved communities come to us with limited academic capital. This means they do not have access to private resources (e.g., people) who can help them navigate the confusing and thick bureaucracies we have established around institutions of higher education. This chapter has discussed a range of challenges these students encounter as they transition *in* to our institutions, transition *through* our institutions, and transition *out* of our institutions. To address these challenges, we discussed several solutions from two fronts. First, we need to use our public resources to add academic capital into our students' lives, and second, we need to consciously re-engineer our students' transitions so they are more intuitive and user friendly.

8   Placing Historically Underserved Students in Selective Universities

During my first and second years of college, I often walked back from dinner at the college cafeteria with a group of friends from Tenaya Hall at Cal Poly San Luis Obispo (a state university in central California). After a brief walk from the dining hall, we typically took a short cut through the side door of the dormitory building, walked through a large general-purpose room that was often used for studying, and made our way back to our rooms. One evening in the middle of my second year, a few of us were coming back from dinner, and as we passed through the general-purpose room, one of my friends pointed to a student sitting in the back with his head down and deep into a problem set of some sort. He said, "That guy just got accepted for transfer to U.C. Berkeley." It was a student I did not know, but I had seen him around from time to time, mostly in the same seat, with the same serious demeanor. I remember glancing at the student as my friend pointed him out. What caught my attention in that small throw-away comment, what kept rolling around in my head for several weeks, was the emphasis he had placed on the student's being accepted for transfer to Berkeley. He said it as though he was impressed.

Like many of our students in the community college, I came from a family that does not have a college-going tradition. I came from a family who loved me deeply but did not have close relatives with bachelor's degrees. In addition to that, I went to a high school where very few people went on to college. As a result, I started Cal Poly with little information about the college experience and very little knowledge about higher education in general. I mostly associated college with sports. I remember moving into the dorms for the first time and having a casual conversation with one of the resident advisors for the hall. He was also a

Cal Poly San Luis Obispo Dormitory

student but an upper classman and interested in being as helpful as possible. In a casual conversation one day, he asked if I had purchased my books for the semester. Classes were starting in a few days, and this was a fairly common question to ask an entering freshman. What I said to myself was, "You have to buy the books?" What I said to him out load was, "No, not yet." I think he could tell I was confused and offered to take me to the bookstore and show me how the process worked. As I look back on this, it is funny, but also understandable. I had spent 13 years in education (K–12) at that point, and in every single grade from the age of five, I showed up to class on the first day, and the instructor handed out the books. I assumed it would be the same at Cal Poly.

There are so many rules and so much information about higher education that first-generation students typically don't know. Their unfamiliarity with academia can make transitioning into college difficult, and we need to recognize this difficulty as educators. First-generation students don't know how financial aid works. They don't understand that you choose a major. They don't understand the difference between a community college, a state college, a public university, a private nonprofit university, a private for-profit university. These are all pockets of knowledge that can help or hinder student success. The important piece of information I did not have as we were returning from dinner, walking through the general-purpose room, and having a friend point out the student who had been accepted to Berkeley was that colleges and universities are ranked. I had no idea thank such ranking existed. I literally thought that people who wanted to go to Cal Poly (a public state college) applied and were accepted. People who wanted to go to Harvard applied and were accepted. This is why his comment about Berkeley (a very prestigious university) puzzled me.

When I discovered that there were ranking systems and academic reputations and public opinion related to the quality of education at various institutions, my competitive side, nurtured from years as an athlete, started to kick in. I had already started down the road of becoming a serious student by that time, and I wanted to know if I could compete with students from these more reputable institutions. This idea stayed with me. I started learning about university and college rankings and reputations. Through this process, I became interested in a few California universities in particular. Eventually I applied for transfer to a number of institutions and accepted an admissions offer from the University of Southern California.

At USC, I noticed a pronounced difference in the educational experience from what I was accustomed to at Cal Poly San Luis Obispo. Most of these differences can be attributed to resources. The facilities were more developed and much nicer than those at the state college I came from. The instructors had lighter loads and often smaller classes, opening up more time-intensive pedagogy options (e.g., more writing assignments). Several students I encountered had much more money in their families, with a few coming from wealth far from what I was accustomed to. The experience was at times intimidating and at other times exhilarating, with a general atmosphere of opportunity and access to professional success after graduation.

I will interject at this point that I am a little uncomfortable with the narrative I just laid out. First, I am not trying to suggest that USC is on a par with Harvard or Stanford. It certainly was not when I was applying for transfer. I am also uncomfortable with much of the ranking system that we use in the United States and how it can make people who attend other institutions feel lesser about their alma mater. Stacy Dale and Alan Krueger conducted a study a few years ago that looked at college rankings and post-graduation success to see if it makes a difference in the development of one's professional life. After controlling for SAT scores, economic background and college ambitions, their findings demonstrated that long-term financial returns are not correlated with the selectivity of the university a person attended (Dale & Krueger, 2011). In other words, students who work hard and have similar aptitudes tend to do about the same after graduation regardless of the school they attended. The study did, however, find one significant exception. When students from disfavored communities attend our most selective universities, they benefit greatly.

Identification of Barriers

This is a problem. Our most selective universities in the United States are simply not admitting community college students at significant rates. While these universities express bold language regarding support for social justice, their record of admitting students from historically underserved communities contradicts their rhetoric. Jennifer Glynn recently grouped all universities by selectivity or competitiveness, placing them into five categories: most selective, highly selective, very selective, selective, and less selective. She then analyzed admissions to each group, looking at high school admissions, community college transfers, and four-year transfers. She found that while the most selective universities enroll about 35,000 community college students each year into their institutions, this number constitutes only about 5 percent of their students. While 14 percent of students admitted by transfer into these institutions, only 5 percent come from community colleges. Of the five categories defined by Glynn, selective universities are the least likely to enroll community college students than all four other groups. Selective universities are nearly twice as likely to enroll transfers from other four-year universities than community colleges and bring in nearly 86% of their student body directly from high schools (Glynn, 2019).

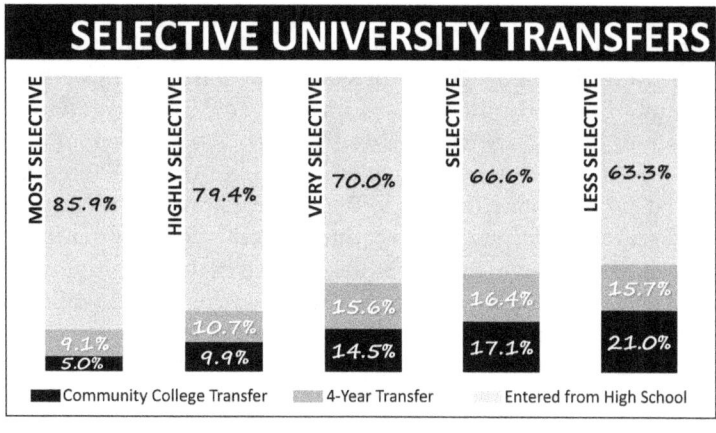

I could understand this bias if community college students were struggling to perform when they transfer to the most selective institutions. However, the academic record shows the contrary. Community college students who transfer to the most selective universities in the country have a higher graduation rate than the students who are admitted directly from high school and the students who transfer from other four-year universities—not lower, not equal, but higher. According to Glynn's analysis, students from community colleges graduate from selective universities at a rate of 74.5 percent. Students transferring from other four-year institutions graduate from the most selected selective universities at a rate of 61.3 percent. Students admitted to highly selective universities straight out of high school graduate at a rate of 72.6 percent. These data need to be shared with every graduating community college student. So many of them I have talked to over the years are very apprehensive about their odds of succeeding after transfer. But the data show that students from historically underserved communities receive better academic preparation in their first few years of college when they attend a community college than when starting out at four-year institutions. These data also raise a very frustrating question: If the most selective universities are committed to social justice and academic excellence, why are they underenrolling community college students?

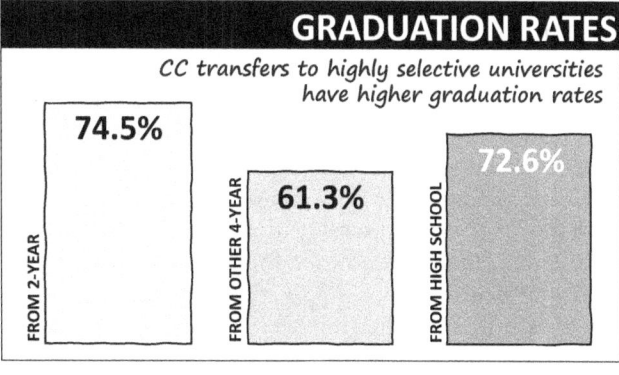

I might also understand this bias with regard to admissions if our most selective universities were silent on the issue of diversity and equity in America, but to the contrary, they are actively engaged in this dialogue across higher education. Most (maybe all) of our highly selective universities speak openly and passionately about their commitment to equity. But their track records with regard to equity-related admissions is very weak. An analysis of the top ten universities in the country according to *U.S. News and World Report* for 2019 (U.S. News and World Report, 2019) reveals a very good example of this. All ten of these universities have overt and unambiguous commitments to equity, access, inclusion, and diversity. They promote and affirm these commitments in their strategic documents and present them as centerpieces of their public relations and outreach materials. Initiatives commonly come out of the provost's office. Special programs devoted to equity are present at most of the universities. Nearly all the graduate schools have adopted language supporting equity. However, their admissions practices fall far below the ambitious intentions of their strategic and publics relations language.

Following is a chart with the top ten universities in the United States (U.S. News and World Report, 2019). They are listed from highest to lowest rank, including the percentage of students at each university who come from a middle- or low-income family and the institution's 2019 endowment.

Rank	University	% From Middle or Low Income[1]		Endowment (2019)
		Students	Americans	
1	Princeton	13.6%	60%	$24.7 Billion
2	Harvard	20.4%	60%	$40.9 Billion
3	Columbia	21.1%	60%	$10.9 Billion
4	MIT	23.4%	60%	$17.4 Billion
5	Yale	16.3%	60%	$30.3 Billion
6	Stanford	18.6%	60%	$27.7 Billion
7	Chicago	24.5%	60%	$8.5 Billion
8	Pennsylvania	16.5%	60%	$14.6 Billion
9	Northwestern	16.8%	60%	$10.8 Billion
10	Duke	16.5%	60%	$8.6 Billion

I find this chart astounding. As indicated previously, there is no question that the rhetoric of these institutions is committed to equity. However, with regard to income diversity in the United States, all ten universities are failing to come close to any proportionate to the American public. According to Chetty (see chart's footnote), 60% of the American public falls into middle-income, lower-middle-income, or low-income categories. But all ten of these universities have student populations of less than 25% from middle-, lower-middle-, or low-income families. The reason for this disparity has nothing to do with resources. All ten have large endowments, with the smallest at $8.6 billion and the largest nearly $50 billion. And all ten are renowned for the intellectual capital of their faculty. They clearly have the money and mind-power to address equity issues in more serious capacities.

I have difficulty squaring their equity rhetoric with such inequitable outcomes given the resources at their disposal. Regardless, if you are an opinion leader in this community

---

1. The income data in the table are pulled from Raj Chetty's work (Chetty, Hendren, Kline, Saez, & Turner, 2014). His work classifies family income by quintiles (1st quintile = poverty, 2nd = lower middle income, 3rd = middle income, 4th = upper middle income, 5th = wealthy). With Chetty's methodology, 60% of Americans fall into quintiles one, two, or three. This is classified as middle or low income in the table.

and reaching an awareness of the disparity in this moment, I hope you will consider *doing* something to change this. If you are an administrator or faculty leader in one of our most selective universities, how will you *lead* to affect this disparity? If you are an elected official or trustee working on higher education policy, what will you legislate? If you are a reporter or researcher who covers higher education issues, what will you *write*? If you are a philanthropist or contributing alumnus, how will you now *donate?* If you are an accrediting or auditing body in higher education, how will you *evaluate?* Now that you know, what will you do?

Recruiting Community College Students

America's most selective institutions are not recruiting from community colleges. Two exceptions are UCLA and UC Berkeley (Cal). Both of these institutions are highly ranked in the United States, and I am sure Glynn would place them in the *most selective* or *highly selective* categories. Both institutions are state funded and under legislative mandates requiring that they enroll a certain percentage of California community college transfer students. Of the top ten ranked universities on this year's list from *U.S. News and World Report*, I have never noticed one of them on any of the three California-based community college campuses where I have worked recruiting students for transfer. And two of the universities on this 2020 list are located in California, with one of them no more than an hour's drive from all three campuses. They are clearly not recruiting from most community colleges.

It is clear that the most selective universities in the United States in general do not understand students from historically underserved communities. As Anthony Jack points out in *The Privileged Poor* (Jack, 2019), disenfranchised students continue to feel disenfranchised when they attend elite universities because of the universities' policies. First, these universities do not seek income balance across the student body. As Raj Chetty has pointed out, students who come from families that make $630,000 per year (the top 1 percent) are 77 times more likely than students from unfavored groups to be admitted to the most selective universities in the United States. These means that the socio-cultural environment on these campuses is dominated by upper-income and wealthy students. Chetty's work also found that 38 highly selective colleges and universities have more students from families who earn $630,000 than students from families making less than $65,000 a year (Chetty et al., 2014).

Anthony Jack (2019) points to several other examples that keep these students feeling marginalized. He gives an example of several colleges closing the college food services during spring break, leaving students who can't afford to eat off campus with food insecurity for up to ten days. He provides an example of an event at one university where individuals who can afford to purchase tickets enter through the front door and individuals who need assistance with the ticker purchase enter through the side door. Another example he gives is the financial aid-related work extended to students at one university, which includes janitorial services in the dorms where mostly Black and brown students are expected to clean toilets of primarily White affluent students, reinforcing stereotypes among peers instead of creating new colleagues across divergent class lines. These and practices like them need to be dismantled and reconstructed in ways that create a more inclusive and egalitarian environment across the academy.

Legacy Admissions

One of the reasons the imbalances described previously exist is legacy admissions: admissions that give additional weight to applicants whose relatives have attended that institution. A recent survey found that 42 percent of private colleges and universities use legacy scoring in the admissions decisions, while only 6 percent or public institutions use the practice (Jaschik, The 2018 Surveys of Admissions Leaders: The Pressure Grows, 2018). Legacy scoring in admissions is prevalent in highly selective private universities and colleges. A 1992 survey found that 74 of the 75 top universities (according to *U.S. News & World Report* rankings) used the practice, and 99 of the 100 top ranked liberal arts colleges used legacy scoring.

A study conducted by Michael Hurwitz estimates that legacy students on average are 3.13 times more likely to be admitted (Hurwitz, 2011) than others. As an example, a recent undergraduate class at the University of Pennsylvania (an Ivy League university) admitted legacy applicants at 41.7 percent during early admissions and 33.9 percent during regular admissions. In contrast, they admitted non-legacy applications at 29.3 percent during early admissions and 16.4 percent during regular admissions (Schmidt, A History of Legacy Preferences and Privilege, 2010).

The policy of legacy scoring and its impact on admissions is important to understand in the context of social justice. Legacy places an emphasis on admitting families that have long associations with universities and colleges, especially the highly selective private institutions. These policies allow more affluent and less diverse families to have an advantage over those from unfavored communities. As Susan Dynarski puts it, "Legacy preferences limit diversity because they replicate in the present the student bodies of the past" (Dynarski, 2018). This policy, of course, creates a disadvantage for community college students, who are generally first-generation students with no college-going traditions in their families. Legacy preference again speaks to the hypocrisy of elite educational institutions, especially private institutions. So many of them publish commitments to social justice, but they quietly hold admissions policies that favor some of the most privileged families in America.

Some people argue that these are private organizations and we should not interfere with their admissions policies. It is their right to run their organizations as they please. If they want to maintain admissions policies that favor privileged communities, it is their right to do so. If you are in this camp, I wonder how you would feel about other private organizations granting privilege to upper-income White families as a matter of policy. Would you be OK with the grocery store having an express lane for wealthy White people? Would you be OK with car dealerships offering a faster sales process for wealthy White people? Would you be OK with online deliveries serving wealthy White families first? Most people I know would say "no" to these questions, so why do we tolerate this with private colleges and universities? Why in the world would we want to grant favorable admissions to a Rockefeller or a Kennedy but make it more difficult for a first-generation Hispanic female from a community college who has the grades to enter an elite school and thereby change the trajectory of her entire life? I don't understand the logic of this at all.

I especially do not understand the logic of legacy admission in the light of a public good. Almost all (probably all) of the private universities and colleges who maintain this discriminatory policy are legally classified as nonprofit institutions. We grant them nonprofit status because they offer a public good. Because of their nonprofit status, they enjoy significant tax benefits and a range of publicly funded privileges. I believe these institutions do offer services that contribute to the public good, especially as it relates to some of their research. However, legacy admissions policies cause public *harm*.

In addition to this unfairness, the institutions are nowhere near exclusively private. We invest vast public funds (tax dollars) in these institutions. They have favorable tax status, meaning they are able to keep much more of their money rather than contributing it to government services. We pay large sums of financial aid to many of their students, helping them pay for the expenses of the private university. We give them very large amounts of federal grant money for research and more. It would be more accurate to describe private universities in the United States as public-private partnerships. With this influx of tax funding going to private organizations, we have a legitimate need to address the discriminatory practice of legacy admissions.

Undermatching

While highly selective universities and colleges have established and stubbornly maintain hurdles that discriminate against admitting students from disfavored communities, community colleges have practices that contribute to this problem as well. The most notably way community colleges work against their students transferring to highly selective universities is a practice known as *undermatching*. Undermatching occurs when students come to us for transfer advice and we encourage them to apply—or match them—to institutions that are below their capabilities. According to Caroline Hoxby, nearly 40 percent of low-income, high-GPA students end up applying to colleges and universities that are non-selective. They could have been accepted to much better institutions, but they were "undermatched" (Hoxby & Avery, 2012).

I have seen this personally throughout my career, especially with low-income and high-GPA students. It is common for these students to be advised to undermatch. Rarely have I seen these students receive direction to aim for institutions that match their academic capabilities and extend significant aid packages. I think many of the personnel who provide the transfer advice are of the false impression that the private highly selective institution will be too expensive for low-income students. However, this impression is simply not true. The *New York Times* conducted an analysis or 31 private institutions and found that low-income families (earning less than $50,000 per year) paid on average $6,000 per year for their education due to the financial packages they received (Paterson, 2019). Many of the most prestigious universities are waiving tuition altogether for low- and middle-income families. For example, at Stanford University, parents with annual incomes below $150,000 and assets typical of that income receive tuition remission—they pay no tuition.

Higher Education Rankings

College and university rankings have been a part of the higher education landscape since the early 1900s (College Rank, 2020). Outcomes and reputation-based evaluations have been conducted in every decade since 1900; however, the interest level surrounding these reports was fairly limited until *U.S. News and World Report* published its first undergraduate ranking in the early 1980s. It became the most widely read college ranking report in history and has continued as an annual report for more than 30 years. During that time, the report has expanded its analysis, modified its methodology, and continued publishing on an annual basis, in spite of the magazine itself ending print publications in 2010.

COLLEGE/UNIVERSITY RANKINGS

Council for Aid to Education	U.S. News & World Report college and university rankings
The Daily Beast's Guide to the Best Colleges	United States National Research Council Rankings
The Economist's "Best Colleges. The Value of University"	Faculty Scholarly Productivity Rankings
Forbes College rankings	The Top American Research Universities
The "Objective" College rankings	Washington Monthly College rankings
Money's Best Colleges	TrendTopper MediaBuzz College Guide
The Princeton Review Dream Colleges	American Council of Trustees and Alumni
Revealed preference rankings	
Social Mobility Index (SMI) rankings	Niche College Rankings

The ranking system has grown to such prominence that other publishers have taken note and joined in the process. The sidebar graphic shows other ratings systems that have entered this space, but none have been able to capture the attention of the public like the annual report released by *U.S. News and World Report*. The report, initially focused on U.S. colleges and universities, has stimulated the development of several rankings that are international in focus, comparing universities across the globe. Some examples include Times Higher Education (THE), QS World university Rankings, the Academic Ranking of World Universities (ARWU), and the U-Multirank (funded by the European Union).

These rankings have become so important in higher education that they are now embedded in some personnel evaluations of senior university executives. In other words, some university presidents are required as part of their evaluation to move the university up in the *U.S. New and World Report* rankings (Gladwell, 2011). The rankings have become so prominent that Wermund has found them specifically included and referenced in university strategic plans (2017). They influence government policy, as governments all over the world and states across the United States try to raise their educational status (Wermund, 2017). They influence philanthropy, with foundations and individual contributors factoring institutional reputation into their decision-making. And they influence how students and parents decide which institutions to attend (Robert Morse, 2011). The rankings system—for better or worse—has emerged as very important to college and universities.

The methodology used by *U.S. News and World Report* has received considerable commentary over the years. In response, the publication has recently settled on an instrument that places emphasis on six key areas (what they refer to as "Ranking Factors"): outcomes, faculty resources, expert opinion, financial resources, student excellence, and alumni giving (Robert Morse E. B., 2019). Following is an expalnation of the relative weight of each factor and what information it includes.

The Outcomes Ranking Factor accounts for 35% of the overall score. These are core measures that speak to the quality of teaching, student services, and student learning. The measure looks at student retention, degree completion, and social mobility. The 2020 assessment added consideration of first-generation students to the degree completion calculation, giving credit to institutions who serve first-generation populations well. The social mobility measure looks at low-income students (Pell Grant recipients) and assesses their graduation rates. As a complement to this measure, *U.S. News* published a ranking of colleges and universities based solely on social mobility at www.usnews.com/best-colleges/rankings/regional-universities-north/social-mobility.

The Faculty Resource Ranking Factor accounts for 20 percent of the overall score. This score focuses on measuring the institution's commitment to teaching by addressing class size, faculty salaries, the proportion of faculty who have achieved the terminal degree in their field, the student-to-faculty rations, and the percentage of the faculty who are full time.

The Expert Opinion Ranking Factor accounts for 20 percent of the overall score. To collect this information, nearly 5,000 academics are surveyed and asked to weigh in on school reputations. Experts include presidents, provosts, and deans of admissions.

U.S. NEWS & WORLD REPORT

Factors	%
Outcomes: Retention, Graduation, Social Mobility (5%)	35%
Faculty Resources: Class Size, Faculty Salaries, FT Faculty with Terminal Degree, Student-Faculty Ratio, % FT Faculty	20%
Expert Opinion: Ratings from Presidents, Provosts, Deans of Admissions	20%
Financial Resources: Avg Spending per Student on Instruction, Research, Student Services, Related Educational Expenditures	10%
Student Excellence: Selectivity, Standardized Tests, HS Class Standing	10%
Alumni Giving: Avg Percentage of Alumni Who Gave to School	5%

The Financial Resources Ranking Factor accounts for 10 percent of the overall score. This measure assesses average spending per student for instruction, research, and support services related to the educational experience. Spending on athletics, housing, and hospitals is not included in the calculations.

The Entering Student Preparedness Ranking Factor accounts for 10 percent of the overall score. This score assesses the academic strength of entering students by looking at the entering student's rank in their graduating high school class as well as entrance exam scores (e.g., SAT).

The Alumni Giving Ranking Factor accounts for the final 5 percent of the overall score. The measure looks at the percentage of alumni who have received a bachelor's degree and have made a financial contribution back to the school.

Throughout this book, I have been arguing that higher education has three great missions: research, teaching, and social mobility. We rely primarily on our R1 and R2 universities[2] to deliver on the research component of this mission. We expect all institutions of higher education to deliver quality teaching and social mobility opportunities. We have indicated that higher education is the great equalizer, and most academics welcome this designation. If we are going to claim this goal as part of the mission—part of the expectation for our colleges and universities—then our raking systems must evaluate our colleges and universities along these lines. Our rankings comprehensively capture research quality, especially if we consider the graduate school rankings and international rankings. A heavy emphasis is placed on research-related measures in their methodologies. Teaching- and learning-related measures are also well captured, especially in the undergraduate comparisons. For example, *U.S. News and World Report* has several measures that serve as strong indicators for teaching. However, its measurement tool provides only token measures for social mobility effectiveness and heavily stacks the scoring system with measures that encourage universities to recruit students from high-income families.

U.S. News and World Report places only 5 percent of its scoring on social mobility. There is also a small amount of consideration for first-generation student success. This measure is folded into the Outcomes section of the scoring. Combined, the two do very little to encourage universities to be effective onramps to the middle class for low- and lower-middle-income students. As we have mentioned, our most celebrated universities skew heavily toward upper-middle- and upper-income students. This emphasis is largely a result of the inherent bias built into the *U.S. News and World Report* scoring system.

Steven Levitt and Stephen Dubner popularized the idea of unintended consequences in their books *Freakonomics* and *Superfreakonomics*. The basic point in both books is that humans respond to a range of incentives, not just economic incentives, and we can predict behavioral tendencies if we understand the incentives. The *U.S. News and World Report* ranking of colleges and universities is having this kind of effect. While I am certain that Robert Morse (the chief data strategist for *U.S. News*) and the people who work with him do not intend for their annual report to incentivize universities to discriminate against students from low-income families

> **PERVERSE INCENTIVES**
>
> "The extent to which U.S. News motivates schools to pick wealthier students is 'mind-boggling.'"
>
> Carol Christ
> Chancellor of UC Berkeley

---

2. R1 and R2 are Carnegie classifications for universities that have very high (R1) or high (R2) levels of research conducted at their university.

and privilege wealthy families, this is the effect his ranking system has had on higher education. As Carol Christ, Chancellor of UC Berkeley, puts it, "The extent to which *U.S. News* motivates schools to pick wealthier students is 'mind-boggling'" (Wermund, 2017).

The measures within the *US News* ranking system that encourage colleges and universities to focus on upper-income students are significant. They include the following:

- Standardized Tests—Entering freshmen with high ACT and SAT scores correlate with higher ranking scores from *U.S. News*. The logic is that these students are smarter and better prepared than lower-scoring students for the rigors of college and therefore an indicator of quality. However, tests like the SAT have been shown to correlate strongly with income and race. This has been substantiated by the College Board itself (the organization that administers the exam). Families with low incomes typically cannot afford to pay for tutors and test preparation services, so they come to the test with the odds stacked against them. If you are a university executive under the expectation to raise your ranking levels, the rational choice is to admit students with the higher scores. This selection preference statistically leads to an increase in the number of high-income and students and a decrease in the number of low-income students and students of color.
- High School Rank—Students who come the highest academic levels in their senior class rank are generally thought to be more prepared for college level work. As such, institutional rankings increase as the number of students from the highest academic levels increases. The logic behind this assumption is straightforward. These students are typically better prepared for college than others. However, these students tend to be from families where education is a priority and often have college-going traditions. Conversely, students from marginalized families tend to live in environments where education is less of a priority or there are fewer educational resources. These differences often translate to their lower-level academic performance and create a bias effect at the university. Upper-income students, who receive a substantial amount of private support for education, are more likely than lower-income students to graduate highly ranked in their class. If you are a university executive under the expectation to raise your ranking levels, this measure clearly calls for you to select highly ranked students; however, the unintended consequence is an increase in the number of high-income and therefore predominantly White students and a corresponding limitation on diverse or low-income students.
- Low-Income Student Completion—This measure is a step in the right direction for *U.S. News and World Report*. Several people have complimented them for the addition. The ranking system has a component that looks at expected and actual completion, rewarding schools that exceed expected completion with additional points. However, when low-income completion is measured rather than low-income volume, colleges and universities are encouraged to select only the most academically prepared students in order to raise completion results. In other words, it is strategically better to admit 100 low-income students who demonstrate a strong likelihood of success rather than admitting 1,000 low-income students who demonstrate that they are *somewhat likely* to succeed but have high potential. The prior helps the university's ranking. The latter helps promote social mobility. This distinction incentivizes universities to select fewer first-generation, low-income applicants, including community college transfer students.
- Faculty Resources—As universities invest resources in faculty, their ranking scores will rise with *U.S. News*. The logic is understandable. The most important relationship for students other than their relationship with other students is their relationship with faculty, and the higher quality the faculty are, the higher quality the educational

experience will be. With that in mind, *U.S. News* looks for high salaries, small classes, high percentages of full-time faculty, faculty with terminal degrees in their field, and favorable student-to-faculty ratios. To meet these expectations, a university must spend a significant amount of money. The high cost for scoring high on this criterion means universities are encouraged to raise tuition and increase their fundraising efforts. Both of these requirements break in favor of high-income families that can afford the tuition increases and are prone to give to the university. If you are a university executive under the expectation to raise your ranking levels, the rational choice here is to increase the number of high-income students and limit the number of low-income students in like proportions.

- Alumni Spending—As the number of alumni who contribute to university increases, their *U.S. News* ranking score increases. Alumni contribution is seen by *U.S. News* as a sign that alumni are satisfied with their undergraduate experience. However, this measure has the unintended consequence of encouraging universities to seek students from high-income families. Students from families who give are more likely to continue giving than students from low-income families. This is a primary reason that legacy is perpetuated at private universities. If you are a university executive under the expectation to raise your ranking levels, the rational choice here is to recruit students who are likely to be contributing alumni and avoid students who are less likely to do so. In other words, increase the number of high-income students and limit the number of low-income students.

- Acceptance Rate—A low acceptance rate translates to higher scores in the *U.S. News* rankings. The logic behind this measure suggests that great schools receive a high volume of applications. Some schools have started gaming the measure with the early decision admissions process (Wermund, 2017). The University of Pennsylvania, for example, has dramatically expanded its early admit process, increasing the number of students who apply while maintaining roughly the same number of overall admits. The unintended consequence revolves around students who apply for early admissions. A recent study (Giancola & Kahlenberg, 2016) focusing on admissions and low-income students found that many more students from upper-income families apply for early admissions compared to applications from students from low-income families. If you are a university executive under the expectation to raise your ranking levels, the rational choice here is to expand your early decision admissions process, but by doing so, you not only increase the number of high-income students but also reduce access for low-income students.

- Spending per Student—The more an institution spends on each student, the better the institution must be. This is the logic behind this measure, and it is scored accordingly by *U.S. News*. As spending per student rises, ranking scores rise. The significance of this need to spend more per student was underscored in a 2014 report (Falciano, Kuncle, & Gnolek, 2014) that asked the question, "What does it take to move into the top 20 for university rankings?" The report found that an institution ranked in the mid-30s would need to increase its spending by about $112 million annually to make the leap.

There are parts of this measure that do correlate to quality; however, basic math helps us understand a hidden perverse incentive. If a university wants to boost its expenditures per student, a logical strategy is to increase the number of students from affluent families and decrease the number of students from low-income families. High-income students almost always need less financial support from the institution, and they have family members who have the means to contribute. As a result, the institution can bring in additional money that will help increase spending per student and/or direct spending to other areas that capture ranking points (e.g., faculty salaries).

- Retention and Graduation Rates—*U.S. News* rankings rise as student retention and graduation rates rise. On the surface, this criterion seems like a solidly positive measure, but students from high-income families are more likely to stay in school and graduate, if for no other reason than finances. Low-income and lower-middle-income students face many financial difficulties, including college expenses. Financial need is one of the reasons (among others) that they often fail to finish. As a result, schools with more high-income students tend to have better retention and graduation rates, which of course leads to higher *U.S. News* rankings. If you are a university executive under the expectation to raise your ranking levels, the rational strategy under this measure is to increase the number of high-income students and limit the number of low-income students.
- Social Mobility—The role higher education plays with regard to social mobility is recognized by *U.S. News* in its ranking system, but it only accounts for 5 percent of the score on the overall ranking. The publication has recently supported a separate report (U.S. News and World Report, 2020) that focuses exclusively on social mobility measures. However, universities and the public primarily focus their attending on the overall ranking. To give greater value to social mobility and incentivize universities to move in this direction, *U.S. News* needs to fold the two together and, in so doing, elevate the scoring devoted to social mobility: move it from 5 percent to something closing to 30 percent. Otherwise, universities will focus on the 95 percent that does recognize social mobility and has several measures baked into the 95 percent that unintentionally encourage universities to favor students from affluent families.

This scoring system has become so important to colleges and universities in the United States that it heavily influences the business model for higher education in America. Imagine that you were a president of a major university and your board stipulated in your contract that you need to move the college up in its rankings. Knowing that the most effective strategies to move up in the rankings will also increase the likelihood of institutional bias against students of color and students from low-income families, what should you do? I think you should say something! We need leaders across higher education to stop the intellectual dishonesty, with mission statements that speak so powerfully about social justice but targeted strategies to increase their rankings with the knowledge that doing so will limit access to their institutions for the families who need access the most.

Solutions and Strategies

Given the previous discussion, we need to support several solutions in a collective effort to transition more students from historically underserved communities as transfers from community colleges into elite universities.

Strategy #30: Establish Proactive Transfer Centers

Transfer centers are centralized locations on community college campuses that provide assistance to students who are planning to transfer to a four-year institution. The services vary greatly including the organization of campus visits, coordination with transfer partners, general information, assistance with application process, and other services. I have worked at three community colleges with very different capacities regarding transfer. One had a transfer program run by an instructional faculty member with a very modest space. The second institution was run by a full-time faculty member with a few staff persons providing support in a substantial space that could accommodate a dozen students of more. The third college had a staff person in the position on a part-time basis with no space for students. While these three cases are only anecdotal, they seem to show a correlation between the different amounts of support provided by each college and the corresponding transfer rate at each college.

Because resources are often limited in transfer centers, the services are geared toward typical students. For this reason, transfer centers focus most (sometimes all) of their attention and resources on transfer to the state-funded universities, where most transfer students intend to enroll. This concentration often leads to a cycle where personnel develop expertise in transfer to these institutions and subsequent biases in their recommendations to students.

However, there are students in community college with unique potential for niche transfer opportunities, including potential to transfer to HBCUs, international institutions, women's colleges, and highly selective universities/colleges that do not receive the same kind of attention as the more traditional receiving institutions. Many students are never provided with information about these opportunities, may be discouraged from pursuing these opportunities, and—if they do decide to move in these directions—are most often required to navigate the process with little support. There are exceptions to this at some community colleges, but they are rare.

Another challenge many transfer centers have is transitioning from passive to active services. There are many reasons for this. Centers have limited resources, limited technical solutions to support active advising, a history of passive advising, and more. Regardless, these centers need to move to a more active approach, especially with regard to low-income, high-GPA students, who are ideal candidates for transfer to highly selective universities and likely to receive financial aid packages that will make their educational expenses equal to or *less* than those for the state university.

I conducted a lightly organized and compressed effort in my district while I was at Norco College. Having developed a cursory relationship with the dean of admissions at the University of Southern California, I decided to identify and encourage low-income, high-GPA students who were nearing transfer status to apply to USC. In January of 2019, I asked the transfer staff person and her manager to develop a list of students at the college who were on track to transfer by June, maintaining a GPA of 3.8 or above and Pell eligible (indicating low income). The process of identifying the students was a little cumbersome, but we eventually found about 30 students who met the criteria. I sent all of them an email indicating that I felt they had a strong chance of being accepted to USC and would likely receive a generous financial aid offer. We offered some light assistance with applying to the college, and I encouraged anyone who was interested to come by my office to further discuss this opportunity. This all happened about two weeks before the applications were due and had all the characteristics of a last-minute campaign.

LOW-INCOME/HIGH-GPA TRANSFERS
Norco College to USC 2019 Experiment

	Applied	Accepted
2017	13	4
2018	11	5
2019	23	12
2020	17	3

Not surprisingly, in the years when Norco College did not encourage these students to apply, the numbers we much lower. However, in the one year when we encouraged students to apply, through a very loose and minimally coordinated campaign, the application numbers and acceptance numbers increased, with most of the students receiving very generous financial aid awards. In 2017, 13 students applied and 4 were accepted to USC. In 2018, 11 students applied and 5 were accepted to USC. In 2019 (the year I encouraged students to apply), 23 students applied and 12 were accepted to USC. In 2020 (the college went back to no targeted encouragement), 17 students applied and 3 were accepted to USC. We need transfer centers throughout community colleges to add this emphasis to their overall strategies.

Strategy #31: Develop Transfer Programs for High-GPA/Low-Income Students

One of the ways community colleges can improve transfer to highly selective universities is with an academic honors program. These programs give students and faculty a chance to increase academic rigor and exploration with students who are interested and committed to the added challenge. Some colleges establish programs where honors classes are established for every student in that class. Other colleges establish an honors track that allows students to pursue additional studies inside non-honor courses. For example, a faculty member may be teaching a history course with 33 non-honors students and 2 honors students. In this scenario, the faculty member meets with the two students to develop additional studies and related work to qualify the students for honors credit.

While many community colleges have honors programs, these programs are still rather rare. In a large study recently completed by the Jack Kent Cooke Foundation, it found that only 17 percent of community colleges examined for this study had honors programs. This low number is concerning because of another finding from the study. When isolating for the community colleges who have honors programs, 96 percent of community colleges with honors programs successfully transferred students to selective four-year institutions. The transfer rate to selective four-year institutions from colleges without honors programs was 82 percent (Glynn, 2019). These results demonstrate how effective honors programs can be for placing low-income and high-performing students into elite universities.

Moving low-income, high-performing community college students to highly selective universities is so important that I think the community college president should take time to make this objective a priority. I would suggest that community college presidents work with a cohort of ten students each year. The cohort should include students who will be eligible to transfer in the present year of the program, are Pell eligible, and have a GPA in the 3.8 range. The president should meet with these students regularly and prepare them for the application process and the cultural transition they will likely need to make as they make the transition. The impact such a practice has on low-income students is so profound that I believe it merits the time and attention from the college president. In addition, when a practice like this becomes known around campus, it may grow and provide incentive to other highly ambitious low-income students and college personnel who would like to provide similar support.

Strategy #32: Change University and College Ranking System

The ranking system that has the most influence in American higher education is the annual report from *U.S. News and World Report*. For several reasons discussed previously, the report incentivizes universities to recruit students from affluent families and establishes a range of disincentives for community college transfer students. This ranking system needs to be completely overhauled or replaced with a system that establishes measures that encourage universities to recruit student from disfavored communities. It is true that *U.S. News and World Report* is a private organization and entitled to measure our colleges and universities in any manner that suits it. It could measure higher education according to the most attractive presidents if it wanted to. It is not using public money to build its instrument, but it has captured so much public attention with its annual report that it is influencing the shape of a very important public asset and influencing how public money is spent. We invest billions of tax money into our public universities and our private universities with publicly funded scholarships, publicly funded research, government appropriations, favorable tax status, and more (Dernoncourt, 2016; Vedder, 2018).

We invest this tax money with three expectations in mind. First, we expect our universities to produce cutting-edge research. Second, we expect all institutions in higher education to teach at the highest levels. Third, we expect all institutions in higher education to promote social mobility in a manner that supports a true meritocracy providing equitable access for all groups in the United States. The *U.S. News* ranking system measures the first two expectations effectively, but this ranking does not place enough measurement emphasis on the third expectation, and we have been experiencing the result for three decades.

One place to start with this reform is with *U.S. News and World Report*'s one-off ranking of universities by their success with social mobility. This analysis has measures that are valid, but the idea of social mobility is not valued sufficiently by *U.S. News* as a cornerstone of American higher education. This is why its main report relegates so few points to social mobility and the much less prominent one-off report provides a deep analysis of social mobility.

Another way that we could correct this imbalance is by collectively giving preference to other reports, ones that place more emphasis on the social justice role higher education needs to play in society. A range of reports address this concept more thoroughly. Opportunity Insights (https://opportunityinsights.org/), for example, has done significant research and related rankings or comparisons of all colleges and universities relative to social mobility. Finally, the federal government may need to play a stronger role in the evaluation of social mobility. It could do this through the accrediting bodies that are empowered by the U.S. Department of Education.

Strategy #33: End Legacy Scoring

Legacy scoring is found primarily in America's most selective universities, with 42 percent of private colleges and universities using the practice as part of their admissions process, while only 6 percent of public institutions use legacy scoring (Jaschik, The 2018 Surveys of Admissions Leaders: The Pressure Grows, 2018). The practice is widely understood to skew admissions toward White, upper-income students. As Rachel Fishman states, "Legacy admissions help to guarantee that a class of students at a school continues to have a proportion of students who are whiter, wealthier, and therefore full-pay at many elite schools" (Fishman, February 2019). As Fishman suggests, it is a discriminatory practice; however, the practice is deeply tied to these institutions' business models, where alumni donations represent significant income for universities, paying for facilities, salaries, student aid, and more (Jaschik, The 2018 Surveys of Admissions Leaders: The Pressure Grows, 2018).

The universities that have built significant portions of their operating expenses and business models around this idea are in a quandary caught between competing moral and financial demands. There is a long history of those at the economic top making themselves comfortable at the expense of minority groups with privilege built on discrimination. Legacy scoring is a classic example. The university personnel and policy makers who support legacy scoring go to great lengths to craft language in support of the practice; however, when the rhetoric is stripped away, their public admission is shocking. Their basic argument is as follows: legacy scoring, which is known to discriminate against students of color and students with low incomes, is needed because it helps build relationships with alumni, who in turn provide money to the university. Discrimination has always existed and persisted because those who benefit from it are reluctant to relinquish the benefit.

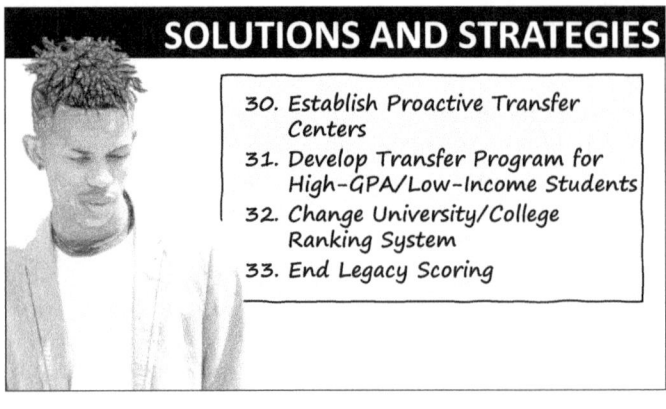

SOLUTIONS AND STRATEGIES

30. Establish Proactive Transfer Centers
31. Develop Transfer Program for High-GPA/Low-Income Students
32. Change University/College Ranking System
33. End Legacy Scoring

It this instance, we find a defense of racism coming from our most prestigious institutions of learning.

We need to recognize this system for what it is and intervene. First, no institution receiving taxpayer funding should be allowed to practice discrimination based on race or income—period. Legacy scoring is a discriminatory practice. As such, all public universities should be required to end legacy scoring, and all private universities that receive public funding should be required to forego all public funding until they end legacy scoring. This would mean that the private institutions that use this practice should not be eligible to receive public research grants, public aid to students, public funding for infrastructure, tax breaks as non-profits, or any other benefit funded by taxes.

On the one hand, this proposal seems controversial. To implement it would be to challenge very powerful institutions (e.g., Harvard). On the other hand, the principle supporting this proposal does not seem controversial at all. To suggest that taxpayers of color and taxpayers from low-income backgrounds can expect their governments (federal, state, and local) to make sure their money is not spent in ways that discriminate against them seems highly reasonable.

Implementation of local, state, and federal policies along these lines would benefit community college transfers significantly. Every year, a portion of community college students graduates with very high GPAs through participation in rigorous courses (e.g., honor programs). However, most of these students come from families where no one has attended elite universities and therefore will not be eligible for legacy scoring. The universities that could change the trajectory of their lives in fundamental ways knowingly stack the admissions selection process against them. We need to advocate for the legislative removal of *all* legacy scoring. It is racist and discriminatory on several levels.

Conclusion

Highly selective universities are a great example of systemic discrimination in the United States. In my experience, they are filled with good-hearted people who have committed their lives to helping students. They themselves are students of history. They understand our long, difficult history with persistent social injustices that maintain social and economic inequality. They speak to these issues openly in lecture halls, through research, and throughout their university's strategic planning documents and openly declare their commitment to these principles in marketing materials. Highly selective universities are filled with individuals who are committed to social justice and sincerely want to build a society that supports upward mobility in a way that meets their commitment to equality.

Nevertheless, they support a set of rules, policies, standards, norms, and traditions that promote the kind of inequality in society they do not individually support. These systems have long histories and corresponding justifications that are rarely challenged and consequently remain.

In the end, there are two great paradoxes that we need to face. First, our most selective universities are filled with individuals who call for equity in society but quietly support institutional practices that discriminate against historically underserved communities. Second, the professionals we look to for dispassionate and scholarly criticism of social institutions are largely silent on the discriminatory practices they support inside their own social institutions. We need to speak to this paradox across higher education and have the courage to openly point to our own sources of systemic race and income discrimination. We need to do this internally with the same rigor and courage that we apply to other sectors in society that have similar practices. Without this kind of internal scrutiny, we will not be able to clean up our own house.

9   Developing Leaders Who Can Effect Institutional Change

My last day on the Norco College campus was June 7, 2019. I remember it vividly because it was commencement and that particular graduation was really special. We had anticipated a larger turnout than the year before and placed significantly more chairs on the field to accommodate what we thought would be a record turnout of graduates, faculty, staff, family members, and friends. The attendance was even greater than we had anticipated. I remember walking onto the field during the procession and looking out over the crowd and seeing hundreds of family members standing in the open parts of the grass, unable to find a place to sit. I am sure it was uncomfortable for many of them, but it gave the entire ceremony a sense of positive energy as overflowing crowds often do.

We proceeded through the ceremonial parts of the graduation smoothly—pledge of allegiance, welcome comments by the moderator, student speech, choir performance, my comments, and so on. At the conclusion of these formalities, the class of 2019 was recognized, and we started the process of bringing each student to the podium. This is always the longest part of commencement and, frankly, as president, it can be exhausting as you enthusiastically congratulate each student and pose for a picture they may keep for a lifetime. However, this was my third graduation ceremony at Norco College, so as students came across the stage, I knew many of them, had spent time with several, and felt a great sense of joy as they bounded across the stage with family members yelling and horns blowing. The entire evening felt personally meaningful and uplifting.

At the end of the ceremony, the dais party was the first to leave, and as we exited the stadium, instead of heading back to my office to change clothes and find my way home, I did something I've never done before. I turned around near the main exit and waited for the crowd to swell and move through the gate. First the faculty exited in two long parallel lines. We high-fived, fist bumped, and hugged. After all the faculty left, four of us (two vice presidents and one faculty member) hung out at the exit of the stadium and did the same with family members and students as they left to go home. We stayed there until most of the crowd was gone. For an hour or more, we greeted people, took pictures with graduates in our ceremonial gowns, said *thank you* to friends and family, exchanged smiles, and generally took in the joy each graduate and those who came with them exuded. It was wonderful.

The four of us eventually walked back to the center of campus and sat in the warm summer evening of inland Southern California. We talked about graduation and the exceptional year it had been for Norco College. The indicators of a healthy college were up. Enrollment, completion, equity, partnerships, fundraising, morale were all trending up. Without question, the college was surging. We all could feel it, and graduation that night confirmed our sense of momentum and optimism for Norco College. I had many good days at Norco College; that day was among the best.

The following Monday, I headed to a meeting at the Riverside Community College District (RCCD) office. District leaders and the three college presidents met for a 2–3-hour meeting in the morning, and at the conclusion of that meeting, I was scheduled to hold a one-on-one with my boss, the chancellor of RCCD. When I stepped into the chancellor's office, I immediately noticed two additional attendees—the vice chancellor of human resources and a person I did not recognize. I moved deeper into the room and introduced myself to the person I did not recognize. We shook hands and exchanged names. He introduced himself as an attorney for the district. The chancellor stood up, said this would be a difficult meeting, said our relationship was not working out, and sat down. The attorney handed me a severance agreement and spoke generally to the document. The vice chancellor handed me an administrative leave notice and also spoke generally to the document. The two of them talked for about 20 minutes with occasional interjections from the chancellor. They finished by taking my phone, laptop computer, keys, and college ID. I don't remember a lot of what they said. I tried to look attentive and professional. I remember trying *not* to look like I was afraid, panicky, small. All I could think about while they were talking was my wife and kids and all the people at Norco College.

I was not technically fired, although that is certainly what it felt like. My contract was bought out "without cause"—no reasons put in writing. I never received an evaluation from the chancellor. I did know we were working through some disagreements, and some of them were difficult. But having my contract bought out was a big surprise. It still surprises me when I think back on that day and the few weeks that followed. The documents were presented to the Board the following day, and while faculty, staff, students, and local elected and civic leaders spoke in protest of the decision for over three hours during the public comments period, everything needed to finalize my departure was board approved at the conclusion of the June 11 Board meeting. Going into my 30th year of work in higher education, I did not have a job.

I have spent a lot of time thinking about this transition in my life—how and why it happened, how these events may have been interrupted, what it means for my future, and more. I keep coming back to the difficulties surrounding institutional change. Most of the colleagues I have worked with agree that we need to make fundamental changes in higher education if we are going to address success rates for historically underserved students. We have discussed the amount of improvement we need to effect in students' lives if we hope to eliminate academic equity gaps, and the gaps are large. There is a growing body of research that points us toward a consistent set of changes that will narrow or close these gaps. However, implementing these changes is frustratingly difficult. Despite our agreement that we need to make changes and our agreement over the kinds of changes we need to make, it can still be perilous for college administrators who try to implement these changes in significant ways. It often aggravates employees who experience the changes in their day-to-day work lives. It creates real pressure points for constituent leaders trying to represent their members.

This problem reveals a great paradox in community colleges. We are proud of the students we serve, concerned that too few of them complete their degrees/certificates, and open about the changes we need to make on behalf of our students. This recognition is approaching omnipresence in the language of our strategic planning documents. However, we have college administrators who are reluctant to direct these changes for fear of losing their jobs, employees who are reluctant to help implement change because they are tired of innovations that do not last, and constituent leaders who are reluctant to lead change with their members because of the consequence these changes represent in the balance of power and distribution of resources. On the one hand, we collectively agree that change is needed; on the other, we are reluctant to make these changes.

When presented with a paradox of this nature—and it occurs routinely—college administrators and leaders of constituent groups across the campus confront a difficult choice. For example, there is a discussion today at many colleges about the idea of Guided Pathways. We discussed this strategy near the beginning of the book. I won't repeat the full discussion here, but you will recall it is a strategy that develops clear and observable pathways that students can easily see and understand as they progress in their academic journey. The strategy has a strong record of success, but implementing it is disruptive. It calls for change in many areas of the college. In an ideal environment, all of the changes that need to be implemented would be carried out in a manner that maximizes student benefits and minimizes disruption in employees' work lives. Some of the changes can be implemented in this manner. We should always be as creative as possible to find solutions that achieve both goals.

However, this balance is simply not possible in all scenarios. There are times when a reform to help students is needed and the reform is disruptive for one or more constituent groups on campus. In these moments, college leaders (board members, managers, faculty leaders, classified leaders, and student leaders) are faced with a difficult question. Do they advocate for the change to help students, or do they advocate to minimize the change to protect the constituents they serve? On paper, this may sound like an easy answer: choose students. But when a person who serves as a leader of a district/college or a constituent group inside a college is actually confronted with this question, the choice is very difficult.

In these circumstances, a leader needs to decide which interest they will advocate for as a first priority and which they will pursue as a second priority. In my experience, community college leaders (including me at times) all too often opt for advocacy on behalf of the comfort of the constituencies they serve rather than the students who stand to benefit from these changes. I have often heard, "As the academic senate president, I am going to fight for faculty"; "As the president of the classified union, I am going to fight for staff"; "As the instructional dean, I am going to fight for my division." And so on. I have not only heard people take these positions; I have taken them myself at times.

Some people consider an environment like this a sign of civic health. Robert Dahl, a classic thinker in political science, argued for this kind of environment under a structure he referred to as pluralism. In a pluralistic environment, he explains, leaders focus exclusively on representing and advocating for their constituents' interests. This motivation is seen as part of the American political tradition, grounded in a political culture of civil disagreement. I believe it is

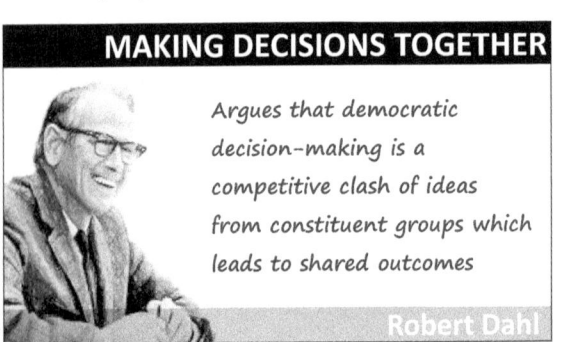

MAKING DECISIONS TOGETHER

Argues that democratic decision-making is a competitive clash of ideas from constituent groups which leads to shared outcomes

Robert Dahl

accurate to say this tradition exists in the United States. We allow for—even encourage—a free market of competing ideas through capitalism, public elections, litigation, peer-reviewed publications, and other traditional activities. The idea that competition and conflict shape ideas into something more consensus based is quintessentially American. To suggest that the United States is a pluralist society is to suggest that it is a country filled with people who have different views, and allowing these views to openly clash in the public sphere may create tension, but it also creates common ground, consensus, and resolution where practical solutions are developed that solve real problems and meet the concerns of most groups involved. It supports the adage of sausage-making. It can be disgusting to watch, but the outcome can be very pleasing and ultimately unifying.

This model of pluralism or factionalism is often applied to higher education, usually discussed within the context of collegial consultation, or shared governance. In a community college setting, we often try to structurally create this sense of shared governance by bringing leaders from all constituent groups into a deliberation and ask them to weigh in on important topics. These deliberations typically include representatives from the academic senate, faculty union, staff union, board, managers, community, students, and district office. In this mix, a problem is presented, an initial solution is proposed, and a dialogue ensues that is supposed to help find the best solution—one that solves the problem and accommodates all or most constituents.

Applying a pluralistic approach to higher education feels appropriate on many levels. It feels democratic. It feels embedded in a tradition of civic dialogue. But embedded in this approach is a major flaw, stemming from the assumption that all groups in the deliberation have close to equal influence. I believe this is mostly true with regard to the groups we invite into college deliberations. I have seen unions, senates, academic divisions, disciplinary departments, and other constituent groups representing employees of the college fare well at different times during shared decision-making. I enjoy environments like this. I like listening. I like participating. I like how it brings us together. I try to build this arrangement into the organizations I belong to. With that said, the constituent group that *never* has influence equal to that of the other constituent groups is our students. They don't have nearly as much influence as the managers, faculty, board members, or staff in these dialogues. Because of their diminished influence, the only time that their interests rise to the top is when the other constituent groups consciously put student interest above their own members' interests. This imbalance of influence, of course, is counterintuitive to our understanding of a pluralistic society. But it is recognizable if we compare it to another social structure, the American family.

In a family unit with one or two parents and several children, or an extended family with multiple adults (grandparents, parents, aunts, uncles, domestic partners, etc.) and even more children, we outright reject the pluralist model. We do not encourage separate interests to compete with each other in family units. We don't expect the adults in the family to advocate for their interests and the children to do the same in a competitive free market of ideas. The power balance and maturity levels are too divergent. We frequently expect the parents and adults in the family structure to subordinate their interests to those of the children in the family. When we list the characteristics of a healthy and functional family, one of those characteristics is the overall willingness and ability of adults in the family to advocate on behalf of the children in the family, even if doing so means the adults may experience loss or need to sacrifice.

By extension, the health of our colleges should partly be measured by each constituent leader's ability to act like a mature adult in a functional family, placing students' interests first and constituent members' interests second. In this sense, constituent leaders across campus do not think of themselves as advocates for their members but see their roles as directing the assets of their constituent group toward initiatives that will have maximum student success. They lend their expertise to an implementation approach that will be as smooth as possible for their constituents. But in the end, this means at times they support some kind of loss for the constituents they represent in exchange for gains the students will receive because of the sacrifice. Adopting this approach is extremely hard; it is rare. But it is a sign of very high emotional intelligence. A question I have been chasing for 15 years as a college leader is, "How do we foster this kind of environment?"

Developing leaders is part of the answer to this question. In my experience, very little attention has been given to this topic. I have held five leadership positions, and while training has been available through state and national associations, little was provided to me by the colleges themselves. The most consistent training I have received has been on compliance-related issues (e.g., knowledge of new federal mandates), technical training (e.g., knowledge of new systems), or strategic planning deliberations where leadership engages in planning. As a college leader, I have not worked in an environment where change management skills were expected, not to mention taught. As a leader in community colleges, I will also admit it is not something I have systematically developed or required from the leaders who report to me. I have always tried to help the people around me learn and grow as they confront new problems and challenges. I have consistently supported conference attendance and outside development activities. I have always supported continuing education. But an intentional professional development strategy and plan for college leaders that prioritizes the interests of students above constituents is one of the areas I look forward to developing.

In 2013, the Aspen Institute wrote a comprehensive report in response to similar concerns. It was concerned that training for community college presidents was insufficient. By conducting analysis of 16 existing training programs, interviewing leaders at several successful community colleges and related organizations, and reviewing pertinent literature, the authors came to two important conclusions. First, training for community college presidents (and by extension, community college leaders) is insufficient. Second, there are five core qualities effective community college leaders must practice: First, college leaders need to have a deep commitment to students and their success. Second, they must be willing to take "significant risks" on behalf of students and their success. Third, they need to think in terms of long-lasting institutional change that will extend beyond their own tenure. Fourth, the need to think strategically with a vision for the college that is built on external partnerships. Fifth, they need to be able to add resources to their institutions (Aspen Institute, 2013).

Solutions and Strategies

As I reflect on Aspen Institute's report, similar literature, and my own personal experience, it seems clear to me that there is a significant lack of training for leaders and for the changes we are trying to make: improving success for students from historically underserved communities. I feel there are specific skills we need to teach our leaders across community colleges. After several years of leading institutional change successfully and at times unsuccessfully, I believe there are six major components a leader must have to be successful with change management. It is the responsibility of the manager to identify these components and develop deep skills for each. They are: 1) develop a clear strategic vision, 2) make equity a strategic prioritization, 3) implement work though teams, 4) manage the "old" and lead the "new", 5) improve through assessment and accountability, and 6) ground all work in the ethic of love.

Strategy #34: Develop and Promote a Clear Strategic Vision

One of my favorite things about being a CEO in higher education is the ability to think and act strategically. I especially enjoy working with the leadership of a college to develop a shared strategic vision. When you ask a group of people who love their college to close their eyes and dream about where they want to take it, the conversation can be magical. Strategic planning is one of the best ways to make change happen, and as we have already substantiated, institutional change is greatly needed if we hope to improve the academic success of students who come from historically underserved communities.

I have successfully led institutional strategic work at three colleges. In all three cases, we were able to make quantifiable improvements to students' lives by developing a clear vision of where we were headed. Developing a vision for any group starts with substantive dialogue across all constituent groups. In my experience, the most successful strategic plans come from the community members who will ultimately implement the plan. As a result, broad-based deliberation and deep listening should always be the starting point for college leaders. From there, amazing ideas can be identified. Clear, compelling, aspirational, and often brilliant goals are found in sincere group dialogue and collective dreaming.

When I was academic senate president at Cerritos College, we launched a program known as iFALCON. It was a habits of mind program built out of a recognized need to help students succeed. Starting as no more than an idea, we developed it into a nationally funded program that was replicated at other community colleges. The program remains active today, using an acculturation model to integrate the campaign across campus. The program helps students envision themselves as successful learners, believe in their ability to succeed, achieve academic and personal goals, and discover connections between personal experiences and academic concepts. It is a simple yet attractive way to talk to first-generation students about success in college and is intended to be used by all personnel at the college with all students at the college. Under this approach, we were able to develop a common nomenclature and approach around teaching students the soft skills they need to succeed.

iFALCON was successful largely because of the time we spent up front talking to faculty, managers, and students about student success, about solutions needed to address student success, and about presentation of the overall approach. I remember one meeting in particular with students. I organized the meeting with them to address "look and feel" issues related to the program, what we would call it, what the graphics would look like, and other topics. This was a very important issue to get right if we wanted it to appeal to students. I came to them with several ideas that I thought were cool and seemed attractive to other faculty members. I was certain one of the several ideas we pitched would resonate, but every single one was turned down by students. They were very kind about the rejections, but there was no mistake that every single proposed idea was a loser for them. I finally threw up my hands and said, how do you want to brand this? A vibrant dialogue followed, and we landed on a tech approach that many computer and device products were using with great success in the 2000s.

By the time I became president of Norco College, I understood the difficulties associated with change and the value of listening and learning from those who are closest to the ground if a successful plan is to be developed. We applied this sense of collegiality to our discussion of the Education Master Plan and Facilities Master Plan. Through a series of workshops extending over nine months, we put people from diverse constituencies into groups and literally asked them to dream about where they would like to see the college go (we used the word *dream*). The quality of discussion in these groups was enthusiastic and inspiring. The ideas they collectively generated far exceeded my imagination and became the foundation of two critical strategic documents for the college. The two plans are shaping the future of the college in a direction that the people of the college enthusiastically embrace because of the inclusive process up front.

The key to successful strategic planning is getting people who know the institution intimately and love the institution to dream, without reservations, together. It ends up being like a conversation with parents about the dreams they have for their children. Using this approach, a leader will develop a vision that far exceeds anything they could do on their own, and once the vision is articulated into a clean narrative, the constituents of the college will embrace it because they are the ones who originally shaped it.

Once a clear vision has been developed for the college through an authentic shared development process and after a narrative of the vision has been developed, it becomes critical to use the college's vision and strategic documents as regular working documents in the college. Many colleges (in my experience, most colleges) do not do this, and that is very surprising to me. They often develop the strategic plan and put it on a shelf. It should be referenced as the document that gives direction to all big decisions. It is the ground that leaders can stand on, arguing that this is the college community's will and we should honor it through implementation. The document should be summarized for easy consumption by the entire campus. It should be graphically communicated with posters, flyers, pamphlets, and websites. It should be the framing document for all major work at the college.

This means that the leadership of the college needs to translate old work into the new strategy. Standardized agendas need to be restructured around the new strategic plan language. Old terminology needs to be replaced with the synonyms now reflected in the plan. Leaders need to help all the people who report to them see how their work aligns with the vision of the college. When custodial workers at the college understand how their work connects to helping students from historically underserved communities find greater academic success, you are on the right track.

The final step in strategic planning for the college takes place around communication. Leaders must accept the challenge of communicating the vision over and over again. This process is endless. Leaders need to tell stories that reflect the vision. They need to find examples that illuminate the strategic plan. They should recognize employees who move the vision forward. They should constantly frame their work around the core strategies of the college. And these measures need to be carried out in a manner that constantly inspires and captures the imagination of those they serve.

My father was a minister for over 40 years. In that time, he served two churches. This is incredible given the kind of turnover that most pastors experience. It is very similar to college presidencies these days lasting on average around two and a half to three years. I spent most of my childhood and adolescent years listening to his sermons on Sunday. As I look back on his career, it impresses me that every Sunday, no matter the topic of his sermon, he could tie it back to the main message of Christianity (salvation) in a fresh way. What he never lost sight of was the vision/direction he was trying to lead and came back to it in a fresh way with a familiar congregation every week.

My point here is not to introduce religion into this conversation but to demonstrate the need to repeat the same message in a fresh way to a familiar audience. This is the kind of consistency leaders need to bring to their constituent members. We need to constantly remind them of where we are headed, why we are headed there, and how their work contributes to this vision. To do this over and over again, leaders must be imaginative and creative, making the old and familiar feel new and fresh every "Sunday."

A final piece of the communication that is essential for meaningful change to take hold is regular celebration of our successes. Keeping your head down and doing the work day to day is important, but we all know how exhausting and draining this can be if it is all we do. We need to pick our heads up occasionally and see the progress we are making. Our strategic plans, if done well, have big aspirational dreams laid out in black and white. But the work we do to get there can be difficult and frankly dreary. Leaders need to keep track of the work being done and how it is adding up to demonstrable successes and victories in the direction of these big dreams. People need to believe that our dreams are achievable, and regularly sharing successes that demonstrate our moving in the direction we have all said we want to go is uplifting. Leaders need to recognize people for work that moves us in our strategic directions. Leaders need to communicate the milestones we are hitting on the way to our goals. Leaders need to help their people occasionally pull their heads up out of the work and celebrate the progress we are making.

Strategy #35: Make Equity a Strategic Prioritization

Every college and university should complete and maintain an equity assessment of the institution. There are a number of ways to complete a study of this nature, but the basic idea is to identify all groups in the institution and measure their success. The study should include access/admissions and completion-related measures. The goal of the study is to quantifiably identify groups that are experiencing academic success and those that are not. From this assessment, disproportionately impacted groups can be identified and specific strategies developed to close the success gap for these groups.

This approach minimizes arguments or persistent beliefs that are not helpful. For example, I still hear arguments from colleagues who suggest we should concentrate on treating everyone the same to eliminate bias. I have also heard colleagues make the argument that we are all diverse in one capacity or other (e.g., Scandinavians are a minority group in the United States). A comprehensive and serious study that assesses measures of completion helps us move the conversation of equity away from politics and into basic social science analysis and problem solving. Assessing the academy with the critical assessment tools we teach in our disciplines helps ground the conversation.

In conjunction with assessment, we must recognize equity at the highest strategic level. It must be included in the Educational Master Plan, the Facilities Master Plan, the Strategic Plan and any other major planning document connected to the colleges. It is important that the goal not be buried too deep in the plan. For example, it should not be a *task* that belongs to an *objective* under a *goal* of a major *strategic initiative*. It should be at the higher or highest levels in the major plans of the institution. Implementation details should come from the comprehensive equity plan that is developed through the decision-making process and treated as an academic priority with buy-in from the major constituent groups across campus. With equity positioned at the highest strategic levels in the institution, the leadership in the institution needs to discuss the issue frequently and make sure the topic remains at the forefront of operations in the institution. With this in mind, college leaders may want to make academic equity the primary focus of the college mission or vision for the institution.

Strategy #36: Implement Work Through Teams

After planning is completed, implementation begins, at which point we need to take great care with teamwork. Doing strategic work is difficult. It is often perceived as an add-on activity. As a result, campus leadership must actively engage in building and coaching teams to get this work done. Leaders should join, build, and oversee the teams that do the work defined by the college's strategic documents. Leadership's assistance with securing places for teams to meet, finding resources needed for teams to work, helping organize the team's work, keeping the team together during difficult times are all important roles they need to play in the development of teamwork throughout the college. Working to solve big problems like the ones we have been discussing throughout this book is difficult. This is why these problems are so widespread and chronic. The work often leads to conflict, but good teams are able to absorb conflict without breaking relationships. Leaders need to help build these teams into strong units *before* the conflict emerges, so the social capital of the group is available when the difficulties arise. Finally, one of the most important roles the leader can play during the grind of implementation is the role of keeping everyone focused on the *why*. When teams fall into difficult periods, their leaders need to remind them of the work they are doing and how it all ties back to helping students from historically underserved communities. Remembering the *why* usually diminishes the passion behind the more trivial disputes we all get caught up in from time to time.

We need big solutions to address the student success and equity-related problems that have been persistent in community colleges. As community college leaders, we should build agendas with the scope to meet these challenges and implement these agendas together in teams. To the greatest extent possible, our teams need to be diverse, with representatives from all constituent groups, including Board members, college administrators, faculty, civic leaders, union members, business leaders, and students. We need to build teams that trust each other, works collaboratively together, leverage individual strengths, hold an unwavering commitment to students, and tackle great challenges.

As we bring diverse constituents together on teams, we need to remind each other that we do not want to operate in a pluralistic model, where individuals are expected to argue for constituent interests. Instead, we are working according to a functional family model, where we help galvanize our constituents and their resources around student success-oriented initiatives. With this approach, leaders are expected to be transparent, open, empathetic, collaborative, and consensus driven. In this model, constituent groups may sometimes lose a little in our effort to help students. The entire model hinges on relationships with high levels of trust. And this leads to the most nerve-racking characteristic associated with leadership in the functional family model—vulnerability.

Dr. Brené Brown, a scholar at University of Houston, has spent the better part of her career looking at the power (and pitfalls) or leading through vulnerability. She captured America's attention in a 2010 TedTalk (www.ted.com/talks/brene_brown_the_power_of_vulnerability?language=en) that went viral with over 45M views (and counting). I was one of those viewers. She excels at bringing deeply meaningful research to popular audiences, and her analysis of the relationship between vulnerability and effective leadership is profound.

To lead a group of people into new territory, into greater levels of success, a leader must be vulnerable with the people they lead. Leaders must be able to aggregate and articulate the aspirations of the group and then set a course in that direction with the open admission that they are not completely sure how to get there. This approach draws people into the endeavor, bringing strengths that the leader does not have, and creates a team that can collectively move in the direction of their dreams. This approach can be powerful, but while Brown's research insists that this is the path of great leaders, she also warns (in a very Brené way) that these leaders will occasionally "get their ass kicked." And because they are leaders operating in an open and transparent manner, the "ass kicking" will take place in the arena, in the public, for all to see.

For many leaders, Brown's advice is counterintuitive. To these people, vulnerability is synonymous with weakness. Vulnerability is the condition that precedes something that none of us want—public embarrassment. I know Brown would agree with these people in the sense that vulnerability can leave leaders exposed. It is a condition where the leader's weaknesses are open and on display. And this vulnerability will be a problem in environments where trust is low, but in environments where good relationships are intact and deep levels of trust have been established, honesty can prevail, unleashing our ability to work together as teams much more effectively. If we are going to have a chance at solving the big challenges we have been discussing throughout this book, we need to build environments where we trust each other deeply and work closely with each other from positions of honesty. We must have the courage to be vulnerable with each other if we hope to build great learning environments for our students.

I have spent a significant amount of time in high-trust environments and unfortunately even more time in fear-based, low-trust environments. The latter are the least productive. In these environments, people rarely work together, and when they do, they are careful to avoid mistakes for fear of reprisal. This attitude leads to extreme incrementalism, with solutions development pointed at the least controversial problems. In other words, very little gets done and none of the hard issues (e.g., the issues this book is trying to address) are resolved. In contrast, high-trust environments, despite the vulnerability wrapped into these environments, are wonderful to work in. In these environments, teamwork is constant. A sense of community develops. The group addresses and works towards solving big problems. These environments are filled with people who trust each other, who have each other's backs, who believe in each other. In these environments, we are able to take risks, try new things, talk openly about our uncertainties, ask for help, admit weaknesses. . . . These are always the environments where big problems are solved because people are able to work together in authentic, meaningful, and productive ways.

In 2019, I saw this play out in a very real way at Norco College. In a high-trust environment across campus, we entered a campus-wide dialogue to reorganize the entire college, with major restructuring in the academic affairs and student services areas. As is typical with reorganization, many of these conversations were difficult. Changing alliances, report lines, office areas, and more is what "begging for conflict" looks like. In the middle of this deliberation, we invited the *Chronicle of Higher Education* on campus to conduct its "Great College to Work For" survey. Knowing the survey would ask Norco College employees a series of poignant questions related to their working environment, I was a little reluctant to proceed. But the survey is only conducted in the spring, and while the timing for us felt unfortunate, we decided to continue.

I remember thinking the results were going to be terrible because we were in the middle of a college-wide deliberation on reorganization, and so some of the meetings were acrimonious. Regardless, the survey was conducted, and a series of questions was asked of the managers, faculty, and staff. There are questions in the survey that are straightforward, like "Do you trust the leadership of the college?" And these questions were asked at a time when I was also leading many college personnel through a difficult reorganization. How could this possibly end well?

When the results came in, we were elated. We ended up being one of only two community colleges in California to receive "Great College to Work For" designation by the *Chronicle*. I attribute this success almost entirely to our efforts to build a functional family-style environment. Working in high-trust environments, focused on big solutions to help students find greater success is exhausting and intense, but it is also very gratifying.

Strategy #37: Manage the "Old" and Lead the "New"

Another skill that innovative leaders need is the ability to navigate in something Clayton Christensen of Harvard calls "The Innovator's Dilemma" (Christensen, 1997).

Christensen captured this idea in 1997 with a book that explored disruptive technologies and their impact on leadership. In a 2016 elaboration on this premise, Charles O'Reilly and Michael Tushman published *Lead and Disrupt* (2016). They argue that when organizations encounter any kind of disruption (technology or otherwise), they must simultaneously keep their "old" business running and explore "new" business in relation to the disruption. The prior is important because it is typically where the primary income for the institution resides, and the latter is important because it charts the future for the institution. Pursuing both is very difficult because the two require different approaches, even different cultures.

Focusing on the "old," on the traditions of an enterprise, is conservative by nature. I do not mean this kind of focus is ideologically conservative; I mean it is culturally and behaviorally conservative. Individuals focusing their energy in this direction are concerned with existing customers. They explore how to bring in more customers like their current base and how to build better relationships with them. The prevailing mindset in this environment focuses on management excellence and efficiency. Getting the trains to run on time, every time, every day, every week is the primary focus and source of pride in this endeavor. The systems, practices, and processes of the institution are to be preserved and incrementally improved day after day in an ongoing quest to perfect the services and products offered to customers. Understanding the mission of the organization, organizing assets around that mission, and implementing with the highest possible quality is the approach that is needed in this environment. Organizations that operate in this manner recognize the successes of their past, understand that these successes have brought them to their present, and commit to continuing in this tradition with ongoing improvement.

Successful organizations will encounter disruption of some sort. A competitor will rise, a technology will develop, a population will shift, an innovation will hit, a new strategy will be introduced, a market will fall, or any number of other circumstances will pose a major challenge to the institution. Disruption of some sort will happen, and when it does, the leadership of the organization must develop a response that charts a new course for the institution. New customers, new services, new products, and new strategies must be factored in, in conjunction with the history of the institution. This kind of thinking requires a progressive approach with largess, risk-taking, tolerance for failure, creativity, scalability, and speed. These environments need leaders rather than managers. They need individuals who will point the trains in a new direction, knowing that the rail system will not run on time for a period while the new direction and required infrastructure to support the new destination are put in place. Organizations that operate in this manner are attempting to break with the past. They are progressive rather than conservative. They believe that an uninterrupted continuation of the past will lead to diminished success, if not failure. Success of the organization lies in the vision of a new future and the boldness to move in that direction.

A good example of this that we are all familiar with is the retail industry transition from brick-and-mortar to online approaches. The transition was difficult, expensive, fraught with learning and adjusting. Many of the businesses that successfully managed their old enterprises (brick-and-mortar) while developing their new approaches (online) are flourishing today. Many of those that did not embrace the new while managing the old are now out of business.

The main point of O'Reilly's work is that great leadership must be able to simultaneously practice both approaches. Supporting the *old* with excellent management and realizing the *new* with bold leadership are part of the same job description. These two approaches clearly butt heads on a cultural level. They come from a different set of assumptions. They require a different set of skills from the executives and line employees responsible for implementation. Regardless, they must coexist for institutions to remain successful during periods of disruption.

The Riverside Community College District and Norco College were in the midst of a disruption when I was hired as the president of Norco College. The external force driving this disruption was related to the population growth that had occurred around Norco College throughout the 2000s. The growth demanded that "little" Norco College expand significantly to offer an appropriate level of education services for the region, and this demand placed a strain on the traditional distribution of resources (and power) across the district. In the end, RCCD's leadership was not able to simultaneously respond to the *new* demands presented by this population growth and the very real *old* demands that continued to challenge the district. O'Reilly reveals this to be a common tension and finds that the *old* business often perceives the *new* business as a threat to the organization and, having the greater share of resources in the organization, often kills or drastically weakens the *new*.

When I think about this duality, this spectrum, and how it relates to higher education, my thoughts first go to tradition. Academics love *old* stuff. We love history. We love reaching back to explain what is to come. Supporting and building on the heritage of a college or university is baked into academia. We are taught to do this in our graduate training. Before we propose anything new in academic thinking, we must conduct a full exploration of history. This is what is known as a literature review. We fully explore what previous thinkers have done to develop an understanding of how we might add to the field. This is a solid practice for moving knowledge and understanding forward. It ensures that we are not overly repetitive, and it forces each generation to build on the shoulders of previous thinkers.

Embedded in this approach is a respect for tradition that is carried throughout the academy. The gowns we wear during graduation ceremonies can be traced to traditions from 12th-century Europe. The earliest universities in Europe were started by the church. In recognition of their religious roots, graduating students emulated the gowns and caps commonly worn by clergy at the time, and now, 900 years later, we are still wearing the medieval clothing during commencement. This respect for the past can also be seen in much of academic architecture. Many universities deliberately honor their past with new buildings that look old. We hold onto old names like the bursar's office, a medieval term from Latin meaning purse-bearer. Higher education is full of examples like this, grounded in our very conservative and traditional leanings.

With that said, these incredibly conservative universities and colleges are also surprisingly progressive. They are often the bastions of new thought, new ideas, new frameworks for approaching the human experience. The very idea of academic freedom comes from the backlash that many academics have received for introducing revolutionary ideas. Tenure for most faculty at research institutions is based on their ability to add new ideas and new findings to their disciplines. The reason that most universities and colleges are now separate from the church is based on academia's inclination to explore new ideas, regardless of their support or contradiction to religious doctrine. This independence has created a long history of conflict between the church and the university. Our past is full of encounters that were tragic, even fatal, for some academics who insisted on presenting ideas that they believed to be true despite their opposition to powerful church forces. Higher education has very progressive leanings.

In many ways, "The Innovator's Dilemma" is holding back the educational reform we need to help historically underserved students succeed. Higher education has long been biased toward the upper-middle- and upper-income families in the United States. Higher education has adopted a value system and culture that favors these families. Higher education recruits students from these families more consistently than students from others lower on the economic scale. Higher education admits vastly more students from these more prosperous families. Also, higher education employs faculty and executives more often from these families. As noted previously, higher education (especially the most selective universities) is primarily made up of a set of institutions that help young people from privileged families maintain their privilege by disproportionately admitting them and therefore disproportionately qualifying them for the most selective jobs and positions in American society.

Recently, dialogue about these biases has emerged, and higher education is slowly coming to the realization that it is part of the growing inequality problem in the United States. This understanding is creating disruption at some colleges and universities—the good kind of disruption. To navigate this disruption successfully, we need to continue managing the *old* parts of our institutions that will remain and simultaneously develop the *new* parts of our institutions that will be added. We need to continue running our institutions using traditional models as a matter of prudence while we develop new models that bring in more students from historically underserved communities and track them all the way through to jobs and positions of prominence in American society. We need to change admissions policies, change pedagogical practices, change student services practices, change government funding distribution for higher education, change private funding distribution for higher education, and much more.

As the *new* business of higher education emerges, O'Reilly's research suggests that the *old* business of the university that has the greater share of resources and power will perceive these changes through a negative frame and work to kill or weaken the innovations that need to transpire. Successful leaders will understand this duality and move forward in both directions as we maintain some of our traditions and dismantle others in our attempt to reverse our 50-year trend of growing inequality in the United States.

Strategy #38: Improve Through Assessment and Accountability

When I was a faculty member, I remember being initially frustrated with the evaluation process. The evaluations I received from peers were almost effusively positive. These of course were flattering, but I was trying to build up an expertise over time and found the overly positive evaluations to offer very little constructive criticism or suggestions for improvement. They did not seem to have a sense of normative excellence and did not use a data-driven approach to inform how close or far I was from this normative standard. As I became a more senior faculty member and started conducting evaluations myself, I quickly understood the complications associated with peer review. Pointing out deficiencies in a colleague's pedagogy or service to the institution can be very complicated and can create a great deal of friction in the workplace. As a result of these complications, what has happened with regard to evaluations at many institutions is a kind of silent agreement where you agree not to look too critically or closely at my work and I will agree to do the same about your work. This has literally created an environment at many institutions in which a recommendation to improve in any area is not taken as constructive criticism that will help with personal development; rather it is received as a possible strike against their performance that is part of their personal record and threatens their job security.

There are many complications associated with evaluations, but we as institutions need to break out of this cycle of meaningless exercises so we are able to do more meaningful and productive assessment of our institutions. An approach that is useful to discuss is program assessment. I had a great deal of success with this approach when I was dean over institutional effectiveness. In this position, I decided to do a comparative assessment of academic programs (disciplines) starting with the initial measure of student retention and completion by course. As I developed the instruments for assessment and started in on the discussion around this approach, I ran into a great deal of consternation. In the politically charged environment of individual evaluations that impact perceived job security, many were generally worried about all evaluations. Regardless of the initial push-back, we moved forward with the project and found that it generated a very strong dialogue about program excellence that was beneficial to program improvement across campus.

Assessment is critical at our institutions. Leadership should make every effort to place all activities of the college into programs, understand how those programs impact the core mission of the college (e.g., student success), and find measures that reasonably reflect the quality of the program relative to the institution's mission. Every employee at the institution should be represented in at least one program. Programs should be measured over time with the expectation that they will improve and to the greatest extent possible be measured against similar programs on campus. It is also critical that faculty and staff see that the assessment process also includes the responsibilities of managers for outcomes. For example, if academic programs are being evaluated, the evaluation needs to bring in the discussion of academic management in the area as part of the conversation. Responsibility for program performance should extend all the way to the college president. The general tone and goal of all the program evaluations should be to help discover best practices and find areas for improvement.

Strategy #39: Build Institutional Values Around Love

The basis for all our work as leaders of the college, the foundation upon which all else is built, should be love. We need to nurture this motivation as a deliberate ethic across leadership. I know some people think that love is exclusively for our private lives—something that we only share with our spouse, partner, family members, and friends. But I believe we are depriving ourselves if we restrict love in this way. Love should be vibrantly alive in all aspects of our lives, including our work as college leaders. Many people, including me, believe love is the highest human expression. When we are loved, in love, being loved, acting in love, we are at our best. We are patient, kind, selfless, and forgiving. We are inclusive, present, fearless, and bold. When we are wrapped in love, we are beautiful. As leaders of the college, we need to talk about this openly and boldly.

We need to love our *students*. We should treat them as family—as our children, grandchildren, nieces, and nephews. From this perspective, we believe our students have something special and unique to offer the world, and we desire to help them discover and nurture what they will offer humanity.

We need to love our *colleagues*. Instead of thinking of the college as a workplace, we should think of it as a community. We are constantly in community and building community by supporting the members of our community with kindness, encouragement, understanding, and forgiveness. From this perspective, we are open to challenging each other to reach our potential. We encourage each other to grow and deliver excellence. We believe that we are capable of brilliant solutions to enduring problems when we work together in teams.

We need to love our *neighbors*. As the community's college, we seek to build enduring relationships with the individuals and organizations in our region. We are committed to working with them to transform lives and the quality of life throughout the region. We aspire to build with them a better culture, polity, community, and economy.

There are few things more gratifying than preparing a gift that is born of your personal talents, crafted with a specific group of individuals in mind, and given as a gesture of love. We all know that in these circumstances the bigger beneficiary is the giver. A leader's job is to think of their work as a gift prepared with love for the intended recipients. If you are able to weave the ethic of love into you daily work, you will receive great joy, and our students will receive you best.

If a leader takes this approach, he or she is joining a long tradition. Plato, Marx, Augustine, Rousseau, Christ, Mohammad, Abraham, the Buddha, Martin Luther King, Gandhi, Mother Teresa, my mother, and your mother—they all suggested that love should be the foundation of our movement through life. I have read several books and heard even more presentations on how we need to treat each other in the workplace. Advice is often presented as a list of core values: "We believe in honesty, openness, transparency, servant leadership, community, student-centeredness, excellence." Many people find these lists vague and difficult to remember. However, if we focus on treating every person from a perspective of love, we don't need the list in front of us. All those core characteristics are in our behavior already when we treat each other with love.

Grounding our institutions in this ethic is how we solve the tendency to advocate on behalf of our members' interest in a pluralist model. Leaders need to encourage those they lead to extend love, especially toward students. If a campus community can think of students as their family members—as nephews/nieces, brothers/sisters, children, or grandkids—it becomes nearly impossible for students to be left behind in the negotiations that transpire across the academy. Seeing students as family members translates into faculty, managers, staff, and board members making sure student interests are heard, considered, and accommodated to the extent possible.

There are many changes that we need to make in our institutions on behalf of historically underserved students. The individuals who will make these changes possible are the college leaders and constituent leaders of groups spread across the campus. However, contemporary community colleges have environments that make these changes very difficult to implement. To counter these difficult environments, we need leaders who can develop compelling visions for our colleges, build great teams in high-trust environments, balance between managing the *old* and leading the *new*, and consciously integrate love as the prevailing ethic of their work.

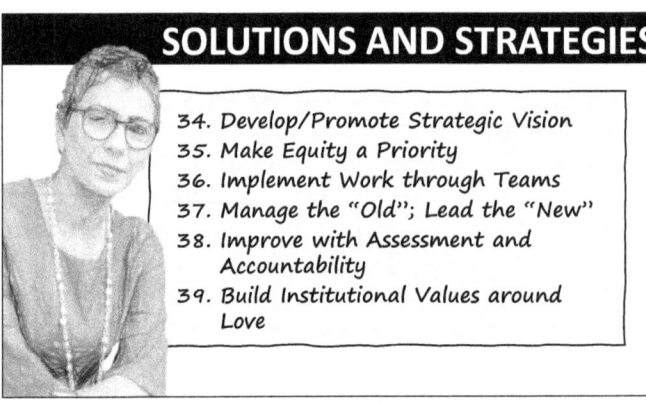

SOLUTIONS AND STRATEGIES

34. Develop/Promote Strategic Vision
35. Make Equity a Priority
36. Implement Work through Teams
37. Manage the "Old"; Lead the "New"
38. Improve with Assessment and Accountability
39. Build Institutional Values around Love

Conclusion

In the face of the injustices we have discussed throughout this book, the main thing we need leaders to do is "end the silence." We need leaders who will not agree to be silent about the conditions that perpetuate the social injustice of underperformance. Institutional underperformance and external underinvestment of institutions is a social injustice. To stay silent on all of the conditions that create this underperformance and underinvestment is to participate in the injustice. Roberts and Rizzo speak to this issue, stating that a primary challenge we face is the need to end "passivism" (2020). They argue that racial discrimination in the United States is perpetuated by a very passive approach that allows patterns of social injustice to continue. We give in to passivism when we stay away from issues related to social injustice because they are uncomfortable and create conflict. We give in to passivism when we let other issues become higher priorities, taking up our time and energy. We give in to passivism when we use anecdotal information and data to fool ourselves and others into thinking we are addressing these issues when we are not. This delusion leads to a kind of willful ignorance of the actual conditions that hold back our students. These practices and others create an atmosphere where unjust hurdles persist.

When leaders in our community colleges implement the strategies we have discussed in this chapter and throughout the book, they are ending the silence, ending passivism, and building institutions that may be able to fulfill the promise of equity we so proudly proclaim in our mission statements across higher education.

10 Implementing the Work of Social Justice in Our Colleges

When I arrived as president of Norco College, one of the first things I decided to do was meet the civic leaders in the community. In most local communities, there are a few hundred civic leaders who have significant influence. They typically include local business leaders, elected officials, nonprofit executives, educational administrators, and leaders of government enterprises in the region. Working with my assistant, we culled through the contacts the previous president left behind and added to that list obvious positions and leaders that were not included on the list. One of the individuals on our list I wanted to meet was the warden of the California Rehabilitation Center (CRC).

CRC is a California state prison, designated a Level II correctional facility for men. Also referred to as a medium security facility, inmates live in open space dormitories rather than the cells we often associate with prison life. There is an armed security perimeter around its 98 acres, but movement in the prison itself is fairly open, although designated time periods give most days a routine structure. According to the CDCR website, the facility housed approximately 3,500 inmates as of December 2019. CRC is one of the older prisons in the state system, with some of the buildings built in 1928. The facility is about a quarter mile as the crow flies from Norco College.

I requested a meeting with the warden, Cynthia Tampkins. She and I eventually developed a strong relationship, but this first meeting, at her facility, was introductory. My plan was to meet with her individually, introduce myself and explore possible ways to collaborate or at least make sure she understood that I was open to collaborating if any opportunities arose. Cynthia is very kind and easy to be around. She is also as strong as you might imagine a prison warden needs to be.

It took about 30 minutes to get through security. I was met by a member of her staff, and we walked together up a very long flight of outdoor stairs to her office, located at the top of a small hill. Her office is in a classic government temporary build that has become permanent. Her staff person escorted me into the building, down a hallway, and into the room where we were to meet.

Expecting to meet with Cynthia one on one, I was surprised when we walked through the door and into a conference room filled with about ten people. CRC, like many other prisons, has an educational staff that works with inmates on technical training (e.g., fire service training) and GED-related education. They also work closely with college personnel if the prison offers college-level instruction. The warden had invited most of the managers from her education team, and also seated at the table was the state system director for all of prison education in California.

I sat down at the conference table, we all introduced ourselves, and they laid out their desire to bring college instruction to the prison.

CRC was currently offering correspondence college courses in partnership with a college located nearly 200 miles from the prison. The program was popular but highly limited given the nature of correspondence through U.S. mail with a partner 200 miles away. They wanted Norco College, a quarter mile away, to offer live instruction at the prison. We talked about the possibilities for a while, and they asked me if I would like to meet some of the college students who were taking correspondence courses. I will admit, I was a little reluctant to agree. I hadn't prepared to meet with her entire team, and meeting a group of inmates was something I had not even imagined. But I could tell they were eager for me to meet their students, so I agreed.

CRC Inmates Taking Exam

A group of four or five walked me to the classroom where inmates were studying. One of CRC's education managers interrupted the students, asked them to gather in a cluster of chairs near the front of the room, introduced me as the president of Norco College, and said that I was considering offering courses at the prison and wanted to get their feedback. I made a few comments supporting the introduction and opened up to the floor to get a sense of their receptiveness to the idea. What followed was a round of eager and probing comments from a group of students who enthusiastically supported the idea. They asked me how many units they would be able to take. They asked me if they could look at our catalog and select courses. They asked me which courses I was thinking about. They asked about articulation of existing units. They asked me if we could build a full AA degree. We talked for about 40 minutes. I left the classroom, walked back down the long stairway, through security, and out to my car.

I sat in my car trying to piece together what had just happened. I was affected by the experience in a meaningful way, but I couldn't put my finger on the reason. I was somewhat emotional about it and altogether surprised. It took a month or more for me to piece together the significance of meeting with the CRC students. Up until the meeting with the students of CRC, I had spent nearly three decades in community college education work. During all those years, I was always taking the posture of selling education. As a professor, I often felt like I was teaching to the disaffected students in the back of the room. I often thought of my lecture as something that needed to convince the students of the value of education. As an administrator, I tried to encourage faculty members to sell our service to students and in the community; I was constantly promoting the virtues of a higher education, especially one that starts with community colleges. What I had never experienced was the reverse. I had never been in a room where students were pleading with me, nearly begging me to bring education to them. This is the energy CRC students brought to me on the day I met with them.

As I shared this story with faculty and managers at the college, several people became enthusiastic about the opportunity of teaching inmates. With this enthusiasm, we went on to develop a model prison education program with CRC. The first graduating class was recognized in January of 2020 with AA degrees in sociology. I am very proud of the program, but what sticks with me to this day is the profound impact education can have on a person's life. And the more difficult their life, the more significant the impact education has. It can literally change the trajectory of an individual's life and very often the trajectory of many members of their family. Standing in front of CRC students, locked up for bad decisions, these students had a palpable, nearly desperate sense of how a collection of courses that add up to a degree could change their odds of success when their time in prison was over.

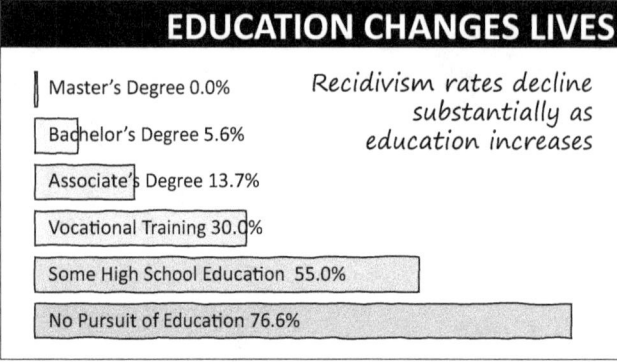

As stated in Chapter 3, education and recidivism have an inverse correlation that is compelling. Inmates who pursue no education while in prison have a national recidivism rate of 76.6 percent. If an inmate pursues some high school education while in prison, their recidivism rate drops to 55.0 percent. Pursuing vocational training drops the rate to 30.0 percent. Achieving an AA degree drops the rate to 13.7 percent, while the completion of a bachelor's degree and master's degree drops the rates to 5.6 percent and 0 percent respectively (Allen, 2006). These numbers are concrete evidence that education changes the trajectory of students' lives. Many of our more traditional students may not have the same consciousness about the benefits they can reap from a successful education, but for students from historically marginalized communities, education can mean the difference between a difficult life and a successful life for their entire family.

Given that community colleges provide the most post-secondary education for students from historically underserved communities, our success is critical. To this end, this book has referenced a large body of literature related to student success for community college students. We have identified 39 strategies that can be implemented to address a range of challenges that our students face.

In terms of implementing the 39 strategies, it is important to think of them as falling into two categories. Some of the strategies can be implemented internally by colleges. These are strategies that have proven effective at the institutional level. Other strategies need to be implemented at the collective level. These strategies are bigger than a single college or institution. They require external changes that need to take place throughout the ecosystem that community colleges operate within. They need governmental and non-governmental organization (NGO) involvement to make them happen. Following is a list of all 39 strategies and how they correspond to these two categories, internal and external changes.

		Internal	External
Initiative 1: Add Academic Capital to Students' Lives (Chap 4 Content)			
Strategy 1	Develop Student Progress Tracking	√	√
Strategy 2	Incorporate New Socializing Agents	√	√
Strategy 3	Focus on Students' Assets	√	
Strategy 4	Increase Diversity of Personnel	√	√
Strategy 5	Expand Counseling Support	√	√
Strategy 6	Nurture Faculty-Student Relationships	√	
Strategy 7	Secure Food/Housing/Health	√	√
Strategy 8	Create Sticky Campus	√	
Initiative 2: Fund Higher Education Equitably (Chap 5 Content)			
Strategy 9	Conduct National Audit		√
Strategy 10	Restructure State Funding		√
Strategy 11	Maximize Student Financial Aid	√	√

		Internal	External
Strategy 12	Build Alumni Connections	√	
Strategy 13	Pursue Federal Grants	√	
Strategy 14	Redirect Social Justice Funding		√
Strategy 15	Alter Tax Status for Institutions That Discriminate		√
Initiative 3: Establish Best Practices (Chap 6 Content)			
Strategy 16	Implement Best Practices for Core Competencies	√	
Strategy 17	Implement Programmatic Standards of Excellence	√	
Strategy 18	Categorize All Activities Under Programs	√	
Strategy 19	Build Physical Spaces to Support Equity	√	
Strategy 20	Expand Professional Development	√	√
Strategy 21	Establish Targeted Support Services	√	√
Initiative 4: Create Intuitive and Supportive Transitions (Chap 7 Content)			
Strategy 22	Implement Guided Pathways	√	
Strategy 23	Develop Intuitive Systems	√	√
Strategy 24	Establish High School Partnerships	√	√
Strategy 25	Articulate Military Training	√	√
Strategy 26	Connect Careers to Learning	√	√
Strategy 27	Establish Common Course Number	√	√
Strategy 28	Build Student-Centered Schedules	√	
Strategy 29	Offer Online Courses/Services	√	
Initiative 5: Place Historically Underserved Students in Selective Universities (Chap 8 Content)			
Strategy 30	Establish Proactive Transfer Center	√	
Strategy 31	Develop Transfer Program for High-GPA/Low-Income Students	√	√
Strategy 32	Change University/College Ranking System		√
Strategy 33	End Legacy Scoring		√
Initiative 6: Develop Leaders Who Can Affect Institutional Change (Chap 9 Content)			
Strategy 34	Develop/Promote Strategic Vision	√	√
Strategy 35	Make Equity a Priority	√	√
Strategy 36	Implement Work Through Teams	√	
Strategy 37	Manage the "Old"; Lead the "New"	√	
Strategy 38	Improve With Assessment and Accountability	√	
Strategy 39	Build Institutional Values Around Love	√	

Leading Institutional Change

From the perspective of implementation, many of the recommended strategies discussed throughout this book can feel daunting. Most of them are big. They will require significant commitment and major resources. Considering the entire list as a whole, it may seem overwhelming. I suspect, however, that you picked up this book and worked through its content because you want to move social justice and equity forward. You clearly see threads of injustice woven into our history and want to eliminate them from the fabric we weave for the next generation. While we cannot remove the inequities perpetuated in our past—we can't remove the perpetrators or the victims—we can help shape our future. More accurately, we are right now shaping our futures partly by the institutions we build and sustain. In this sense, our decisions today impact the extent to which tomorrow will continue marginalizing specific groups or shift to including all groups. If we as college leaders today decide to maintain the historical structures discussed in this book, we are deciding to continue marginalizing specific communities. If we decide to reform these structures with many of the strategies discussed in this book, then we are making the choice to build a more inclusive society. Either way, we are making a choice.

I acknowledge that leading change for social justice and equity is extremely difficult. The leader is put into situations where they must persuade people in power, people with power, to make changes that are often not in their immediate self-interest. Many of the people who hold elevated positions in higher education come from communities that have historically benefitted from the social structures that currently exist, and to alter these structures is to remove their advantage, their leverage, their privilege. It is in their personal interest to keep these rules in place.

This is largely why it is so difficult for minority population groups who experience discrimination to change the course of that experience. Discrimination against economically disadvantaged populations is how the majority population creates an unequal environment with the odds stacked in their favor. The group in power extracts resources from the group that is out of power, creating privilege for one and hardship for the other. Asking people with power to cede some control to a group with less power is difficult. Getting them to actually carry it out is improbable. And the entire process is professionally dicey.

For example, most of higher education is filled with faculty who support equity and social justice. However, when the factual claim is made that public four-year universities serving whiter and higher-income students receive more tax dollars than community colleges, which serve much higher proportions of students from marginalized communities, rarely do our four-year colleagues, which often teach social justice from the lectern, agree that the tax imbalance is discriminatory and should be adjusted. I cannot point to one instance where they have actively lobbied to effect this change for the sake of social justice. Instead, they mostly ignore this issue, and when it is discussed, they provide well-developed, long, complicated, and historical arguments that give explanations for this unequal and discriminatory distribution of public resources, obscuring obvious inequality behind a mountain of complicated arguments that get codified through legislation, written into education policy, and established through legal precedent. All of this serves the purpose of bolstering the legitimacy of conditions that deprive resources from one group so another group can prosper.

Self-interest group loyalty plays out in thousands of different scenarios across higher education. When a union advocate knowingly protects a faculty member who has demonstrated racial bias in the classroom and refuses to "turn on" the faculty member, the advocate is choosing to preserve union power rather than address social injustices. When a college manager refuses to implement difficult equity policies because it may strain relationships and jeopardize future prospects for promotion, the manager is choosing to maintain or accumulate administrative power rather than address social injustices. Boards, academic senates, departments, divisions, legislatures, and others have been asked for decades to implement reform to make conditions better for students from historically marginalized communities, but when the request requires the surrender of some power, it is commonly denied behind some kind of complicated and abstract justification. When people are asked to choose between preserving their own power or correcting a social injustice, they historically develop a complicated justification for choosing to preserve their power.

I believe these general examples are the main reasons we look at the list of changes that need to be made and find our hearts racing. Leading change for social justice and equity feels good when you consider the group you are helping, but when you consider the group you are opposing, the notion of implementing the needed changes can feel personally and professionally risky. Leaders doing work in this space must navigate complicated political terrain. The only approach I have found to be successful (and it has not always been successful) is to focus *everything* around students. The "why" behind every strategy mentioned in this book must be connected to students somehow. Why are we doing strategy X? Because it will help students through Z. This needs to be the dialogue around every proposed strategy. It is the only argument that has the potential to bring all of us together. If justifications and dialogue for strategies focus on state compliance, district stability, union solidarity, academic freedom, management efficiency, balanced budgets, and the like, there will be constituent groups that launch compelling counter-arguments based in power calculations that slow or stall the progress toward these important social justice initiatives.

It takes a while to build justifications for all these initiatives around student-centered arguments, but this is critical. For example, one of the strategies mentioned in an earlier chapter is to develop hiring practices that increase institutional diversity. There are many arguments that can be made in support of this goal—arguments that explain the "why" behind this strategy. One set of arguments can be made around compliance. There are many federal, state, and local policies that speak to diversity issues. Building arguments that suggest we need to comply with these laws is a legitimate way to explain why we need to develop hiring practices to increase diversity. Another set of arguments can be made around empowerment of employee groups. For example, at most institutions of higher education, there is a disproportionately high percentage of White faculty and a disproportionately low percentage of brown and Black faculty relative to local, state, and national population distributions. Bringing employee groups into balance with larger population distributions empowers groups that have been historically marginalized. Arguments along these lines can be used to explain why we need to hire with diversity in mind. I have been at institutions where both approaches have been used, and they usually spiral into difficult disagreements. Few people respond positively to compliance-based arguments, and discussions around proportionality of employees often brings out the sharp edges of identity politics.

In contrast, if the "why" is built around students, if we focus on the idea that our students need to first experience people who look like them to feel like they are part of the institution and then experience people who do *not* look like them to prepare them for the extremely diverse workplaces they will entering, the college community receives this initiative in a much different light. They may see hiring for diversity as a difficult strategy to implement, but if they see it as something that will help our students succeed (and nearly everyone I have worked with is interested in helping students succeed), they are likely to accept it. With this approach, the conversation can still become about power, but it will be about empowering students. For this reason, framing these strategies around student success is essential.

After all the student-centered framing work is done, three critical conversations toward the development of a comprehensive implementation plan need to be organized. A major challenge during all of these conversations will be to keep the conversations framed around empowering students and protect the dialogue from slipping into all the other distractions that can potentially detail progress.

The first conversation that needs to be held is with the *executive team*. The make-up of this team varies from college to college, but regardless, it is typically a small team that

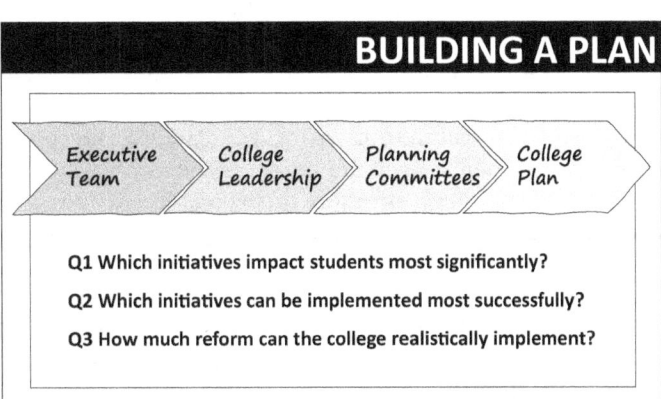

meets regularly to direct the most important strategic work of the college. This team needs to be introduced to this work with regard to how you anticipate moving the college toward greater equitable student success by closing performance gaps, especially completions. Each initiative needs to be discussed in broad strokes, relying primarily on student success framing. The team should understand not only the overall goal of each initiative but its approach. Achieving this level of understanding may take a couple of meetings. During the dialogue, there are three questions that need to be addressed: 1) Which initiative will impact students most significantly? 2) Which initiatives can be implemented most successfully? 3) How much reform can the college manage?

In the discussion around these three questions, the group should identify initiatives that are already been established at the college and are functioning successfully. The group should review all strategic planning documents of the college (educational master plan, facilities master plan, technology plan, and equity plan) to determine if any of the initiatives you are introducing have already been identified by previous planning groups (initiatives with different names might have many common features). The group should collectively think about resources that are available to the college and how they could be used for various initiatives. This discussion will help with the second and third questions in particular when the group assesses the likelihood of successful implementation and how much change is feasible. The product that should emerge from this conversation is the first draft of a plan. It may not include all the narrative explaining the plan but a prioritization of initiatives, suggested timelines, outline of activities, objectives and goals, groups involved in the deliberation leading to the plan, and parties/groups responsible for implementing the various activities of the plan.

As the conversation with the executive team is near completion, a second important conversation should start with *college leaders*. This group is also defined differently from college to college. I always try to define this group with fairly broad strokes. I typically include all managers, committee chairs, department chairs, senate leaders, union leaders, and community advisors in this group. These are the individuals on a college campus who have their finger on the pulse of particular constituents and have communication access with the members of their constituencies. Bringing them into the same kind of dialogue that was held with the executive team can further shape prioritization of initiatives, tighten up student-centered framing, reveal unanticipated hurdles, and secure early allies.

One of the discussions that needs to take place during this dialogue pertains to the role of each college leader. All too often, college leaders enter a dialogue from the perspective of constituent advocate. In this role, they see themselves as making sure that their constituents are represented, that no decisions diminish the existing powers and privileges enjoyed by their constituents, and that they might influence decisions in a direction that adds powers and privileges to those they represent.

This is an understandable role but not the exclusive role college leaders must play. They need to be reminded that as leaders, they have significant influence over a set of college resources and part of their job is to help strategically point those resources in a direction that will help improve the academic success of students. Each leader has a significant influence over the attitudes their constituents adopt, the kind of work they support, and the level of effort their constituents put into the work. In this sense, the relationship between the CEO and college constituent leaders is symbiotic. The president needs to listen to college leaders. They have meaningful insight and a strong sense of public opinion from their constituents. At the same time, they will need to help the president implement the strategy once it has been articulated. Breaking down old structures that hinder student success will not be possible without the college leadership on board. The CEO and the constituent leaders need each other to succeed.

When I was president of Norco College, we were nearing completion of a major plan to improve equity and student success at the college. Some of the activities were already being implemented, and very important plans were being set in motion on several other fronts. The plan called for reform across the college. We had developed the plan through a long deliberation with the executive team, college leaders, planning committees, all-campus meetings, and more. As the reality of the plan started to take hold, dissenting voices began to emerge with department faculty in particular. During one department chair's meeting, the faculty chairs started expressing deep frustration with all the pushback from their faculty. I was not in the meeting, but the VP of instruction was, and during the heated exchange, he texted me and recommended I walk across campus to listen to the group. As I walked from my office to the classroom where they were gathered, I made a point of centering my thoughts on the kind of success students had been experiencing, our general frustration with the low success, and our collective desire to significantly improve on their success, in particular their graduation rates.

I entered the room. The department chairpersons were seated in a circle, and they appeared frustrated. All of them felt beaten up from their own faculty pushing back on the program of change laid out in our new educational master plan document. We were in the middle of a full campus reorganization. We were implementing guided pathways deeply. We were in agreement with the goal of closing the equity gap and all that this goal implied for pedagogical change. And several other fundamental changes that had their constituents under stress and registering their frustration with individual chairpersons. I can sympathize with how difficult it is to lead through this kind of reform. I have been in the position of receiving criticism from my colleagues before, and it can sting. Faculty are very smart, they are trained to be critical, they usually have strong oratory skills, and the job security that comes with tenure can make them fearless. So, I listened for a good 45 minutes as the faculty chairs redirected this heat in my direction. Each was professional and respectful, but they were also direct. Eventually, they asked to hear from me.

I was careful to sincerely recognize the difficult situation they were in and tried to communicate a sense of empathy. I told them I was willing to revisit everything in the plan, but I did not want to back down on the idea of effecting major change for students. I talked about the frustration of watching students' success numbers, especially the numbers for marginalized groups, stay relatively flat for 30 years and that my greatest fear was spending a career that amounted to zero or very subtle change in these numbers. As we talked about students, and the impact success has on their lives, the impact failure has on their lives, I could feel the tone in the room shift. Every department chair moved from a posture of frustration to a posture of advocacy. It was not a shift in advocacy for my position, the position of administration, or anything like that. It was a shift in the direction of advocacy for students, especially students from historically underserved communities.

It is true that faculty can be difficult to work with at times, for all the reasons I mentioned previously. I have a few emotional scars to prove this, and I am sure I delivered my share of them when I was a faculty member. But I will say this with a very high degree of confidence: I have never worked with a group of people more passionate about students than the faculty at Norco College, Crafton Hills College, and Cerritos College, and all the other community college faculty I have had the pleasure of knowing over the years. If you want to create a passionate agenda of work for your college, frame it sincerely and genuinely around student success, and faculty will fuel it like no other constituency group.

The third dialogue takes place through the *planning process* and the committees associated with this process. Most colleges have some kind of decision-making process that includes collective input. This kind of arrangement is usually required by accrediting bodies and is certainly part of academic tradition. After the initial conversation with the executive team and the college leadership has helped give some structure to the initiatives and how they are be prioritized, a more structured conversation can start working through the planning process and shared decision-making process. This conversation needs to cover much of the same ground covered in the previous two conversations. Conversations need to be tightly framed around student success. With this frame, committees should explore which initiative will have the most significant impact on students, which initiatives can be implemented with the highest likelihood of success, and how much reform can be successfully absorbed and implemented by the institution. During these conversations, information collected during prior conversations should be presented to help initiate the dialogue from a more developed starting point. However, similar ground will definitely be covered during this phase.

To help formalize findings during this phase, it may be advisable to collect opinions from committee members and others involved in the conversation. The opinions should not be collected until the dialogue has matured and all individuals participating in the analysis have an understanding of each initiative and how the initiative will help students. There are many ways to design an instrument for collecting opinion. I recommend the design in the following figure.

Analysis of Strategic Priorities

Listed below are several strategies we are considering for implementation at the College. Please review each one and indicate the extent to which you believe 1) the strategy will help our students experience greater success, and 2) we will be able to implement the strategy successfully.

		Strongly Agree	Agree	Disagree	Strongly Disagree	Not Sure/No Opinion
S1	Develop Student Progress Tracking					
	This strategy will help our students succeed					
	This strategy can be implemented successfully at our college					
S2	Incorporate New Socializing Agents					
	This strategy will help our students succeed					
	This strategy can be implemented successfully at our college					
S3	Focus on Students' Assets					
	This strategy will help our students succeed					
	This strategy can be implemented successfully at our college					
S4	Increase Diversity of Personnel					
	This strategy will help our students succeed					
	This strategy can be implemented successfully at our college					
S5	Expand Counseling Support					
	This strategy will help our students succeed					
	This strategy can be implemented successfully at our college					
S6	Nurture Faculty-Student Relationships					
	This strategy will help our students succeed					
	This strategy can be implemented successfully at our college					

During this phase, committee members should be encouraged to take the dialogue back to their constituents for input. They need to be reminded of their role through a similar conversation held before with college leaders. The committee(s) may want to sponsor public forums for collecting information during the deliberation process and proactively take the deliberation out to other meetings.

One of the major reforms I helped organize at one college was a complete reorganization. The reorganization moved managers, staff, and departments into new areas; modified functions across multiple areas; and genuinely had an impact on most areas of the college. The approval and deliberation process we used include 50+ meetings! As president, I personally attended over half of the meetings and presented the proposal at several. During the course of those meetings, the reorganization plan was presented, comments were collected, the plan was revised based on comments that seemed to reflect shared opinion, and the cycle continued over a six-month period. The early meetings were highly contentions; some of the comments made in public meetings were even hostile. By the time we reached the later meetings, comments we extremely mild, with nuanced suggestions for improvement. The plan eventually built its way into a document that was unanimously agreed upon by the governing committees of the college and presented to our governing board with no opposition and significant praise from a range of constituent leaders. While I am not so sure I would repeat 50+ meetings, the lesson I take from that experience is the importance of upfront and inclusive deliberation for major decisions. If leaders take appropriate time during the deliberation process, they will find the approval and implementation processes much more stable and collectively accepted than they would be with a top-down implementation.

The conclusion of the shared deliberation process should lead to a final draft from the committee. The draft should detail the process that was followed, summarize the data collected during the process, and clearly present the plan/strategy for improving equitable student success at the college. The plan needs to communicate a clear picture and vision for where we are headed. This picture will be very important during the implementation phase, as opinions inevitably heat up. There may be other steps involved in the strategic planning process after the main committee work is completed. For example, the final draft is usually formally received by the president and forwarded to the district and board. Minor revisions may occur in these final steps, but more commonly, these are formalities. After the committee has completed its work, the implementation phase can be organized.

Implementation of the plan is the process of making ideas reality. It is extremely complicated, as indicated by the percentage of failed institutional change initiatives. According to a 2013 survey of global business executives, about 54 percent of large-scale institutional change initiatives succeed, and approximately 46 percent fail (Aguirre, von Post, & Alpern, 2013). The study finds that these initiatives fail for three main reasons (respondents could record any number of reasons.):

First, many fail because of change fatigue (reported as a reason by 65 percent of respondents). They are launched in an environment where many changes are already underway. In this environment, employees are already emotionally and physically drained from the current list of initiatives when the new initiative is introduced. As such, there is not enough time or enthusiasm to implement the new call for change, and the initiative fails.

The second most common reason for failure relates to insufficient leadership expertise (reported by 48 percent of respondents). Many initiatives fail because the institution does not have the leaders needed to implement the kind of change called for in the initiative.

The third most common reason for failure is lack of engagement (reported by 44 percent of survey respondents). In these cases, CEOs and the executive team try to implement change by dictating the changes that need to occur across the institution. Communication is mistaken for engagement. Consequently, the personnel expected to carry out the work feel disconnected from the importance of the change and are unable to see its value to the institution. In these circumstances, employees may delay implementation, wait for executive turnover, or even go so far as to sabotage the initiative with deliberately poor implementation.

Thirty-eight percent also indicated they have been in situations where they did not agree with the changes they were required to implement.

Failed implementation for any reason carries a cost. The most obvious cost is that the needed change does not happen. In the context of this book, if an institution develops a comprehensive plan to improve student success and eliminate equity gaps, a failed implementation means the unacceptable success rates for their students remain unchanged, with all the achievement gap inequities intact, and the injustices the institution is trying to address remain. Another cost associated with failed implementation is wasted time, resources, and energy. All of these are investments made during the planning process and the initial implementation phase. The planning and initial implementation for a significant change initiative can span two or three years, meaning significant resources are wasted if the change initiative is not successfully implemented. Finally, employee morale can be negatively affected with failed implementation. College personnel who invest heavily in the plan do so because they are excited about helping students find greater success. If the initiative fails during implementation, involved employees are often left feeling discouraged. They may start to doubt the capabilities of the college's leadership, begin to question the sincerity of their own colleagues, and even pull away from the notion that we can meet these enduring challenges.

I have watched, joined, and led institutional initiatives intended to change student success for many years. There are several approaches to implementation I have seen that elicit a range of results. The first I will mention is obviously the worst approach, but it is surprisingly common. I have seen so many efforts start and end with the plan. Writing a solid plan is difficult and is definitely gratifying when it has been completed. I have definitely felt the euphoria of holding a finished, well-designed, and approved plan in my hand.

But all too often, this accomplishment is treated like as the final step. Outside requirements (e.g., accreditation) often stipulate the development of a plan to improve in a particular area, and I have watched a number of well-intentioned colleagues deliver on this requirement. They write the plan, put it on a shelf, post it to a webpage, file it on a shared drive, and move on to the next required project. A plan on a shelf does nothing. It is equivalent to giving architectural drawings to a homeless person and claiming you have done something to improve their situation. A plan is meant to bring order to implementation.

Another pitfall I have seen with regard to implementing institutional reform is assigning major projects to people without the leverage to implement work at an institutional level. I have seen this happen at many institutions trying to close the equity gap. Most institutions acknowledge the equity gap as a critical problem. This is an important step. To address this, I have seen most institutions approach this challenge by assigning a director or dean to develop and implement some kind of equity plan. This can work if the individuals responsible for tasks are provided with institutional resources. For example, if it is continually clear that the president and the executive team are supporting and monitoring the work and intervening when help is needed, the initiative can move forward. But if the individual responsible for results is left to implement this very complicated challenge on their own, with limited authority to effect institutional change, the initiative will not succeed.

Occasionally, I have seen the CEO take complete charge of institutional initiatives. CEO involvement in institutional change is necessary for success, but a CEO who slips into an authoritarian approach will cause implementation to suffer. As Aguirre, von Post, and Alpern found, this approach is the second most likely reason implementations fail. A heavy-handed approach from the CEO causes important players in the institution to feel disengaged. It strips them of the decision-making authority and creativiey they need during the dynamic process of implementation. It creates a decision-making bottleneck, with the CEO having to make decisions that quickly outstrip the amount of time they can make available to the project. This approach often leads to poor quality decision-making as important individuals with unique perspectives and expertise are excluded from input for lack of deliberation.

An approach I was initially drawn to over the last few years but have subsequently pulled away from is the idea of placing implementation into the shared governance structure that most colleges have adopted. The idea behind this approach is appealing on the surface. Most institutional initiatives have component parts. For example, in Chapter 3, we discussed the need for a Guided Pathways approach to help improve student success. Implementing this approach touches on many areas of the institutions. Curriculum, teaching, counseling, student information systems, student activities, and more are eventually impacted by this strategy. A full plan developed for a Guided Pathways approach will require work across the institution by multiple programs.

On two occasions, I have participated in a well-intentioned implementation approach that identified a large scope of work and assigned the work to various committees already established at the college. Committees were asked to oversee the required work and report out to the overarching strategic planning committee on their progress. In both instances, the implementation suffered because the committees usually met only once or twice a month. They did not have budget or personnel resources to assign to their projects, and they had no authority to require work to be completed, both of which are often essential to complete the assigned task.

The implementation approach to institutional change that works most effectively is one that assigns the work of implementation to the college leadership. I am not necessarily referring to the official college leaders defined in the college organization. I am talking about the people on campus who make things happen. Some of these individuals do come from the official positions, but not always. For example, at one institution where I worked, I remember two vice presidents in particular. One I enjoyed working with very much. She was an effective leader. She was able to move the institution forward, even when the work that needed to be done was difficult. She had a colleague VP who was actually her senior. I tried to work with him a few times, in spite of warnings I received from other faculty members. He was clearly motivated by fear, afraid of offending anyone out of concern for job security. He had a long history defined by incremental if not imperceptible change or improvements. The two VPs were recognized by the college's organization chart as having equal authority, but with regard to real impact and influence on the institution, there was no comparison. She was a leader. He was not.

There are also individuals in every institution who have limited official authority but deeply impact the institution through their unofficial leadership. Aguirre, von Post, and Alpern refer to this dynamic as cultural power. They are not using the term *culture* to refer to race, ethcnicity, or heritage. They are talking about institutional culture, which is often recognized as the unofficial or unwritten set of rules and norms that have influence over an institution. In most (maybe all) institutions, there are individuals who effectively navigate these unofficial structures so effectively that their influence can be as significant as an effective president or vice president. These individuals, the ones with real influence, whether that influence is derived from official or unofficial structures, need to be on the implementation team.

Once these individuals are identified, they need to be assembled into an implementation team that is collaborative, egalitarian, and empowered. The group may need a little encouragement and support to get off the ground, but collaborative leadership is one of the most important aspects of contemporary leadership (Stokes, Baker, DeMillo, Soares, & Yaeger, 2019).

I pulled a group like this together when I was president. It included college vice presidents; presidents from the academic senate, classified senate, and student senate; union leaders from the faculty and staff bargaining units; and the chair of the overarching strategic planning committee for the college. These individuals had no history of meeting as a combined group. As president, I deliberately tried to set a tone of openness and trust. Once individuals became comfortable with the meeting atmosphere (this happened quickly), the group took off and became very productive.

When the most influential members of a college community come together and commit to working collaboratively, very significant changes can happen at a rapid pace. When a change agenda is being implemented at an institutional level, we can expect that members of the college community will push back against different changes. They will often turn to their constituent group leaders for advocation and representation. Having most of the constituent leaders on the team gave us the ability to address these issues quickly and effectively. When constituent leaders can talk about our concerns with each other, relationships strengthen, and problems are solved on much tighter timelines. Instead of having conversations between groups and individuals over several meetings where some attend and others do not, the all-inclusive meeting with the right players becomes very powerful for directing change across an organization.

For the group to be successful, they will need resources, and it is the CEO's job to make sure these resources are provided. First, they need to be empowered to do the work. To empower this group, they need to be formally recognized and introduced by the college president to the campus community and referenced regularly through the implementation period. Once the campus community recognizes their collective position, it is up to the president to set a positive tone. The members of this team, especially the faculty, will need time. The president may need to help remove other duties from their work lives by paying for part-time faculty or administrators to take responsibilities off team members' plates. The group will need a small budget for things like travel, conference attendance, off-campus meetings, and other expenses. The group will need access to key personnel. They may need clerical support from time to time and will definitely need support to track all the work and measure results from the work as it progresses, which may require support from research-related services at the college.

Conclusion

A theme that emerges in this book is the idea that social justice work in higher education is difficult. This kind of work is difficult in higher education and any other sector of society that seeks reform under this umbrella. It is often disruptive and requires significant change in multiple areas across an institution. Ironically, to implement social justice reform, leaders need to practice a high level of management expertise that moves forward in a methodical, predictable, and measured manner. Leaders need to thoroughly understand the reforms that are needed and possible, reforms that will effect change in equity. They need to follow established planning processes that are embedded in our institutions. Through these processes, we need to prioritize and sequence the work we plan to do carefully, taking time to frame all of the work around a desire to help students succeed. Throughout the process, we need to listen, collaborate, and deliberate with our colleagues. Finally, leaders need to find the resources needed to support effective implementation and ongoing operations. All of these very traditional management skills are needed if we hope to implement the social justice reforms that will break from many of the other very traditional practices that allow inequities to persist. In this sense, conservative and traditional implementation techniques are needed to bring about progressive social justice reform.

11 Social Justice Reform in the Community College Ecosystem

In the mid-1990s, I ran for city council. It was my first concentrated venture into the civic area after spending years studying political science as an undergraduate and graduate student. I had worked on a few campaigns before this one, but the city council race was the first with my name on the headline. I enjoyed the process, met a lot of good people, and worked very hard in the evenings and weekends to encourage people to vote for me, but in the end, I lost by one or two percentage points. Soon after the campaign, I was introduced to a regional consultant who did a lot of political and government relations work in the area, and he offered me the opportunity to do some political and campaign consulting work through his office. I was still teaching full-time but able to engage in some very interesting political and government consulting work through this opportunity.

One of the first contracts I landed through his office was as a fundraiser. Shortly after my campaign loss, I was at a friend's apartment. He had managed my campaign for city council, and we were trying to find consulting work. We ended up calling an acquaintance who was running for county supervisor. It was still early in his campaign, and we knew he was still putting his team together. In the phone conversation, we learned that he was looking for someone to lead his fundraising effort, and we suggested that we would do a great job for him. I remember him asking us, with a bit of surprise in his voice, "Do you know how to run a fundraising campaign?" I said "Yes," happy he did not ask, "Have you ever run a fundraising campaign?" I had never actually run a large fundraising effort, but, having run for office recently and with a background in political science, I felt confident I knew the basic structure of such an effort and could learn the details quickly. He agreed over the phone to bring us on board. The next day, I went to the library and checked out four books on campaign fundraising.

1996 Campaign Photo
Kids Are Wiped Out!

As I suspected, the structure for campaign fundraising was not super complicated. It has become more complex in recent years with the development of online contributions, but the basic strategy in the mid-1990s boiled down to reviewing public records to find people who 1) historically give to political campaigns or 2) own significant assets in policy areas that could be impacted by the candidates running for office. Once we identified the individuals, we contacted them, told them about the candidate and his policy positions, and asked for contributions. We brought the candidate in near the end to help make the closing requests. We implemented this strategy and had strong success. In fact, we outraised the other candidates in the campaign by a significant margin.

This effort led to several other campaigns and government outreach contracts. I worked to persuade voters to support candidates, contribute money to causes, support school bonds, lean favorably toward various issues, vote for local measures, and so on. All of these efforts held a common structure. They were campaigns prescribed for a defined area—an assembly district, a school district, the city boundaries, a region. And to influence opinion in the defined area, we had to identify all the opinion leaders and reach out to them directly with a compelling message.

Throughout those years, what always surprised me was how easy it is to identify regional opinion leaders and how accessible they are. Regional opinion leaders are typically those who run the regions' businesses, governments, schools, nonprofits, faith-based organizations, and similar institutions. The leaders of these organizations are typically eager to be known and willing to engage in conversations about the state of the region and how we might shape its future. I often talked to my students about the accessibility of these networks. They are easy to join and easy to access. It takes some effort, but almost none of the individuals in these local and regional networks are hiding. In my experience, they are eager to participate in regional dialogues. I know many Americans feel disillusioned about democracy. At the local and regional level, I find these processes open and accessible.

When I eventually became a college president, I was eager to apply these skills to my work and immediately started in on identifying the region's opinion leaders, reaching out to them, and participating in their organizations. I found local, regional, state, and federal offices in our service area remarkably open. When I was president of Norco College, we had at least six big initiatives that needed regional support and partnerships: veterans' education, prison inmate education, STEM/photonics education, dual enrollment with high schools, and the development of a mixed-use campus. Without going into the details on each initiative, they all had components to them that were bigger than Norco College; bigger than the Riverside Community College District; and only possible through large, multifaceted regional partnerships. We felt that any one of these initiatives could help build the college in several capacities. Our goal was to pitch all of these to the region's civic leaders with the understanding that most would not find traction. We felt that if one or two could establish a footing and start to take shape, we could succeed with a strong development strategy.

To our surprise, all six received enthusiastic support and continued to mature while I was at the college. This experience demonstrated another characteristic of civic involvement that surprised me. While civic leaders are accessible and actively engaged in a regional dialogue, most of them are heavily consumed with the understandable burdens of running their own organizations—managing their business, city, nonprofit, faith-based organization. While they routinely make time to participate in regional dialogues, I find that the immediate demands in their civic lives are so significant that they often do not have time to develop plans for regional development. As a result, there are not a lot of voices contributing to innovative ideas for regional development. If community colleges can conceive of initiatives that enhance the college *and* improve the region, they can get momentum through local and regional collaborations.

Community colleges operate in an ecosystem. This ecosystem is made up of 1) the civic, business, and government organizations in the college's service area; 2) a range of elected officials, government agencies, and education interests in the college's state capital; 3) a similar set of offices and organizations in Washington, DC; 4) the four-year institutions the college most commonly transfers students to; and 5) a few national organizations that are active in community college education. These groups have a tremendous amount of influence over the success of our institutions and consequently the success of our students. They can influence resources, participate in partnerships, affect public opinion, write legislation, and much more. If they are strong proponents of our work, they can use their influence to add resources. If they are not supportive or ambivalent, they can cause resources to diminish.

As discussed in Chapter 10, there are 39 strategies that colleges can implement to narrow or close the equity gap in our colleges. Some of the strategies can be implemented internally by colleges, while others need to be implemented across the community college ecosystem. For convenience, the table of 39 strategies and the extent to which they require internal work, external work, or both appears subsequently (this is the same table that was presented in Chapter 10).

		Internal	External
Initiative 1: Add Academic Capital to Students' Lives (Chap 4 Content)			
Strategy 1	Develop Student Progress Tracking	√	√
Strategy 2	Incorporate New Socializing Agents	√	√
Strategy 3	Focus on Students' Assets	√	
Strategy 4	Increase Diversity of Personnel	√	√
Strategy 5	Expand Counseling Support	√	√
Strategy 6	Nurture Faculty-Student Relationships	√	
Strategy 7	Secure Food/Housing/Health	√	√
Strategy 8	Create Sticky Campus	√	
Initiative 2: Fund Higher Education Equitably (Chap 5 Content)			
Strategy 9	Conduct National Audit		√
Strategy 10	Restructure State Funding		√
Strategy 11	Maximize Student Financial Aid	√	√
Strategy 12	Build Alumni Connections	√	
Strategy 13	Pursue Federal Grants	√	
Strategy 14	Redirect Social Justice Funding		√
Strategy 15	Alter Tax Status for Institutions That Discriminate		√
Initiative 3: Establish Best Practices (Chap 6 Content)			
Strategy 16	Implement Best Practices for Core Competencies	√	
Strategy 17	Implement Programmatic Standards of Excellence	√	
Strategy 18	Categorize All Activities Under Programs	√	
Strategy 19	Build Physical Spaces to Support Equity	√	
Strategy 20	Expand Professional Development	√	√
Strategy 21	Establish Targeted Support Services	√	√
Initiative 4: Create Intuitive and Supportive Transitions (Chap 7 Content)			
Strategy 22	Implement Guided Pathways	√	
Strategy 23	Develop Intuitive Systems	√	√
Strategy 24	Establish High School Partnerships	√	√
Strategy 25	Articulate Military Training	√	√
Strategy 26	Connect Careers to Learning	√	√
Strategy 27	Establish Common Course Number	√	√
Strategy 28	Build Student-Centered Schedules	√	
Strategy 29	Offer Online Courses/Services	√	

		Internal	*External*
Initiative 5: Place Historically Underserved Students in Selective Universities (Chap 8 Content)			
Strategy 30	Establish Proactive Transfer Center	√	
Strategy 31	Develop Transfer Program for High-GPA/Low-Income Students	√	√
Strategy 32	Change University/College Ranking System		√
Strategy 33	End Legacy Scoring		√
Initiative 6: Develop Leaders Who Can Affect Institutional Change (Chap 9 Content)			
Strategy 34	Develop/Promote Strategic Vision	√	√
Strategy 35	Make Equity a Prioritization	√	√
Strategy 36	Implement Work Through Teams	√	
Strategy 37	Manage the "Old"; Lead the "New"	√	
Strategy 38	Improve with Assessment and Accountability	√	
Strategy 39	Build Institutional Values Around Love	√	

The Need for Ecosystem Changes

Most of America is calling for social justice. A majority of us (58 percent) believe race relations in the United States are bad, and most (56 percent) believe this problem is getting worse. A clear majority indicates we do not want racism to be part of our society, and a recent survey found that 75 percent of Americans believe diversity strengthens us and should be nurtured (Horowitz et al., 2019). I know there are people who do not care for this idea. Their expressions range from dispassionate academic disagreement to blind hate. Although some resistance to efforts for social justice was found in our own survey results and is consistently present in national polling, we are at a turning point in America where large majorities recognize racism and discrimination, see it as a problem, and want to do something tangible to eliminate it.

There are at least three basic ways the public sector can address discrimination in the United States. First, we can do the steady and tedious work of research. This is something that our universities and a few nonprofits have done well. Documenting the histories of each group and describing the social constructs that support biased decision-making is important work. It helps us understand the problem and develop meaningful solutions. The weakness with this approach, however, is that it relies on people in power to institute change when they see the evidence of this discrimination in their own institutions. However, people in power rarely volunteer to make changes to benefit people out of power, regardless of evidence. And if the change requires that these leaders surrender, or lessen, their power, the likelihood of change is extremely low. In this sense, research may be better understood as a necessary prelude to meaningful action.

A second way discrimination can be addressed by the public sector is through the law. Making discrimination illegal is an approach that has achieved significant gains. Through local, state, and federal legislation, we have eaten away at hate-based practices. Through court proceedings and subsequent precedents, we have removed important structures and practices that lead to unjust discrimination. A major strategy used by social justice organizers has been to leverage the findings in research, bring these findings to the greater public's attention through carefully planned demonstrations, and use the resulting swell of public opinion to end unjust practices by replacing them with new laws, policies, and precedents. Like the first method discussed in the prior paragraph, this approach directs our civic leaders—people in power—to make changes to their institutions, but it comes at them with greater force than reasoning and research alone. This approach brings the influence of government authority.

A third way to address discrimination against marginalized groups is to help individuals from these communities occupy positions of power at levels proportionate to their populations. I believe this is the most effective way to eventually rid our country of discrimination. The most common pathway to positions of influence and power, the most common route to a position at or near the top of our civic and private institutions, goes through higher education. It is rare to become a leader in legislatures, corporations, and nonprofits without a bachelor's degree. It is basically impossible to lead law firms, hospitals, educational institutions, court rooms, medical practices, and engineering firms without formal education. To place individuals from marginalized communities into positions of power in the United States, we must move students from these communities successfully through our institutions of higher education. And as we have pointed out several times in this book, of the sectors in higher education, community colleges are most focused on working with students from disfavored communities.

For America to move forward with social justice work—and most Americans want to move forward in this direction—community colleges must be strong. This is the core premise of this book and an idea I have been chasing for many years. To build strong community colleges, we need to make internal and external changes. External changes are needed throughout the ecosystem in which community colleges operate. The system includes regional and national universities; local governments, civic, and business organizations; state legislatures, agencies, and non-governmental organizations; a range of federal government and non-government entities; and similar organizations.

At the local and state levels, community colleges collaborate well with government and civic sectors. Most community colleges are organized at the county level with locally elected or government-appointed trustees/board members from the community. This structure makes for solid professional (and personal) relationships between community colleges, unified school districts, local municipalities, county agencies, and other civic organizations.

With education policy and funding heavily influenced by state government, community colleges typically have strong relationships with their state agencies. Most of the states have a community college state system office, and college leaders are often active in their state capitols. In contrast, community colleges do not generally have such strong ties to the federal government. We have a few national organizations like the Association of Community College Trustees and the American Association of Community Colleges that express our national interests, but our level of involvement in Washington is thin compared to that of our four-year and K–12 colleagues. As "community" colleges, we are strong in our backyards. But we are clearly not as strong in Washington, D.C. As a result, federal legislators and agency personnel hold high levels of consciousness for the issues impacting four-year and K–12 institutions, with community college challenges often an afterthought.

The absence of a strong federal agenda for community colleges is deeply concerning when we recognize the community college sector as an engine for social justice and consider the students we serve. The health of our community college systems should be a major component of the federal government's strategy for education specifically and should be part of all strategies to promote upward mobility in America.

To get a sense of what a comprehensive federal agenda for community colleges might look like, I first assessed the policy recommendations published by ACCT (2020) and AACC (2020). Both organizations have adopted federal policy recommendations and have collaborated in the development of these recommendations. They have been very active in national agendas supporting community college completion rates and equity, supporting significant research and training in these areas. Their emphasis on completion and equity has been promoted as a national agenda for community colleges, with much of the work in these areas directed at community college leaders and some of the work directed at federal actors.

The policy recommendations ACCT and AACC have concentrated on for 2020 place an emphasis on five core areas. First, they recommend greater support for low-income students through reauthorization of the Higher Education Act, modifications to Pell funding, support for college promise programs, assistance with food insecurities, and tax code revisions to benefit low-income families. Second, they recommend strengthening of workforce development education with expanded funding for students and programs, placing emphasis on colleges that serve students from marginalized communities. Third, they recommend the development of several accountability/student-success measures. Some of these include development of a shared national database for outcomes, revisions to success measurements, and revisions to financial regulations related to risk assessment. Fourth, they ask for a reduction in the regulatory environment that burdens many community colleges. Fifth, they recommend support for several historically underserved student groups. Some of these include Dreamers, military veterans, formerly incarcerated people, low income earners, and international students.

ACCT and AACC have developed strong recommendations; however, my initial feeling after reviewing both associations' proposals was that the list was incomplete. So, I decided to go back through the literature, review all my notes, and develop a list of all the strategic recommendations that help marginalized students experience greater academic success. Once I had gone through the list, I looked at each strategic recommendation with an eye to federal assistance. Where might the federal government be able to assist with the implementation of these recommended strategies? This process led to six possible areas of assistance from the federal government. Some of the recommendations under the six areas replicate those supported by AACC/ACCT, and none of them conflict with the two organizations' recommendations. The six recommended policy areas and corresponding details are literature-based suggestions that should be considered in a comprehensive national agenda for community colleges.

The federal government can strengthen community colleges by *expanding federal aid* to students. This may include policies that help keep community colleges affordable (e.g., college promise programs), expand financial aid funding (e.g., Pell Grant), fund housing solutions for housing-insecure students, and fund food solutions for food-insecure students.

The federal government can strengthen community colleges by *promoting equity*. This may include policies that increase funding for support services to students from historically underserved communities; support national best practices that encourage equity-mindedness; allow DACA/Dreamer students to pay the same in-state tuition rates as other state residents; recognize the community college segment as essential to national social justice efforts; support diversity in hiring at community colleges; develop a national score card on equity for all community colleges; and require faculty, staff, and administrators to receive training in equity-mindedness in pedagogy, service, and management.

NATIONAL AGENDA ITEMS

1. Increase funding/resources for students
2. Close access/completion equity gaps
3. Improve transfer rates from CCs to universities
4. Support job placement
5. Fund higher education sectors equally
6. Develop strategic systems

The federal government can also strengthen community colleges by *helping improve transfer*. This may include policies that support common course numbering for GE-related courses in community colleges and four-year institutions (e.g., History 101 is the same throughout the state), support the recognition of all AA/AS degrees as transferring in to four-year institutions at the junior (third year) level, sponsor a national scholars program to encourage low-income/high-GPA students to transfer to highly selective universities, encourage the university ranking systems (e.g., *U.S. News and World Report*) to place greater emphasis on social mobility in their overall score, support diversity-balanced admissions at four-year institutions, end legacy scoring for admissions in universities, and support one integrated educational system (K–16) to align curricula and make transitions more seamless.

In addition, the federal government can strengthen community colleges by *supporting job placement* of CTE students. This effort might include processes that map CTE programs to jobs on a national scale, expand federal funding (e.g., Perkins) for development of CTE programs, support government data-sharing with community colleges for job placement tracking and CTE program recruitment, and develop a national apprenticeship program/network.

Further, the federal government can strengthen community colleges by *equalizing higher education funding*. This may include policies that conduct and maintain a comprehensive report on higher education funding across all higher education segments (how much government money is invested in CC, state college, public university, private university students), call for equal investment in all students (community college students should receive comparable funding to four-year students), balance federal spending between research and teaching/learning, encourage social justice-related nonprofits to invest as much in community colleges as they do in four-year institutions, support increased funding for counseling services in community colleges, and support an increase in the proportion of full-time faculty at community colleges.

Finally, the federal government can strengthen community colleges by *supporting systems development*. This may include policies that support development of a national data mart measuring major outcomes, development of models for multi-year scheduling, development of a means for student progress tracking, development of a volunteer network to support students, data-sharing between high schools and community colleges for seamless enrollment, a means to articulate military training into college credit, and a way to grant credit for prior learning for working adults.

These areas constitute a broadened scope of work for federal government to play in building agency across the community college sector. To further assess the validity of these recommendations and develop prioritizations for the necessary work, we asked community college personnel and students to weigh in on these recommendations through a national survey. The survey was constructed around the six policy areas described previously. With the help of almost 60 volunteers (trustees, college presidents, administrators, faculty, staff, community college alumni, community members, and elected officials), the survey was administered throughout June, July, and August of 2020.

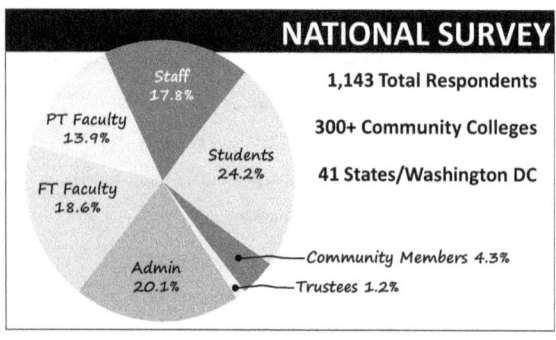

NATIONAL SURVEY
1,143 Total Respondents
300+ Community Colleges
41 States/Washington DC

Staff 17.8%
PT Faculty 13.9%
Students 24.2%
FT Faculty 18.6%
Admin 20.1%
Community Members 4.3%
Trustees 1.2%

Distribution of the survey was carried out through several phases. We asked state system leaders to support the survey and distribute it to the community college leaders in their state. We contacted district CEOs and asked them to distribute the survey to college/campus leaders throughout their districts. We reached out directly to over 1,100 college CEOs/presidents and encouraged them to distribute the survey to college personnel and students. We reached out directly to individual community college personnel. Finally, we posted the survey broadly across several social media feeds.

Over 1,100 respondents contributed their opinions through the survey, with 24.2 percent of respondents representing students, 20.1 percent administrators, 18.6 percent full-time faculty, 17.8 percent staff personnel, 13.9 percent part-time faculty, 4.3 percent community members, and 1.2 percent trustees. College personnel were distributed across 41 states and Washington, D.C. Over 300 community colleges and related organizations contributed to the data. Respondents represented major race/ethnicity groups in the United States, with 1.7 percent identifying as American Indian/Native American/Alaska Native, 43.4 percent identifying as Asian, 4.0 percent identifying as Black/African American, 10.7 percent identifying as Latinx/Hispanic, 0.6 percent identifying as Native Hawaiian/other Pacific Islander, 35.5 percent identifying as White/Caucasian (Non-Hispanic), and 4.0 percent identifying as mixed race.

Findings From Policy Area 1: Increase Funding/Resources for Community College Students

According to a recent report released by the Century Foundation (2019), private four-year institutions throughout the United States spend an average of $72,000 per full-time equivalent student, public four-year institutions spend an average of $40,000 per FTES, and community colleges nation-wide spend an average of $14,000 per FTES. It is true that many of the private and public four-year institutions have research as part of their mission, while community colleges do not. This naturally means four-year institutions cost more to run. But even when spending calculations are controlled for research, private four-year institutions spend three times more than community colleges and public four-year institutions spend 60 percent more than community colleges.

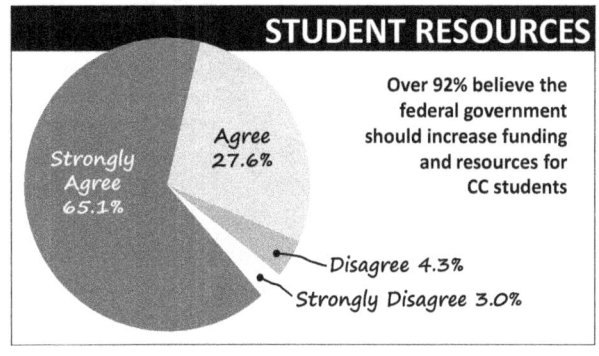

Given that community colleges serve a much higher proportion of students from historically underserved communities, this disparity of public funding (and private funding) is inequitable.

To assess the extent to which the federal government should increase funding and resources for community college students, we asked community college personnel to weigh in on four possible ways the federal government could provide help: 1) support keeping community colleges affordable, 2) increase financial aid funding for students, 3) support/fund solutions for housing-insecure students, and 4) support/fund solutions for food-insecure students. Averaging the scores across all four suggestions, we found the following: over 92 percent of respondents indicated that the federal government should play a role in increasing funding/resources for community college students. Of these, 65.1 percent indicated that they *strongly agree* with this position, 27.6 indicated that they *agree*, 4.3 percent indicated that they *disagree*, and 3.0 percent indicated that they *strongly disagree*.

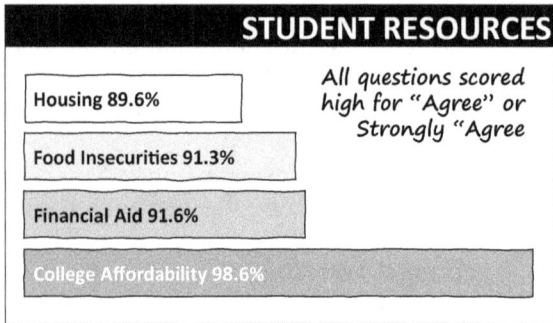

Of the four suggestions, the one addressing college affordability received the most support, with 98.6 percent of respondents indicating that they *agree* or *strongly agree* that the federal government should play a role in keeping community college affordable. The suggestion at the second-highest level of support, with 91.6 percent of respondents saying they *agree* of *strongly agree*, asks that the federal government increase financial aid for students. Regarding food insecurities, 91.3 percent of respondents believed the federal government should do something to help. The suggestion with the least amount of support, but strong support nonetheless, was the one involving housing insecurities, with 89.6 percent of respondents indicating the federal government should do something to help students with housing problems.

Findings From Policy Area 2: Close Access and Completion Equity Gaps

Students from marginalized communities are underrepresented in higher education. Many are underrepresented with regard to admissions/enrollments, especially at our country's most selective universities. All marginalized communities are underrepresented at commencement ceremonies, with disproportionately low percentages receiving bachelor's degrees. To assess federal government involvement in helping close access and equity gaps, we asked community college personnel to weigh in on seven possible ways the federal government could provide help: 1) increase support for students from historically underserved communities;

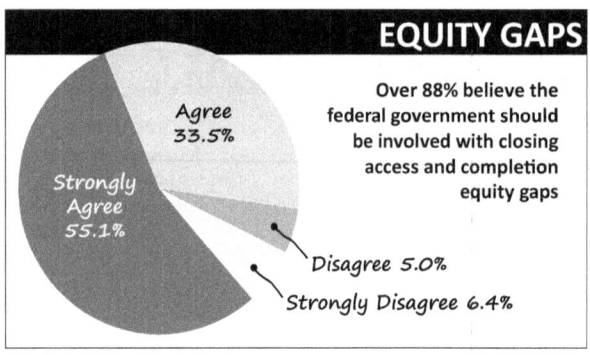

2) support a national best practices dialogue around equity-mindedness in pedagogy, service, and management; 3) allow DACA/Dreamer students to receive the same educational services as U.S. citizens; 4) recognize community colleges as essential to national social justice efforts; 5) support diversity in hiring at community colleges; 6) develop a national scorecard on equity for all community colleges; and 7) require community college employees to complete equity-mindedness training. Averaging the scores across all seven questions, we found that over 88 percent of respondents indicated that the federal government should play a role in closing access and completion equity gaps. Of these, 55.1 percent indicated that they *strongly agree* with this kind of support from federal policy, 33.5 percent indicated they *agree*, 5.0 percent indicated that they *disagree*, and 6.4 percent indicated that they *strongly disagree*.

All seven suggestions individually received very strong support from community college personnel. The suggestion that received the strongest support calls for federal support to increase diversity in hiring. More than 92 percent of respondents indicated that they *agree* or *strongly agree* with federal support in this area. The weakest level of support was found for the need for a national equity scorecard, although support for the scorecard still registered high, with 82.1 percent supporting federal assistance in this area. Having all community college personnel participate in some kind of federal equity training was supported by 86.0 percent of respondents. Providing Dreamers and DACA students with the same benefits as U.S. citizens was supported by 86.6 percent, and federal support for students from historically underserved communities was endorsed by 90.6 percent. Some kind of federally sponsored/supported dialogue about education and equity was supported by 91.1 percent of respondents. Finally, having the federal government recognize community colleges as instrumental in national efforts to promote social justice was supported by 91.3 percent of survey respondents.

EQUITY GAPS — Strongly Agree or Agree
- Equity Scorecard 82.1%
- Equity Training 86.0%
- Access/Support for Dreamers 86.6%
- Resources for Historically Underserved 90.6%
- Best Practices Dialogue on Equity 91.1%
- CCs as National Social Justice Engine 91.3%
- Diversity in Hiring 92.4%

Findings From Policy Area 3: Improve Transfer Rates from Community Colleges to Four-Year Institutions

About 80 percent of community college students indicate they intend to transfer from their community college to a four-year institution and pursue a bachelor's degree. About 30 percent of these students successfully transfer within six years (Community College Research Center, 2020a). To assess potential government involvement in helping improve transfer rates, we asked community college personnel to weigh in on seven possible ways the federal government could provide help: 1) support common course numbering for GE courses in community colleges and four-year institutions (e.g., History 101 would be the same throughout the state), 2) make sure all public four-year institutions receive students with AA/AS degrees at junior level (third year) status, 3) sponsor a national scholars program to encourage low-income/high-GPA students to transfer to highly selective universities, 4) encourage the university ranking systems (e.g., *U.S. News and World Report*) to place greater emphasis on social mobility, 5) support diversity-balanced admissions at four-year institutions, 6) end legacy scoring for admissions in universities (legacy scoring gives preferential admissions to applicants whose relatives attended the university), and 7) support one integrated educational system (K–16) to align curricula and make transitions more seamless.

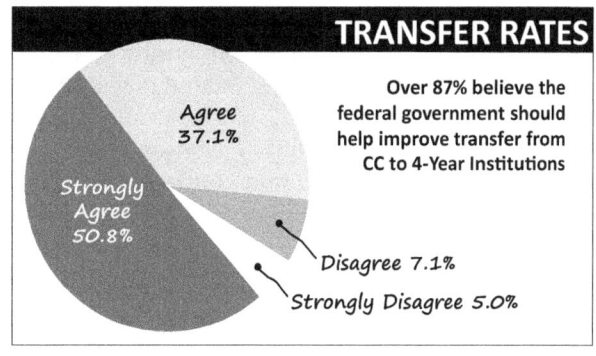

TRANSFER RATES
- Strongly Agree 50.8%
- Agree 37.1%
- Disagree 7.1%
- Strongly Disagree 5.0%

Over 87% believe the federal government should help improve transfer from CC to 4-Year Institutions

Averaging the scores across all seven questions, we found that over 87 percent of respondents indicated that the federal government should play a role in helping improve transfer rates, with 50.8 percent indicating they *strongly agree* with this kind of support from federal policy, 37.1 indicating they *agree*, 7.1 percent indicating they *disagree*, and 5.0 percent indicating they *strongly disagree*.

TRANSFER RATES

Strongly Agree or Agree

- Integrated K–16 81.4%
- Univ Ranking Systems 84.1%
- Diversity Balanced Admissions 85.5%
- Legacy Scoring 87.8%
- National Scholars Program 90.9%
- AA/AS Transfer as Junior 91.4%
- Common Course Numbering 93.8%

All seven suggestions individually received very strong support from community college personnel. The question that received the strongest support calls for federal help with developing a common course numbering system for GE-related courses across two-year and four-year institutions at least at the state level. While some states have already completed this work, most have not. Just under 94 percent of respondents indicated they *agree* or *strongly agree* with federal support for this suggestion. The weakest level of support was found for the need for an integrated K–16 curriculum and transition process, although support for this integration still registered high, with 81.4 percent supporting federal assistance in this area at the *agree* or *strongly agree* level. Encouraging university ranking systems like *U.S. News and World Report* to place greater emphasis on the work universities are doing to promote social mobility was supported by 84.1 percent of respondents. Helping expand diversity consideration in four-year admissions practices was supported by 85.5 percent, and removing legacy scoring from all admissions practices was supported by 87.8 percent of respondents. Development of a national scholars program with particular emphasis on helping low-income/high-GPA students transfer from community colleges to selective universities was supported by 90.9 percent. Finally, making sure all AA/AS transfer degrees are recognized by four-year universities at the junior level, or third year, was supported by 91.4 percent of survey respondents.

Common course numbering is often controversial with faculty because it touches on curriculum and academic traditions that recognize faculty as the primary architects of college curriculum. The controversy that is often raised involves faculties' academic freedom to develop curricula. Common course numbering typically removes a degree of flexibility for faculty by aligning curricula across community colleges and four-year institutions, most often at the state level. This practice puts some restraint on faculty; however, community college students receive great benefit from this approach because it makes the transfer process and academic preparation for transfer considerably less confusing. Based on our survey findings, community college faculty recognize this benefit for students and strongly support the federal government's assistance in establishing common course number of some sort. Isolating faculty survey responses on this question, we found that 92.4 percent indicated they *agree* or *strongly agree* with the need for federal government to help develop common course numbering. Sixty percent indicated they *strongly agree*, 32.4 percent said they *agree*, 5.2 percent said they *disagree*, and 2.3 percent said they *strongly disagree*.

Findings From Policy Area 4: Support Job Placement for Career and Technical Education Students

American business leaders and legislators have voiced concern over the skills gap, a phenomenon in the economy today where the number of available workers with requisite skills is not sufficient to fill jobs available in the United States. This skilled worker shortfall has placed growing scrutiny on the long tradition of career technical education in American community colleges. With as many as 20 percent of community college students working on degrees or certificates that lead directly to jobs (Community College Research Center, 2020b), the successful transition from community college to the workplace is critical for student success and the strengthening of our economy. To assess potential government involvement with placing CTE students into jobs, we asked community college personnel to weigh in on five possible ways the federal government could provide help: 1) provide national mapping of career technical programs to jobs, 2) expand federal funding for development of CTE programs, 3) support government data-sharing with community colleges for job placement tracking and CTE program recruitment, 4) develop a national apprenticeship program/network, and 5) develop national standards for work-based learning and community college education. Averaging the scores across all five questions, we found that over 94 percent of respondents indicated that the federal government should play a role in helping improve job placement for CTE students, with 57.8 percent indicating they *strongly agree* with this kind of support from federal policy, 36.6 indicating they *agree*, 3.8 percent indicating they *disagree*, and 1.9 percent indicating they *strongly disagree*.

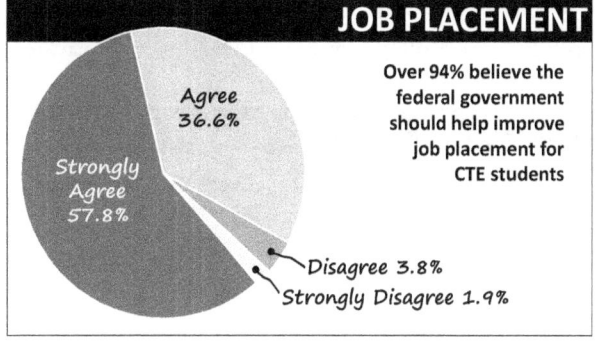

All five questions individually registered strong responses, with some of them receiving scores among the highest in the overall survey. The suggestion that received the strongest support in this subset recommends federal help with mapping CTE programs in community colleges to jobs. Over 96 percent of respondents indicated they *agree* or *strongly agree* with federal support for this capacity. The lowest level of support was found for the need for developing national work-based learning standards, with 90.7 percent supporting federal assistance in this area at the *agree* or *strongly agree* level. Expanding federal funding for CTE programs (e.g., Perkins) was supported by 93.7 percent of respondents. Bringing the federal government into the development of a national apprenticeship programs or network of some sort was supported by 95.4 percent, and making federal data available to community colleges through a data-sharing agreement to help with tracking and recruiting received 95.6 percent favorability from respondents.

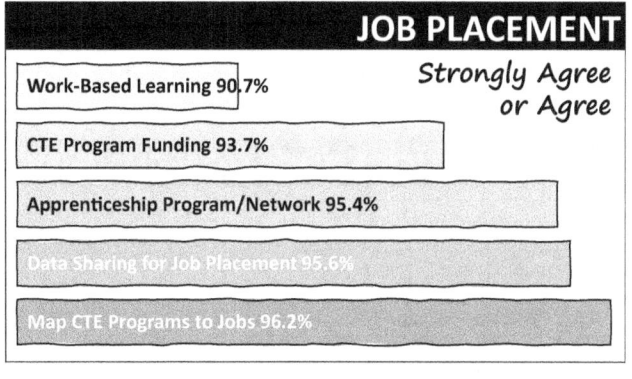

Findings From Policy Area 5: Fund Higher Education Sectors Equally

Funding for higher education from government, non-profit, and private sources is wildly unequal, with community colleges receiving the least of any higher education sector. Given that community colleges serve the majority of students from marginalized communities, this inequity is problematic on multiple levels. To assess the federal government's role in establishing equal funding across higher education sectors, which translates to equal investment in all student groups, we asked community college personnel to weigh in on six possible ways the federal government could provide help: 1) develop a report on funding across all higher education segments (how much money is invested in community college, state college, public university, and private university students), 2) call for equal investment in all undergraduate students (community college students should receive comparable funding to four-year students.), 3) increase balance between federal spending on research and teaching/learning, 4) encourage social justice-related nonprofits to invest as much in community colleges as they do in four-year institutions, 5) support expansion of funding for counseling services in community colleges, and 6) support an increase in the proportion of full-time faculty in community colleges. Averaging the scores across all six questions, we found that over 90 percent of respondents indicated that the federal government should help equalize funding across all segments of higher education, with 53.2 percent indicating they *strongly agree* with this kind of support from federal policy, 37.2 percent indicating they *agree*, 5.5 percent indicating they *disagree*, and 4.1 percent indicating they *strongly disagree*.

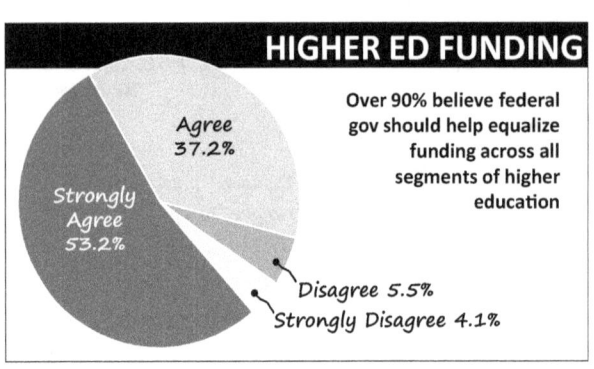

All six suggestions in this subset elicited mostly favorable responses from survey respondents. The suggestion that received the strongest support in this subset recommends that the federal government develop a national report on higher education by segment. Over 94 percent of respondents indicated they *agree* or *strongly agree* with federal support in this area. The lowest level of support was found for the idea of funding all undergraduates equally across higher education segments. For this suggestion, 87.5 percent of respondents marked *agree* or *strongly agree*. Redirecting more nonprofit funding toward community colleges received 89.3 percent support. Establishing greater balance between federal spending on research and federal spending on teaching/learning was supported by 89.8 percent of respondents. Increasing the proportion of full-time faculty and counselors was supported by 90.7 percent and 90.9 percent, respectively.

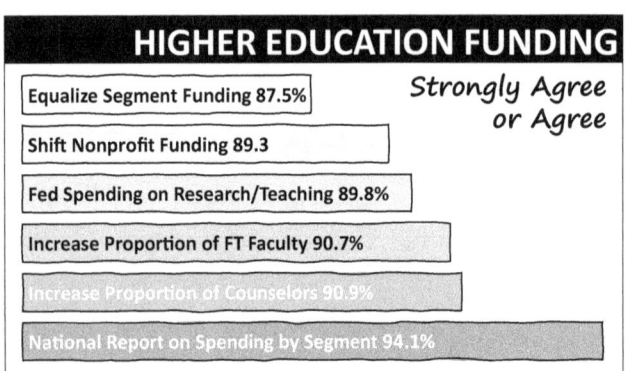

Findings From Policy Area 6: Develop Strategic Systems

Community colleges are increasingly faced with the need for sophisticated operational systems to support strategies that close enduring academic equity gaps; however, many of the systems needed are available only to institutions with much larger budgets, or the systems have not been developed at all because community colleges as a segment do not offer enough financial benefit to private companies that have the capacity to develop the solutions. To assess the federal government's possible role in helping develop these systems, we asked community college personnel to weigh in on

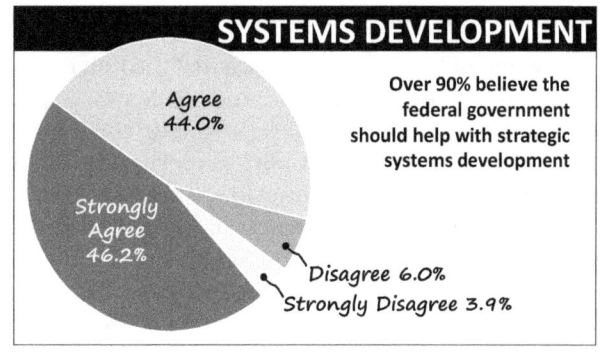

seven possible solutions: 1) national data mart measuring major outcomes (e.g., enrollment, course completion, graduation, transfer) for all community colleges; 2) multi-year scheduling tool allowing students to map out their entire academic plan; 3) student progress tracking instrument allowing college personnel and students to monitor real-time progress toward degree completion; 4) national volunteer network to add academic capital into students' lives; 5) data-sharing between high schools and community colleges for seamless enrollment/transition; 6) tool for scaled articulation of military training, recognizing veterans' prior learning for college credit; and 7) credit for prior learning tool, granting credit for skills learned during employment. Averaging the scores across all seven questions, we found that over 90 percent of respondents indicated that the federal government should play a role in helping develop strategic systems, with 46.2 percent indicating they *strongly agree* with this kind of support from federal policy, 44.0 percent indicating they *agree*, 6.0 percent indicating they *disagree*, and 3.9 percent indicating they *strongly disagree*.

All seven questions in this subset elicited mostly favorable responses from survey respondents. While responses were strong, this subset was the only subset to average less than 50 percent in *strongly agree* responses. The question that received the strongest support in this subset recommends that the federal government assist with data sharing between high schools and community colleges to make the transition more seamless. Over 93 percent of respondents indicated they *agree* or *strongly agree* with federal support in this capacity. The lowest level of support was for a national data mart to measure community college outcomes, with 87.0 percent of respondents saying they *agree*

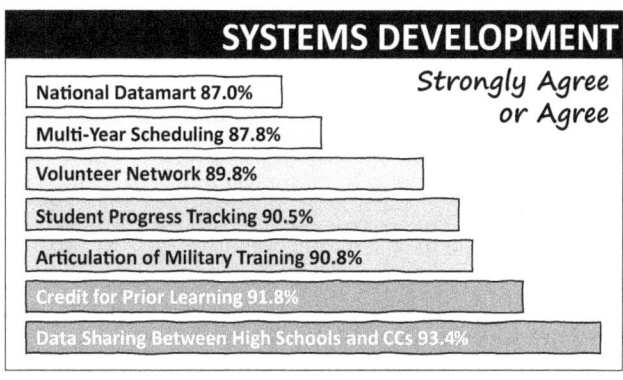

or *strongly agree* with this suggestion. The federal government being involved with a multi-year scheduling solution received 87.8 percent support. Developing a national volunteer network to add academic capital into students' lives received 89.8 percent support from respondents. Federal participation in tracking student progress along their academic journey was favored by 90.5 percent. Development of a national recognition of military credit was supported by 90.8 percent of respondents. Finally, granting credit for prior learning in the workplace was supported by 91.8 percent of respondents.

Discussion of Survey Findings

The review of literature suggested that the federal government should consider providing six areas of assistance to community colleges. The six were evaluated with several policy questions under each area. Aggregated scores for each show strong support for all six. The area with strongest support was related to job placement. Over 90 percent agreed or strongly agreed that the government should assist in this area. Expanding resources/aid for students was the second most supported, with 92.8 percent. Funding higher education sectors equally received support at 90.4 percent. Federal assistance with the development of strategic systems garnered 90.2 percent. Bringing the federal government into efforts to close access and completion equity gaps was supported by 88.6 percent. Improving transfer from community colleges to four-year institutions was supported by 87.8 percent.

	Strongly Disagree	*Disagree*	*Agree*	*Strongly Agree*	*Agree + Strongly Agree*
Job Placement	1.9%	3.8%	36.6%	57.8%	94.3%
Funding/Resources for Students	3.0%	4.3%	27.6%	65.1%	92.8%
Equal Funding for Ed Sectors	4.1%	5.5%	37.2%	53.2%	90.4%
Strategic Systems Development	3.9%	6.0%	44.0%	46.2%	90.2%
Access/Completion Equity Gaps	6.4%	5.0%	33.5%	55.1%	88.6%
Improve Transfer Rates	5.0%	7.1%	37.1%	50.8%	87.8%

In all, the review of literature suggested federal policy support for 36 policies in six different policy areas. All 36 policy areas received strong support from community college personnel in the NPACC survey, with every policy recommendation attaining more than 80 percent *agree* or *strongly agree* from survey respondents. Twenty-two of the 36 policy recommendations received 90 percent or higher agreement from respondents. These results point to a very strong convergence between research-based recommendations for federal support of community colleges and opinion from practitioners in America's community colleges.

Policy	*Policy Area*	*Agree + Strongly Agree*
Support keeping community colleges affordable	Funding/Resources for Students	98.6%
Provide national mapping of career technical programs to jobs	Job Placement	96.2%
Support government data sharing with CCs for job placement tracking and CTE program recruitment	Job Placement	95.6%
Develop a national apprenticeship program/network	Job Placement	95.4%
Develop a report on funding across all higher education segments (how much money is invested in each sector?)	Equal Funding for Ed Sectors	94.1%
Support common course numbering for GE courses in CCs and four-year institutions	Improve Transfer Rates	93.8%
Expand federal funding for development of CTE programs	Job Placement	93.7%
Support a solution for data-sharing between high schools and CCs for seamless enrollment	Strategic Systems Development	93.4%
Support diversity in hiring at CCs	Access/Completion Equity Gaps	92.4%

Policy	Policy Area	Agree + Strongly Agree
Support a solution to grant credit for prior learning for working adults	Strategic Systems Development	91.8%
Increase financial aid funding for students	Funding/Resources for Students	91.6%
Make sure all public four-year institutions receive students with AA/AS degrees at junior level (third year) status	Improve Transfer Rates	91.4%
Support/fund solutions for food-insecure students	Funding/Resources for Students	91.3%
Recognize CCs as essential to national social justice efforts	Access/Completion Equity Gaps	91.3%
Support a national best practices dialogue around equity-mindedness in pedagogy, service, and management	Access/Completion Equity Gaps	91.1%
Sponsor a national scholars program to encourage low-income/high-GPA students to transfer to highly selective universities	Improve Transfer Rates	90.9%
Support expansion of funding for counseling services in CCs	Equal Funding for Ed Sectors	90.9%
Support a solution to articulate military training into college credit	Strategic Systems Development	90.8%
Develop national standards for work-based learning and CC education	Job Placement	90.7%
Support increase of full-time faculty in CCs	Equal Funding for Ed Sectors	90.7%
Increase support for students from historically underserved communities	Access/Completion Equity Gaps	90.6%
Support development of a solution for student progress tracking	Strategic Systems Development	90.5%
Increase balance between federal spending on research and teaching/learning	Equal Funding for Ed Sectors	89.8%
Support development of a volunteer network to support students	Strategic Systems Development	89.8%
Support/fund solutions for housing-insecure students	Funding/Resources for Students	89.6%
Encourage social justice-related nonprofits to invest as much in CCs as they do in four-year institutions	Equal Funding for Ed Sectors	89.3%
End legacy scoring for admissions in universities	Improve Transfer Rates	87.8%
Support development of a solution for multi-year scheduling	Strategic Systems Development	87.8%
Call for equal investment in all students (CC students should receive comparable funding to four-year students)	Equal Funding for Ed Sectors	87.5%
Support development of a national data mart measuring major outcomes	Strategic Systems Development	87.0%
Allow DACA/Dreamer students to receive the same educational services as U.S. citizens	Access/Completion Equity Gaps	86.6%
Require CC employees to complete equity-mindedness training	Access/Completion Equity Gaps	86.0%
Support diversity-balanced admissions at four-year institutions	Improve Transfer Rates	85.5%

Policy	Policy Area	Agree + Strongly Agree
Encourage the university ranking systems (e.g., U.S. News and World Report) to place greater emphasis on social mobility	Improve Transfer Rates	84.1%
Develop a national score card on equity for all community colleges	Access/Completion Equity Gaps	82.1%
Support one integrated educational system (K–16) to align curriculum and make transitions more seamless	Improve Transfer Rates	81.4%

In addition to the 36 policy questions in the survey, respondents were invited to submit comments on any of the survey questions or anything they thought the survey may have overlooked. About 250 respondents (22 percent) submitted comments. Two of the most frequent comments either expanded on ideas presented in the survey or raised issues that community colleges should implement internally that were not germane to federal government involvement (i.e., improve how counseling is delivered, improve internal processes).

The most emphatic comments, often expressed with a degree of frustration, tended to be related to social justice and federal government involvement. As more than one respondent noted, the survey had an underlying bias that presumed that community colleges should be actively involved in social justice work and that the federal government should increase its level of support for this work. These respondents are correct with regard to this underlying assumption. In fact, this assumption was clearly expressed in the introduction to the survey, stating that "The goal of this survey is to develop a data informed, national agenda for community colleges. The agenda will be used to advance federal support for community colleges and the vital role they play in social justice and equity."

With this presumption, the survey did not ask respondents to weigh in on their thoughts about social justice overall or their attitudes about community colleges playing a role in social justice. There were also no overt questions about whether the federal government should be involved with community colleges in the first place. The premises of the survey led to some energetic opinions in the comments section, with 40 to 50 individuals (approximately 4 percent of respondents) opposing the idea that community colleges should be involved with social justice and the notion that the federal government should be assisting.

General push-back on social justice came from negative comments regarding race/ethnicity considerations in admissions as well as hiring and other academic decision-making processes. Some comments opposed the calculation that social constructs help some groups and hinder others, arguing that marginalized group characteristics should be minimized or eliminated in favor of more emphasis on individual merit. A few comments expressed frustration with equity-mindedness approaches. Some comments recommended DACA/Dreamer students receive *less* support than citizens. A few respondents expressed concern for maintaining academic standards under a social justice agenda.

Some respondents also expressed a general distrust of the federal government. Others were concerned over increased federal taxes, feared that federal programs might take resources from other federal services, felt that federal involvement would add a compliance drag on community colleges, expressed negative views of Secretary of Education DeVos, or expressed dissatisfaction with the role the federal government has played in K–12 education. Many comments reflected concerns about the system of federalism that we already work under in the United States, where the balance between local, state, and federal control is often a source of contention.

While the most emphatic comments opposed social justice and federal government involvement, the overwhelming majority of respondents supported these two goals. Averaging the scores for all 36 policy questions, a little over 90 percent indicated they *agree* or *strongly agree* with the policy suggestions, while a little less than 10 percent indicated they *disagree* or *strongly disagree*. In other words, over 90 percent support the concept of community colleges doing work in the social justice space, and over 90 percent are in favor of the federal government playing some kind of role.

A few comments emerged from bargaining units (unions). Some respondents voiced concern over the lack of institutional support for part-time faculty. Some called for federal assistance in supporting unions. A few commented on the unequal pay between part-time and full-time faculty as well as the disparities between university pay and community college pay. Others criticized unions for extending protection to individuals who practice racial discrimination or bias.

Federal government assistance with infrastructure issues was raised by a few respondents. Some recommended assistance with large construction projects as well as technology. Perhaps fueled by the pandemic and its impact on educators' lives while the survey was being administered, several called for help with communications technology and federal assistance for students who may not have access to the technology needed for online or web-enhanced instruction. Some respondents recommended federal help in moving away from large private technology systems and into more affordable ones.

A few comments were made about programs and services. There were calls for greater emphasis on STEM and arts education. Expanding mental health services was addressed several times, as was the need for childcare services. CTE education, experiential learning, non-credit education, competency-based learning, technical colleges, and credit for prior learning were all addressed in a group of comments on workforce development issues. These comments indicate legitimate needs that many community colleges have besides those that we have identified as proposals for a national policy agenda.

This survey helps identify six policy areas with specific policy recommendations under each that can frame a national agenda for community colleges. To implement these recommendations, there are four basic approaches the federal government can take: 1) support or expand existing federal programs that focus on community colleges in a manner that addresses some of the concerns raised in the survey, 2) expand existing federal programs focused on social justice issues into the community college sector to address survey related issues, 3) launch new federal programs that support the survey's policy recommendations, and 4) incentivize states and higher education boards to move in these policy directions as conditions to receive federal funding.

First, federal programs are doing some of this work already. The community college sector needs to identify these programs and support or request their expansion with regard to some of the specifics addressed in the survey. For example, two offices in the Department of Education are designated to work with community colleges and promote community college initiatives. These resources could be expanded to help implement some of the policy recommendations of the survey.

Second, there are existing federal programs promoting social justice, but they have not targeted community colleges. For example, Housing and Urban Development (HUD) has provided technical assistance to public-private partnerships for housing, but this agency has not been involved with funding community college housing projects. HUD could expand its work to help address housing for housing-insecure students. We need to identify programs and work with their managers and corresponding legislators to find ways that they can expand their work throughout the community college sector.

Third, some of these recommendations will need to be established as new federal programs or funded by the federal government and established by an outside organization through a competitive bidding process. America's College Promise Act is a good example of

200 *Reform in the Community College Ecosystem*

a new policy that was originally proposed in 2015 and has been reintroduced every year since. The bill has not passed (yet), but it is a good example of a new program that would make two years of community colleges free for many students needing financial assistance. This would be a new program that addresses the number-one policy recommendation in the survey.

Fourth, the federal government commonly influences the behavior of other governmental and civic organizations by attaching requirements to federal funding. This is a strategy that could be used to encourage states and college/university boards to move in the policy directions recommended by this survey. For example, to eliminate legacy scoring for admission to some universities, thereby depriving less affluent applicants of a space, the federal government could stipulate the absence of this practice as a requirement to

	Existing Education Progs	Existing Social Justice Progs	Possible New Policy/Prog	Possible Incentives
1. Increase Funding/Resources for Students				
Support keeping community colleges affordable (0.986)				
Increase financial aid funding for students (0.916)				
Support/fund solutions for food-insecure students (0.913)				
Support/fund solutions for housing-insecure students (0.896)				
2. Close Access/Completion Equity Gaps				
Support diversity in hiring at CCs (0.924)				
Recognize CCs as essential to national social justice efforts (0.913)				
Support a national best practices dialogue re equity in pedagogy, service, and management (0.911)				
Increase support for students from historically underserved communities (0.906)				
Allow DACA/Dreamer students to receive the same educational services as U.S. citizens (0.866)				
Require CC employees to complete equity-mindedness training (0.86)				
Develop a national score card on equity for all CCs (0.821)				
3. Improve Transfer Rates from CCs to Universities				
Support common course numbering for GE courses in CCs and 4-year institutions (0.938)				
Make sure all public 4-year institutions receive students with AA/AS degrees at junior level (0.914)				
Sponsor national scholars program for low-income/high-GPA student transfer to selective univs (0.909)				
End legacy scoring for admissions in universities (0.878)				
Support diversity-balanced admissions at 4-year institutions (0.855)				
Encourage the university ranking systems to place greater emphasis on social mobility (0.841)				
Support integrated educational system (K16) for curriculum alignment and seamless transitions (0.814)				
4. Support Job Placement				
Provide national mapping of career technical (CTE) programs to jobs (0.962)				
Support government data sharing with CCs for job placement tracking and CTE recruitment (0.956)				
Develop a national apprenticeship program/network (0.954)				
Expand federal funding for development of CTE programs (0.937)				
Develop national standards for work-based learning and CC education (0.907)				
5. Funding Higher Education Sectors Equally				
Develop report on funding across higher education segments (0.941)				
Support expansion of funding for counseling services in CCs (0.909)				
Support increase of full-time faculty in CCs (0.907)				
Increase balance between federal spending on research and teaching/learning (0.898)				
Encourage social justice nonprofits to invest as much in CCs as they do in 4-year institutions (0.893)				
Call for equal investment in all students (0.875)				
6. Develop Strategic Systems				
Support a solution for data-sharing between high schools and CCs for seamless enrollment (0.934)				
Support a solution to grant credit for prior learning for working adults (0.918)				
Support a solution to articulate military training into college credit (0.908)				
Support development of a solution for student progress tracking (0.905)				
Support development of a volunteer network to support students (0.898)				
Support development of a solution for multi-year scheduling (0.878)				
Support development of a national data mart measuring major outcomes (0.87)				

receive any federal funding. This is not a far stretch. Federal stipulations are already in place that prohibit overt racism or race-based discrimination in institutions that accept federal funds. Most scholars agree that legacy scoring embeds racial and income bias into the admissions process. Requiring the removal of these practices before federal funds are made available to universities seems consistent with existing requirements.

These four basic strategies describe the next round of work that will need to be completed in the development of a national agenda. The following table suggests how this work might be organized.

While there is additional work that needs to be done, there are three specific recommendations for community college leaders (trustees, managers, faculty leaders, staff leaders, and anyone else involved in community college leadership) that come out of this survey: 1) claim our central role in social justice and upward mobility, 2) formally adopt a comprehensive federal agenda, and 3) engage through collaborative activism.

Recommendation #1

Community college leaders need to claim our central role in social justice and upward mobility. Throughout my career, I have grappled with our role in higher education and what makes us unique in the sector. Many of us are frustrated with narratives that explain our work in pejorative terms. Descriptions of community college work often feel externally constructed and derivative of university work. The notion that community colleges are primarily filled with students and personnel who are not quite university caliber is a common refrain held in popular culture and echoed across the university system where most of us are trained.

We need to reject this framework and vocally embrace the unique and special mission of American community colleges. We are not ineffectual renderings of the university; rather, community colleges are institutions of higher education whose central role is equity. The work of the community college is the work of social justice, and we carry out this mission in society at a greater volume, with greater intentionality, and through greater expertise than most of our four-year colleagues. Community colleges unconditionally and uncompromisingly embrace the idea of promoting social mobility through education. This dedication is not as strongly evidenced at most of our four-year institutions. In this sense, community colleges are central to a national strategy to end systemic inequality, discrimination, and racism. This needs to be our pedestal, and a consciousness of this role in society starts with community college leaders recognizing this role, embracing it, and claiming it out loud to the constituents we serve.

Recommendation #2

Community college leaders need to formally adopt a comprehensive federal agenda. This action recognizes that community colleges function in an ecosystem supported by a range of institutions and resources. Local, regional, state, and federal institutions make up this ecosystem, and their interaction with community colleges has an impact on the education our students receive. The survey clearly supports the idea that the federal government is part of this ecosystem but is not participating in a prominent enough manner. The federal government needs to direct greater attention, support, and resources toward community college students. A critical step we can take to elicit greater support from the federal government is to formally adopt an agenda that clearly articulates the role we expect the federal government to play in community college education.

Our national organizations have already adopted federal policy agendas, but, given our survey results, they need to broaden their official recommendations. State organizations representing community colleges often have federal recommendations and should consider broadening or adopting some or all the issues raised in our survey. At our colleges and districts, elected or appointed board members should go through the deliberative process of articulating their expectations for federal support through adoption of a federal agenda. Constituent organizations like senates and unions often establish policy goals and need to make sure these are extended to the federal government. Finally, regional civic organizations that regularly establish federal policy goals should be invited to include some of these ideas into their own agendas.

Recommendation #3

Community college leaders should engage through collaborative activism. To encourage the federal government to move in these policy directions, we need to build greater levels of collaboration throughout the community college sector. This task is difficult because of the dispersed nature of the sector. There are several national organizations that do work on behalf of community colleges; some do advocacy work in Washington. Throughout the country are organizations that represent their community colleges at the state level. Sometimes these are organized as chancellors' offices, others are run by executive directors of a state association, and others have commissions under the state department of education. Most colleges are organized and led by a local board of governors, often at the county level. Community college board members are typically elected or appointed by a state elected official (e.g., the governor). Within all of the organizations are constituent groups organized at state and federal levels themselves. Senior managers, faculty, staff, and trustees have organizations that represent the interests of their constituencies across the 50 states and in Washington, D.C. Very often, the political, government relations and communications arms of these organizations are directed at efforts to lobby against each other for greater pieces of the existing community college pie. This is part of the process and will probably always be part of our system's deliberation; however, we need to channel the considerable assets we share toward an effort to grow the overall size of the pie for the community college sector.

It may be too expensive for many colleges to organize collaboration through these groups in Washington; however, local members of the House of Representatives, U.S. senators, and federal agencies often have local or regional offices that are close to our colleges. Through local resources, we can create compelling pressure for a federal agenda through regular meetings in these offices using a collaborative approach where trustees, managers, senates, unions, and local civic leaders collectively lobby under a unified agenda.

Conclusion

Community colleges serve a higher proportion of students from historically underserved communities than any other sector in higher education. Because they are underserved, they typically start their journeys further back and must complete them with fewer resources. This speaks to the core reason they have lower success rates. We have discussed this disparity thoroughly in other areas of the book along with specific strategies that need to be implemented if we hope to address many of the challenges these students face. To be successful in these reforms, we must face two difficult challenges. Both are difficult, but I also believe they are achievable. First, we must face the improvements we need to make internally. As James Baldwin put it, "Not everything that is faced can be changed, but nothing can be changed until it is faced." In the previous chapter (Chapter 10), we discussed the first challenge, identifying ('facing") the strategies that are likely to require internal work. As leaders in community colleges, we need to address these with a high degree of professionalism, urgency, and collaboration.

Facing our internal challenges is critical, but equally important are a set of issues that we must address outside our colleges. We must face the challenge of ecosystem reform. How we collaborate across our civic ecosystems and how the institutions inside these systems collaborate with us are essential. The entire system needs to address issues related to funding for community colleges; collaboration in the work around access, job placement, and transfer; solutions development; and more. Our best work in these areas has historically taken place at the local and state levels. Both of these areas have room for improvement, but the area that has been the weakest over the years, and the part of our ecosystem that needs greater collaboration, is the federal government.

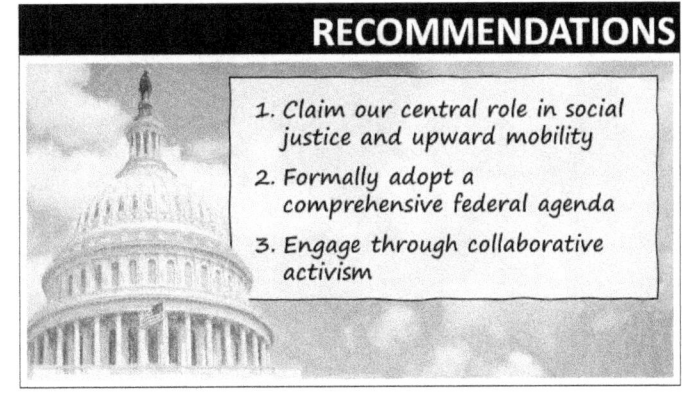

RECOMMENDATIONS

1. Claim our central role in social justice and upward mobility
2. Formally adopt a comprehensive federal agenda
3. Engage through collaborative activism

12 Caution and Courage

My favorite essay in all of American politics is *Letter from a Birmingham Jail*, by Dr. Martin Luther King, Jr. The letter was written in early April of 1963, after Dr. King and others were jailed for participating in a series of marches and sit-ins protesting racial segregation throughout Birmingham, Alabama. The "Birmingham Campaign" was organized by the Southern Christian Leadership Conference (SCLC). As president of SCLC, Dr. King was in Birmingham at the request of one of SCLC's Alabama affiliates to help organize a series of protests against the particularly brutal brand of racism that he described as "engulfing" Birmingham. The residents and civic institutions of the city were hardline segregationists, with separated areas for "whites" and "coloreds" strictly enforced for restaurants, theaters, drinking fountains, restrooms, and lodgings. The police department had a documented record of brutality against African Americans, including children and seniors.

Voting rights were systematically suppressed, and there was much more injustice rooted in the community's segregation policies and practices.

To bring attention to these injustices, SCLC organized a series of non-violent protests, including mass meetings, lunch counter sit-ins, marches on city hall, boycotting of downtown merchants, kneel-ins at churches, sit-ins at the public library, mass voter registration at the county courthouse, and general demonstrations of protest. As described in his letter, these protests were intended to create public pressure that would bring Birmingham's White decision-makers to the table for negotiations aimed at overcoming racial injustices. Instead, the residents and power structures of Birmingham reacted with significant force and violence in an attempt to shut the protests down and preserve segregation's hold on the city. Their goal was to fulfill the promise Governor George Wallace had declared a few months before during his inaugural address: "Segregation now, segregation tomorrow, segregation forever."

Reacting to the protests, many private citizens physically and verbally accosted African Americans peacefully sitting at "white only" lunch counters. They accosted peaceful marchers, church attendees, people standing in line to register to vote. Some went so far as to react by bombing the homes of Black leaders. Some White residents inflicted hate speech, bodily injury, damage to personal property, and acts intended to kill. The city and state allowed these crimes against African Americans to stand with little or no intervention and eventually joined in on the attacks, turning high-pressure fire hoses against protestors, beating passive demonstrators, *siccing* police dogs on African Americans peacefully marching in public areas, arresting protestors for minor and trumped-up charges and more. Images from the Birmingham Campaign still shock us today. Captured in simple and indisputable black-and-white photographs are the brutality, indignity, and injustices civil rights protestors suffered in this era and the hate-filled actions directed at them by private citizens and local government officials.

Dr. King was among those arrested in Birmingham for disobeying a court ruling that called for an end to the protests in Birmingham. He was held in solitary confinement—he would end up staying there for eight days—and allowed only one visitor, Clarence B. Jones, his attorney. I recently listened to a podcast interview with Jones (2019) in which he retells the story of the letter.

Jones first met with Dr. King on Saturday, the day after his arrest, and arrived with deep concern over the other protestors who had been arrested. Most of them were young, poor, and unable to post bail. Their parents were highly concerned about their condition, and Jones wanted to talk to Dr. King about raising funds through SCLC to help bail them out. Jones recalls being frustrated with Dr. King at the time because he was completely uninterested in talking about the need for bail. Instead, he was preoccupied with a letter that had been published the day before in a local Birmingham newspaper. On the day of Dr. King's arrest (Good Friday), an open letter signed by eight White clergymen from Alabama was published in the *Birmingham News*. The letter criticized Dr. King's approach as "unwise and untimely" and commended the Birmingham Police Department for its restraint throughout the protests.

Dr. King was so worked up about it that Jones was unable to talk to him about anything other than the letter. Dr. King had already started working on a response, writing in the blank spaces of the newspaper, on napkins, paper towels, and scrap pieces of paper. At the end of their meeting, he gave the writings to Jones, who smuggled the work out in his pockets and under his shirt. This routine went on two times per day over the course of four or five days. Jones would take handwritten notes out and smuggle blank paper in, hidden under his shirt. Dr. King's chief of staff typed everything up, following the arrows and notes that explained how his disparate written pieces fit together into what eventually became the *Letter from a Birmingham Jail* and now stands as one of the great essays in American political literature (Capehart, 2019).

In the letter, Dr. King explains why he is in Birmingham. He lays out a four-phase approach to nonviolent campaigns, explaining how they had arrived at the fourth phase of nonviolent protests. He talks about constructive nonviolent tension, positive peace, and negative peace. He pens the famous line "justice too long delayed is justice denied." He captures the toxic sting of racism through the eyes of his children. He speaks of his disappointment with White Protestant, Catholic, and Jewish leaders. And over the arc of the essay, he describes a country where White Americans are permitted to enjoy the fruits of the American Dream while Black Americans suffer unimaginable pain (sometimes as severe as lynching) whenever they insist that they should be able to enjoy the same benefits. Referencing the lunch counter sit-ins, where Black men and women sat at lunch counters for "Whites Only" and suffered extreme abuse as a result, Dr. Kings writes "when these disinherited children of God sat down at lunch counters, they were in reality standing up for the best in the American dream." The letter's moral high ground is the idea that access to the freedoms of America is for every man and woman, regardless of race. Many parts of the essay are gripping, but the part that strikes me every time I read the letter is his direct challenge to "white moderates."

This paragraph is nearly 60 years old, but it could have been written last week, given how relevant it is to today's environment and how insightfully it describes the reasons racism (and xenophobia, and sexism, and homophobia, and religious intolerance, and other forms of discrimination) persists. We live in a democratic country were most

> I must confess that over the last few years I have been gravely disappointed with the white moderate. I have almost reached the regrettable conclusion that the Negro's great stumbling block in the stride toward freedom is not the White Citizen's Council-eror the Ku Klux Klanner, but the white moderate who is more devoted to "order" than to justice; who prefers a negative peace which is the absence of tension to a positive peace which is the presence of justice; who constantly says "I agree with you in the goal you seek, but I can't agree with your methods of direct action;" who paternalistically feels he can set the timetable for another man's freedom; who lives by the myth of time and who constantly advises the Negro to wait until a "more convenient season." Shallow understanding from people of goodwill is more frustrating than absolute misunderstanding from people of ill will. Lukewarm acceptance is much more bewildering than outright rejection.

people do not want racism to be part of our society (Horowitz et al., 2019), yet it persists. Why?

The reason it persists in society is *not* because of the Ku Klux Klan, neo-Nazis, white nationalists, skinheads, and holocaust deniers. The reason it persists is because of "moderate decision-makers" who hold power across a range of public and private institutions, insisting that they oppose all forms of discrimination but too often refusing to take concrete actions to end this behavior in society. They constantly find reasons to put off meaningful action indefinitely. Like the eight clergymen from Birmingham, our "moderate decision-makers" agree that racism has no place in their institutions, but when presented with concrete solutions to address racist or discriminatory behavior, they find the means *untimely* and too *disruptive.*

As I mentioned in a story earlier in the book, I once was offered the opportunity to secure $24 million that would have been used to build housing for homeless students and housing-insecure military veterans. I received two criticisms from my boss as I tried to press for accepting the resources: The funding timeline was too compressed, and receiving the funding would create several problems throughout the district with the other two colleges not receiving any funding. I was harshly criticized for bringing a solution that was too disruptive and inconvenient.

Without reservation, I agree with the criticism. The timeline was tight, and the funding would have created an internal stir. As a result, the district rejected the money because its decision-makers were "more committed to order than to justice," as Dr. King would put it. With the decision to reject the funding, the district's order was preserved, but the injustice of homeless students remained. The students who could be sleeping in college-funded rooms today are still sleeping in cars and under bridges.

I have been working in community colleges for 30 years and have personally engaged in probably thousands of hours of sincere dialogue from college leaders about improving student completion rates and closing the equity gap. Throughout this period, the completion gaps have remained, with students from disfavored communities experiencing less academic success than students from more privileged communities. A recent study out by UPenn (The Pell Institute for the Study of Opportunity in Higher Education and PennAHEAD, 2018) shows that these gaps have become worse over the last several decades. The report classified all families in the United States into four income groups: quartile 1 (wealthy families), quartile 2 (upper-middle-income families), quartile 3 (lower-middle-income families, and quartile 4 (low-income or poor families). The assessment looked at college completion for dependent family members 24 years old or less between the years of 1970 and 2016. It found that BA/BS completion rates have increased slightly for poor families, moving from 22 percent to 25 percent. They have improved a little more for lower-middle-income families, moving from 23 percent to 33 percent. They have increased the most for those from upper-middle-income families, moving from 26 percent to 59 percent. And wealthy family members have gone from a high completion rate of 55 percent in 1970 to an even higher rate of 75 percent in 2016. The gaps are clearly widening. Students from upper-middle-income and wealthy families are now experiencing much greater college success than their colleagues from families with lower incomes. The data from this study are frustrating, even counterintuitive. Everyone I have worked with over the years (literally everyone) wants these gaps to narrow, if not close. Yet they persist—and even grow.

BA/BS COMPLETION RATE

% of family members completing college by income shows widening gaps

1970:
- Poor 22%
- Lower-Middle 23%
- Upper-Middle 26%
- Wealthy 55%

2016:
- Poor 25%
- Lower-Middle 33%
- Upper-Middle Income 59%
- Wealthy 75%

I have been involved with equity gap work at three colleges and have had quantifiable success at all three. The successes in all three colleges involved substantive change across the institution, and making the changes was at times extremely difficult. There were days I got in the car and cried on the drive home. There were days I pulled over, bought a pack of cigarettes, smoked one or two, and threw the rest away. I endured many sleepless nights. There were two trips to the hospital thinking I may be in the middle of a cardiac episode (both were stress related). At all three colleges, there were moments when I/we had to confront powerful forces in the institution who opposed change and often expressed their opposition in deeply personal ways. In these moments, department/division personnel, unions, senates, executives, governing board members, even long-time friends and colleagues reacted to these changes with negativity, even hostility, and I responded poorly at times as well.

There are many reasons we often respond to reform in ugly ways. Humans have a basic need for order and continuity. Significant change is usually *de facto* criticism of the status quo. Our jobs are wrapped up in our identities, and so touching our work is touching us at a very personal level. Change requires additional work in the transition for people who are often already overworked. There are understandable reasons people react so intensely to the changes that need to be made if we hope to attain equitable success for all student groups.

One major reason these difficult exchanges take place in higher education is our relatively flat and democratic environments. Open dialogue, inclusive dialogue, shared decision-making, and representative constituent groups are wrapped into a fairly egalitarian environment that is filled with deliberation. These are, of course, qualities in our academic environment that most of us, including me, cherish, nurture, and defend. However, they can make institutional reform very difficult. Richard Neustadt, one of the classic researchers in political science, explains this point when he writes about decision-making in the executive branch. He argues that the U.S. president has a huge job—one of the biggest in the world—and in order for him (someday her) to get his job done, he must rely heavily on help from a range of constituent groups, including congress, the courts, the media, state and local government leaders, business leaders, party leaders, other heads of state, government agency heads, public opinion, and the like.

The thing that makes the job of the president particularly difficult is that we expect him to do this huge job well, and he has an array of constituents at his disposal that can help, but none of them are *required* to help. He is dependent on them for success, but almost none of them are dependent on him for their personal job security. In fact, if leaders of a constituent group decide to oppose the president, they can do so openly, and typically their jobs will not be threatened.

For example, the president needs Congress to enact legislation. If it opposes him, he has very little recourse. The president needs the media to help explain challenges and solutions to the public. If those in this sector oppose him, there is not much he can do. The same applies to the president's relationship with most constituent groups. This reliance on other powerful actors leads Neustadt to conclude that the most important skill for successful presidents is his power of persuasion.

Leadership in colleges and universities, especially those in positions of CEO, are in a very similar predicament. The job is not as big as the U.S. president's. We don't have jobs that impact lives on a national or global scale, but the environment is very similar. College presidents have a job to do, but to do it well, they need support from important constituent groups. The academic senate, classified senate, bargaining units, academic division/department leaders, management organization, governing board members, community organizations, business leaders, locally elected officials, and more are part of a complicated, delicate, and fragile lattice that must be built if any institutional change is to be implemented effectively. The entire lattice is built on trust, and if any constituent group pulls away and takes an active oppositional stance, initiatives can come crashing down, especially when the initiatives are young. And when these initiatives fall, the leader (i.e., CEO) is usually held accountable for the crash.

So, the predicament around social justice issues that most presidents find themselves in is as follows: On the one hand, there are glaring inequities in higher education. There is no dispute about this. Students from disfavored communities are routinely ground out of our institutions before they complete their degrees. This happens at an alarmingly higher rate than for students from privileged communities. This discrepancy is clearly observable across multiple, duplicated, peer-reviewed, and longitudinal studies. On the other hand, CEOs live in the decision-making environment described previously. They realize that addressing these inequities will require substantive institutional change, and with the environment described previously, the odds of success are low and the chances of losing their job over an initiative crash are high.

This is how we end up with well-intentioned leaders who do very little to change the outcomes for students from disfavored communities. This is how we have ended up talking about closing the completion gap for 50 years, only to see it widen under our leadership.

This is the phenomenon that creates the "white moderates" Dr. King referenced. "I agree with you in the goal you seek, but I can't agree with your methods of direct action" is the refrain that generated so much frustration for Dr. King. It is a refrain that acknowledges how perilous direct action can be. This phenomenon is alive and palpably present today. It is why *Letter from a Birmingham Jail* is still relevant. Written nearly 60 years ago, it poses an important question all leaders who want to do equity work in higher education must answer: In the face of grave inequities across higher education, will you respond with caution or courage?

If you are honest with yourself, this is a difficult question to answer. I know it is for me. To help answer this question, I would like you to walk through one last scenario with me. Imagine in your town there is a summer camp for kids run by the town. It is a day-camp where kids can meet other kids, enjoy the outdoors, learn crafts, and generally have fun for two weeks. It is not anything your kids or grandkids attend, and while you personally do not help run the program, you are a town employee in another department and support the program whole-heartedly. You know several of the people who help organize the camp each year. One day, you are on a walk through your neighborhood, and one of the day-camp parents who lives in the neighborhood stops you. The parent, someone you know and trust, proceeds to tell you about a town employee who works at the camp and how this person has been particularly harsh with some of the day-campers. The employee does not appear to have done anything illegal, but as the parent describes his behavior, it is clear he is making some kids feel bad, emotionally upset, discouraged, and withdrawn. His behavior has at times been so emotionally egregious that a few kids have left camp crying. From the description, it is clear that this behavior is entirely inappropriate, but there is no evidence, and you are only professionally acquainted with the employee. What would you do in this situation?

You would probably take the problem home with you. Talk it over with your spouse, partner, or a close friend. You might run through the avenues that are available to you. You could approach the person directly. You may need to approach the person's boss. Could this matter escalate to the town council? What if the accusation is false? How will the person react? Should you bring HR into the conversation? Will this embarrass the town government? Are there legal consequences associated with this matter? Could you be liable for reputation damage? Will his union representatives get involved? Will the parent back you up if the matter gets complicated? How will your colleagues view you if they hear you have stepped into this matter?

My gut says that nearly all of us will feel empathy for the child or children. We will all believe something wrong has happened and needs intervention. We will also recognize how complicated it could become if we address the issue in an official manner. Many of us may find a middle ground where we take some kind of minor action of notifying someone unofficially and leave it at that.

Now, think through the same scenario, and this time, imagine that it is your child, or grandchild, or a child that you know and love deeply who was subjected to this treatment. You are aware that your child had been acting a little strange lately, and when the neighbor tells you of the incident(s), the neighbor references your child as one of the victims. Your child is one of the kids who was emotionally abused by the town employee at the day-camp. You realize why your child has been unusually withdrawn and upset lately. As you walk home, you picture your child confused as the staff member yelled. You picture your child sitting alone. As you drive to work the next morning, you picture your child feeling hurt, isolated, and humiliated because an adult who was trusted to nurture them and the other kids hurt them instead.

I suspect your response now will not be small. It will not be carefully measured to protect your professional reputation. You will not give long consideration to all the possible hurdles in front of you. With almost no effort, your response will be one that transcends personal *caution*, and you will act with *courage* on behalf of a person you love.

When we love someone deeply, we are our best selves. This is when we actually seem like we were made in the image of God. We are focused, fearless, selfless, directed, forgiving, patient, intentional, caring, courageous, empathic, kind, and caring. We hope for them, celebrate their successes, tend to their pain, stand in their defense, fight at their side, without end. This book has covered substantial territory. It has laid out detailed and ambitious work that we need to do on behalf of our students. But the most important act we can extend to our students, the one practice that brings every strategy into focus, is love. If we love our students like they are our own family members, we will effortlessly find the courage it takes to reimagine, redesign, and reform higher education into a social justice engine where all student groups find equitable academic success.

Works Cited

AACC: American Association of Community Colleges. (2020, August 17). *Community college agenda for the 2020 presidential candidates.* Retrieved from www.aacc.nche.edu/wp-content/uploads/2020/02/AACC_Presidential_Campaign_Proposals_Final2020.pdf

About the Children. (n.d.). *AdoptUSKids.* Retrieved September 24, 2020, from www.adoptuskids.org/meet-the-children/children-in-foster-care/about-the-children#:~:text=According%20to%20the%20most%20recent,old%20(in%20some%20states)

ACCT and AACC. (2020, August 17). *2020 Community college federal legislative priorities.* Retrieved from www.acct.org/files/NLS%202020%20Green%20Sheet%20-%20FINAL.pdf

ACLED. (2020, September). Demonstrations & political violence in America: New data for summer 2020. *ACLED.* Retrieved from https://acleddata.com/2020/09/03/demonstrations-political-violence-in-america-new-data-for-summer-2020/

Agarwal, K. (2018, January 1). Inside higher ed: College-in-prison programs flourish, but for how long? *American Historical Association.* Retrieved from www.historians.org/publications-and-directories/perspectives-on-history/january-2018/inside-higher-ed-college-in-prison-programs-flourish-but-for-how-long

Aguirre, D., von Post, R., & Alpern, M. (2013, November 14). Culture's role in enabling organizational change. *Strategy.* Retrieved from www.strategyand.pwc.com/gx/en/insights/cultures-role-organizational-change.html

Alaska Native Groups & Cultures. (2020, September 14). *Alaskaweb.org.* Retrieved from http://alaskaweb.org/native/gps&cults.htm#:~:text=In%20general%2C%20there%20are%20three,by%20their%20language%20and%20geography

Allen, R. (2006). *An economic analysis of prison education programs and recidivism.* Atlanta, GA: Emery University, Department of Economics.

American Nonprofit Academy. (2020, May 4). All too rare: A gift underscores a persistent lack of support for community colleges. *American Nonprofit Academy.* Retrieved from https://americannonprofitacademy.com/nonprofit-news/all-too-rare-a-gift-underscores-a-persistent-lack-of-support-for-community-colleges/

Applied Educational Systems. (2019, July 31). 78 Career and technical education facts for 2019. *Applied Educational Systems.* Retrieved from www.aeseducation.com/career-technical-education-facts-that-prove-its-awesome

Ashford, E. (2019, January 3). A better understanding of Asian students' needs. *Community College Daily.* Retrieved from www.ccdaily.com/2019/01/better-understanding-asian-students-needs/

Aspen Institute. (2013, June 21). Crisis and opportunity: Aligning the community college presidency with student success. *aspeninstitute.org.* Retrieved from www.aspeninstitute.org/publications/crisis-opportunity-aligning-community-college-presidency-student-success/

Barham, J. A. (2019, September 13). The 100 richest universities: Their generosity and commitment to research. *The Best Schools.* Retrieved from https://thebestschools.org/features/richest-universities-endowments-generosity-research/

The Best Schools. (2019, July 9). Prison education: Guide to college degrees for inmates and ex-offenders. *The Best Schools.* Retrieved from https://thebestschools.org/magazine/prison-inmate-education-guide/#:~:text=By%202017%2C%2034%20of%20the,in%20courses%20for%20college%20credits

Bialik, K. (2017, November 10). The changing face of America's veteran population. *Pew Center for Research*. Retrieved from www.pewresearch.org/fact-tank/2017/11/10/the-changing-face-of-americas-veteran-population/

Bielak, D., Murphy, D., & Shelton, J. (2020, January 8). "Billion dollar bets" to create economic opportunity for every American. *The Bridgespan Group*. Retrieved from www.bridgespan.org/insights/library/big-bets/billion-dollar-bets-to-create-economic-opportuni

Bragg, D. D., Endel, B., Anderson, N., Soricone, L., & Acevedo, E. (2019, July). What works for adult learners. *JFF*. Retrieved from www.luminafoundation.org/wp-content/uploads/2019/08/what-works-for-adult-learners.pdf

California Community College Chancellor's Office. (2020a, January 2). *Management information systems data mart*. California Community College Chancellor's Office. Retrieved from https://datamart.cccco.edu/DataMart.aspx

California Community College Chancellor's Office. (2020b, September 2). *Data mart*. Sacramento, CA: California Community College Chancellor's Office.

California Community College Chancellor's Office. (2020c, April 20). *Management information systems data mart*. California Community College Chancellor's Office. Retrieved from https://datamart.cccco.edu/DataMart.aspx

California Community College League. (2019). *Fast facts 2019*. California Community College League. Retrieved from https://ccleague.org/sites/default/files/pdf/state-advocacy/fast_facts_2019_final.pdf

The Campaign for College Opportunity. (2015, September). *The state of higher education in California—Asian American, Native Hawaiian, Pacific Islander report*. The Campaign for College Opportunity. Retrieved from https://collegecampaign.org/wp-content/uploads/2015/09/2015-State-of-Higher-Education_AANHPI2.pdf

Capehart, J. (2019, April 18). How MLK's famous letter was smuggled out of jail: 'Voices of the movement' episode 3. *The Washington Post*. Retrieved from www.washingtonpost.com/opinions/2019/04/18/how-mlks-famous-letter-was-smuggled-out-jail-voices-movement-episode/

Carapezza, K. (2017, March 15). National survey shows high rates of hungry and homeless community college students. *NPR*. Retrieved from www.npr.org/sections/ed/2017/03/15/520192774/national-survey-shows-high-rates-of-hungry-and-homeless-community-college-studen

Carnevale, A. P., Smith, N., Melton, M., & Price, E. W. (2015). *Learning while earning: The new normal*. Georgetown University, Center on Education and the Workforce. Retrieved from https://cew.georgetown.edu/cew-reports/workinglearners/

Cause, L. R., Holtzman, T., Gault, B., Croom, D., & Polk, P. (2019, April 11). Parents in college by the numbers. *Institute for Women's Policy Research*. Retrieved from https://iwpr.org/publications/parents-college-numbers/

The Center for Community College Leadership. (2018, April). *Money left on the table: An analysis of Pell Grant receipt among financially-eligible community college students in California*. The Campaign for College Opportunity. Retrieved from https://education.ucdavis.edu/sites/main/files/ucdavis_wheelhouse_research_brief_vol3no3_online_1.pdf

The Century Foundation. (2019, April 25). Recommendations for providing community colleges with the resources they need. *The Century Foundation*. Retrieved from https://tcf.org/content/report/recommendations-providing-community-colleges-resources-need/?agreed=1

Chen, G. (2020, June 15). The catch-22 of community college graduation rates. *Community College Review*. Retrieved from www.communitycollegereview.com/blog/the-catch-22-of-community-college-graduation-rates#:~:text=As%20shown%20in%20the%20graph,rate%20stands%20at%2028%20percent

Chen, J. (2017, March). Nontraditional adult learners: The neglected diversity in postsecondary education. *SAGE Open*. Retrieved from www.researchgate.net/publication/314262633_Nontraditional_Adult_Learners_The_Neglected_Diversity_in_Postsecondary_Education

Chen, X., & Nunnery, A. (2019, October). *Profile of very low and low-income undergraduates in 2015–16*. U.S. Department of Education Undergraduates in 2015–16. Retrieved from https://nces.ed.gov/pubs2020/2020460.pdf

Chetty, R., Hendren, N., Kline, P., Saez, E., & Turner, N. (2014). Is the United States still a land of opportunity? Recent trends in intergenerational mobility. *American Economic Review*, 141–147.

Christensen, C. M. (1997). *The innovator's dilemma*. Boston, MA: Harvard Business School Press.

Coggeshall, W. L., Murke-Storer, M., Correa, M., & Tidd, S. (2019, December). Correctional education (post-secondary education). *Washington State Institute for Public Policy*. Retrieved from www.wsipp.wa.gov/BenefitCost/Program/735

College for America. (2017, June 7). Addressing the college completion gap among low-income students. *College for America*. Retrieved from https://collegeforamerica.org/college-completion-low-income-students/#:~:text=Its%20latest%20research%20released%20in,percent%20of%20middle%2Dincome%20students

College Rank. (2020, January 5). The history of college rankings. *College Rank*. Retrieved from www.collegerank.net/history-of-college-rankings/

Community College Research Center. (2015). *The movement towards pathways*. Community College Research Center. Retrieved from www.aacc.nche.edu/wp-content/uploads/2017/09/TheMovementTowardPathways.pdf

Community College Research Center. (2020a, June 22). *Community college FAQs*. Community College Research Center. Retrieved from https://ccrc.tc.columbia.edu/Community-College-FAQs.html

Community College Research Center. (2020b, March 29). *Community college FAQs*. CCRC Community College Research Center. Retrieved from https://ccrc.tc.columbia.edu/Community-College-FAQs.html

Contardo, J., & Tolbert, M. (n.d.). *Prison postsecondary education: Bridging learning from incarceration to the community*. Retrieved from http://johnjay.jjay.cuny.edu/files/ContardoTolbert_Paper.pdf

Couloute, L. (2018, October). Getting back on course: Educational exclusion and attainment among formerly incarcerated people. *Prison Policy Initiative*. Retrieved from www.prisonpolicy.org/reports/education.html#:~:text=Of%20all%20formerly%20incarcerated%20people%20with%20in%2Dprison%20GEDs%2C%20less,complete%20at%20least%20some%20college

Dale, S., & Krueger, A. B. (2011, June). Estimating the return to college selectivity over the career using administrative earnings data. *National Bureau of Economic Research*. Retrieved from http://www.nber.org/papers/w17159.

Darling-Hammond, S., Michaels, E., Allen, A., Chai, D., Thomas, M., Nguyen, T., . . . Johnson, R. (2020, September 10). After "the China virus" went viral: Racially charged coronavirus coverage and trends in bias against Asian Americans. *Health Education & Behavior*. Retrieved from https://journals.sagepub.com/doi/full/10.1177/1090198120957949

Davis, R. J. (2006, July). College access, financial aid, and college success for undergraduates from foster care. *NASFAA*. Retrieved from https://files.eric.ed.gov/fulltext/ED543361.pdf

De Alva, J., & Schneider, M. S. (2015, April 6). Rich schools, poor students: Tapping large university endowments to improve student outcomes. *AIR American Institute for Research*. Retrieved from www.air.org/resource/rich-schools-poor-students-tapping-large-university-endowments-improve-student-outcomes

Dernoncourt, F. (2016, December 4). How much public funding do private universities in the United States receive, directly or indirectly? *Academia*. Retrieved from https://academia.stackexchange.com/questions/81056/how-much-public-funding-do-private-universities-in-the-united-states-receive-di

DeVol, R. (2016, October 23). Address income inequality through investing in CTE skills training. *Huffington Post*. Retrieved from www.huffpost.com/entry/address-income-inequality_b_12577306?guccounter=1&guce_referrer=aHR0cHM6Ly93d3cuZ29vZ2xlLmNvbS8&guce_referrer_sig=AQAAAAxHboAmAECXeMjid4xU4rg8v6PiGC8HGJgXm9Yu1bH8gaLVTL0ovaquEUD8Isdcy71NB80U5Ss000LE8-cGmSanBrrDAk7upaChZ4vEW3

Doar, R., Bowman, K., & O'Neil, E. (2016, August 8). 2016 Poverty survey: Attitudes toward the poor, poverty, and welfare in the United States. *American Enterprise Institute and Los Angeles Times*. Retrieved from www.aei.org/publication/2016-poverty-survey/

Dworsky, A., & Pérez, A. (2009). *Helping former foster youth graduate from college*. Chapin Hall at the University of Chicago. Retrieved from www.careerladdersproject.org/docs/ChapinHallCampusSupportPrograms.pdf

Dynarski, S. (2018, September 28). At elite colleges, racial diversity requires affirmative action. *The New York Times*. Retrieved from www.nytimes.com/2018/09/28/business/at-elite-colleges-racial-diversity-requires-affirmative-action.html

EAB. (2019a, October 8). 60% of adults have considered returning to college but worry about cost. *EAB*. Retrieved from https://eab.com/insights/daily-briefing/adult-learner/adults-have-considered-returning-to-college-but-worry-about-cost/

EAB. (2019b, October 23). Adult learners: Who they are and what they want from college. *EAB*. Retrieved from https://eab.com/insights/daily-briefing/adult-learner/adult-learners-who-they-are-what-they-want-from-college/

Education Commission of the States. (2018, June). Transfer and articulation statewide common course numbering. *Education Commission of the States*. Retrieved from http://ecs.force.com/mbdata/MBquest3RTA?Rep=TR1802

Education Data. (2020, February 27). Percentage of high school graduates that go to college. *Education-data.org*. Retrieved from https://educationdata.org/high-school-graduates-who-go-to-college/

Education Encyclopedia. (2019, December 12). Community colleges: The history of community colleges, the junior college and the research university, the community college mission. *Education Encyclopedia—StateUniversity.com*. Retrieved from https://education.stateuniversity.com/pages/1873/Community-Colleges.html

educationdata.org. (2020a, August 3). College enrollment & student demographic statistics. *educationdata.org*. Retrieved from https://educationdata.org/college-enrollment-statistics/

educationdata.org. (2020b, September 14). College enrollment & student demographic statistics. *Educationdata.org*. Retrieved from https://educationdata.org/college-enrollment-statistics/

Edwards, C. (2010, March). Public-sector unions. *Cato Institute*. Retrieved from www.cato.org/sites/cato.org/files/pubs/pdf/tbb_61.pdf

Ellis, S. K. (2019, June). Accelerating acceptance 2019. *GLAAD*. Retrieved from https://www.glaad.org

Espinosa, L., & Baum, S. (2019, February 19). OPINION: Black students' 'unprecedented and unequal' college debt should cause alarm. *The Hechinger Report*. Retrieved from https://hechingerreport.org/opinion-black-students-unprecedented-and-unequal-college-debt-is-cause-for-alarm/

Fain, P. (2019, May 23). Wealth's influence on enrollment and completion. *Inside Higher Ed*. Retrieved from www.insidehighered.com/news/2019/05/23/feds-release-broader-data-socioeconomic-status-and-college-enrollment-and-completion

Falciano, V., Kuncle, R., & Gnolek, S. (2014). Modeling change and variation in U.S. News & world report college rankings: What would it really take to be in the top 20? *Research in Higher Education, 55*, 761–779.

Fishman, R. (2019, February 25). Pushing for radical change in admissions. *New America*. Retrieved from www.newamerica.org/education-policy/in-the-news/pushing-radical-change-admissions/

Fry, R., & Cilluffo, A. (2019, May 22). A rising share of undergraduates are from poor families, especially at less selective colleges. *Pew Research Center*. Retrieved from www.pewsocialtrends.org/2019/05/22/a-rising-share-of-undergraduates-are-from-poor-families-especially-at-less-selective-colleges/#:~:text=In%202016%2C%2020%25%20of%20dependent,with%2029%25%2020%20years%20earlier

Fuschillo, A. (2018, August 14). The troubling student-to-counselor ratio that doesn't add up. *Education Week*. Retrieved from www.edweek.org/ew/articles/2018/08/14/the-troubling-student-to-counselor-ratio-that-doesnt-add.html

Gerda Hagenauer, S. E. (2014, May 21). Teacher–student relationship at university: An important yet under-researched field. *Oxford Review of Education*. Retrieved from www.tandfonline.com/doi/full/10.1080/03054985.2014.921613

Giancola, J., & Kahlenberg, R. (2016, January). True merit: Ensuring our brightest students have access to our best colleges and universities. *Jack Kent Cooke Foundation*. Retrieved from www.jkcf.org/research/true-merit-ensuring-our-brightest-students-have-access-to-our-best-colleges-and-universities/

Gier, N. (2018, September 2). An update on unions in higher education. *Idaho State Journal*. Retrieved from www.idahostatejournal.com/opinion/columns/an-update-on-unions-in-higher-education/article_dfbd130f-37fa-5561-9ddd-d87a267e87ac.html

Gladwell, M. (2011, February 6). The trouble with college rankings. *The New Yorker*. Retrieved from www.newyorker.com/magazine/2011/02/14/the-order-of-things

Glynn, J. (2019, January). Persistence: The success of students who transfer from community colleges to selective four-year institutions. *Jack Kent Cooke Foundation*. Retrieved from www.jkcf.org/research/persistence/

Goldrick-Rab, S., Baker-Smith, C., Coca, V., Looker, E., & Williams, T. (2019). *College and university basic needs insecurity: A national #RealCollege survey report*. Philadelphia, PA: The Hope Center, Temple University.

Green, E. L., & Waldman, A. (2018, December 28). "I feel invisible", Native students languish in public schools. *The New York Times*. Retrieved from www.nytimes.com/2018/12/28/us/native-american-education.html

Green, K. C. (2018, July 22). The Babel problem with big data in higher ed. *Inside Higher Ed*. Retrieved from www.insidehighered.com/blogs/digital-tweed/babel-problem-big-data-higher-ed-1

Gregor Aisch, L. B. (2017, January 18). Some colleges have more students from the top 1 percent than the bottom 60. Find yours. *The New York Times*. Retrieved from www.nytimes.com/interactive/2017/01/18/upshot/some-colleges-have-more-students-from-the-top-1-percent-than-the-bottom-60.html

Helhoski, A. (2018, October 16). 2018 FAFSA study: Students missed out on $2.6 billion in free college money. *Nerdwallet*. Retrieved from www.nerdwallet.com/blog/2018-fafsa-study/

Henshaw, A. (n.d.). LGBT college statistics. *Campus Explorer*. Retrieved September 16, 2020, from www.campusexplorer.com/college-advice-tips/DC54CA9B/LGBT-College-Statistics/

Hill, C. B., Kurzweil, M., Pisacreta, E. D., & Schwartz, E. (2019, January 10). Enrolling more veterans at high-graduation-rate colleges and universities. *ITHAKA*. Retrieved from https://sr.ithaka.org/publications/enrolling-more-veterans-at-high-graduation-rate-colleges-and-universities/#:~:text=According%20to%20Student%20Veterans%20of,by%20the%20end%20of%202015

Horowitz, J. M., Brown, A., & Cox, K. (2019, April 9). Race in America 2019. *Pew Research Center*. Retrieved from www.pewsocialtrends.org/2019/04/09/race-in-america-2019/

Hoxby, C. M., & Avery, C. (2012, December). The missing "one-offs": The hidden supply of high-achieving, low income students. *The National Bureau of Economic Research*. Retrieved from www.nber.org/papers/w18586

Hsin, A., & Xie, Y. (2014, June 10). Explaining Asian Americans' academic advantage over whites. *PNAS*. Retrieved from www.pnas.org/content/111/23/8416

Hurwitz, M. (2011). The impact of legacy status on undergraduate admissions at elite colleges and universities. *Economics of Education Review*, 480–492. Retrieved from www.sciencedirect.com/science/article/abs/pii/S0272775710001676?via%3Dihub

Jack, A. A. (2019). *The privileged poor: How elite colleges are failing disadvantaged students*. Cambridge: Harvard University Press.

Jaschik, S. (2013, June 7). The deceptive data on Asians. *Inside Higher Ed*. Retrieved from www.insidehighered.com/news/2013/06/07/report-calls-end-grouping-asian-american-students-one-category

Jaschik, S. (2018, September 24). The 2018 surveys of admissions leaders: The pressure grows. *Inside Higher Ed*. Retrieved from www.insidehighered.com/news/survey/2018-surveys-admissions-leaders-pressure-grows

Johnson, K., & Urquhart, J. (2020, September 4). White nationalism upsurge in U.S. Echoes historical pattern, say scholars. *Reuters*. Retrieved from www.reuters.com/article/us-global-race-usa-extremism-analysis/white-nationalism-upsurge-in-u-s-echoes-historical-pattern-say-scholars-idUSKBN25V2QH

Jones, C. B. (2019, April 18). Voices: How MLK's famous letter was smuggled out of jail. *J. Capehart, Interviewer*.

Jynnah, R., & Noe-Bustamante, L. (2019, June 3). Facts on U.S. Immigrants, 2017: Statistical portrait of the foreign-born population in the United States. *Pew Research Center*. Retrieved from www.pewresearch.org/hispanic/2019/06/03/facts-on-u-s-immigrants/

Kahlenberg, R. D. (2015, May 28). How higher education funding shortchanges community colleges. *The Century Foundation*. Retrieved from https://tcf.org/content/report/how-higher-education-funding-shortchanges-community-colleges/?agreed=1

Kelly, R. (2017, December 12). Survey: 94% of students want to use their cell phones in class. *Campus Technology*. Retrieved from https://campustechnology.com/articles/2017/12/12/students-want-to-use-their-cell-phones-in-class.aspx

Kesslen, B. (2019, June 10). 'Homophiles': *The LGBTQ rights movement began long before Stonewall*. Retrieved from NBC News: https://www.nbcnews.com/feature/nbc-out/homophiles-stonewall-there-was-growing-gay-rights-movement-n1015331

Lawrence, S. (2009). *Social justice grantmaking II*. New York City: The Foundation Center.

Levine, E. (2019, November 7). Are colleges and universities meeting the online learning challenge? *EdTech: Focus on Higher Education*. Retrieved from https://edtechmagazine.com/higher/article/2019/11/are-colleges-and-universities-meeting-online-learning-challenge

Libassi, C. (2018, May 23). The neglected college race gap: Racial disparities among college completers. *Center for American Progress*. Retrieved from www.americanprogress.org/issues/education-postsecondary/reports/2018/05/23/451186/neglected-college-race-gap-racial-disparities-among-college-completers/

Lopez, G., & Krogstad, J. M. (2017, September 25). Key facts about unauthorized immigrants enrolled in DACA. *Per Research Center*. Retrieved from www.pewresearch.org/fact-tank/2017/09/25/key-facts-about-unauthorized-immigrants-enrolled-in-daca/

Lopez, G., Ruiz, N. G., & Patten, E. (2017, September 8). Key facts about Asian Americans, a diverse and growing population. *Per Research Center*. Retrieved from www.pewresearch.org/fact-tank/2017/09/08/key-facts-about-asian-americans/

Mack, D. (2019, November 25). Access to higher ed for incarcerated students is essential to criminal justice reform. *The Hill*. Retrieved from https://thehill.com/opinion/criminal-justice/471944-access-to-higher-ed-for-incarcerated-students-is-essential-to

Marcus, J. (2017, April 21). Community colleges rarely graduate the veterans they recruit. *The Atlantic*. Retrieved from www.theatlantic.com/education/archive/2017/04/why-is-the-student-veteran-graduation-rate-so-low/523779/

May, L. C. (2020, March 18). Resilience and resistance: Fighting for higher education in prison. *Inside Higher Ed*. Retrieved from www.insidehighered.com/views/2020/03/18/prisoner-describes-his-and-other-inmates-struggles-access-higher-education-opinion

Mayer, A., Kalamkarian, H. S., Cohen, B., Pellegrino, L., Boynton, M., & Yang, E. (2019). *Integrating technology and advising: Studying enhancement to colleges' iPASS practices*. New York: Community College Research Center, Teachers College, Columbia University.

Minthorn, R. Z.-T.-H.-A. (2020, January 28). Indigenous perspectives on native student challenges in higher education. *Higher Education Today*. Retrieved from www.higheredtoday.org/2020/01/28/indigenous-perspectives-native-student-challenges-higher-education/

Moore, J. C. (2019). *A brief history of universities*. Switzerland: Springer Nature.

Morin, R. (2011, December 11). The difficult transition from military to civilian life. *Pew Research Center*. Retrieved from www.pewsocialtrends.org/2011/12/08/the-difficult-transition-from-military-to-civilian-life/#:~:text=While%20more%20than%20seven%2Din,11%2C%202001%2C%20terrorist%20attacks

National Center for Education Statistics. (2019a, December 12). *Fast facts*. National Center for Education Statistics. Retrieved from https://nces.ed.gov/fastfacts/display.asp?id=66

National Center for Education Statistics. (2019b, December 19). *Fast facts*. National Center for Education Statistics. Retrieved from https://nces.ed.gov/fastfacts/display.asp?id=75

National Communication Association. (2019, November). *The impact of socioeconomic status on college enrollment*. National Communication Association. Retrieved from www.natcom.org/sites/default/files/publications/NCA_CBrief_Vol9_10.pdf

National Working Group on Foster Care and Education. (2014, January). *Fostering success in education: National factsheet on the educational outcomes of children in foster care*. National Working Group on Foster Care and Education. Retrieved from https://cdn.fc2success.org/wp-content/uploads/2012/05/National-Fact-Sheet-on-the-Educational-Outcomes-of-Children-in-Foster-Care-Jan-2014.pdf

Nelson, C. (2010, December 21). Defining academic freedom. *Inside Higher Ed*. Retrieved from www.insidehighered.com/views/2010/12/21/defining-academic-freedom

The New York Times. (2017). Economic diversity and student outcomes at America's colleges and universities: Find your college. *The New York Times.* Retrieved from www.nytimes.com/interactive/projects/college-mobility/

O'Reilly, C. A., & Tushman, M. (2016). *Lead and disrupt.* Stanford, CA: Stanford University Press.

Paterson, J. (2019, February 5). Elite colleges a better bet for low-income minority students, ranking finds. *The New York Times.* Retrieved from www.educationdive.com/news/elite-colleges-a-better-bet-for-low-income-minority-students-ranking-finds/547681/

Pechan, C. (2019, December 12). Looking back and moving forward—philanthropy in the 2010s. *Fluxx Blog.* Retrieved from https://blog.fluxx.io/looking-back-and-moving-forward-philanthropy-in-the-2010s

Pell Institute. (n.d.). *Estimated bachelor's degree attainment rate by age 24 for dependent family members by family income quartile: 1970 to 2017 (.xls).* Pell Institute. Retrieved from http://pellinstitute.org/indicators/reports_2019_data.shtml

The Pell Institute for the Study of Opportunity in Higher Education and PennAHEAD. (2018). *Indicators of higher education equity: 2018 historical trend report.* The Pell Institute for the Study of Opportunity in Higher Education and PennAHEAD. Retrieved from http://pellinstitute.org/downloads/publications-Indicators_of_Higher_Education_Equity_in_the_US_2018_Historical_Trend_Report.pdf

Pew Research Center. (2013, June 13). A survey of LGBT Americans. *Pew Research Center.* Retrieved from www.pewsocialtrends.org/2013/06/13/a-survey-of-lgbt-americans/

PNPI. (2019a, November 9). Fact sheets: Veterans in higher education. *PNPI.* Retrieved from https://pnpi.org/veterans-in-higher-education/#:~:text=Veterans%20in%20Higher%20Education,-Since%201944%2C%20the&text=This%20assistance%20has%20expanded%20access,a%20postsecondary%20degree%20or%20credential

PNPI. (2019b, October 24). Profile of very low and low-income undergraduates in 2015–16. *PNPI.* Retrieved from https://pnpi.org/profile-of-very-low-and-low-income-undergraduates-in-2015–16/

PNPI. (2020, September 14). Native American students in higher education. *PNPI.* Retrieved from https://pnpi.org/native-american-students/#:~:text=17%25%20of%20Native%20American%20students,to%2013%2C600%20in%202017%E2%80%9318

Porter, S. R., & Stephens, C. M. (2010, November 8). *The causal effect of faculty unions on institutional.* Ames, Iowa: Department of Educational Leadership and Policy Studies, Iowa State University. Retrieved from file:///C:/Users/breec/Downloads/SSRN-id1705713.pdf

The Postsecondary National Policy Institute. (2018, 9 November). Fact sheets: Veterans in higher education. *The Postsecondary National Policy Institute.* Retrieved from https://pnpi.org/veterans-in-higher-education/

Radford, J. (2019, June 17). Key findings about U.S. immigrants. *The Pew Research Center.* Retrieved from www.pewresearch.org/fact-tank/2019/06/17/key-findings-about-u-s-immigrants/

Robert Morse, E. B. (2011, January 27). Students say rankings aren't most important factor in college decision. *U.S. News and World Report.* Retrieved from www.usnews.com/education/blogs/college-rankings-blog/2011/01/27/students-say-rankings-arent-most-important-factor-in-college-decision

Robert Morse, E. B. (2019, September 8). How *U.S. News* calculated the 2020 best colleges rankings. *U.S. News and World Report.* Retrieved from www.usnews.com/education/best-colleges/articles/how-us-news-calculated-the-rankings

Roberts, S. O., & Rizzo, M. T. (2020). *The psychology of American racism.* Washington, DC: American Psychologist.

Sawyer, W., & Wagner, P. (2020, March 24). Mass incarceration: The whole pie 2020. *Prison Policy Initiative.* Retrieved from www.prisonpolicy.org/reports/pie2020.html

Schmidt, P. (2010). A history of legacy preferences and privilege. In R. D. Kahlenberg (Ed.), *Affirmative action for the rich: Legacy preferences in college admissions* (p. 59). New York: The Century Press.

Schmidt, P. (2015, April 15). Unionization pays off for community-college instructors. *Chronicle of Higher Education.* Retrieved from www.chronicle.com/article/Unionization-Pays-Off-for/229353

Shema, H. (2014, April 19). The birth of modern peer review. *Scientific American.* Retrieved from https://blogs.scientificamerican.com/information-culture/the-birth-of-modern-peer-review/

Signe-Mary McKernan, C. R. (2017, October 5). Nine charts about wealth inequality in America (Updated). *Urban Institute.* Retrieved from http://apps.urban.org/features/wealth-inequality-charts/

Smith, A. A. (2015, June 8). 2 + 2 shouldn't = 5. *Inside Higher Ed.* Retrieved from www.insidehighered.com/news/2015/06/08/two-year-transfers-are-finding-not-all-their-credits-go-them

Smith-Barrow, D. (2018, December 1). From foster care to college. *The Hechinger Report.* Retrieved from https://hechingerreport.org/from-foster-care-to-college/

Sorrell, C. (2017, May 26). 51 Useful aging out of foster care statistics: Social race media. *National Foster Youth Institute.* Retrieved from www.nfyi.org/51-useful-aging-out-of-foster-care-statistics-social-race-media/#:~:text=More%20than%2023%2C000%20children%20will,care%20will%20become%20instantly%20homeless.&text=There%20is%20less%20than%20a,any%20point%20in%20their%20life

Stauffer, A. (2019, October 15). Two decades of change in federal and state higher education funding: Recent trends across levels of government. *The Pew Charitable Trusts.* Retrieved from www.pewtrusts.org/en/research-and-analysis/issue-briefs/2019/10/two-decades-of-change-in-federal-and-state-higher-education-funding

Stevens, A. H., Kurlaender, M., & Grosz, M. (2018). Career technical education and labor market outcomes: Evidence from California community colleges. *The Journal of Human Resources, 2.*

Stokes, P., Baker, N., DeMillo, R., Soares, L., & Yaeger, L. (2019). *The transformation-ready higher education institution: How leaders can prepare for and promote change.* American Council on Education (ACE). Retrieved from www.acenet.edu/Documents/The-Transformation-Ready-Higher-Education-Institution-Huron-ACE-Ebook.pdf

TED: The Economic Daily. (2017, May 22). 69.7 percent of 2016 high school graduates enrolled in college in October 2016. *TED: The Economic Daily.* Retrieved from www.bls.gov/opub/ted/2017/69-point-7-percent-of-2016-high-school-graduates-enrolled-in-college-in-october-2016.htm

Tinson-Johnson, N. (2018, January 11). Being a poor college student: The unexpected barriers no one talked about. *HuffPost.* Retrieved from www.huffpost.com/entry/being-a-poor-college-student-the-unexpected-barriers_b_5a57a234e4b02f870f8dc38b

Trotta, D. (2019, March 5). Some 4.5 percent of U.S. Adults identify as LGBT: Study. *U.S. News.* Retrieved from www.reuters.com/article/us-usa-lgbt/some-4-5-percent-of-u-s-adults-identify-as-lgbt-study-idUSKCN1QM2L6

U.S. Census Bureau. (2020, August 3). Quick facts: Population estimates, July 1, 2019. *U.S. Census Bureau.* Retrieved from www.census.gov/quickfacts/fact/table/US/PST045219

U.S. News and World Report. (2019, December 20). U.S. Best colleges. *U.S. News and World Report.* Retrieved from www.usnews.com/best-colleges

U.S. News and World Report. (2020, January 6). Top performers on social mobility: National. *U.S. News and World Report.* Retrieved from www.usnews.com/best-colleges/rankings/national-universities/social-mobility

Vedder, R. (2018, April 8). There are really almost no truly private universities. *Forbes.* Retrieved from www.forbes.com/sites/richardvedder/2018/04/08/there-are-really-almost-no-truly-private-universities/#35c1acca57bc

Vespa, J. E. (2020, June). Those who served: America's veterans from World War II to the war on terror. *U.S. Census Bureau.* Retrieved from www.census.gov/content/dam/Census/library/publications/2020/demo/acs-43.pdf

Wachter, M. L. (2007, July 19). The rise and decline of unions. *SSRN.* Retrieved from https://ssrn.com/abstract=1001458

Wade, L. (2015, June 2). Gay men are more likely to graduate college than anyone else. *Business Insider.* Retrieved from www.businessinsider.com/gay-men-are-more-likely-to-graduate-college-than-anyone-else-2015-6

Wermund, B. (2017, September 10). How U.S. News college rankings promote economic inequality on campus. *Politico.* Retrieved from www.politico.com/interactives/2017/top-college-rankings-list-2017-us-news-investigation/

White, B. P. (2016, April 19). Beyond a deficit view. *Inside Higher Ed*. Retrieved from www.insidehighered.com/views/2016/04/19/importance-viewing-minority-low-income-and-first-generation-students-assets-essay

The Williams Institute, UCLA School of Law. (2019, January). LGBT demographic data interactive. *The Williams Institute, UCLA School of Law*. Retrieved from https://williamsinstitute.law.ucla.edu/visualization/lgbt-stats/?topic=LGBT#density

Windmeyer, S. (2016a). Finding your campus roadmap for LGBT progress. *INSIGHT into Diversity, 88*(2), 36–37.

Windmeyer, S. (2016b, April 15). The path forward: LGBT retention and academic success. *INSIGHT into Diversity*. Retrieved from www.insightintodiversity.com/the-path-forward-lgbt-retention-and-academic-success/

Woetzel, J. B. (2019, January). Navigating a world of disruption. *McKinsey and Company*. Retrieved from www.mckinsey.com/featured-insights/innovation-and-growth/navigating-a-world-of-disruption

Wong, A. (2015, September 1). The subtle evolution of Native American education. *The Atlantic*. Retrieved from www.theatlantic.com/education/archive/2015/09/native-american-education/402787/

Ziegler, A. (2010, June 28). Smart phones beating out computers. *The Daily Nebraskan*. Retrieved from www.dailynebraskan.com/smart-phones-beating-out-computers/article_ae5025a2-cd67-5b58-a0a5-6a06a1660b0f.html

Index

Note: **Boldface** page references indicate photos. *Italic* references indicate figures and boxed text.

AA/AS completion rates: earnings and 123; of fire fighters 120; of incarcerated or formerly incarcerated students 50–51, 169; industries near community college and 130; of JFK high schools students 128; negative socialization and 66; new job openings in California requiring (by 2030) 123; recidivism and 50–51, 170, *170*; recognition of, supporting 188; transfers and 191–192; workforce development and 130
AACC 186–187
academic capital: academic counseling services and 70–72; defining 3; faculty-student relationships and 72–73; food insecurities and, addressing 73; gaps in 56; health insecurities and, addressing 73; housing insecurities and, addressing 73; institutional diversity and 70; new socializing agents and *63*, 68; overview 75; socializing agents and 62–66, *62*, *63*; sticky campus and 73–75; strategies for building 66–75, *74*; students' assets and 68–70; TEDx Talk on 3–4; tracking students and 66–68
academic counseling services, expanding 70–72
academic freedom 98
academic success gaps, quantifying 57–60
acceptance rate measure 145
access to higher education: for African American students 26–28, *27*; for foster care students 44–46, *45*; for incarcerated or formerly incarcerated students 52, *52*; for indigenous students 36–37, *36*; for Latinx students 29–32, *31*; for LGBTQ+ students 42–43, *43*; for low-income students 54, *55*; for military veteran students 46–48, *48*; for Southeast Asian students 33–34, *34*; for working adult students 39–40, *40*
access to opportunity 10
accountability and leadership development 164–165
ACCT 186–187
Achieving the Dream (ATD) 117
ACT scores 144

AdoptUsKids report 44–45
ADT (Associate Degree for Transfer) program 132
advising, proactive 124
affirming approach 103
affirming educational environment 102–103
African American communities 69
African American students 19–21, *20*, 26–28, *26*, *27*, 58–59, *59*
aging out of foster care system 45
Aguirre, D. 179
Alpern, M. 179
alumni connections, building 89
Alumni Giving Ranking Factor 143
alumni spending measure 145
American Association of University Professors (AAUP) 98
American College Health Association 42
American Council on Education (ACE) 49, 115, 129
American Dream 8–10, 16, 63, 82–83
American Indian College Fund 36
American Indian population 34–36; *see also* indigenous students
American School Counselor Association 71
America's College Promise Act 199–200
Amnesty International report 35
Anti-Defamation League (ADL) 13
Applied Educational Systems study 123
apprenticeship education 130–131
Asian population in United States 33, *33*
Asian students *see* Southeast Asian students
Asian subgroups 32–33, *33*; *see also* Southeast Asian students
Aspen Institute's report 156
assessment and leadership development 164–165
assets-based approach 68–70
audit, conducting and maintaining national 87

BA/BS completion rates: of African American students *27*, 28, 59, *59*; community college students and 2; of foster care students *45*, 46, 59, *59*; gaps in 207, *207*; of high-income

students 15–16, *16*; of incarcerated or formerly incarcerated students 52, *52*, *59*, 60; income levels and 15; of indigenous students 36–38, *36*, 59, *59*; of Latinx students 31–32, *31*, 59, *59*; of LGBTQ+ students 42, *42*, *43*, 59, *59*; of low-income students 16, *16*, 54–55, *54*; of middle-income students 16, *16*, *55*; of military veteran students 48–49, *48*, 59, *59*; of Southeast Asian students 33–34, *34*, 59, *59*; of underserved students 2–3, 16–17, *17*, 59, *59*; of underserved students at selective universities 137, *137*; of working adult students 40–41, *40*, 59, *59*
Bailey, Thomas R. 117
Berkeley 135–136
bias: in American society 8–9; dialogue about, emerging 164; enrollment 91; in nonprofit funding 81–84; in other funding sources 84–86; in public education funding 78–81; in teacher evaluations 99; in underserved students' funding 86; *see also* discrimination
Big Data, leveraging 125
Bill and Melinda Gates Foundation 117
"black box" jobs 12, *12*
Black students 19–21, *20*, 26–28, *26*, *27*, 58–59, *59*
Bridgespan Group study (2020) 82–83
Brown, Brené 160–161
Brown v. Board of Education (1954) 26, 28, 80
Bureau of Indian Education 35
Bureau of Justice Statistics 50
Bush, George W. 41

"cafeteria model" of education 117
California Community College Association for Occupational Education 122
California Community College system 18–19, 81, 89, 120, 139
California Polytechnic University (Cal Poly) 7, 135–136, **135**
California Rehabilitation Center (CRC) program 168–169, **169**
California State Academic Senate 1–2
California State University (CSU) system 33, 121–122
Campaign for College Opportunity report 33
Campus Explorer report 44
Campus Pride Index 43
Campus Pride survey 43
caseload approach 71–72
Century Foundation reports 81, 84, 86
Cerritos College 1–2, **1**, 68, 93–94
Cervantes, Sabrina **76**, 77
challenge pillars students face 117–119
Chetty, Raj 15, 138
Chinese Exclusion Act 32
Chinese immigrants to United States 32
Christ, Carol *143*, 144
Christensen, Clayton 161–162
Chronicle of Higher Education 161
Civil Rights Movement 26

cleanliness of campus, need for 74
"cold civil war" in United States 10
collaborative activism 202
collaborative solutions in higher education 2
collective bargaining in higher education 97
college completion rates *see* AA/AS completion rates; BA/BS completion rates
college pathways, defining all 67, 117–118
college properties, designing to support equity 106–107
communal experiences on campus, design for 74
Community College Research Center (Columbia University) 69, 117
Community College Review 43–44
community colleges (CCs): challenges of, unique 25–26; community and 130; disproportionate funding at, arguments for 86; ecosystem of 183–184; endowments 84–85, *85*; enrollment in, unique 25; private giving to 84; role of in America 3; social justice education and 4–5, 90; as social justice institutions 83; social mobility and 90; teaching focus of 97; transitions from 120–124, *120*, *121*; transitions to 113–116; underserved communities and 83; uniqueness of 4–5; *see also specific name*; student composition of community colleges
Completion by Design (CBD) initiative 117
connectedness, need for 72, 74
connecting careers to learning 129–132
continuous learning, building capacity for 82–83
contract education 131
core competencies of teachers 100–103, *100*
course milestones 125
course numbering, shared 132, 191–192
course success rates 18–21, *19*, *20*
COVID-19 pandemic 32, 53, 134
Crafton Hills College (CHC) 22–24, 115, 129
"crimmigration" 30
CTE (career technical education) courses 122–124, 188, 192–193, *193*, **200**
cultural norms and discrimination 13–14
cultural power 179
customer relationship management (CRM) 71

DACA (Deferred Action for Childhood Arrivals) 30–32, *31*, 187, 198
Dahl, Robert 154, **154**
dairy science 6–7
"Data Gumbo" 127
data as punishment culture 126
data as resource culture 126
degree maps 124
Demos report (2015) 55
Department of Veterans Affairs 47
Developmental Education Initiative (DEI) 117
DeVos, Betsy 36
Diaz, Adam 22–24, **22**, **23**
dirt data 126

discrimination: against African Americans 9, 26–27; from cultural norms 13–14; against economically disadvantaged populations 172; empowering marginalized groups and 186; against immigrants 30; against indigenous populations 9; from individuals and groups 12–13, *13*; institutional 14–15; against Latinx 28; law in addressing 185–186; against LGBTQ+ people 41–43; from public policy 13; public sector in addressing 185–186; research in addressing 185; social science disciplines working on 8–9; against Southeast Asians 9, 32
disruption 162–163
diversity 9, 21, 37, 70, 138, 173, 185, 190–191
Don't Ask, Don't Tell policy 41
DOS (disc operating system) 127
Dreamers 30, 32, 187, 198
Dubner, Stephen 143
Dynarski, Susan 140

EAB.org 124
economic gaps in United States 10–12, *10*, *11*
Education Advisory Board (EAB) 38–39
educational goal changes 118–119
educational system, supporting integrated 191
EducationData 39
Emancipation (1863) 26
empirical reality 8
employment in United States 11–12, *11*, *12*
endowments 84, *84*, *85*
enrollment: barriers to 112; bias 91; in California Community College system 89, 120, 139; in colleges 25, 36, 78; in community colleges, unique 25; in CTE courses 123, 131; of foster care students 46–47; high school graduates and college 78; high school partnerships and 128, 183, 188, 195; of incarcerated and formerly incarcerated students 52; of indigenous students 36–37; limited 118; of low-income students 54–55; of military veteran students 48; online 134; open 112; progress in 60; in Puente program 107; in selective universities 137, *137*; in state-funded universities 147; targets 58–59, *58*; of working adult students 39–40; year-over-year increases and, problem with targeting 57; *see also* access to higher education
Entering Student Preparedness Ranking Factor 143
entertainment in America 8
equality, shared value of 8–9
equity gaps: big change needed to address in U.S. society 2–3, 207; in course success rates 19–21, *19*, *20*; in retention rates *18*, *19*, *20*; social justice reform in colleges and closing 187, 190–191, *190*, *191*, **200**; *see also* inequality
equity as strategic priority 159
evaluation of teachers 95–96, 98–99

Every Student Succeeds Act (ESSA) 35–36
ex con students 49–53, *51*, *52*, *59*, 60, 168–170, *170*
Expert Opinion Ranking Factor 142

factionalism 155
Faculty Resource Ranking Factor 142
faculty resources measure 144–145
faculty-student relationships, nurturing 72–73
faculty unions 97–98, *97*
federal grants, pursuing 89–90
FERPA (1974) 126
financial aid, maximizing 88–89
Financial Resources Ranking Factor 143
Fishman, Rachel 149
food insecurities of students, addressing 73
foreign-born residents in United States 30, *30*
foster care students 44–46, *44*, *45*, 59–60, *59*
Foster Youth Program 77
full-time equivalent student (FTES) funding 81, *81*, 84
funding higher education equitably: alumni connections and 89; endowments and 84, *84*, *85*; federal grants and 89–90; financial aid and 88–89; full-time equivalent students and 81, *81*; national audit and 87; nonprofit funding bias and 81–84; Norco College situation and 76–78; overview 91–92; private funding sources bias and 84–86; public education funding bias and 78–81, *80*, *81*; social justice funding and 90, *90*; social mobility and 82–83, *82*; state funding and 87–88; strategies for 87–91, *91*; tax status of institutions that underserve marginalized students and 91

Gateway Community College 121–122
GED 52
GE packages, shared 132
G.I. Bill 48, 114
GLAAD/Harris poll 43
globalization 12
Glynn, Jennifer 137, 139
"good trouble" 3, *3*
graduation from college *see* BA/BS completion rates
graduation rate measure 146
Gramsci, Nicole 51
grants, pursuing federal 89–90; *see also specific name*
"Great College to Work For" survey 161
"Great Equalizer" 15–19, *15*
Green, Kenneth 127
"grey box" jobs 12, *12*
GUI (graphical user interface) 127
Guided Pathways (GP) framework 116–117, 124–125, 154, 179

Hafliger family 6–7
Harvard endowment 84, *84*
Harvard's admissions policies scandal 32

hate crimes in America 9, 41
health insecurities of students, addressing 73
Hernández, César Cuauhtémoc García 30
higher education: academic freedom and 98; affirming environment and 102–103; collaborative solutions in 2; collective bargaining in 97; community and, embracing 102–103; core competencies in 100–103, *100*; impact on society 15–16; influence in society and 17; Latinx issues and 29; low-income students in 80, *80*; middle-income students in 80, *80*; race and ethnicity in 79–80, *79*; rankings of colleges and universities 141–146, *141*, *142*; recidivism rates and 50–51, *51*; student centeredness and 100–102; types of, common 79, *79*; *see also* access to higher education; community colleges (CCs)
Higher Education Act (1965) 50, 187
high-income students 15–16, *16*
high school partnerships 127–128, 183, 188, 195
high school rank measure 144
Hispanic students 19–21, 28–32, *29*, *30*, *31*, 58
historically Black colleges and universities (HBCUs) 26
historical perspective of United States and social injustice 8–10, 21
homophobia 14
Hope Center (Temple University) 73
housing insecurities of students, addressing 73
Hoxby, Caroline 141
Huffington Post 54
Hurwitz, Michael 140

IBM 127
iFALCON program 157
immigrants and immigration issues 30, *30*, 32–33
impact investing 82–83
imperfect learning 119
implementing social justice in colleges: California Rehabilitation Center program and 168–169; challenge of 180; collaborative 180, *180*; collective strategies 170; college leaders and *173*, 174, 179; compliance issues and 173; cultural power and 179; executive team and 173–174, *173*; faculty's reactions to social justice education and 172; failure of, reasons for 177–178; Guided Pathways framework and 179; heavy-handed approach and 178–179; importance of 170; institutional change and 171–180; internal strategies 170; overview 180–181; planning committees and *173*, 175–176; resources for 180; self-interest group loyalty and 172; share governance approach and 179; strategies for 170, **170–171**; student-centered framing and 173–174, *173*, *176*; successful 180–181
incarcerated and formerly incarcerated students 49–53, *51*, *52*, *59*, 60, 168–170, *170*

income distribution in United States 53, *53*
income level of families' impact 15
Indian Appropriations Acts 35
Indian Removal Act (1830) 35
indigenous students 19, 21, 34–38, *36*, 42, 59, *59*
industry partnerships 130–131
inequality: economic 10–12, *10*, *11*; low-income 10–11, *10*; middle-income 10–11, *11*; of opportunity 9; *see also* equity gaps
"Innovator's Dilemma, The" 161–164
institutional activities categorized as programs 105–106
institutional change *see* implementing social justice in colleges; leadership development
institutional discrimination 14–15
institutional diversity 70, 173
intuitive systems, developing 125–127, *125*
iPASS program 69

Jack, Anthony 139
Jack Kent Cooke Foundation 148
Jaggars, Shanna S. 117
Jenkins, Davis 117
JFK High School students 128
jobs: "black box" 12, *12*; federal government supporting placement in 188; "grey box" 12, *12*; in "old" versus "new" economy 11–12, *11*, *12*, 38–40, *40*, 131; transitioning from college to 122–124; 20th-century 129; 21st-century 129
Jobs, Steve 127
Joint Services Transcript (JST) 115
Jones, Clarence B. 205

Kamehameha Schools (Hawaii) 35
Kennedy, John F. 26
King, Martin Luther, Jr. 3, 204–206, **204**, 209

L.A. Times survey of poverty line 84
Latinx students 19–21, 28–32, *29*, *30*, *31*, 58–59, *59*
leadership 100–103, *100*
leadership development: accountability and 164–165; assessment and 164–165; decision-making and 154–155, *154*; equity as strategic priority and 159; managing the "old" and leading the "new" and 161–164; at Norco College 152–153; overview 166–167; passivism and, ending 166–167; shared governance and 155–156, *155*; strategic vision and 157–159; strategies 156–166, *166*; teamwork and 159–161; values built around love and 165–166; vulnerability and 160–161
learning process 95, *95*, 119
learning-to-earning connection and integration 119, 129–132
legacy admissions 139–141
legacy scoring, ending 149–150, 191
"Letter from a Birmingham Jail" (King) 3, 204–205, *206*, 209

Levitt, Steven 143
Lewis, John 3, **3**
LGBTQ+ students 41–44, *42*, *43*, 58–59, *59*
Literature review approach 100
Lopez, Brenda 61–62, **61**, 65
love, values build around 165–166, 209–210
low-income inequality 10–11, *10*
low-income student completion measure 144
low-income students 15–16, *16*, 53–57, *53*, *54*, *55*, 58, 80, *80*
Lumina Foundation 117

Magna Charta Universitatum 98
major, selecting college 118
management skills 100–103, *100*; *see also* leadership development
managing the "old" and leading the "new" strategy 161–164
Mann, Horace 15–16
MAP (Military Articulation Program) 129
Maslow, A. 73
mass shootings in United States 9
May Revise 76–78
Mendez v. Westminster School District (1946) 28
Meredith, James 26
meta-majors 124
Miami Dade endowment 84, *85*
Microsoft 127
middle colleges 128
middle-income inequality 10–11, *11*
middle-income students 15–16, *16*, *55*, 80, *80*
military education information 126
military occupation specialization (MOS) 115, 129
military training articulation, developing solutions for 129
military veteran students 46–49, *47*, *48*, 59, *59*
millennial attitudes toward LGBTQ+ people 43, *43*
mission-related investing 82–83
"model minority" 32–33
Morse, Robert 143

National Association of Student Financial Aid Administrators 46
National Center for Education Statistics (NCES) reports 2, 16, 39, 55
National Foster Youth Institute 45
National Veteran Education Success Tracker 48
National Working Group on Foster Care and Education report (2014) 45
Native Alaskans 34–36; *see also* indigenous students
Native Americans 34–36; *see also* indigenous students
Native Hawaiians 34–35; *see also* indigenous students
Navy Enlisted Classifications (NECs) 129
needs hierarchy 73
negative socialization 66
Neustadt, Richard 208

new socializing agents *63*, 68
New York Times analysis of college tuition 141
nonprofit funding bias 81–84
nontraditional adult learners (NALs) 38–41, *39*, *40*, 58
Norco College: California Rehabilitation Center program and 168–169, **169**; disruption at 163; Foster Youth Program at 77; funding higher education equitably situation and 76–78; leadership development at 152–153; Lopez at 61–62, **61**, 65; Lopez's experience at 61–62; military training articulation at 129; professional support at 5; social justice education at 168–169, 175; transfers at 121; Veterans Resource Center at 76–77; workforce training at 131
normative ideals 8

Obama administration 35
Obama, Barack 41
occupational specialties 115, 129
Onboarding 16, 111–113, *113*, 116, 124, 128
online courses and services 133–134
opinion leaders 183
opportunity for college education 7–8
O'Reilly, Charles 162, 164
Outcome Ranking Factor 142

passivism, ending 166–167
pathways to careers, establishing viable 82
pedagogy 96–97, 100
peer review 96, 98–99
Pell Grants 50, 55, 148
Perkins program 123
perverse incentives 143–144, *143*
Pew Research Center 30–31, 42, 46
physical surroundings of students, designing to support equity 106–107
place-based strategies, creating 82
pluralism 155–156
political campaign fundraising 182–183
poor students *see* low-income students
Postsecondary National Policy Institute (PNPI) 36, 42
posttraumatic stress disorder (PTSD) 45–46
poverty 54, 84; *see also* low-income students
Princeton University 79
prison students 49–53, *51*, *52*
private funding sources bias 84–86
proactive advising 124
proactive transfer centers, establishing 146–148, *147*
professional development 107
program-related investing 82–83
progress tracking students 66–68, 124
Public Agenda and Kresge Foundation study (2018) 39
public education funding bias 78–81
public education as "Great Equalizer" 15–19, *15*
public policy and discrimination 13
Puente program 107

race relations in America 9, 185
racism 9, 14–15, 185, 204–206
Rainbow Community 41
Ranking Factors 142–143
ranking systems, changing 148–149, 191
recidivism and education 50–51, *51*, 169–170, *170*
Redesigning America's Community Colleges study 117
residential campuses and stickiness 74
resources, relevant 124–125
retention rate measure 1465
retention rates 18–21, *18*, *20*
Riverside Community College District (RCCD) 5, 153, 163
Rizzo, M. T. 166–167
Roberts, S. O. 166–167
Rolfe, John 26
Royal Society of Edinburgh 98
"Rust Belt" states 38

SAT scores 144
schedules, optimized 125
schedules, student-centered 132–133
segregation 204
self-interest group loyalty 172
separate but equal doctrine 80
services skills 100–103, *100*
Shepard, Matthew 41
signage on campus, need for 74
slaves/slavery 9, 26
social genome model (SGM) 82
social injustices in United States 8–10, 12–15
socializing agents 62–66, *62*, *63*
social justice education: community colleges and 4–5, 90; faculty's reactions to 172; literature on best practices in 4; new areas for discussion in 4; at Norco College 168–169, 175; personal development and 5; self-interest group loyalty and 172; takeaways from book 4–5; *see also* implementing social justice in colleges
social justice funding 90, *90*
social justice missions of foundations 82–83
social justice reform in colleges: AACC and 186–187; access and equity gaps and, closing 187, 190–191, *190*, *191*, **200**; ACCT and 186–187; agenda, need for 16; caliber of students at community colleges and, rejecting stereotype of 201; caution versus courage in responding to 209–210; challenges facing *16*, 207–208; changes to college ecosystem and, need for 185–189; collaborative activism and 202; ecosystem of community colleges and 183–184; equalizing funding of higher education sectors and 188, 193–194, *194*, **200**; equity gaps and, closing 187, 190–191, *190*, *191*, **200**; equity and, promoting 187; federal aid and, expanding 187; funding and resources and, increasing 187, 189–190, *189*, *190*, **200**; job placement and, supporting 188, 192–193, *193*, **200**;
literature review 196, **196–198**, 198–201; love and 209–210; national agenda items for 187–188, *187*, 201–202; national survey and 188–189, *188*; negative responses to 207–208; opinion leaders and 183; overview 202–203; political campaign fundraising examples and 182–183; predicament surrounding 208–209; recommendations for 202, *203*; strategic systems and, developing 188, 194–195, *195*, **200**; strategies for 184, **184–185**; transfer rates and, improving 188, 191–192, *191*, *192*, **200**
social mobility 82–83, *82*, 90, 143, 146, 192, 201
social movements 10–11, 26
social service programs, improving 82–83
social unrest related to social justice issues 9
Southeast Asian students 19, *20*, 21, 32–34, *33*, *34*, 59, *59*
spending per student measure 145
standardized tests measures 144
standards of excellence for programs, implementing 103–105
state funding, restructuring 87–88
state prison education programs 51–52, *51*
STEM education 61–62, 199
sticky campus, creating 73–75
storytelling in communicating ideas 8
strategic vision, developing and promoting clear 157–159
student centeredness 100–102, 132–133
student challenges 117–119
student composition of community colleges: academic success gaps and, quantifying 57–60; African Americans 26–28, *26*, *27*, 58–59; foster care youth 44–46, *44*, 59–60; incarcerated and formerly incarcerated people 49–53, *51*, *52*; indigenous groups 34–38, *36*, 42; Latinx 28–32, *29*, *30*, *31*, 58; LGBTQ+ 41–44, *42*, *43*, 58–59; lives of, typical 24–26; low-income people 53–57, *53*, *54*, *55*, 58; military veterans 46–49, *47*, *48*, 59; overview 24–25; Southeast Asians 32–34, *33*, *34*, 59; working adults 38–41, *39*, *40*, 59
student experiences on campus: academic freedom and 98; best practices in core competencies and (teach, serve, manage, lead) 100–103, *100*; evaluation of teachers and 95–96, 99; faculty unions and 97–98, *97*; institutional activities categorized as programs and 105–106; learning process and 95, *95*; overview 108; pedagogy of teachers and 96–97, 100; peer review and 96, 98–99; physical surroundings and 106–107; professional development and 107; standards of excellence for programs and 103–105; strategies for maximizing 100–108, *107*; support services and 107–108; teaching methods and, individual 93–95
student information systems (SIS) 126
student journey 16–17, *17*, 65–66, *65*, 109–112, *111*

student progress, informing individuals and college personnel about 67–68
students' assets and academic capital 68–70
students' assets, focusing on 68–70
student-to-counselor ratios 67
student-to-faculty ratios 63
success in higher education 2–3, 21, 126; *see also* AA/AS completion rates; BA/BS completion rates
Supplemental Nutrition Assistance Program (SNAP) 73
support services, establishing 107–108

Taslitz, Howard 93–94, **93**
tax status of institutions that underserve marginalized students, altering 91
teaching: evaluations of teachers 95–96, 98–99; excellence, defining 99; learning and 95, *95*; pedagogy 96–97, 100; research situations versus 96
team-based caseload approach 71–72
teamwork 159–161
technology 12
tenure process 96, 97
top ten universities: disfavored student groups at 17; income level of students at 138, **138**
tracking students 66–68, 124
Trail of Tears 35
transitions/transfers: AA/AS completion rates and 191–192; apprenticeship education and 130–131; bureaucracy of 111; from community college to jobs 122–124; from community college to university 120–122, *120*, *121*; connecting careers to learning and 129–132; contract education and 131; course numbering and, common 132, 191–192; federal government in improving 188; GE packages and, shared 132; from government programs to community college 116; Guided Pathway framework and 124–125; for high-GPA/low-income students 148; from high school to community college 113; high school partnerships and 127–128; industry partnerships and 130–131; intuitive systems and 125–127, *125*; from military to civilian life 46–48, *47*; from military to community college 114–115; military training articulation and 129; online courses and services and 133–134; overview 134; proactive transfer centers and 146–148, *147*; to selective university 135–139, *137*; social justice reform in colleges and improving 188, 191–192, *191*, *192*, **200**; strategies for successful 124–134, *134*; student-centered schedules and 132–133; student journey 109–112, *111*; transitioning IN 112–116, *112*; transitioning OUT 119–124, *119*; transitioning THROUGH 116–119, *116*; Tyreese situation and 109–111; of underserved students in selective universities 135–139, *137*; workforce training and 131; from workplace to community college 113–114
Tribally Controlled Community College Assistance Act (1978) 35

Trump administration 36
Tushman, Michael 162
Tyreese (student) 109–111, **109**

Umoja program 68–70
underenrollment 33, 137, 190
undermatching 141
underserved communities: community colleges and 83; funding bias against students from 86; quality of education in 80–81; socialization process in 63–64; student journey and 65–66, *65*; support for students from, lack of 64–65
underserved students in selective universities: BA/BS completion rates of 137, *137*; barriers and, identifying 136–139, *137*, *138*; at Cal Poly 135–136; legacy admissions and 139–141; legacy scoring and, ending 149–150; overview 150–151; proactive transfer centers and 146–148, *147*; ranking systems and, changing 148–149; recruiting 139; strategies for increasing 146–150, *150*; transfer programs for high-GPA/low-income students and 148; transfers and 135–139, *137*; undermatching and 141; at USC 136
unions, faculty 97–98, *97*
University of Connecticut 122
university endowments 84–85, *84*
University of Mississippi 26
University of North Carolina special program 55
University of Pennsylvania 140, 145, 207
University of Southern California (USC) 7, 136
University of Wisconsin study (1917) 54
unrest related to social injustices 9
UPenn study (2018) 207
Urban Institute report (2017) 10
U.S. Census Bureau 26, 29, 36, 47, 53
U.S. Department of Defense 126
U.S. News and World Report college rankings 17, 79, 138, 141–143, *142*, 148

values built around love 165–166
Veterans Affairs 126
Veterans Resource Center 76–77
veteran students 46–49, *47*, *48*, 59, *59*
von Post, R. 179
vulnerability 160–161

Wallace, George 204
Walnut Street jail (Philadelphia) 50
White, Byron 69
white nationalism 13, *13*
Williams Institute (UCLA School of Law) report (2019) 42
workforce development and training 129–131
working adult students 38–41, *39*, *40*, 59, *59*
World Economic Forum (2019) 11, 39
Wounded Knee massacre (1890) 35

"zero-blind" approach 98–99